Resources for Teaching

The Winchester Reader

Contributors

Donald McQuade

Robert Atwan

Alix Schwartz

Julia Sullivan

Bedford Books *of* St. Martin's Press
BOSTON

For information, write: St. Martin's Press Inc.
175 Fifth Avenue, New York, NY 10010

Editorial Offices: Bedford Books *of* St. Martin's Press
29 Winchester Street, Boston, MA 02116

ISBN 0–312–04879–3

Acknowledgment

Opal Palmer Adisa, "I Will Not Let Them Take You (for Jawara)." Copyright
© 1990 by Opal Palmer Adisa. Reprinted by permission of the author.

Preface

The Winchester Reader is a unique book, demanding, we feel, a unique instructor's manual. We have especially designed the manual to escort you through our distinctive "bite-sized" chapters. Permitting a wide spectrum of themes and topics to be covered in a syllabus, these small, focused chapters will also support varied compositional and rhetorical approaches. You can use the clustered selections to show two (or more) sides of an argument; to demonstrate a range of viewpoints on a topic; to contrast a theoretical or expository essay with an experiential or narrative essay on the same subject; to portray a similar theme enacted in different genres, such as an essay or short story; to compare an ironic and straightforward (or humorous and serious) account of an issue; or to examine different prose styles manipulating the same theme. These are only a few of the combinations covered in this manual.

The Winchester Reader is unique in its freedom from apparatus, its many, many juxtapositions, its distinctive thematic arrangement, and its high proportion of less-known contemporary writers outside the usual composition canon. Realizing that the usual discussion-question format doesn't suit our purpose, we want to offer instructors more than a simple assortment of isolated questions (with or without answers) that they can recycle for the classroom. We have agreed that instructors need a more closely integrated, hands-on initiation to the book's 41 chapters, 124 selections, and 140 epigraphs than a conventional question-driven format furnishes. We have decided, therefore, to organize the manual around thorough, essaylike entries with strategic advice for teaching each chapter and each selection. Questions for class discussion and some of the responses they might generate *do* appear throughout the entries, but they are embedded, part of the overall approach to the chapter and the selection.

This comprehensive compilation of teaching strategies demonstrates our concerted plan to interweave classroom-tested practices and speculative — and innovative — suggestions about specific ways of working effectively with the chapters and selections. Each manual chapter begins with a section entitled "Working with the Chapter," which incorporates general questions about the theme itself: Why do we cluster these selections? What do they have in common? What thematic contrasts and comparisons arise? How can this chapter work for you in the classroom? Whenever relevant, this chapter survey also includes some of the ways in which the epigraphs can be used to stimulate discussion or deepen the intellectual context in which selections can be considered. (Note: Each epigraph receives useful commentary appropriately situated in each chapter.) In general, "Working with the Chapter" will help you decide on the best ideas and issues to emphasize in class. It also carries practical suggestions for the most productive lines of inquiry to pursue with your students.

In "Working with the Chapter," we also propose an innovative method for using reading to generate writing. We call this "A Writing-before-Reading Exercise." With this feature we reverse the usual compositional procedure. Instead of assigning a text to read and then asking students to write about (or from) it, you can invite students to draft an essay on a theme or topic first and *then* read how other writers have handled it. This exercise affords your students two advantages: (1) they have an opportunity to assert their own voice into the public or literary discussion of a theme or idea; and (2) they are prepared to read the selections later with a writer's eye, having already considered and written about the subject. We recommend that this "prereading" assignment be composed as a first draft.

Students can then revise their essays according to what they learned from the selections. A follow-up assignment ends each chapter.

Instructional support in this manual also includes suggestions for working with each selection. These suggestions take the form of detailed essays on every selection in the book. Each entry-essay includes varied interpretive and pedagogical elements: strategies for stimulating and leading class discussion, analysis and criticism of literary passages, and relevant background information. Connections with other selections in the book and ideas for further reading and research appear under the heading "Additional Activities." The manual also has some additional texts that can be copied and introduced for in-class work. "Generating Writing," which follows the essay for each selection, suggests writing assignments. Additional writing assignments are included in "Writing about the Chapter," the last section in each manual chapter. For convenience and alternative arrangements, the manual also includes two tables of contents: a rhetorical listing with which you can organize selections around familiar structures and patterns and another with which you can focus on such elements of composition as tone, diction, style, and organization.

We hope this manual will facilitate an open, unencumbered, and mutually respectful dialogue between you and your students in which productive reading and writing can flourish. *The Winchester Reader* is first and finally a *reader*. We want it to convey reading at its most spirited and most challenging. Thoreau said that the act of reading is also "the process of *being read,* as finding your fate in your capacity for interpretation of yourself." We can think of worse fates.

Contents

The First-Person Singular

Writing for Oneself

Joan Didion, On Keeping a Notebook

Toi Derricotte, Diary: At an Artist's Colony

William Safire, On Keeping a Diary

WORKING WITH THE CHAPTER

As instructors of writing, we know that when our students are learning to write, they are simultaneously learning to think. And journals, diaries, and notebooks — writing done for oneself — can enhance the writer's ability to think for himself or herself. Because journals are innocent of the motives driving more public forms of writing — the desire to impress, or persuade, or instruct an audience — journals can be a site for pure exploration, for unfettered expression of the writer's thoughts and feelings.

Teaching Strategies

Point out to your students that Anne Frank keeps a diary primarily "to bring out all kinds of things that lie buried" deep in her heart. And Alice James finds in her diary an "outlet" for her "emotions, sensations, speculations and reflections."

Joan Didion records her experiences in her notebook with the sole intention of remembering "what it was to be me": for that reason her most successful entries are those which capture the essence of an experience so that it can be relived by her future self. Her conception of writing for oneself accords well with William Safire's statement that the "central idea of a diary is that you are not writing for critics or for posterity but are writing a private letter to your future self." Henry David Thoreau, who, like Didion and Safire, often *does* write for posterity, considers his journal a place for working out his ideas for himself, a place in which he can associate with his *own* "loftiest thoughts." Each of these professional writers acknowledges the worth of sometimes writing for oneself. The entire chapter on "Writing for Oneself" provides a perfect opportunity to talk about audience, and to explore the advantages of purely exploratory writing, which doesn't acknowledge any audience more alien than one's own future selves.

The personal sense of audience that underlies all the selections and epigraphs in this chapter determines the shape of writings done for oneself. The writer's thought carves its own path on the page, sometimes inching along, but more often racing forward, pursuing the messy truth. Sometimes the path is concrete, as for the women and men on the Overland Trail, discussed in the epigraph by John Mack Faragher. Travel diaries are a major type of writing for oneself; they often take the episodic shape of the writer's journey. In a sense, though, travel diaries only make literal the guiding principle in all journals: to record the writer's spiritual, intellectual, or emotional journey, the gradual quest to understand oneself and the world. Toi Derricotte explores her feelings about her own racial identity, and her reactions to the racism around her, in the pages of her diary. Because she is her own primary audience, her main purpose is understanding; she doesn't have to cut off her thinking prematurely to achieve a coherent thesis statement. Awareness of a broader audience will bring the urge to focus and organize one's words, certainly part of the purpose of a course in writing. But the kinds of writing done in a journal, free of the watchful eye of critics and posterity, are equally worth fostering.

A Writing-before-Reading Exercise

Ask your students if they have ever kept a diary or a journal. Do they have a notebook in which they record their thoughts and observations? For those who already have a diary, journal, or notebook, the purpose of the assignment is twofold: (1) to continue following their habitual pattern of writing in their journal, and (2) to begin analyzing that pattern. Have them consider these questions: When do you normally write? How much do you normally write? What are some of the factors that can affect the frequency or length of your entries? Why do you write? How do you feel about the writing you do in your journal, both the process of writing and the product? Who is your audience for this journal? Do you ever reread earlier journal entries? Do you ever show your journal to anyone? Do journal entries ever form the basis for more polished, public pieces of writing?

If some students have never kept a journal, this is their chance to give it a try. Tell them that they'll need nothing more complicated than a writing implement, a little time, and something congenial to write upon. This surface can vary from a blank book with ornate cover to a spiral-bound notebook, or just scratch paper stapled together along one edge. For just one week, they should try to write in their journal once a day. Ask them to consider questions such as these: What kinds of things do you find yourself writing down? What kinds of things do you find yourself leaving out? What is the underlying logic in your method of selection? Do you like keeping a journal? From your week's experience, can you imagine benefits that might come from such an activity?

WORKING WITH THE SELECTIONS

Joan Didion

On Keeping a Notebook

Teaching Strategies

Probably the main difference between a notebook and an essay is the intended audience: the first is written for oneself and the second with a public audience in mind. An intriguing hybrid is born when an author such as Didion writes an essay on the topic of keeping a notebook. She writes that "your notebook will never help me, nor mine you" (para. 17), but the experience of writing an essay inspired by her experience in writing a notebook transforms the previously irrelevant "you" into a viable audience.

This vacillating sense of audience sets off tensions in Didion's essay. Whereas she writes the notebook in order to "remember what it was to be me," the essay reveals the hopes and anxieties of her former selves to a much wider audience, transforming self-exploration into confession. Of course she's not completely comfortable with the confessional mode, with the emphasis on herself. Therefore, although she makes fun of a society that expects us "to affect absorption in other people's favorite dresses, other people's trout," she doesn't focus her essay unwaveringly on the "implacable 'I'," as she claims to do in her notebook. And she embeds the details about others — about the man at the hat-check counter and the Greek shipping heiress — in a statement on the impossibility of cashing in on such details in one's writing. "On Keeping a Notebook" provides ample internal evidence to falsify its own claim: that notebooks are filled with "bits of the mind's string too short to use" (para. 11).

Didion's essay adds an intriguing twist to a discussion on writing for oneself. Ask students to identify her audience for the piece. Do they feel that they are being addressed? If so, what might be her intention toward them? If they believe she is trying to persuade them about the benefits of keeping a notebook, refer them to paragraph 4, in which she expresses the opinion that "Keepers of notebooks are a different breed altogether, lonely and resistant rearrangers of things, anxious malcontents, children afflicted apparently at birth with some presentiment of loss" (para. 4). Because she wouldn't have to persuade anyone born with the compulsion to take up a notebook, nor would she be able to persuade someone born without the compulsion to do so, who might her audience be? Have your students point to specific evidence that this essay, unlike the notebook from which it derives, *is* meant for a public audience, and have them point to specific evidence that it also fulfills an exploratory function for Didion herself. What might she have learned from writing this essay that she would not have learned if all these notebook entries had remained just that — random entries in a notebook?

To facilitate a discussion of truth versus fact, you might want to ask your class what Didion means when she says of her first notebook entry that "perhaps if I were analytically inclined I would have found it a truer story than any I might have told about Donald Johnson's birthday party or the day my cousin Brenda put Kitty Litter in the aquarium" (para. 5). In what sense is her fantastic story truer than what actually happened? What is Didion setting up as a contrast to truth? How does the sample *diary* entry in paragraph 6 differ from the sample *notebook* entry with which she opens the essay?

Diaries, according to Didion and many other purveyors of the form, are built upon a sense of the discontinuity between one's past and present selves. You might ask your class why Didion withholds the identity of the girl in the plaid silk dress, who is introduced in paragraph 2, until paragraph 9. Can they point to other places in the essay where she embodies her past selves in language that suggests they are separate people? Didion emphasizes "keeping in touch" with the people one used to be. Have them identify the specific ways in which her essay conveys the success of her attempts to keep in touch. Have them point out and discuss the ways in which her essay creates a sense of distance between the present and past selves instead. Ask them how this distance ties in with other feelings expressed in the essay, or with other feelings about writing as a whole.

Additional Activities

Didion distinguishes in her essay between the truth and "an accurate factual record," a distinction that can also be found in "Family Stories," particularly in "No Name Woman" by Maxine Hong Kingston (see Chapter 12). If you begin the semester by having the students write personal essays, you might be able to avoid receiving tediously factual accounts by turning to the examples set by Didion and Kingston. Francine du Plessix Gray's "I Write for Revenge against Reality" (see Chapter 40) might also bring out an interesting parallel.

Generating Writing

1. In paragraph 8, Didion creates an extended metaphor drawn from the world of finance. Her ironic tone suggests that she rejects the value system implied in this metaphor. Ask your students to name precisely what she is rejecting. To what extent is it possible for

a writer to remain uncontaminated by such a system? What value system does she endorse instead? Does the evidence in the essay suggest that she consistently upholds these values? Encourage students to draw specific evidence from the essay to support their assertions.

2. Didion begins her essay with a cryptic entry from one of her old notebooks. She has to perform an act of interpretation on that entry, reading between the sparse lines, and an act of memory, reconstructing the incident and, eventually, its significance. Suggest to members of your class who have kept a notebook, journal, or diary for a number of years that they choose an entry that would be meaningless to anyone else. Have them write an essay in which they reconstruct the incident that prompted them to write the entry. Ask what the incident meant to them then. What does it mean to them now? Has its meaning changed along with their perspective? Give them the option of juxtaposing two or more entries, in order to bring out a pattern that would not otherwise have been noticeable.

Toi Derricotte

Diary: At an Artist's Colony

Teaching Strategies

Whereas the essay by Joan Didion includes excerpts from her notebook, Toi Derricotte's piece consists solely of entries from her diary. Nevertheless, the issue of audience is a live one in this selection as well. Referring to her earlier work, she writes, "when I began writing *The Black Notebooks,* I wrote mainly to myself, although at the back of my mind was the idea that maybe someday, I would get the courage to make it public" (para. 18). She writes with a double consciousness, trying to understand herself and to "write for the larger human community" (para. 18). Didion feeds us only small tastes of her notebook, giving the impression of vast stretches of purely personal material that we'll never see, but Derricotte renders her diary for the time spent in the artists' colony a public document by publishing it in its entirety. By making public a genre that is personal by definition, Derricotte is able to negotiate the distance between her contradictory desires, as they are expressed in the first diary entry: "I will be silent. I want him to like me. I want to tell him how he hurts me. I want to speak."

You might begin by asking your students how they felt when reading Derricotte's diary. Did they feel as if they were eavesdropping on her personal thoughts? In what ways does this diary resemble others they've encountered, including their own? Does the author seem to grow to understand herself better by writing this diary? To what extent and in what specific ways does her diary fit in the classification "Writing for Oneself"? If students feel that the political subject of this selection makes Derricotte's mission seem directed more toward social change than personal knowledge, ask them if they can imagine any ways in which the political can simultaneously be deeply personal. Encourage them to discover how the political operates on a personal scale, in Derricotte's diary and perhaps in their own lives.

Once you have dealt with the subject of the selection, you may want to address more formal matters. Does this diary *formally* resemble others they've read? For instance, does the writing seem polished or unpolished? Have them point to specific passages to support their impression. Is it possible to read this selection as a story written in the form of diary entries? What kinds of evidence would they offer for such a reading? What difference would it make in their reading of this selection if they were to decide to call it a story rather than a diary?

In this selection, Derricotte sets up a tension between speaking and silence. You might ask your students how she convinces her readers that it is difficult to choose between these options. What are the consequences of each alternative? How does the fact that her skin color allows her to pass for white contribute to the tension between speaking and not speaking? Do students think she resolves the tension by the end of the selection? Why or why not? How could the very act of writing and publishing "In an Artist's Colony" resolve that tension?

Because it is essential that they understand the complex workings of racism, you might want to ask your class what Derricotte means by "the internalized process of racism within me" (para. 17). Judging from the evidence in the selection, how does she feel about her color? What *is* her color? Why is this characteristic important? What is the function of the diary entry called "Saturday Night"? Ask students to describe their reactions to the information, taken from the *New York Times,* that 60 percent of the people in the United States could be genetically classified as black.

Additional Activities

You might structure a chapter around the intersection of the personal and the political realms. Other writers in this volume whose contributions illustrate the principle that the personal is political include Bernice Johnson Reagon, June Jordan, Alice Walker, Brent Staples, Adrienne Rich, Itabari Njeri, Nancy Mairs, Shelby Steele, and Gloria Steinem, among others.

Generating Writing

1. Ask students to write an essay answering this question: is Derricotte or is she not setting herself up as a representative of her race in this selection? They should be able to find evidence to support both possibilities. Ask them to explain how these two seemingly opposite impulses can coexist in one piece. Where might Derricotte herself draw the line marking the extent to which she sees herself as a representative of blacks? How might she define that role? In contradistinction to what? How does the presentation of this piece as a series of diary entries help her to define her position?

2. Early in this selection, Derricotte writes that she doesn't like to "lose control" of her identity (para. 6). Assign an essay in which students explore the issue of control in Derricotte's writing. They might want to follow their exploration on at least two levels: (1) the actions related by her written words, and (2) the written words themselves. That is, they might discuss the control she exhibits in her interactions with other artists in the colony, as well as the control evident in her way of shaping the telling of those interactions. Why does control matter to her? Does it have the desired effect on the reader — your students?

William Safire

On Keeping a Diary

Teaching Strategies

William Safire's contribution to this chapter on personal writing is strikingly *im*perso-nal. He considers the subject of a distance, speculating about the possible reasons for the "atrophy of the personal diary" in a way that gives us no clue as to which, if any, of these possibilities affect him; he gives excerpts from three diaries, none of which is his own, or even the diary of a person whom he knows; he poses four rules for *other* people who might be intimidated by diaries; and then, after ironically revealing that he no longer keeps a diary, he signs off. If students have already found signs of reluctance in Didion and Derricotte to reveal themselves fully to a public audience for their private writings, they will have no trouble discerning an even more extreme reluctance in Safire.

You might begin by asking your students to compare and contrast Safire's essay to the two other pieces in the chapter. Ask them to identify the sources of the diary excerpts in Didion and Safire, for example. Have them characterize the tone of each piece. Ask them to locate specific features that contribute to Safire's tone. Do they find a greater distance between Safire and his subject than between either of the other writers and her subject? If so, what is the effect of this distance? Does it make them more or less inclined to take his word, to accept, for example, his opinion on the "art of the diarist in its pure form"? Does a definition of a diary's "pure form" seem compatible with the nature and purposes of diaries as your students have experienced them?

Gail Godwin, in an essay titled "A Diarist on Diaries," concurs with Safire's observation that the number of diarists has declined. How many students in your class keep a diary? Have the students who do not keep diaries speculate about the reasons for that decline. Godwin suggests that some of her friends do keep diaries but don't admit it. Ask why a person might keep his or her diary-writing propensity a secret. Safire lists a few of the stereotypes currently attached to diarists. Can your students think of any other common conceptions about diaries and the people who write in them? In his epigraph, John Mack Faragher suggests differences in the diaries written by men and women. Do such generalizations hold true for the diarists in your class? Have gender stereotypes affected your students' decisions about whether or not to start a journal in the first place, and how to characterize that journal if they do keep one?

You might also ask if Safire conceives of diaries as having primarily a private or primarily a public function. Have your students consider his statement that "Diaries remind us of details that would otherwise fade from memory and make less vivid our recollection" (para. 5), and his example of that principle. Is there some dissonance between the statement and the example? And if it is true that "you are not writing for critics or posterity but are writing a private letter to your future self (para. 10), then why does he compare Barrymore's style with "the insecure jottings-down of most of us on little expense ledgers" (para. 15)? Ask them to speculate on how Safire's own career as a journalist affects his attitude toward diaries.

Additional Activities

You might teach Safire along with "Happy New Year" by Russell Baker (see Chapter 15). Each has a surprise conclusion that simultaneously justifies the essayist's pessimism and undermines his overall credibility.

You might also teach Safire in conjunction with more consistently ironic pieces such as Jonathan Swift's "Modest Proposal" (see Chapter 27) and Judy Brady's "I Want a Wife" (see Chapter 22), in order to facilitate a discussion on irony.

Generating Writing

Here is an assignment that will elicit non-traditional essays. Have your students imagine that they have spent the day with William Safire and Joan Didion, back in the days when Safire still kept a diary. The student may choose to spend an ordinary day with them, or to be present at an earth-shaking event. At the end of the day, when both Safire and Didion have fallen asleep, your student creeps into their rooms and steals a peek at the diary of the former and the notebook of the latter. What does the student find in each? Your students may of course feel free to adapt this fantasy in any way they see fit, and to write it from any point of view and in any form that best suits their ideas, as long as they aim to capture the difference between Safire's concept of "diary" and Didion's concept of "notebook."

WRITING ABOUT THE CHAPTER

1. Have students look over the notes they made before reading the selections, in which they analyzed their own journal-writing habits. Ask them to use this rough analysis, and any insights they have picked up while studying this unit, to write their own version of "On Keeping a Journal (or Notebook, or Diary)." Have they discovered some basic principles or rules they'd like to share? Are they now able to articulate their own motives for writing a journal so that a reader of their essay might be motivated to start a journal too? Ask them to write their essays in the first person, as did Didion, Derricotte, and Safire, and to try to capture some of the personal flavor of the writing they do for themselves in this essay written for others.

2. If you want to assign a research paper, have your students go to the library for the diary of a famous person, preferably someone whose life work (in any field) they admire. Have them read the diary and then analyze the uses to which the writer puts the diary form. Is the diary a close friend and confidant, as it is for Anne Frank, or an emotional outlet, as it is for Alice James? Or is it a place where its author can explore her or his thoughts, as Thoreau does in his journal? Is it a witty collection of gossip about famous people, written with an eye to eventual publication? Is it a place to record dreams, or fantasies, or ideas for poems or novels yet to be written? Have each student use excerpts from the diary he or she has chosen to support a thesis about the function or functions of that diary.

3. Read the manual chapter "Writing Informally about Reading." If you decide to assign journals to your students, you might consider using this assignment with the one on "Writing for Oneself," or at any other time during the semester. Have each student choose a journal entry in which he or she came to an unexpected insight while writing in the journal. Each student should revise that entry, creating a polished piece to be handed in along with a photocopy of the original journal entry. This exercise will show students how ideas can often appear in rough form when we are not straining to produce them, and that revising such an idea can be easier than staring at blank paper until an idea springs full-blown into one's head. If your students are doing team journals, you might have them collaborate on an essay based on an idea they've been discussing in their team journal.

2

Ambitions

Frederick Douglass, Learning to Read and Write

Russell Baker, Gumption

Amy Tan, Two Kinds

WORKING WITH THE CHAPTER

At the heart of many American childhoods is the excitement of growing up with the American Dream, with the prospects — as well as the pressures — defined by ambition to "make it" or to "get ahead." That dream can take, of course, many forms, as the selections from Frederick Douglass, Russell Baker, and Amy Tan demonstrate. The three come from entirely different racial backgrounds and cultural contexts, and yet their experiences share at least one major feature: their context is dramatically shaped by a still-prevalent American myth: no matter who one is or where one comes from one can become — with ambition, hard work, and dedication — extraordinarily successful.

As you work through these selections with your students, you might focus on the similar patterns of behavior behind these American childhood encounters with the American myth of ambition as well as the ways in which these very different young people come to recognize and understand the everyday limits of their own human possibilities. The epigraph by Mario Puzo is a convenient précis of the process that *many,* but certainly not all, American youngsters undergo as they reconcile their distinctive vision of their own possibilities with the pressures and constraints imposed by devoted parents or by repressive laws and social customs.

An even more provocative version of the same idea can be found in the passage from James Truslow Adams: the painful irony implicit in a simplistic rendition of the American Dream. Although he observes that the "very foundation of the American Dream of a better and richer life for all is that all, in varying degrees, shall be capable of wanting to share in it," he does not mention that *many* Americans, and especially those of color, were excluded from access to the tools — reading and writing — that would enable them to participate vigorously and freely in converting that dream into daily reality.

The material reprinted in this chapter demonstrates that not all Americans can dream the same dream. Russell Baker says of his sister, "Doris could have made something of herself if she hadn't been a girl." The mother depicted in Amy Tan's story is unconsciously bound to a stereotypical version of the Chinese-American rendition of the dream. In a similar vein, Frederick Douglass makes it clear in the passage reprinted from his *Narrative* that the fundamental freedom to read, write, and educate oneself, so widely assumed by nineteenth-century white Americans, was simply unavailable to slaves. In this sense, you might want to open a discussion of the thematic and stylistic relations among these three selections by exploring how race and gender skew the notion of ambition around which is built the mythical American Dream — both in the way it can be initially imagined and the extent to which it can be realized by *all* Americans.

These three authors also express personally the tensions evident when different visions of an individual's ambition clash. Each of the principal figures must face conflicting visions of ambition that others have for them. They must, finally, declare their right to articulate that ambition for themselves. Each author powerfully states that theme.

Teaching Strategies

You might want to launch a discussion on "ambitions" in American society by bringing the issue home to your students: what ambitions do they harbor, for themselves and for American society? Brainstorming a list of those ambitions will stir a good deal of conversation about equal access — what chance do *all* their peers, as well as *all* Americans have to realize those ambitions?

One of the most interesting aspects of discussing this theme in class — and following it up with writing exercises — might well be exploring the origins of the ambitions your students find they still have. The strong presence of mothers links Baker's account with Tan's. Douglass's ambition is driven by the irresistible urge to be free, both intellectually and politically. It would be productive to examine how Douglass's and Baker's autobiographical — and Tan's fictional — accounts show that they have satisfied their ambitions. (Here, the epigraph from Stephen Crane will prove very useful. Students will quickly gather and perhaps fully appreciate what Crane means when he says, "I am disappointed with success.") So too, you might take up what it means that two of these selections are autobiographical, the other fictional. How does this difference affect their response to each selection?

A Writing-before-Reading Exercise

Each of us has grown up in a sociocultural and economic context shaped at least in part by some version of the American Dream, and, more particularly, by belief in the benefits of personal ambition. As preparation for working with these three renditions of the belief in ambition, have students spend time in class writing out the principal characteristics of the dream as they have heard it reported by, say, parents, relatives, friends, and teachers. Then have them draw up a personal list of those characteristics, especially those which have surfaced in their own lives. They should write out as many of these characteristics as possible. They can readily draw on these notes in order to write a personal essay recounting the specific way in which the American belief in ambition has significantly affected their lives.

WORKING WITH THE SELECTIONS

Frederick Douglass

Learning to Read and Write

Teaching Strategies

The selection from Frederick Douglass's *Narrative* is an excellent introduction to the complexities around the idea of individual ambition in American culture. His own ambition — to educate himself and to understand his relation to and place in mid-nineteenth-century American society — is constrained by his racial identity and by the willful exclusion of black Americans from the satisfaction and power of either being educated or educating themselves.

Douglass's account of his "stratagems" for educating himself to read and write are often painfully ironic: his educating himself despite formidable odds is mirrored by his mistress's need to learn how to resist her human instincts and train herself to comply with her husband's refusal to permit one of his slaves to read and write. The opening paragraph is the sensible place to begin discussing Douglass's use of irony. You might ask your students to characterize the tone of voice they hear, for example, in the phrase, "It is due, however, to my mistress to say of her . . ." (para. 1). Does his attitude toward his "mistress" remain consistent throughout the essay, or does it change? If so, to what?

Perhaps the most ironic moment in the selection is Douglass's account of his mistress's ambition. He reports that "She was not satisfied with simply doing as well as he [her husband] had commanded; she seemed anxious to do better." This line serves as an extremely painful reversal of Douglass's own goal to educate himself.

At several other moments in this passage Douglass develops a similarly strong ironic attitude toward his own self-education. The main fact of slavery, that it "proved as injurious to her [his mistress] as it did to me," emphasizes the irony of repressing others. Other moments, particularly when Douglass talks about the disadvantages of educating himself and about how he "envied my fellow-slaves for their stupidity" — give you ways of extending this productive discussion of a compositional skill that many students have difficulty practicing successfully.

The Douglass selection is also an excellent help in teaching other compositional skills, including organization, sentence structure, and diction. You might want to ask your students to describe the overall structure of the selection; directing them to the opening paragraph should prove fruitful; they will come to realize that Douglass organizes his account of learning to read and write around the statement, "I was compelled to resort to various stratagems." Asking your students to list — and then to describe — each "stratagem" in detail will strengthen their confidence in responding to subtler aspects of the essay. So too, some extended conversation about the implications of choosing the word *stratagems* will bring out Douglass's attitude toward his own ambitious efforts to learn to read and write.

Discussing the overall organization of the Douglass selection might well lead easily into detailed consideration of his sentence structure. Have students describe how Douglass builds sentences in the opening two paragraphs. Once they can describe how these sentences are constructed, they are ready to take up the larger question of the effects such structures elicit in readers. Being able to describe how Douglass's sentences work — and to discuss the effects they produce — certainly will prepare students to consider whether or not his sentence structures remain consistent throughout the selection. Such an exercise in close reading can inform a similar exercise in examining Douglass's diction, as well as whether it, too, remains consistent.

This selection also demonstrates that Douglass works very effectively with figurative language. Ask students to consider the passage in which he uses an anecdote to describe his having "finally succeeded in learning to write" (para. 8). When he was sent on errands, he invariably carried a book and bread: "This bread I used to bestow upon the hungry little urchins, who, in return, would give me that more valuable bread of knowledge." This passage might well serve as the focal point of some conversation about Douglass's "stratagems," but it could also open up extended discussion of the advantages of drawing on figurative language — and especially metaphor — to make a crucial point clear. In this same vein, you might ask students to find other examples of successful metaphors in the selection as well as to identify what makes each successful.

The selection also lends itself to productive class discussions and writing assignments on broader social and cultural themes and issues. Encourage students to recognize the social, political, and cultural issues in this selection by inviting them to reflect on the circumstances in which they learned to read and write. Recounting the events and circumstances that led to their developing these enabling — and ennobling — skills will enable them to practice their own ability to write narrative essays and to establish a clear purpose for their essays.

Douglass's prose demonstrates that narration depends for much of its effectiveness on generous use of details enhanced by the writer's clear sense of direction and purpose. As you teach the narrative, you might want to discuss the effects of Douglass's choice of details in the incidents he recounts. As you pursue this line of questioning, students will begin to recognize the relation between the writer's selection of details and his overall purpose in writing the piece. (Douglass introduces very little of the dialogue that often reinforces vivid narration. You might want to ask students to speculate on how lack of dialogue affects this selection.)

Additional Activities

In an especially provocative scene, Douglass reports that his mistress, full of fury and apprehension, snatched a newspaper from him. "From this time I was most narrowly watched. If I was in a separate room any considerable length of time, I was sure to be suspected of having a book, and was at once called to give an account of myself . . ." (para. 3). Have students consider the ways in which the speaker in Russell Baker's essay and Amy Tan's story are also "narrowly watched." Although the circumstances in which they are forming their personal identity are obviously very different, these three writers do address this issue in terms similar enough to warrant some attention. Have your students discuss the similarities and the differences in the ways in which — and how closely — Douglass, Baker, and Tan are "watched." What forms of surveillance surface in each writer's account of his or her ambition?

The Douglass selection also works extremely well with the three selections in Chapter 3 ("Moments of Recognition"). You might ask students to identify the moment in Douglass's account of his learning to read and write that proved to be a moment of recognition for him, a turning point in his way of seeing himself as well as his relation to the world around him.

Generating Writing

1. The Douglass selection points to a profound change in the narrator's self-image once he discovered the enabling acts of reading and writing. Consider asking students to prepare the first draft of an essay in which they re-create the *specific* sociocultural and political circumstances amid which they learned to read and write. To complete this exercise successfully, they will need to spend a great deal of time recalling the event that is associated most clearly in their minds with learning to read and write. They will also need to remember to set that occasion in an appreciable social, cultural, and political context for their readers.

2. Here's another possibility for giving students an occasion to write successfully about their reading the Douglass selection. As the selection demonstrates, the myth of American success, and the personal ambition that recharges that myth, can often be complicated, or simply erased from one's list of possibilities, by racial and sexual stereotypes and discrimination. Ask students to draw on their reading of Douglass to pursue this issue in analyzing contemporary media. They could examine a current or recent issue of a popular American magazine addressed to teenagers and select an advertisement promoting some aspect of the American dream of success. After studying the advertisement, they could write an expository or argumentative essay in which they analyze the individual success imagined in the ad and then demonstrate how that ideal trades on (or is subverted by) some racial or sexual stereotype.

Russell Baker

Gumption

Teaching Strategies

Effective writers often bring the full weight of experience to the words they write. From Russell Baker's essay, we can assume that he picked up this talent, at least in part, from his mother. She has the remarkable ability of making abstract words concrete. To demonstrate, have students look carefully at the phrasing around the word *gumption*: "allocated all the gumption" and "Have a little gumption." Baker's mother invariably converts "gumption" into a measurable commodity: Doris has enough of it, her mother remarks, for ten people. You might then ask students to examine how these words and phrases from his mother's mouth — and from Baker's pen — help us to understand and appreciate the legacy Baker inherited from his mother.

You might follow through by asking students to point to other abstract words and phrases and then discuss how these gain material strength from the syntax in which they are presented. Such an exercise could lead quite naturally and productively to discussing the overall effects that writers produce when they transform the abstract into the concrete.

You could pursue a related issue of language along similar lines. Near the end of his essay, Baker talks about his mother's "bottomless supply of maxims" and follows it immediately with an example: "An apple a day keeps the doctor away" (para. 60). How does Baker prepare us for this dramatic moment? Ask students to locate other examples of such clichés and maxims throughout the selection. What are the implications of each — for Baker's mother? for Baker?

The maxims and clichés that Baker draws on also help structure his account of his youth and his "decision" to be a writer. You might work with students to explore the effects of repeating, for one, the cliché "bump on a log." What other clichés reappear in the essay, and with what effects?

So too, productive class discussion might well focus on the ways in which Baker's use of cliché seems to reinforce conventional gender identities. In many respects, conventional gender definitions and restrictions function in much the same way, and with the same effects, as Baker's use of maxims. You might ask students to explore this issue by identifying the ways in which gender stereotypes are presented in this essay. To whom or what are these stereotypes most often attributed? The paragraph about asking boys if they wanted to grow up to be president is an interesting example, and its attention to Lincoln is another chance to compare and contrast the sociocultural assumptions in this paragraph with those in the James Truslow Adams epigraph. A class discussion of this sociocultural — and finally compositional — issue might well conclude by your asking students to sketch the female equivalent to young boys being asked if they wanted to grow up to be president, and, as Baker says, being "asked it not jokingly but seriously" (para. 6).

Considering the language associated with gender identities might well open up a related and extremely important issue in the essay: agency. Students shouldn't have much difficulty explaining that it is Baker's mother who articulates the ambition he is expected to enact, but they may have a much harder time describing precisely how Baker goes about achieving this effect compositionally. The presentation of dialogue should prove a helpful focus. Reminding students that Baker's mother speaks first and insistently for him (as is evident in the repetition of "she said") should help them understand whose ambition is finally the most important to realize. Baker reinforces that sense by ascribing the mother's ambition for the boy to God, as in the line: "My mother replied that I was blessed with a rare determination to make something of myself" (para. 12). This line of attribution is reinforced in other parts of the essay by Baker's use of religious imagery, as in "bestowed" and "chasuble." This strain of images culminates in Baker's own expression of his faith in language, as is amply evident in the final two paragraphs of the essay.

One of Baker's acts of faith in language is his use of metaphors. Working with your students on this aspect of Baker's style should prove very fruitful. A good place to begin might be his use of the phrase "embarked on the highway of journalism" or his description of his "threadbare relatives."

Your students may not be regular readers of Baker's columns, nor might they know that he is widely regarded as one of America's most insightful and humorous columnists. Students can help strengthen their own writing by analyzing the strategies Baker uses to create his humorous effects. Have them identify those humorous moments and examine the strategies he uses to create this effect. Consider the scene in which Baker announces that he would like to be a garbage man. What devices does he use to evoke a humorous response?

Baker gains much of his success as a columnist from deft use of irony. Ask your students to locate — and then analyze — his use of this technique in the essay. Some of his handling of irony becomes rather complex. Consider his treatment of gender as an issue in accomplishing one's ambition. What tone do your students imagine when they read the sentence: "Doris could have made something of herself if she hadn't been a girl" (para. 3)? Does Baker encourage his readers to take this line ironically? What about the next sentence: "Because of this defect, however, the best she could hope for was a career as a nurse or schoolteacher, the only work that capable females were considered up to in those days"? How does Baker's use of *capable* here color his readers' response?

Additional Activities

Compare and contrast Russell Baker's and Frederick Douglass's ideas of "a perfect afternoon." What activities might both writers find themselves drawn to? In what specific ways might that shared activity be similar and different for each?

Baker's essay and Tan's story move toward a similar dramatic point: both speakers learn something significant from their mothers, but not what either mother apparently had intended. Ask students to identify as specifically as they can the dream or personal goal each mother tried to articulate for her child. You might follow up with questions focusing on how that expectation was foiled in each instance. What, finally, did each youngster learn from his or her mother, and how did the incidents they recount enable them to understand their mothers better?

Generating Writing

1. Russell Baker describes his idea of "a perfect afternoon" in paragraph 2: "lying in front of the radio rereading my favorite Big Little Book, *Dick Tracy Meets Stooge Viller.*" You might ask your students to engage in a similar imaginative exercise. Have them write the first draft of an essay in which they describe with as much detail as possible what they imagine themselves doing on "a perfect afternoon." They should describe what they would be doing and where they would be doing it and should also characterize the reaction their parents would have to such activity or inactivity.

2. Baker provides an interesting angle on whether ambition is limited by gender. He reports that his sister Doris "could have made something of herself if she hadn't been a girl" (para. 3). Give your students a chance to follow up on this provocative moment by asking them to write an essay telling about some incident in which gender was, as for Baker's sister, a "defect." Ask them to prepare a narrative demonstrating that a person's gender was regarded as a "defect." They will, of course, also need to attend to the way in which the problem was resolved, or why it wasn't.

Amy Tan

Two Kinds

Teaching Strategies

Amy Tan's story is excellent for getting students to respond to and practice point of view in writing. One of Tan's most appreciable accomplishments in this story is her ability to control the reader's response by gradually shifting her point of view about the events as well as the "raised hopes and failed expectations" that are the dramatic center of this story. The center of gravity in the story gradually shifts from Tan's account of the mother's hopes and dreams — and her daughter's subservient relation to them — to the daughter's struggles to articulate her own independence and her own sense of identity.

Your students may quickly notice that the story begins with the daughter's efforts to recount — and satisfy — her mother's ambition that her daughter will be recognized as a "prodigy." Tan's repeating this word, and reinforcing it by recurrent use of the word *genius,* creates a thematic focus for the first part of the story. The mother dominates the daughter's syntax and her sense of her own abilities, as we see from the start — in her repeating the phrase "You could." This phrasing is also an ironic commentary on both mother's and daughter's failed efforts to accept their visions of themselves and each other. The "you" imagined here can be applied to mother and daughter if it is also regarded as generic, as we see in paragraph 4 when the speaker reports that "We didn't immediately pick the right kind of prodigy." This generic "you" is enacted throughout the essay as the daughter tries on various identities as a "prodigy." She says: "I pictured this prodigy part of me as many different images, and I tried each one on for size." None fits. The reality of the mother's work as a domestic and of the daughter's attention to their "formica-topped kitchen table" invariably intercedes.

The daughter gradually tries to assert control over the ways in which her ambition will be articulated by trying to define the word *prodigy.* She reports that she has "new thoughts," filled with "lots of won'ts. I won't let her change me, I promised myself. I won't be what I'm not." Yet these efforts to establish a sense of ambition for herself separate from her mother are subverted by the daughter's slipping into the language of childhood: into the nursery-rhyme world of "the cow jumping over the moon" and later of a baby "that had something in its pants."

Tan draws engaging similes to illustrate the states of consciousness she seeks to render. Early in the story, the daughter describes her mother's repeated attempts to adjust the sound of their television set: "She got up — the TV broke down into loud piano music. She sat down — silence. Up and down, back and forth, quiet and loud. It was like a stiff, embraceless dance between her and the TV set" (para. 19). Go over this passage with your students, showing how this dramatic moment might serve as a metaphor for the structure of this story about "raised hopes and failed expectations." You could ask them to trace movements of mother and daughter away from and toward each other. Pursue this line of questioning by asking them to notice when — and how — mother and daughter embrace with shared hopes and expectations. And then close the discussion by asking how the story's final paragraph reinforces — or complicates — this "dance" between mother and daughter.

The piano lessons with Mr. Chong serve much the same dramatic function as the moment in which Tan describes her mother's relation to the television set. These lessons also serve as flawed enactments of the mother's dream about her daughter as a prodigy. Rather than realize her mother's vision, these lessons, Tan writes, taught her daughter how she "could be lazy and get away with mistakes, lots of mistakes" (para. 40). They became her opportunities to act out her determination "not to try, not to be anybody different."

Even the "failed expectations" of the daughter's performance in a local talent show (she calls it a "fiasco") do not relieve her of the burden of her mother's ambition. The issue of the daughter's obedience is finally settled in a dramatic confrontation that results in the daughter's shouting, "I wish I weren't your daughter." "Then I wish I'd never been born!" "I wish I were dead! Like them" [her twin baby sisters who were killed in China] (para. 78).

Tan presents no simple resolution to the daughter's refusal to be what her mother wanted her to be. "Neither of us talked about it again, as if it were a betrayal that was now unspeakable. So I never found a way to ask her why she had hoped for something so large that failure was inevitable." The story ends with a repetition of another version of silence.

Additional Activities

The selections from Douglass, Baker, and Tan are linked by the fundamentally human effort of trying — of young people struggling to face representations of their future that have been insistently provided for them. For Baker and Tan, this dilemma might be summarized in this line from Tan's story: "Why don't you like me the way I am?" (para. 30). For Douglass, the issue is *not* whether this or that identity is the "right" one, but whether he will be allowed to assert — or even imagine — any identity at all for himself. The interweaving of racial, class, and gender issues in these three essays should make it productive for you to work with them in class, particularly in discussing nature *and* origins of the futures imagined for these young people. It's not simply who articulates and controls one's ambition but what the origins of that inherited ambition are, and how those origins are tied into problematic racial, class, and gender identities.

Another link among these three selections is obedience. The three young people come to the conclusion that they cannot obey the dictates of others, especially in defining their individual identities. The daughter in Amy Tan's story summarizes this belief most succinctly: "Unlike my mother, I did not believe I could be anything I wanted to be. I could only be me" (para. 79). Direct attention to determining the specific ways in which the characters of these three young people can be linked as well as differentiated.

Generating Writing

Amy Tan recounts with haunting specificity and clarity a mother's disappointment in her daughter's struggles and finally her failed efforts to live up to the ambitious expectations set for her — to be a "prodigy" or a "genius." Ask students to write about a time in their lives — however roughly similar it might be — when they, too, did not satisfy the ambitious expectations one (or both) parents established for them. Following Tan's example in "Two Kinds," students should spend time establishing the sociocultural and familial context within which this conflict over expectations occurred. So too, they will need to present a portrait of the parent detailed enough to warrant the attention he or she commands in their lives. Finally, they ought to show how this conflict over "raised hopes and failed expectations" was resolved.

You might want to encourage students to write about how racial, class, and gender issues restrict the vision of individual ambition articulated by *any* American. Encourage them to read through a recent issue of a popular American magazine and identify either an advertisement or an article about individual ambition. Ask them to analyze the sociocultural, economic, and political assumptions embedded in the piece of writing and to determine the extent to which the advertisement or article accounts for racial, class, and gender differences in presenting its writer's vision of ambition.

WRITING ABOUT THE CHAPTER

1. Have your students carefully reread the essays they draft before they read the three selections in this chapter. Invite them to rewrite that draft. In what specific ways has the reading — and the class discussion — they have engaged in affected their plans to revise

that earlier draft? What specific compositional skills will they now try to apply to their own drafts that they hadn't thought of when they first prepared them?

2. As a prelude to another writing exercise, ask students to reread Russell Baker's essay and Amy Tan's short story. Both Baker and Tan learn something significant from their mothers, but not what either mother had intended. Similarly, most of us have had to face a dream or goal one (or both) of our parents established for us during childhood. Ask your students to recall such a goal — and the circumstances within which it was presented — and write an essay in which they recount an incident highlighting the conflict between the dream someone else articulated for them and their own interests. They might use this incident to illustrate the fact that they did not meet the expectations set for them.

3

Moments of Recognition

George Orwell, Shooting an Elephant

Langston Hughes, Salvation

John Updike, A & P

WORKING WITH THE CHAPTER

The structure we give our experience is built in part on the flashes of insight we have from time to time; these brief illuminations seem to focus our perceptions and help us understand our lives and the world around us. Much of our religion and philosophy is dedicated to fostering and explaining moments of recognition, encouraging us to use what we learn in our instants of clarity to help us through the rest of our days. Literature, too, is an attempt to capture and analyze these moments. When we read of someone else's insight, we experience that insight with them and share their revelation; we learn from others' recognition as we learn from our own.

Teaching Strategies

This chapter includes several perspectives on moments of recognition. The chapter epigraphs provide a context for discussion, and the selections illustrate the process of enlightenment. The best place to begin discussion may be with the chapter title. What do students think it means? What is it that is recognized in a "moment of recognition"?

James Joyce's *epiphany* is the name most often used for the sudden leap of understanding. Read closely the epigraph with the definition. You may want to ask the class to bring in various dictionary definitions. What is the original meaning of the word? How does Joyce's use of it draw on and expand its religious significance? Discuss Joyce's hero's belief that the writer's role is to "record these epiphanies with extreme care." Does the class agree?

Michael Dorris gives the example of Native-American initiation ceremonies as an instance of socially sponsored moments of recognition. What do students make of Dorris's assertion that Native-American teenagers were "expected to alter self-conception in a split-second vision"? Many Native-American tribes would not give children a permanent name at birth; instead, their adulthood rituals were supposed to provide or inspire an individual's name, just as the ritual clarified their role in the tribe and their own sense of self. One of the most interesting aspects in this culture of initiation is that self-awareness comes all at once, as the product of an unusual and challenging experience, rather than bit by bit in daily life. Dorris describes the Native-American initiation rituals as the adolescent's search for something "that would transform him." Does our culture have its own structures or institutions whose purpose it is to provide a "moment of personal, enabling insight"?

In his epigraph, Arnold Van Gennep describes how change occurs in persons and societies. The epigraph's source, *The Rites of Passage* (Chicago: University of Chicago Press, 1960), is focused on the thresholds passed over during transformation. It is these thresholds, Van Gennep believes, which we commemorate in our social rituals — the boundary between two states is a symbol for our transition through them. Discuss how this idea relates to the epiphany concept. How might these thresholds prompt heightened perception of the states they link and divide? How does the passage between two social or psychological states intensify awareness of the change this transition involves?

How does the quotation from Van Gennep put Dorris's epigraph into context? Does it help students think of analogous rituals and ceremonies from our own culture? You might want to look at these epigraphs in conjunction with Hughes's "Salvation." How is his "religious experience" portrayed as an expected stage in his development as an African-American adolescent? How is it different from the Native-American rituals described by Dorris?

What threshold did Orwell cross in shooting the elephant? How might that have been the kind of transformative experience to which Dorris refers? How would the experience differ from the initiation ritual? Ask students to focus on the attitudes of the people, both Burmese and English, surrounding Orwell. How might their perception of the threshold Orwell crossed differ from his own? Is an essential sympathy between the subject and the society around him necessary for an epiphany? Is it necessary to a rite of passage?

How might Updike's "A & P" be seen as a response to the challenge implicit in the Joyce epigraph? How does the narrator's age — nineteen — seem to affect his response to his moment of realization? How might this be seen as a narrative of initiation? Over what thresholds might Van Gennep say the narrator passes?

A Writing-before-Reading Exercise

Ask students to call to mind a moment when they experienced a flash of insight. What were the circumstances? How did their perception of the situation, and of themselves and the world around them, change? Did this moment of recognition have any lasting influence on their behavior or their way of constructing their experience? What lesson, if any, did it teach them?

WORKING WITH THE SELECTIONS

George Orwell

Shooting an Elephant

Teaching Strategies

This is one of Orwell's most accessible essays, and though the experience he recounts is exotic, students should certainly be able to identify with his sense of being trapped in an impossible situation. Make sure they are clear about the context of the elephant incident; ask if they understand why Orwell, an Englishman, was a police officer in Burma. How do the circumstances of British rule over India seem to have contributed to Orwell's personal and political consciousness? Of what kind of government was Orwell a representative? How might he have been perceived by the Burmese?

Discuss Orwell's style in this essay. How would students describe his tone? What kind of diction does he use? What does his attitude toward himself and his actions seem to be? How is this attitude conveyed? Ask the class to pick out specific passages in which Orwell distinguishes between his attitudes at the time he shot the elephant and his attitudes when writing the essay. How does he create a sense of distance between his current and his former selves?

You might want to talk about the essay's structure, and how it contributes to our understanding of the author's moment of recognition. How does the essay begin? The first sentence is arresting and informative: "In Moulmein, in Lower Burma, I was hated by large numbers of people . . ." (para. 1). What is the effect of the word *hated* here? What is the effect of his focus on the first person? The essay could have begun with a sentence like, "During the British reign over India, the colonial police were despised." Would the essay's force have been substantially diminished by such an opening?

Orwell begins by relating various ways in which the Burmese expressed hatred for him and other Europeans. After providing some context, he discusses his conflicting feelings about his job and the people around him (para. 2). How is paragraph 2 organized? Are Orwell's objections to imperialism expressed clearly? Does the alternation in the opening paragraphs between attacks on the British Empire and disgust with the Burmese people mirror the ambivalence Orwell must have felt when he shot the elephant? How do these paragraphs set the stage for the coming revelation?

Orwell is very clear about the meaning he attaches to the experience of shooting the elephant. He describes it as "something . . . which in a roundabout way was enlightening," an incident that "gave me a better glimpse than I had had before of the real nature of imperialism" (para. 3). How does his description of the incident coincide with Joyce's definition of "epiphany"? Discuss this comparison with the class.

Talk about Orwell's way of relating the elephant episode. What kind of language does he use? What is his tone? Orwell refers to the elephant here as *it* rather than *he;* why? What do students make of the phrase, "had turned the van over and inflicted violences upon it" (para. 3). Might this be an attempt to reproduce the idiosyncratic English of the Burmese witnesses? How does Orwell's tone change when he discovers the dead man? Does this change in tone reflect a change in attitude toward the elephant? Might this be the rhetorical equivalent of sending for the elephant rifle?

Describe Orwell's attitude toward the crowd. Why might he feel this way about them? Why would they make him "uneasy"? Notice his care in pointing out that the Burmese are no different from "an English crowd" (para. 5). Why might it be important to him to make this connection?

How many revelations does Orwell experience? The first seems to be when he stops on the road. "As soon as I saw the elephant," he writes, "I knew with perfect certainty that I ought not to shoot him" (para. 6). Is this insight invalidated by his next perception, "suddenly I realized that I should have to shoot the elephant after all"? How did these two realizations work together to enable his main epiphany, that "when the white man turns tyrant, it is his own freedom that he destroys"? The impossibility of reconciling his moral decision with the social pressures around him lead Orwell to understand just how dangerous are the forces that create those social pressures.

The piece does not end with Orwell's moment of recognition, however. What effect does the account of the elephant's death have? What does Orwell's chief preoccupation seem to have been at the time? What do his chief interests seem to have been at the time of writing? The description of the elephant's death seems wrenching — why? Ask the class to discuss the irony of the concluding sentence, "I often wondered whether any of the others grasped that I had done it solely to avoid looking a fool" (para. 14). What does this admission tell us about Orwell's isolation from his fellow Europeans and their isolation from one another? How might that alienation contribute to the dangerous state of affairs that Orwell first perceived while facing the crowd and the elephant?

Additional Activities

Interested students might want to read Orwell's novel *Burmese Days* (New York: Harcourt, Brace, 1950), a fictional account of experiences very similar to Orwell's. How are the themes in this essay echoed in the novel? Does the novel genre give Orwell the freedom to present various points of view on the conflict between Burmese culture and British imperialism? Some students might want to report on Orwell's other works, and his treatment there of similar themes. In *1984* and *Animal Farm*, as in the essay, moments of revelation are accompanied by shocking violence. Must leaps of perception be violent, or inspired by violence? Why might Orwell link the two?

Generating Writing

1. Ask students to recall an incident in their own life when social pressure drove them to do something they knew to be wrong. What realizations did the event help them to reach? How did their experience parallel Orwell's? How did it differ from his?

2. How does Orwell use language to convey emotional states? Have the class analyze his style in this essay, especially focusing on tone and diction. What kind of imagery is used? What kinds of verbs and sentence structures are employed? How does style help create the essay's powerful effect?

Langston Hughes

Salvation

Teaching Strategies

Hughes is best known today for his influential poetry; ask students if they are familiar with his work. Does his prose seem particularly poetic? Read the opening paragraph aloud with the class. How does Hughes capture the rhythm of speech? The paragraph includes diction that evokes the thirteen-year-old Hughes ("going on thirteen," "my Auntie Reed's") as well as the revival-meeting rhetoric ("very hardened sinners," "brought to Jesus"). What is the effect of this allusion to the spoken word? How does it help to characterize the author as a boy?

What is significant about the age at which Hughes had this experience? Many religious groups — Native Americans, believers in Judaism, and some Christian denominations — feel that the moment when children are ready to become part of the spiritual community comes at the beginning of adolescence. Certainly his Aunt Reed's friends and fellow worshippers seem to have thought him ready for this step. What does the class think? Might it not be difficult for a twelve-year-old to think seriously about such issues like salvation and damnation? What do students have to offer from their own experience?

What does the class make of the young Hughes's conviction that he would, when he was saved, see Jesus? How do they take the statement, "I had heard a great many old people say the same thing and it seemed to me they ought to know" (para. 2)? Is Hughes the adult writer being ironic at the expense of his younger self? What kind of comment does this belief make about the way in which children receive religious training?

Why does Hughes decide to pretend to be saved? How much influence does Westley's pretense, and the congregation's response to it, seem to have on him? How great an influence does embarrassment seem to have? Discuss Hughes's rationalization, "God had not struck Westley dead for taking his name in vain or for lying in the temple. So I decided that maybe to save further trouble, I'd better lie, too" (para. 11). Discuss Hughes's impossible situation. What might have happened if he had waited until he saw Jesus, in some satisfactory way, before he said he was saved? How did the congregation's pressure toward piety work against the young Hughes's actual piety and belief?

How does Hughes react to the success of his deception? Talk about the effectiveness of the essay's final paragraph. Does the closing run-on sentence convey the voice of a frightened, upset twelve-year-old? What is the essential paradox of Hughes's revelation? Talk about the irony of Hughes's "salvation." Can those nurturing institutions — a loving family and a devout and caring church — wind up doing a child tremendous harm?

Additional Activities

Students interested in Hughes may want to read and report on his work and career. Do the themes raised in this essay recur throughout Hughes's work? Why might he focus so much on the experiences of children?

If the film *Marjoe* (1972; directed by Howard Smith and Sarah Kernochan) is available, you might want to assign it for class or individual viewing. (A video version of the film is distributed by RCA/Columbia Pictures Home Video.) This biography of a child evangelist is an interesting contrast to Hughes's depiction of an early religious experience.

Generating Writing

1. How would students describe the mood of this essay? Ask the class to write a brief essay analyzing how Hughes uses language to create this mood. They should pay special attention to diction; what kind of vocabulary does he employ? Are Hughes's family and the congregation portrayed sympathetically? How does their portrayal help heighten the essay's sense of conflict?

2. Have students discuss an incident from their own life in which community expectations caused them to go against their own conscience. How did the experience make them feel? Did it force them to reexamine some of the community's values? How can too much good will produce bad results?

John Updike

A & P

Teaching Strategies

Ask the class to characterize the story's narrator. You may want to ask someone to read the first few sentences aloud; how does Updike use Sammy's speech to reveal his character? How might we stereotype a nineteen-year-old man who works as a cashier in a supermarket? Would we be likely to expect him to be particularly insightful? How does Updike undermine these expectations?

How does the narrator relate to the people around him? Talk about his perceptions of the girls in bathing suits. How does he see them? What criteria does he use to judge them? How do students react to the attitudes Sammy and his co-workers express? You might want to discuss his comment, "You never know for sure how girls' minds work (do you really think it's a mind in there . . . ?)." Why might Sammy have, or claim to have, this opinion of women? What is gender's part in developing the story? What role does class play? Is age a factor here as well?

What does Sammy's overall view of the world seem to be? Is he an optimist? A cynic? How does his language distance him from his emotions and from the people around him? What feelings and attitudes might his habits of language and thought be meant to hide?

Discuss the manager's comment to the girls. Although his disapproval may seem ridiculous today, it would have been quite shocking to shop in a bathing suit in the early 1960s. Nearly all high schools, and many colleges, still had dress codes at that time, and people were quick to express opinions about others' grooming and attire. Why does Mr. Lengel speak to the girls? Is his comment motivated only by their appearance, or might it reflect other tensions in the town? Sammy stresses the difference in status between the girls and the manager; he describes his favorite as "getting sore now that she remembers her place, a place from which the crowd that runs the A & P must look pretty crummy" (para. 18). Why does Sammy choose to identify with the girls rather than with Mr. Lengel?

Why does Sammy quit? What, finally, is his motivation for this action? How would students define his epiphany? Do they agree or sympathize with the new view of the world to which this experience has brought him?

Additional Activities

Students interested in further reading might want to look at Ring Lardner's short story, "Haircut," from *Haircut and Other Stories* (New York: Random House, 1984). Like Updike, Lardner uses the distance between narrator and author for dramatic effect. How are the stories different? How is Lardner's narrator unlike Sammy? Why does Lardner's narrator fail, finally, to grasp the reality of the situation he describes?

Generating Writing

1. Invite students to retell this story from the perspective of one of its other characters. How would this character evaluate the situation at the A & P? How might Sammy appear to this character? What might he or she make of Sammy's decision to quit his job?

2. How close is Updike's perspective to his narrator's? Ask the class to read the story closely and distinguish between Sammy's attitudes and those which seem, by implication, to be the author's. Tone might be a help in making this distinction. What does Updike seem to think of the narrator? What would he like us to think? How does his choice of narrator make the story more effective? How might the story be different if the narrator were, rather than a nineteen-year-old grocery clerk, an adult, Harvard-educated writer — someone like Updike himself?

WRITING ABOUT THE CHAPTER

1. In each of these stories, a moment of recognition comes in opposition to social and community pressures. Does epiphany necessarily entail isolation from society? Must heightened understanding of problems or situations involve separation from society? Why, or why not?

2. From their work with the chapter, how would students explain its title? How has their reading changed their views of recognition and revelation? Which of the selections did they find most affecting? Which did they think gave the clearest illustration of an epiphanic moment?

3. Ask the class to return to the Writing-before-Reading exercise. How might they revise their description of their own moment of recognition after working with the chapter selections? With which of the authors do they feel most sympathy? If they were to turn their experiences into literature, would they write them as an essay? as a short story? or in some other genre? What might they hope to convey to their readers?

4

Places in the Heart

E. B. White, Once More to the Lake

Gretel Ehrlich, The Solace of Open Spaces

David Bradley, Ringgold Street

WORKING WITH THE CHAPTER

The Edward Abbey epigraph opens with a seeming contradiction: "This is the most beautiful place on earth. There are many such places." Ask your students to explore the significance of his words: how can line 1 retain its meaning in the context of line 2? This is one way to lead them to explore the all-important notion of subjectivity in this chapter. Each place described in the selections — a remote lake in Maine, an open range in Wyoming, and a city street in Philadelphia — is special not because of its intrinsic, objective features, but because of its effect on the writer. Eudora Welty's analogy also suggests an intimate relation between the "sense of place" and the landscape of the writer's mind: she writes in an epigraph to this chapter that place "is forever astir, alive, changing, reflecting, like the mind of man itself." Even D. H. Lawrence, who writes that the "spirit of place is a great reality," speaks of the *people* who are "polarized" in a locale. You might want to ask your students to infer what they can about the people who chose these places to write about. How does the "spirit of the place" each describes reflect his or her own spirit?

Teaching Strategies

The essays in this chapter are extraordinarily rich in associations and possibilities. If you teach this chapter early in the semester, and you would like to assign a piece of descriptive writing to your students, you might focus the discussion of these selections on the author's strategies for creating a sense of place. One good way to achieve this focus is to have your students close their eyes and try to visualize the place described in the essay they have just read. What do they see with their minds' eye? What details stand out in memory? What senses do those details appeal to? After they have exercised memory in this way, have them open their eyes and find the specific passage or passages that triggered the mental images. Have them analyze these passages to discover the author's strategies for making an impression on the reader. (This exercise also works during the peer editing of student papers: if one's classmates remember an image or phrase, the student who wrote it will know where his or her writing is most effective; if nothing stands out in memory, that will send a different, but equally important, message.)

If it is later in the semester, and you are at work on improving your students' analytical skill, you might want to focus on point of view instead. The obvious answer to the question of perspective in this chapter is simple: all three essays are written in the first person. But if you push harder on the question, you will lead students to insights about the essays. You might start by asking them to scrutinize the common metaphors for point of view, including *point of view* itself, and *perspective*, and *standpoint*. What do these words imply? What do these authors view? How does their "perspective" (in every sense of the word) affect what they view? Where do they "stand" in relation to the places they describe? You might also ask how the verb tenses affect the point of view in "The Solace of Open Spaces," as opposed to "Once More to the Lake" and "Ringgold Street." This question could lead in a number of directions, among them considering the question of distance, fine tuning the distinction between *narrator* and *author*, or discussing nostalgia.

If your discussion of point of view leads to a discussion of the relative objectivity of different genres and media, you might ask your students to bring a nonessayistic representation of a place to your next class meeting. This might be a photograph, a painting, a passage from a novel or a poem, or even a song, with or without lyrics. Ask students to examine the ways in which the traces of point of view are betrayed in each genre, and how the creator's point of view affects the consumer's impression of the place being represented.

A Writing-before-Reading Exercise

Before your students read the essays in this chapter, have them take a few moments to think of a place they hold dear — a childhood playground, a favorite high-school hangout, their old neighborhood. Ask them to think about what makes this place special. What are the most vivid details they can recall about this place? What images do they associate with the place? What emotions does recollection of the place elicit? What word might they choose to describe their dominant image of the place? If you have time, you might want to ask students to do some mapping on the topic of the places in their hearts, once they have decided which place they will focus on. Because maps are spatial, they are particularly well suited to this topic. Just make sure that they do not take your instructions *too* literally — you don't want a road map to the place, or a scale drawing. Be sure they include such things as images and associations. You might suggest they start with a graphic representation of the place, and add words to convey the emotions or memories they associate with each graphic detail. Alternatively, you might help them avoid a too-literal reading of your instructions by suggesting that they structure their maps according to a principle other than geography, that they create maps starting, for example, with their five senses.

Having identified and explored their own places in the heart, ask them to describe those places in writing. Assign a rough draft of an essay in which they make their writers see — and appreciate — the place closest to their heart. What details would they choose to make this place vivid for readers who have never seen it? What emotion or emotions would they emphasize?

WORKING WITH THE SELECTIONS

E. B. White

Once More to the Lake

Teaching Strategies

This essay is a modern classic, and deservedly so. It is a joy to teach, because every detail works to create a coherent whole, demonstrating that equation so dear to the English instructor's heart: form is inseparable from content. Vladimir Nabokov used to tell his students always to value the *how* over the *what,* but never to confuse it with the *so what.* "Once More to the Lake" is an essay with almost no *so what.* We like to begin by challenging our students to identify the smallest points of style imaginable — White's use of the definite pronoun *the,* for instance, or his use of the conjunction *and.* If they ask themselves why it's "the dragonfly" rather than "a dragonfly" in paragraph 5, or why White prefers parataxis (linking by coordinating conjunctions) over syntaxis (linking by subordinating conjunctions), their answers will always lead them to a profounder understanding of the ideas and emotions in the essay.

Furthermore, analyzing almost any passage in the essay will lead the student eventually to consider everything else in the essay. Take the metaphor with which White opens paragraph 6: "We caught two bass, hauling them in briskly as though they were mackerel." Ask your students to analyze this metaphor. They might notice that it's unusual in that it yokes two similar entities — it's surprisingly unsurprising, as metaphors go. Ask them why White might have created such a metaphor. Someone might mention that whereas these bass are freshwater fish, mackerel live in the sea. This observation could lead to a discussion of the sea versus lake motif that runs through the essay. What does the sea represent to White? to his son? in the context of World War II? What does the lake represent? The surprising lack of surprise might lead someone to mention White's surprise at other unsurprising occurrences; an example from the same paragraph might be, "When we got back for a swim before lunch, the lake was exactly where we had left it," which observation leads White to comment that this "seemed an utterly enchanted sea." Ask students where the sense of enchantment comes from. Do they find other indications of a supernatural feeling of wonder occasioned by contact with the natural world in this essay? This line of thought might lead to a discussion of the religious imagery in the essay, and an attempt to characterize White's spiritual position. Yet another response to the question about the bass-and-mackerel comparison might be to call attention to the analogy's being drawn from the natural world. This clue might lead your class to look at his other metaphors drawn from nature, to see how they function in the essay. What is the effect of the metaphor comparing outboard motors to mosquitos (para. 10)? How does that metaphor help reintegrate the new sound into nature, erasing the difference that White initially claimed for them? This line of questioning might lead students to consider the opposing forces in the essay: change and stasis, a sense of time circling versus a sense of time moving forward. Another student might call the bass-and-mackerel metaphor redundant — why describe something by comparison to something that's nearly identical? Ask your students to find other examples of redundancy in this essay, on different scales. They might find phrases such as "the years were a mirage and there had been no years" (para. 5) or the pervasive use of repetition. Or they might jump to psychology and point to White's sense of his own redundancy: If his child replaces him, then he has no place. This line of thought will lead to analysis of the final scene, in which generation and death come together in one chilling sensory image. Many students might have felt that this ending comes out of nowhere in this essay about "jollity and peace and goodness" (para. 9). Then lead an exploration into the early signs of White's ambivalence, his anxiety about his own mortality. You might also point out that the Freudian reading prompted by the final scene is supported by the earlier suggestion of a primal scene from White's boyhood at the lake, where "the partitions . . . were thin and did not extend clear to the tops of the rooms" (para. 2).

Additional Activities

White's classic essay raises classic issues about reading and writing that enable us to help students discover a great deal about their own resourcefulness with language and their ability to use it to express the ideas they want or need to express. Yet, in addition to the mastery of language highlighted in the essay, White also explores several important themes that link it with other selections.

A fundamental choice that writers routinely make is diction. Discuss White's choice of words and describe it in a few paragraphs. What makes White's word choices so effective? Compare and contrast White's diction with, say, George Orwell's in "Shooting an Elephant." Choose examples of distinctive diction and then discuss the similarities and differences.

You might apply the same basic exercise to other aspects of each writer's prose style, including the syntax and rhythms of their sentences and the devices with which they build unity into their paragraphs. This classroom exercise can be readily extended to any other "classic" essays in this collection. A still more informative exercise would be to do a comparison and contrast of stylistic features in less celebrated essayists. Studying stylistic features in White and less celebrated writers will not only introduce your students to "canon" issues in the first-year composition course but also help demystify these texts.

White has the ability to weave thoroughly engaging metaphors into the fabric of his sentences. Ask students to identify several of the most memorable metaphors and describe what is so distinctive about them. Then they should read the selections in Chapter 33, "The Power of Metaphor." Also, they might explain how White's metaphors exemplify (or challenge) the assumptions about figurative language in the selection from Lakoff and Johnson's "Metaphors We Live By."

Broaden this discussion by comparing and contrasting stylistic features in White's and other essays by unfolding the thematic links among them. The scene in which the father shares the feeling of his son's icy cold bathing suit is a strong bridge to the selections in Chapter 3, "Moments of Recognition"; it is a provocative example of an epiphany. As such, it offers rich possibilities for discussing connections to (and distinctions from) the moments of discovery inscribed in these other essays.

White's essay offers another perspective on the theme of father–son relations featured in Anderson's "Discovery of a Father" (Chapter 20). Students might compare and contrast this relationship and its consequences in each story. How does each writer control the language that expresses this theme?

Generating Writing

1. Assign an essay in which your students analyze the doubling motif in "Once More to the Lake." How does White's eerie feeling "that he was I, and therefore, by simple transposition, that I was my father," form the core of this essay? How does White reinforce this main theme on other levels of the essay, in style, imagery, rhythm, and so on? What are the larger implications of this eerie sensation?

2. Assign an essay in which your students analyze one metaphor from the essay (other than the metaphor(s) you have already discussed in class), tracing all its implications and connections throughout the essay to their logical conclusions.

3. If any students find the unassailable coherence of "Once More to the Lake" uncongenial, have them write an essay arguing against the value system that places a high premium on artistic coherence and unity. They might want to argue, say, from a cultural perspective that offers other aesthetic values, or from the standpoint of a feminist critic of the male academy. They might want to offer — and analyze — another essay as an alternative to the traditional values demonstrated in White's prose.

Gretel Ehrlich

The Solace of Open Spaces

Teaching Strategies

An engaging account of a writer's efforts to express the beauty and power of the Wyoming landscape, both as a place in nature and a site for living and working, Ehrlich's essay is laden with opportunities to learn about the art of writing. It is a first-rate introduction to the craft of description and enables students to observe the dramatic encounter between the landscape and its inhabitants.

Perhaps the most effective way to start is to focus on Ehrlich's skill in writing description. What overall impression does she create of the Wyoming landscape? What are the major characteristics of the landscape? Explore the connection between her description of the land and the people who inhabit it. You could pursue this point by asking students to point to — and explore the implications of — those moments in which Ehrlich discusses how the people of Wyoming have adapted to the distinctive features of the landscape. Have they literally taken on the characteristics of the landscape? Through Ehrlich's description, students should be able to infer principles and procedures for writing effective description.

One of the most prominent strategies in Ehrlich's essay is her recurrent use of metaphor. Examine paragraph 1 for her use of figurative language. Ehrlich creates a striking image of sheep who "drift across dry land, tumbling into draws like water and surge out again onto the rugged, choppy plateaus that are the building blocks of this state." Why is the figurative language in this sentence so effective? Identify other moments in the essay when Ehrlich draws on metaphor to strengthen descriptions and accelerate the pace of her prose.

Consider Ehrlich's skillful use of transitions. Have students notice how she shifts abruptly from one topic to another, from physical description to personal experience, from historical facts to character sketch. Then ask them to examine more carefully how she connects these moments by association rather than logic. This essay demonstrates that transitions are more than simply connecting words; ideas can hold passages together without such explicit transitional words as *however, consequently,* and *therefore.*

Have students identify, in the passages they judge to be the most effective descriptions, the kinds of sentence structure Ehrlich typically uses. What do your students gather from these passages about the structures most appropriate for the descriptions they write?

Students should notice how Ehrlich balances her account of Wyoming with a series of apparent contradictions. Life in Wyoming is replete with "violent swings" and "slow accumulations." Explore how, in describing weather conditions, she emphasizes both features. Look for other oppositions she describes and show how these apparent oppositions affect her portrait of the West.

You can extend this discussion by calling attention to Ehrlich's ability to blend generalization and detail. What specific effects does she create with this mixture? The *movements* of her prose reflect the language and sentence structure that she attributes to Wyoming residents (see paras. 16–18). Ehrlich's talk about "the skin and bones of thought," "dropped" verbs, and "compressed" language might help students with diction, syntax, paragraph development, and overall rhythm and structure in their own essays.

You could easily broaden the focus of this discussion to include the organization of Ehrlich's essay. Ask students to write out, and then discuss in small groups, the principles of organization with which Ehrlich ensures unity and coherence in her paragraphs and the essay as a whole. With what themes does she connect the parts of her essay? How does she use time (and especially the seasons) to order her essay?

Ehrlich combines personal experience with character sketches and descriptions of the landscape. She begins and ends by recounting a personal experience. Students could compare and contrast the accounts of personal experience that frame her essay. What effects does she achieve by opening and closing with her own experience? With what point of view does she open the essay? Does it remain consistent throughout?

Ehrlich dedicates much of her essay to unfolding her personal response to living in Wyoming. Ask students to reread carefully the opening paragraph and to assess the effects of her opening. You might ask them to discuss, for example, the significance of her reporting that she has "just awakened from a nap." What scene does she awaken to, and with what consequences? When and with what effects does Ehrlich return to develop (and complicate) the elements introduced in the opening paragraph?

Consider the place Ehrlich creates for herself in the essay as well as the ways in which Wyoming has affected her. Why did she go to Wyoming in the first place? Students shouldn't have any difficulty explaining why she went there and what she expected to find. But then they ought to follow through and discuss her response when she arrived there. Ask if they see clearly how the "open spaces" of Wyoming provide "solace" for Ehrlich.

Ask students to explain what Ehrlich means when she says, "We might also learn how to carry space inside ourselves in the effortless way we carry our skins." Have students explore the connections between her point here and what she says in her final paragraph. What does she mean when she says that "we build *against* space"? How do people living in Wyoming "build *against* space," and how do they see themselves in relation to "open spaces"?

Next, consider Ehrlich's management of her thesis, that space "can heal what is divided and burdensome in us." What does she achieve by holding the statement of her thesis until the penultimate paragraph? What effects would she have gotten by presenting her thesis at the beginning? Understanding the architecture of Ehrlich's essay will both enrich students' appreciation of her accomplishments as a writer and strengthen their skill in composition.

Additional Activities

The Ehrlich selection can be taught effectively with many essays in *The Winchester Reader*. Try it with Chapter 33, "The Power of Metaphor." Her use of metaphor and its structural contribution illustrate the principles Lakoff and Johnson discuss in their account of the metaphors "we live by."

Because Ehrlich blends description, historical narrative, personal experience, and character sketch, the essay shares much with Mary Gordon's essay on Ellis Island in Chapter 7. Students might compare and contrast Ehrlich's apparent fondness for and identification with people living in the West with Mary Gordon's affectionate depiction of and identification with the immigrants who enter their new world through Ellis Island.

Ehrlich moves beyond stereotypical treatments of residents of the West. Read her essay along with Chapter 22, "Resistances to Stereotypes." Ehrlich's essay will lend an engaging twist to students' thinking and writing about that chapter.

Generating Writing

1. Ask your students to describe some public or private place that gives them "solace." Have them write an essay describing that place with enough detail to enable readers to appreciate both the place and the writer's reasons for seeing it as a source of solace.

2. As preparation for developing their essays on the Ehrlich essay, ask what she means when she talks about the Western Code. What can they infer about its rules? How is this code articulated and handed down from one generation to the next?

As soon as they feel comfortable explaining this Western Code, ask them to prepare the first draft of an essay in which they articulate the principles that governed some code of behavior in their own life. For this writing exercise they will need to decide on a suitable form. Which would be more effective, a narrative essay retelling an anecdote that illustrates this code of behavior? A descriptive essay? An expository one? In any case, they will need to attend to the "rules" that govern this code of behavior.

David Bradley

Ringgold Street

Teaching Strategies

Because the setting of this essay is all-important, you might want to make a blackboard map of Ringgold Street. Or you might have a group of students collaborate on making the map, using the details in the essay's first two paragraphs. A second group of students might add the details gleaned from paragraph 6, both about North 24th Street and the setup of Bradley's apartment there. Invite students to discuss the significance of geography and architecture in "Ringgold Street." Bradley himself admits to "anthropomorphizing" the houses along the street. Ask them how the architecture of a building reflects the needs and values of the people who live in (or design) that building. You can follow up by asking them to discuss what the architecture in this Philadelphia neighborhood tells us about that neighborhood's social structure.

Probably the most interesting questions about architecture's significance in this essay are on the essayist himself. Ask students to identify Bradley's place in the carefully outlined world of "Ringgold Street." They will probably notice that when he lives in Aspen Park he is outside Ringgold Street, in a position from which he can look into the homes of the neighbors across the courtyard. Although he keeps protesting that he is not a voyeur, your students will probably find that the distinction he draws is not entirely convincing. He writes, "Let me be clear about this: I never *observed* the people of Ringgold Street. I just saw and heard them, as you catch glimpses and snippets of sound through windows as you walk down a street" (para. 8). One might ask the difference between *observing* and *seeing*. Bradley is careful to stress his passivity ("Fate brought me to live on Ringgold Street" [para. 12]), and indeed seeing is more passive than observing, but when he starts looking through his neighbors' garbage cans it becomes difficult to believe that he's just catching random glimpses of their lives.

You might here want to shift the discussion away from the literal structure of Ringgold Street to the structure of the essay. Students should notice that two distinct kinds of narrative strategies alternate throughout the essay. Have them characterize each. They should be able to notice, for one, that the sections beginning with fragments identifying the time of day on Ringgold Street lack the first-person pronoun that appears in the intervening sections. They might also notice that the third-person sections take place after Bradley has moved to Ringgold Street himself. This observation might lead them to try to place Bradley within the sections lacking the first person: if he lives on Ringgold Street, then where is he in the narrative? They might sense that the third-person sections aren't completely objective — someone, for instance, must be inferring that the woman "steps gingerly" from her house because it is being renovated — and they might recognize the pattern of observation and inference as Bradley's own modus operandi, thinly disguised. In fact, clues appear throughout the essay that the "bearded black man" who first appears in paragraph 3 is David Bradley: both of them are joggers, neither works a regular nine-to-five job, and the bearded man wears a shirt "bearing the faded logo of a recently popular Canadian lager" — Moosehead beer (para. 12), perhaps?

You will want to discuss the evidence that Bradley sets it up so that the reader's activity parallels his own: we have to read between the lines to piece together his identity in the same way as he reconstructs his neighbors' and the former inhabitants' lives by sifting through their trash and junk mail. Ask students if they feel as if they have been made complicit in this act of voyeurism. Does the idea that he is merely "reading" his neighbors' lives make his voyeuristic "sport" (para. 14) seem more innocent? Does Bradley's narrative strategy so draw the reader in that he or she is convinced by his resolution "that if you kept your eyes and ears open to it you could learn almost anything about people whose lives would be fascinating if you took the time to think about them" (para. 25)? Help students examine the choice Bradley set up in those final paragraphs — between "a real place with real people or . . . a place that I loved but which was largely fantasy," between the "mundane" and "magic." He ends up choosing to "leave reality alone." In a sense, however, the dichotomy he has set up is a false one: after all, he invents the Champagne Clansman's ACLU membership, the Sunbather's brother, and the Parisian's Maxwell House (para. 25) just as surely as he invented the spicy earlier versions of their lives. What overall impression of David Bradley do your students carry away from this essay?

Additional Activities

You might want to connect your discussion of "Ringgold Street" to the selection in Chapter 5, "The Power of Names." When Bradley finds that "he has no choice but to give [his neighbors] names" (para. 8), he makes it sound as if naming is a benign activity, but the power of the bestower of names is undeniable: he creates their identities by naming them.

Because Bradley is an outsider on Ringgold Street, "a raw newcomer of doubtful religion and an ethnic identity that made some of them uneasy" (para. 14), his essay will also work well in conjunction with the issues of us and them discussed in Chapter 8, "Bridging Distances." Similarly, many issues in Chapter 14, "Public Space," will reverberate with David Bradley's essay.

Generating Writing

1. Assign an essay in which your students explore Bradley's relationship to his neighbors, both past and present. When he lives in Aspen Park, he begins to think of the people he observes as his "real neighbors" (para. 8). Does this attitude change when he lives on their block? What does actual contact with the inhabitants of Ringgold Street do to his attitude toward them? Have your students examine any signs of his emotional involvement, and pay special attention to his reaction to the "ghosts."

2. There's a moment in this essay when a cliché comes to life in an almost chilling way: Bradley sees a For Sale sign and "suddenly I saw *myself* living on Ringgold Street." The italics emphasize that he has suddenly encountered himself, as if in a mirror. Assign an essay in which students examine Bradley's shift in perspective, the 180-degree turn whereby he finds himself living in the apartments he used to observe, looking out into the very apartment he previously inhabited. How does his reversal determine the structure of the essay? What is the relationship between the Bradley who lives in Aspen Park and the Bradley who lives on Ringgold Street? Why does he use the third person pronoun to describe the persona who lives among and interacts with the inhabitants of Ringgold Street? How does the dual point of view in this essay affect the reader? To what extent do Bradley's two personae merge in the final paragraphs, when the distinction between the two narrative styles breaks down? How would your students rate this ending's resolution?

WRITING ABOUT THE CHAPTER

1. These essays *feel* very different when we read them, and the authors create our reactions mostly by their distinctive use of point of view and organization. Ask your students to write an essay examining how these essays are set up. How, for example, are Gretel

Ehrlich's "open spaces" and the loss of "distinction between background and foreground" reflected in the essay's organization? To what extent and in what ways is the organization of White's "Once More to the Lake" determined by patterns of repetition? How does the architecture of Ringgold Street, and David Bradley's shifting position within and around it, produce his essay's organization? How do the authors situate themselves within the setting each describes, and where do we, as readers, find ourselves in relation to these authors and their "places in the heart"?

2. Have students revise their Writing-before-Reading exercise, applying what they have learned by reading the selections in this chapter. Ask them to identify which specific features of their essays also appeared in one or more of the essays they read. What other specific features might they also adopt for their purposes? Have them consider, for example, how the writers' skillful choice of details demonstrates their affection for their special place. Also have them consider reworking the point of view they established in the first draft of this essay.

3. Although all the selections in this chapter are about places for which the writers feel deep affection, each also shows traces of mixed feelings. Have your students write an essay exploring the writers' mixed reactions to the places in their hearts. Which writer do they find the most ambivalent? How is this ambivalence primarily conveyed — in direct statements or selection of details? Is the writer's ambivalence resolved by the end of the essay? (This assignment might also take the form of a first-person essay in which the student writer describes a place for which he or she has both positive and negative feelings. Have them write an essay in which they convey the complexity of their emotional attitude toward that place.)

5

The Power of Names

Maya Angelou, "What's Your Name, Girl?"

Mary McCarthy, Names

Paul Gruchow, Seeing the Elephant

WORKING WITH THE CHAPTER

If you want a theme that your students will readily "identify" with — this may be it. Few subjects hit closer to home, especially among young people still struggling with a sense of identity. The topic lends itself to wide-ranging discussion. You can talk about the ways in which our names can be used and abused by others as a system of oppression, as Maya Angelou dramatizes in a vividly portrayed vignette from her autobiography; or how personal names and nicknames form the contours of our social world (as Mary McCarthy illustrates in a penetrating reminiscence of a Catholic childhood); or how names in general connect us to the larger themes of history and language, as Paul Gruchow observes in a beautifully choreographed — though little-known — contemporary essay that is ostensibly about a famous American landmark but gradually branches out into a compelling meditation on the power of names.

Teaching Strategies

One place to begin discussion, of course, is with the first epigraph, a quotation that springs to mind whenever anyone considers the meaning of names. Students have probably heard the expression "What's in a name?" but only those who've read the play in high school may know that it comes from Shakespeare's *Romeo and Juliet.* The three selections in this chapter are perhaps unusual in that they don't quote Juliet's famous question; practically every newspaper or magazine piece on the topic uses it for either a title or an opening. The quotation provides you with a question for discussion that will move the class from personal matters to an essential problem of language: is there a fundamental connection between what a thing is and what it's named? Would a rose by any other name really smell as sweet? What if, one writer suggests, roses were called "scarletina stinkworts"? Would our response be the same?

If you work through these epigraphs in class, it would be a good idea to get the class thinking about Juliet's question — is she right or is she naive? The tragedy of *Romeo and Juliet,* of course, is that names, especially family names, have an established and identifying power that is not easily dismissed. This power is recognized by writer Haig A. Bosmajian, who in the epigraph comments directly on Juliet's "What's in a name?" by answering "Plenty!" Bosmajian's comment points us toward names and oppression, an issue that is at the heart of Booker T. Washington's eloquent observation about the relation between personal names and African-American identity. You might want to expound upon Washington's point in class by commenting that the connection between names and identity — the subject of Maya Angelou's essay — has been a dominant issue in African-American literature from the middle of the nineteenth century and has been directly addressed by such prominent black essayists as Ralph Ellison ("Hidden Name and Complex Fate") and James Baldwin (*Nobody Knows My Name*).

Finally, our names not only have a personal, social, or political significance, but, the early twentieth-century French anthropologist Lucien Lévy-Bruhl observes in his epigraph, they possess a profound cultural meaning as well. In many cultures, people don't go out and purchase a book on "What to Name Your Child," seeking some cute or original name for their newborn. For many groups, naming is an important initiation ritual in which an infant is transformed into "a definite human being" and becomes a member of the community. The parents don't already have a name picked out before the child is born — how could they? The name must come from the child: the parents must determine which ancestor is reincarnated in the newborn and name the infant accordingly.

These four epigraphs cover a lot of intellectual ground. They will help open up discussion and suggest a number of ways into the selections. Because nothing seems more personal than one's name, however, an effective way to begin considering the theme is to invite students to draft an essay in which they reflect on their own names.

A Writing-before-Reading Exercise

At one time or another nearly all of us have received a name or nickname — from family, friends, neighbors, or enemies — that we didn't like or didn't want. Ask your students to consider a name that they may have been stuck with. What was it? Who gave it to them? How did the name come about? What didn't they like about the name? Were they able to get rid of it, or do some people still call them by that name? How deeply did the name alter their self-image? After considering these questions, they might draft an essay describing as specifically as they can how someone else's name for them affected their sense of identity.

WORKING WITH THE SELECTIONS

Maya Angelou

"What's Your Name, Girl?"

Teaching Strategies

As mentioned earlier, the problem of one's personal name has been a persistent theme of black writers in America. Maya Angelou's selection, an episode from the first of her autobiographical works, *I Know Why the Caged Bird Sings*, comes out of this tradition. Angelou brings the issue directly into focus toward the middle of the selection (para. 30) when Margaret says that "Every person I knew had a hellish horror of being 'called out of his name.' It was a dangerous practice to call a Negro anything that could be loosely construed as insulting because of the centuries of their having been called niggers, jigs, dinges, blackbirds, crows, boots and spooks." You might want to begin discussing the selection with this passage. One point to explore in class is the connection that Angelou makes here between a personal name and a racist epithet. If your class doesn't see why Margaret finds the name "Mary" insulting, then the point of the episode is lost.

The class should realize, of course, that nothing is wrong with the name "Mary" in itself. Some students might take Margaret's anger literally and simply assume that she hated the name Mary or that she saw it as an unflattering nickname. Some discussion, then, is required about the reason for Mrs. Cullinan's calling her out of her name. Once Mrs. Cullinan's motives are understood, the class can consider how the episode ends. They should now be able to see that Margaret's anger is legitimate — the wrong name (Mary) is immediately followed by a racist epithet ("little black nigger"), as though the two were indeed equated in Mrs. Cullinan's mind. In other words, to Margaret, being called "Mary" was always equivalent to being called "nigger." But why does Mrs. Cullinan finally scream, "Her name's Margaret, goddamn it, her name's Margaret!" Clearly, Margaret has won her point; but there seems more to this ending than that sort of victory. Trying to interpret the episode's conclusion could lead to some interesting open-ended class discussion about the extent of Mrs. Cullinan's own awareness of what the name Mary really meant. Ask your class, too, if they find it significant that the broken plate Mrs. Cullinan throws actually hits Miss Glory.

After you've examined how the theme of personal name and identity works in the episode, it would be instructive for the class to see how skilfully Angelou incorporates into the account other examples of names and language. Students may think, for example, that the opening paragraphs have little to do with the naming issue at the center of the story. It is a good idea then to point out that the word *debutante* in paragraph 1 is odd. Students should begin to see how this rather improper name in the social context of Margaret's childhood establishes a pattern of metaphor and irony throughout (the language of "finishing school," and so on) and leads to Margaret's learning the proper names for all Mrs. Cullinan's fancy tableware, which, Margaret says, "were additions to my vocabulary and in fact almost represented a new language."

The theme of this chapter has naturally led us to focus our suggestions on names and language. But the larger issue here (most students will not need to be reminded of it) is racism and oppression, and how a young girl with plenty of grit and a remarkable sense of humor overcame both.

Additional Activities

The verbal patterns in "What's Your Name, Girl?" can be pointed out to students quite easily and directly. Not so obvious to them, perhaps, will be the allusions to Lewis Carroll's comic masterpieces, *Alice's Adventures in Wonderland* and its sequel *Through the Looking Glass*. Angelou, of course, casually refers to Alice and the Cheshire cat, but the allusions to Carroll run deeper in the episode, which despite its serious racist topic has a comic undertone. Margaret, like Alice, has suddenly entered a strange world in which she needs to learn new rules and in which bossiness and the conflict between master and servant predominate. Alice, too, is thrown into a world where "mid-Victorian values" (Margaret's phrase) are continually being enforced and challenged; Mrs. Cullinan is a kind of "Ugly Duchess" (Margaret often comments on her looks); and we see a version of the Mad Tea-Party. But the most significant parallel with the Alice books is names and their meaning, a topic explored in the "Humpty Dumpty" chapter of *Through the Looking Glass* (incidentally, one of the words that Humpty Dumpty "defines" is *glory*). Most students should be aware of the Alice books, but for some additional discussion you might want to read appropriate passages to the class. Or you could construct a research assignment asking students to write about the parallels they find between Maya Angelou's selection and the "Alice" books.

Generating Writing

Dishware is dominant throughout the Angelou selection. You might ask students to focus on the symbolic meaning of dishes in the episode. They should consider carefully what dishes represent to Mrs. Cullinan, to Miss Glory, and to Margaret herself. How are they used to establish a sense of order and value? How does Bailey's suggestion that Margaret destroy them solve her dilemma? What does destroying the dishes mean to each of the major figures in the episode? By paying close attention just to Angelou's way of using dishes in the episode, your students should begin to see how a writer can transform small or ordinary details into thematic and symbolic significance.

Mary McCarthy

Names

Teaching Strategies

If a finishing school is an ironic metaphor for Angelou, it s a reality for Mary McCarthy, a contrast that pairs these two selections perfectly for classroom discussion. So different in social context yet so similar in dilemma, the two will enable students to realize just how widespread the problem of names is.

Like the Angelou episode, Mary McCarthy's "Names" is part of a full-length autobiography, *Memories of a Catholic Girlhood* (1957). The section we reprint deals with her life as an eighth grader in a Seattle convent school. She has just undergone a religious crisis, and here she becomes engaged in another sort of rebellion: her resistance to a mysterious nickname given her by other girls. The episode divides into three parts: a general discussion of names, a comic misunderstanding between herself and the nuns over menstruation, and her reaction to the "hated" nickname. To get discussion started you might introduce this overall structure so that students can begin to consider how these various parts come together as a thematic whole.

McCarthy opens with a list of girl's names. Students might consider what these names have in common and what they mean to McCarthy. Students should see that McCarthy contrasts different groups and two types of names: exotic names and common names. This contrast is one students will readily recognize, for many have opinions about names they like or don't like, and the reasons often break down into "that's too ordinary" or "that's unusual." Carrying the common name Mary, McCarthy is herself attracted to exotic or foreign names.

The point in this general discussion of names, however, is McCarthy's observation about the special significance Catholics give to names (a generalization to which students might take exception, because they've just seen how important names also are to black Americans). Still, they should understand why McCarthy believes that "your name is your fortune and it tells you what you are or must be." To get discussion flowing, you might ask how many in the class know what their names mean and if they were named after a religious or historical figure. You might also ask whether they believe that names have these deeper meanings for an individual.

That this opening section is relevant to the piece as a whole should be apparent to students: McCarthy provides both social and religious reasons for attaching so much importance to names. We need this information to see why the nickname later disturbs her. Mention too the bit of foreshadowing in this first part; she pointedly ends the essay with a more distinct definition of her name than she offers at first.

But the second part of the selection — the account of her "absurd situation" — will surely seem disconnected from the theme and the entire piece. You might ask directly what connection McCarthy's "menstruation" episode has to the general theme of names. This may prove to be a difficult question and it may elicit varied responses. The most literal response, of course, is that these events — the menstruation episode and the nickname — happened at the same time and thus have a close narrative connection. But though

McCarthy establishes that this interpretation is correct, it doesn't get at the thematic relation of the episodes. You may have to probe a little deeper in discussion.

Here are a few suggestions that are worth exploring. The mistaken menstruation itself is directly connected to the problem of naming. Notice that neither the nuns nor McCarthy says anything that might eliminate the absurd misunderstanding. The convent is a world of euphemism, a truth that McCarthy acknowledges when she says, "I was conscious of a funny constraint; I did not feel it proper to name a natural process, in so many words, to a nun."

But McCarthy makes further connections between menstruation and naming. The menstruation episode, she says, is important because it became yet another pretense, one that led to shame and guilt. She pretended "to have become a woman" — a new identity — just as she had earlier (and would later) pretend to be identified by specific names, the "hated" nickname one of them. The shame and guilt she felt about keeping up this pretense, we can imagine, easily became attached to the mysterious nickname "Cye," which she then construed must mean something negative or mocking, something "horrible." Besides being directly connected with names and pretense, then, the menstruation episode provides readers with a psychological context for understanding her hatred of the nickname. Students will see that this is a quite complex psychological account of an adolescent crisis. Some students may not believe McCarthy's explanation for the bleeding but will, despite her report, accept the nun's interpretation that she was afraid of what was really happening and was trying to pretend it wasn't.

Why "Cye"? Intriguingly, McCarthy has no answer and your class may want to speculate about what the letters C Y E could possibly stand for. But the name's literal meaning is not as important as what it meant symbolically. Your class may want to consider, too, whether McCarthy felt something about this name was true, in the sense that she claims the nickname "found her out." The nickname, like Angelou's "Mary," became a sign of McCarthy's outsider status, her "wrongness." And like Angelou's Margaret, she ultimately resists the "imposed" name and reestablishes her real name. You might ask your class how her new identity — her "fresh start," she calls it — is still based on the meaning of her real name. And what is she "bitter" about?

Additional Activities

This selection is a good opportunity for open class discussion about our psychological attitude toward first names. Mary McCarthy raises a lot of issues about names and our reactions to them. She was a student in the 1920s. Ask your class if they think attitudes toward first names have changed much since McCarthy's childhood. Try taking an informal poll. Do young people still prefer "exotic" names to "common" ones? Do their names differ much from those of their parents? What about their grandparents? How many in the class share the names mentioned in McCarthy's reminiscence? If they could easily rename themselves, how many would do so? Would the change be from common to exotic or exotic to common?

Generating Writing

McCarthy believes that our first names mean something. Do your students know what their first names mean? Ask them to do a bit of research on their first names — checking etymology, meaning, or religious background, and so on — and then write an essay in which they (1) discuss the meaning of their name as clarified by their research, and (2) discuss how much they believe the name's meaning has to do with their identity.

Paul Gruchow

Seeing the Elephant

Teaching Strategies

In this reflective essay, the writer talks not about his own name but the power of names in general. It's an unusual essay and students may not be wholly prepared for its discursive movement, as Gruchow proceeds from describing the pioneers on the Oregon Trail to visiting one of the major sites along the trail, Independence Rock, continuing to a meditative conclusion about the Vietnam Memorial and the role of names in American history. The essay is an opportunity to address the discursive approach an essayist may take with a topic and to show students how an essay can be a frame for several elements. Gruchow works into the essay (1) historical narrative (the Oregon Trail and Independence Rock), (2) his own experience in climbing Independence Rock, and (3) his vision of the power of names.

It would be a good idea in teaching this piece to ask students to find the break in its two-part structure — the division between Gruchow's historical narrative and his personal experience. Invite students to look over the essay again in class. They should soon see that the break occurs with the paragraph beginning, "I climbed the rock myself one August day . . ." (para. 13). Once they've seen this division and are aware of how the first part of the essay is historical and the second personal, they can observe how this break also marks a major shift in pronouns. Gruchow generally uses "you" throughout the first part of his essay, and "I" in the second. If you concentrate discussion on these pronouns, students will be able to form a good sense of the essay's movement.

You may need to ask students to consider Gruchow's use of *you*. Whom do they think it includes? Why does he use this pronoun instead of *they*? Ask them to substitute *they* or *them* in the opening sentences and comment on the different effect. What effect do they think Gruchow wants to establish?

Then there's the elephant. Not a real elephant like the one George Orwell was forced to deal with in "Shooting an Elephant," (see Chapter 3), but a symbolic elephant that, as Gruchow points out, has become part of the American idiom. It's not a well-known expression and you might want to inquire if anyone had ever heard it. Though Gruchow offers a gloss for this pioneer expression (see para. 6), make sure students understand what it means, both literally and figuratively. They must also see the connection between the elephant and the theme of naming; this metaphor was the "name" the pioneers gave to their experience. The phrase comes up throughout the essay and in different contexts.

But though the pioneers added many expressions to our language, Gruchow mainly mentions in this essay their own names as they are chiseled into Independence Rock. It's this direct, personal experience with names and naming that moves the essay from the past and brings it into the present. In discussing this section you might want to call attention to the family of vacationers Gruchow finds on Independence Rock. Ask students about their significance: why didn't Gruchow merely ignore them when he wrote the essay? Why do they think he decided to include these people as part of the experience?

Gruchow then takes his essay through another turn, which you may want to discuss in class. After the family leaves and he has the mountain and the moment to himself (para. 18), students may begin to detect a change in tone as the writer's experience becomes increasingly visionary. To get discussion started, ask how Gruchow establishes the mood for this solitary moment; how do setting and atmosphere contribute to this mood? Gruchow makes a surprising leap as the names on the mountain remind him of the names on the Vietnam memorial. Suddenly, we are no longer in the pioneer past but in recent history, where we see that names still hold great power.

Students might discuss the ways in which Independence Rock and the Vietnam War Memorial are both different and alike. But their discussion ought to touch on the connection Gruchow finds between names and knowing. With names, he says, "we lay claim to anything — to a place, or a plant, or a person, or an idea." You might want to wrap up discussion with this statement by asking how it brings all the details of the essay together — the elephant, the rock, the carved names, the Vietnam Memorial. Try looking closely in class at the last two sentences in the essay, starting with "I wandered among all those names. . . ." Invite someone to read it aloud. Then open discussion about the meaning of the final sentence. Can the students speculate about what Gruchow means by his "own elephant"? And why doesn't he *name* where he is heading?

Additional Activities

"Seeing the Elephant" has many similarities to the essays in Chapter 4, "Places in the Heart." You might want to assign it with, say, Gretel Ehrlich's "The Solace of Open Spaces." Notice that Gruchow picks up the phrase, "the spirit of place" that D. H. Lawrence uses in one of the epigraphs to Chapter 4. How does the phrase apply to both Gruchow's and Ehrlich's essays? Invite the class to consider whether there really is something that we can call the "spirit of place," or whether they think the phrase is merely a poetical way of speaking.

Generating Writing

The expression "seeing the elephant" can provide an interesting collaborative research and writing assignment for your class. Divide the class into groups and ask each group to explore the origins and meaning of the expression. They will need to look into various sources, such as books on the Oregon Trail, the history of the American West, and the American language and expressions, and assorted articles. You might then want to set up a panel in which each group reports on its findings and discusses the relative merits of the sources and interpretations.

WRITING ABOUT THE CHAPTER

1. The Angelou and McCarthy episodes are good examples for handling the Writing-before-Reading exercise. Both writers deal with their response to unwanted names imposed on them by others. After they read these selections, ask students to go back over their draft and revise it according to ideas or techniques they learned from the selections.

2. If you prefer to ask for an essay on names in general, here's a suggestion that might inspire some class controversy. A *New York Times* writer wondered if "a child's name tells more about the parents than it does about the child." You might raise the question and invite students to respond in an essay that will incorporate their reading and class discussion.

3. A large part of the aura about such recent memorials as the Vietnam War Memorial and the Ellis Island memorial surely has to do with the vast lists of names at the sites. People come from all over to view these names and sometimes to make rubbings of them. Ask the class to speculate about this trend in recent history. In preparing for discussion, you might ask students to choose either the Vietnam or the Ellis Island memorial and research its architecture and philosophy. How important were the names to the designers of each monument? What controversies surrounded them? One writer, for example, objected to the Vietnam War Memorial because he saw it as a monument designed to show failure and defeat.

6

Divided Identities

Kesaya E. Noda, Growing Up Asian in America

Adrienne Rich, Split at the Root:
An Essay on Jewish Identity

Shelby Steele, On Being Black and Middle Class

WORKING WITH THE CHAPTER

In an epigraph to this chapter, Jan Clausen draws on the work of Jacqueline Rose, who "paints a picture of identity as a deceptively smooth façade hiding an endless turmoil of contradictory impulses and desires." The essayists whose works make up this unit have pushed aside that façade to expose their own divided identities. Although it might be impossible to discover a person with a completely *un*divided identity, the divisions within the authors in this unit are exacerbated because each is a member of an ethnic minority group. As Gloria Anzaldua points out that people who are "exiled from what is considered 'normal,' white-right" too often "internalize this exile" and "split apart" from themselves. For such writers as Kesaya E. Noda, Adrienne Rich, and Shelby Steele, "the act of writing," Anzaldua says, is "the quest for the self."

This quest requires great courage on the part of the writers. They have to take an honest look at themselves and their societies. Adrienne Rich has to disinter a part of her identity that had been repressed from fear of discrimination. Shelby Steele has to struggle to reconcile his loyalties to his own race and his own class, just as Kesaya Noda struggles to understand the difference between a self-definition based on her own culture and one based on internalized messages from the dominant culture. The writers achieve varying degrees of success in finding a resolution for their divided identities. But each writer learns from his or her "creative self-confrontation," as Erik Erikson names it, and we and our students can certainly learn by reading the accounts of their struggles with the issues of divided identity.

Teaching Strategies

Discuss how well each author resolves his or her divided identity. Do your students find all the resolutions equally compelling? Do they find that any of the authors reconcile the two sides of their identities by choosing one side over the other? Are any successful in finding a resolution that encompasses all the conflicting forces? Ask them which resolutions could function as solutions on a larger social scale, and which are more purely personal.

Erik Erikson, in an epigraph to this chapter, expresses impatience with people who are experiencing identity crises. To the question "Who am I?" he prefers the question,

"What do I want to make of myself, and what do I have to work with?" Ask your class if the writers in this chapter would make Erikson impatient. Or do they ask and answer the questions he poses? What are the implications of the two parts of his question? Which of the writers address the question of self-making, and which address that of the materials with which to make oneself? What, if anything, separates Noda, Rich, and Steele from the adolescents to whom Erikson apparently refers?

A Writing-before-Reading Exercise

Have each of your students brainstorm a list of the identities that comprise her or his overall identity. Remind them not to limit themselves: they should write down every possibility that comes to mind. Then have them choose two or three items from the list and write a rough draft describing how these identities interact.

WORKING WITH THE SELECTIONS

Kesaya E. Noda

Growing Up Asian in America

Teaching Strategies

This essay at first seems structurally simple. Your students will notice the three main divisions, which might lead them to expect Kesaya Noda to treat each facet of her identity separately before moving to the next. Actually, though, the elements of one's identity are not so easily compartmentalized: in her essay the issues accumulate, so that race issue becomes inseparable from gender, for example. Within the parts of the essay as well, her structural choices will probably not be transparent to your students upon first reading. Draw their attention to the section entitled "I am a Japanese American" and ask them to characterize the transition between the episode in which she rages at her parents about their response to the internment camps and the episode in which her car gets stuck in the sand at her uncle's ranch. Encourage them to think about the relations among the parts of her essay. Unlike Adrienne Rich and Shelby Steele, Noda does not always make her thinking explicit: the reader must often supply the connections suggested by her juxtapositions.

Similarly, her problem with the issue of divided identity will at first seem simpler than it is. After all, she makes it quite clear from the beginning that the schism lies not within her, but between the inside and the outside. It's the people who are not Japanese, the media and other ignorant people, who are confused, not her. From what Noda writes in paragraph 2, it seems all she has to do is ignore the external messages in order to be grounded and comfortable within her identity. But evidence shows that Noda has internalized some of these ignorant voices, the ones that say "You are other. You are less than. You are unalterably alien." Have students identify places in the text where they can tell that those voices have affected her, and altered her own self-image. Ask what strategies she has used to overcome those voices.

Noda's ideal of pluralism is illustrated not only at the end of the essay, as a solution to the problems of divided identity, but throughout the essay. Have students analyze the scene at the Shinto shrine, where contrasting cultures coexist. Also have them interpret the Japanese folk song and the anecdote recounted in the Epilogue. How compelling do they find her solution? Can they see evidence in these three anecdotes — about the shrine, the nursemaid, and the Muslims — that pluralism is *not* a fully satisfactory resolution?

Additional Activities

If you would like to use this essay to help you teach composition, at least two features of her writing will illustrate the principle that form and content are complementary. Have your students examine the sentence structure in paragraph 3. They should notice a predominance of sentences in the passive voice. Even a sentence that begins in the active voice soon falls victim to the passivity pervading the entire passage: "The Japanese fell natural heir to the same anti-Asian prejudice that had arisen against the Chinese." Ask them to describe the effect of all these passive constructions. Do these sentences allow them to imagine an agent for the racism they describe? Where, in fact, are the people who are oppressing the Japanese? What is the effect of their virtual absence from this essay? How is Noda's use of passive constructions mirrored in the thematic content of the essay?

Noda obliquely draws our attention to the second compositional feature that you might want to emphasize when she says of her mother that she "speaks with her life as much as with her tongue." Ask how that principle might also be applied to her writing by Kesaya Noda, her "mother's daughter." This question could spark a discussion about the advantages of showing rather than telling in one's writing. You will have an excellent example close to hand in Noda's account of her mother: she shows a couple of episodes in which her mother demonstrates her own brand of strength, and lets us draw our own conclusions.

Generating Writing

1. Have your students focus on the opening line of Noda's essay, "Sometimes when I was growing up, my identity seemed to hurtle toward me and paste itself right to my face." Ask them to think about the significance of her emphasis on the *face*. Suggest that they think about the concept of "passing" in connection with this question. Then assign an essay in which they explore the differences between visible ethnicity (as with Noda and Steele) and invisible ethnicity (as with the third-generation German Americans mentioned by Noda, or with Adrienne Rich). They will probably want to draw on all three essays in this unit for their papers, in which they explore the advantages and disadvantages of each possibility.

2. You might also assign an essay in which your students explore Noda's relation to history. In paragraph 1, she seems to dissociate herself from the history of her race: she writes, "Events that had happened quite apart from the me who stood silent in that moment connected my face with an incomprehensible past." Does her attitude toward history change during the essay? How?

Adrienne Rich

Split at the Root:
An Essay on Jewish Identity

Teaching Strategies

Adrienne Rich opens her essay about Jewish identity by foregrounding the act of writing: "For fifteen minutes I have been sitting chin in hand in front of the typewriter, staring out at the snow." It is clear from the beginning that Rich's exploration of her own identity will be inextricable from the "dangerous" act of writing. Although "Split at the Root" is too well written to be a genuine first draft, it still bears the marks of "peeling back" (para. 11) of the layers of her personal history in order to expose the root. Encourage students to examine the time frame in the opening pages of the essay, where Rich backtracks first to 1960, then further back, to her own birth, and then further again, to describe her father's upbringing. We are privy to the procedure by which she realizes that she can tell the story of her own childhood only in the context of her father's life. See if your class can discover other textual evidence of the messy writing process in the prose of this essay, among whose final insights is a powerful statement about writing itself: "we can't wait to speak until we are perfectly clear and righteous. There is no purity and, in our lifetimes, no end to this process."

As she puts in the foreground the role of the writing process, Rich focuses on the complex role of language itself. Rich's father taught her, among other things, to feel "the power of language." Explore that power with your students. Where in the essay do they see language as a force that protects and perpetuates a racist status quo? Have them think about both words with positive connotations, such as "Christian," and words with negative connotations, such as "Negro" and "Jew." Ask your class where connotations come from, and how they function. Where in the essay do they see language as a force against racism? How does Rich use language against silence as a tool for resistance?

Encourage them to discuss the power of silence as well. Rich says that she "had no language for anti-Semitism itself"; that she couldn't ask "Why do they hate us so?" because she had no way to say "we" that included both her and the victims of the Holocaust. See if your students can come up with other examples, from their own experience, of concepts that they previously found impossible to think about because they didn't have the language with which to name them. Rich writes that the world in which she grew up "was christian virtually without needing to say so." Can your class think of other examples from everyday life of ideologies that seem so "natural" or "transparent" that they are hardly open to question?

To question the ideology of the culture in which she was raised, Rich must break a family secret. Specifically, she must break her father's silence, in order to speak up about the conflicting parts of her own identity. Your students may be troubled by Adrienne Rich's focus on the conflicts — Christian versus Jew, North versus South, them versus us, and the "white marble statue of Christ" in a "black ghetto" hospital, to name a few. They may wonder why she doesn't just accept her father's "measured" explanation in paragraph 30, in which he says "I am a person, not simply a Jew." After all, Rich herself admits that she has, at times, wanted to "say merely *I am a woman; I am a lesbian*." Help them to understand why Rich was not satisfied with her father's answer, and why she didn't, or couldn't, just choose to begin her own individual identity at her own individual birth. Explore the issues of heritage and community in her essay, and discuss the consequences of a society in which individuals are responsible only for themselves.

Additional Activities

"Split at the Root" would work very well in a larger discussion of Chapter 32, "Language and Politics." You might consider assigning a double-entry journal, to be kept during the time you have devoted to the issue of language and politics in your course. In this journal, each student would write down words heard in daily life — on television or in the movies, in the classroom or the dorms — in the left-hand column. On the right, the student would write any inferences he or she could make about the particular word in the specific context. Have them pay special attention both to the connotations of words and the unspoken assumptions behind the choice of words. This concentration might be difficult at first, for users of a language too often take it as transparent. but this exercise should sensitize your students to the political consequences of language, especially if you have them share their entries with each other a day or two after you give the assignment. In this way, the students who are baffled will get a jump start from the students who are already noticing lots of implications in the words they hear.

Rich's essay would also connect nicely with Maxine Hong Kingston's "No Name Woman" (see Chapter 12). Both writers must break a family secret to find their own identities. And Rich's attempts to come to terms with her Jewish heritage have much in common with Kingston's attempts to understand her Chinese heritage. Also, each author finds herself in a double bind, forced to commit an act of betrayal whether she speaks or keeps silence.

Generating Writing

1. Rich speaks of the small daily betrayals, the response of "silence and then amnesia" upon hearing a racist or sexist joke. Ask students to think back to a time when someone told a racist or sexist joke in their presence. How did they feel? How did they react? Did they later wish they had reacted otherwise? Have them write an essay based upon a personal narrative about a bigoted remark, but also ask them to move beyond the personal narrative form to speculate in an expository mode about the larger causes and effects of such humor.

2. Rich describes the clothing and jewelry that her father urged the female members of his family to wear. Ask your students if they have ever had the experience of being judged by the clothes they wore. Do they ever judge people by their clothing? Have they ever based their opinion of a person on such external details, only to realize later that they were off the mark? Ask your students to write on clothing as a sign system. Which items of dress produce what specific impressions? What are the social implications and consequences of such a system?

Shelby Steele

On Being Black and Middle Class

Teaching Strategies

Shelby Steele places his exploration of his own divided identity in a historical context. Make sure your students understand that when Steele characterizes the dynamics of being black and middle class, saying that "the positive images of one lined up with the negative images of the other, so that to identify with both required either a contortionist's flexibility or a dangerous splitting of the self," these images could describe his situation in the 1980s and in the 1960s with equal accuracy. But the times changed even if he didn't: although he was both black and middle class in both decades, that divided identity posed different problems for him, and suggested different solutions, in each period. Ask your students why Steele chose to identify with the black half of his identity instead of the middle-class half during the "racially turbulent sixties." Was he completely comfortable with that choice? How does he justify or explain it in the essay? More than once he compares the ethnic consciousness of the blacks in the 1960s to wartime patriotism. What is the effect of this comparison? And what is the effect of his metaphorical use of the word *bigamist* to describe himself in paragraph 13?

If your students are competent readers, they should be able to identify and discuss without much trouble the decision Steele made in the 1960s about the "two indispensable parts" of his identity. To answer questions about Steele's position in the 1980s, however, they will have to read between the lines. Ask them to identify Steele's resolution to the problem of divided identities. Do they think he has found a solution that combines his class and his race, or that he has chosen to side with the middle class? Some evidence shows that he believes he has decided in favor of an option that will betray neither side of his identity: he talks of showing lower-class blacks "the entire structure of principles, effort, and sacrifice that puts one in a position to buy a ticket any time one likes." And he acknowledges, in the last paragraph, that "actual victimization" does exist, and that we should "resist [it] with every resource." Still, given the aim of his essay, that acknowledgment doesn't carry much weight. As he says, the victimization model is not really relevant to his situation, and he doesn't show us any Blacks for whom it is relevant.

If some of your students feel that Steele has chosen to identify with the middle class at the expense of his race, encourage them to offer evidence to support their assertion. If they are having a hard time pinning down the source of their opinion, you might direct them first to paragraph 6, in which he lists "the work ethic, the importance of education, the value of property ownership, of respectability, of 'getting ahead,' of stable family life, of initiative, of self-reliance" as middle-class values, making it clear, by contrasting the value system of racial identification, that this is just one possible value system, the one preferred by middle-class Americans. By the end of the essay, however, he lists the same values as "a necessity": "in the eighties and beyond . . . racial advancement will come only from a multitude of individual advances." Individualism has transformed from one possible world view to the only possible world view.

It might be profitable to juxtapose Shelby Steele with Arnold Rich, from the essay "Split at the Root." Steele says that when he was in high school he believed his "class-conditioning was the surest way to overcome racial barriers." You might have your students compare this belief with Arnold Rich's faith that "With enough excellence, you could presumably make it stop mattering that you were Jewish." The ways in which the Rich family and the Steele family distance themselves from other, less acceptable members of their race — the "pushy" or "loud, hysterical" Jews or the "imaginary character named Sam" — have much in common. Of course, Steele is much more conscious of the implications of his dissociation from members of his race than is Arnold Rich — or at least we must assume he is, from only the evidence in the two essays. Ask students to compare *and* contrast the two men.

Also ask your students if *they* feel that Steele has been victimized because of his skin color (whether or not he considers victimization an appropriate paradigm for himself). What, for example, does he mean by his "vulnerability on a largely white campus"? How does he distinguish "vulnerability" from "victimization"? This is a difficult question. Have students reexamine the passages in which Steele discusses the concept of vulnerability. Discuss the relation of vulnerability to the double bind, to his ambivalence about his race, and to his repression of that ambivalence. Ask students if they can tell from the essay who or what is putting Steele and others like him in a vulnerable position. Could it be other blacks, such as the friend whose remarks appear in the opening paragraphs of the essay? Or could it be the entire system of class and race? If that is the source, how would vulnerability differ from victimization? They might find it easier to get a handle on the distinction — or to decide there is no real distinction — if you ask them to suggest a way in which the black faculty group could have approached their situation, in accordance with their feelings of vulnerability rather than "within a framework of victimization."

Additional Activities

Steele describes his recognizing the pattern in his life of class and race as a "sort of slow-motion epiphany"; he compares his epiphany to "the suddenly sharp vision one has at the end of a burdensome marriage when all the long-repressed incompatibilities come undeniably to light." You might teach Steele's essay in conjunction with the pieces in Chapter 3, "Moments of Recognition." This combination would nicely illustrate genre distinctions, because the selections in "Moments of Recognition" are primarily narrative, whereas Steele's epiphany is triggered by an event that he narrates, but the remainder of his essay is argumentative. As a follow-up writing assignment, you might want to have students write two essays on the same incident, one implying the significance of the epiphany, and the other spelling out its significance and exploring it in an expository mode.

Steele's essay, along with the selections in Chapter 2, "Ambitions," would also combine well to spark a discussion and critique of the American Dream.

Generating Writing

1. Steele writes that identity is "a form of self-definition, facilitated by images of what we wish our membership in the collective to mean." Invite your students to brainstorm some images that have helped them to define their collective identity — as a citizen of their native land, as a member of an ethnic group, as a person of a specific class, and so on. Have them write an essay in which they explore a few powerful images, interpreting the significance of the images — both positive and negative — and their effect on the student's sense of his or her own identity.

2. Steele's ends with the metaphor of a moving train. Can your students think of any literal actions that might fulfill the requirements of that metaphorical solution? Can they conceive of any ways of putting Steele's insight about the inappropriateness of the victimization model to work without sacrificing community? This essay assignment could be set up as a research paper: you would instruct students to research programs and people who have worked to improve conditions for racial minorities, and then to hold their methods up to the pattern proposed by Steele. Do the programs they have researched show results? What do their guiding principles seem to be?

WRITING ABOUT THE CHAPTER

1. Have students look again at the drafts they wrote before reading the selections. Is there a conflict between the parts of their identities described in this draft? If so, have them write a new draft, in which they trace the conflict to its sources. Have they unconsciously absorbed dominant stereotypes of people of their own race or religion? Have they felt pressure either to identify with or distance themselves from parts of their own identity? If some students find, even after reading and discussing the selections, that their identities are conflict-free, they should use the second draft to explore the source of the harmony they feel.

2. You might also assign an essay in which students explore the theme of betrayal in one or more of the essays in this chapter. In what sense does betrayal attach itself to both sides of a double bind? How can both speaking out and preserving silence about one's ethnicity be seen as instances of betrayal? Who would the writer be betraying in either case? At what cost? Which acts of betrayal do the authors you have chosen to write about choose to make? Why? What are the results?

3. Arnold Rich was the only Jew at the military school he attended in his youth. Shelby Steele writes of being one of a small group of blacks on a "largely white college campus." Each has known what it feels like to be the only one of his ethnicity in a classroom, and, no doubt, the only one of his ethnicity in the workplace, in a restaurant, at a park. Ask students if they have ever had the experience of being the only person of their race or gender in a public place. Perhaps a woman student majoring in one of the hard sciences will be able to report on one such experience. How did it feel to be the only woman in a class full of men? How often did she raise her hand in class? If students in your class have never experienced what Arnold Rich and Shelby Steele, along with countless other members of minority groups, have experienced, you might suggest this extra-credit activity, to sensitize students to this condition. Suggest that interested students go, individually, into situations where they know they will be in the minority, preferably the only person who doesn't fit in. White students might consider a predominantly black church, or a Japanese Noh play, or a cultural event sponsored by local Pakistanis. Some students may choose to sit in on a class at your school: perhaps a man would attend a women's studies class, or a woman a graduate course in physics. Of course, to visit such a class for one hour is not the same as to attend for an entire semester, but they should feel some effects nonetheless. Have them write up a report on how it felt to be one of a very small minority, if only for an hour.

The Social Fabric

7

What Is an American?

J. Hector St. Jean de Crèvecoeur, What Is an American?

Ishmael Reed, America: The Multinational Society

Mary Gordon, More than Just a Shrine:
Paying Homage to the Ghosts of Ellis Island

WORKING WITH THE CHAPTER

In the current global climate, national identities are more problematic than ever. What is a national culture in an age of tolerance, disarmament, and instantaneous information? How are peoples and states to maintain their cultural integrity while taking part in movements toward internationalism? Challenges to culture affect the United States peculiarly; our way of life is our biggest export, but as we ship it out for our overseas customers, we are constantly revising the product from within.

Teaching Strategies

Ask students what being an American means to them. How do they think the concept has changed over their own lifetime? How might they like it to change further? Discuss these ideas in depth; you might want to review a typical American college student's day and talk about the aspects of the experience that are specific to this country. What does the American student have in common with students in Europe? In the other industrialized nations? In the whole world?

How familiar are students with the "melting-pot" metaphor for our nation? Discuss the expression and their experience of it. The Emerson epigraph is an early expression of this idea; arguing against politicians seeking to bar further immigration, Emerson claims that strength will come to our nation by combining diverse elements into an alloy of humanity.

Arthur Schlesinger, Jr., offers a hundred-and-fifty-year progress report on the melting pot idea; do students agree with him that "recent years have seen an astonishing repudiation of the whole conception?" What do they make of his feeling that we now celebrate diversity at the expense of unity? Which, if either, of these values is more important to our society? The passage quoted from Ralph Ellison's *Invisible Man* opposes Schlesinger's position; ask students to restate, in their own words, Ellison's critique of the ideal of assimilation. Draw their attention to his punning rejection of white values. Must persons of color become "colorless" if they are to succeed in American society? How does our culture make space for non-European values? How does it exclude them in the interest of preserving unity?

In his epigraph, Enrique López sketches the self-portrait of a boy trying desperately to reconcile pride in his Mexican heritage with the desire to be part of "the gringo world." How do conflicts in racial and ethnic identity complicate growing up? It is difficult enough for children to decide who they are; if they constantly receive messages about their own identities that are based on stereotypes and slurs, self-definition is infinitely harder. Ask the class how much they identify with López. Does their view of themselves and their place in society change from day to day, even from moment to moment? Discuss López's closing statement, "it was small comfort to know that other minority groups suffered even worse rebuffs than we did." Would that, in fact, be any comfort at all? Should it be?

The Emerson epigraph should be taken together with the selection from Crèvecoeur as a way into the historical background for the idea of the American. Which groups are mentioned by Emerson and not by Crèvecoeur? How might that difference reflect the patterns of forty years of immigration? What kinds of attitudes toward America do both men seem to share? How do they differ?

With which of the selections would Schlesinger be most likely to agree? Might he and Gordon see eye to eye on some aspects of the importance of Ellis Island? Might Ishmael Reed critique their views as being too centered in the experience of European immigrants and overlooking the claims of Americans of color? How are Schlesinger's views the logical development of Emerson's and Crèvecoeur's?

How are Ellison's, López's, and Reed's viewpoints similar? Why might we expect them, as persons of color, to have the same perspectives on immigration and assimilation? How do they differ and why? Point out to the class the marked difference between López's investment in white society and the radical separatism of Ellison's hero. Where does Reed fit into this continuum? Where do students themselves feel our emotional investment should be, in the values of society as a whole or in those of our own racial or ethnic group?

A Writing-before-Reading Exercise

Ask the class to come up with their own definition of an American. Who is the most typical American they know? How is this person's experience representative of our cultural identity? Have students briefly present and discuss their conclusions. Encourage the class to debate the merits of their choices; how do students' perceptions of what it means to be an American differ?

WORKING WITH THE SELECTIONS

J. Hector St. Jean de Crèvecoeur

What Is an American?

Teaching Strategies

Students may find a number of things about this selection confusing, beginning with its author's name. Do we think of the French as among America's earliest settlers? Why might their contributions be overlooked? You may want to tell students that Crèvecoeur's *Letters from an American Farmer* (from which this selection is drawn) originally attributed the letters to a fictitious "Farmer John." Why might Crèvecoeur have chosen to present himself as the editor, rather than the author, of the letters? What value might the persona "Farmer John" have had?

The structure of *Letters from an American Farmer* is simple: the letters purport to be from an American farmer to an educated English friend, explaining American thought and customs, and offering descriptions and opinions of interesting or controversial aspects of American society. Individual letters deal with such widely varying topics as the American landscape, Native American customs, and the institution of slavery. Throughout the work, "Farmer John" makes a constant effort to anticipate his English friend's prejudices and preconceptions about American life, and to clarify points that a European might presumably find obscure. What might be the motivation for this literary structure? Who does Crèvecoeur's intended audience seem to have been?

Discuss Crèvecoeur's first sentence with the class. How does it help establish the "author" as a born American? What authority might that give him? How is that ironic because of the real author's identity? Ask students if Crèvecoeur's presentation of American history seems selective. Whose contributions does he — or his "American farmer" — overlook? What implications does a view of our history as the product of English immigration and efforts have?

How does Crèvecoeur characterize Europe in his opening paragraph? He says, for example, that "we have no princes, for whom we toil, starve, and bleed." What might be the force of this unfavorable comparison? Crèvecoeur goes on to state that "we are the most perfect society now existing in the world." Discuss this claim with the class. What might he mean? How accurate was this claim at the time it was made? How accurate might it be today? Ask the class to extrapolate from this paragraph Crèvecoeur's ideas on what constitutes a perfect society. How do they coincide with the ideals of the American Revolution? How do they coincide with today's social ideals? What exception might we take with them?

Crèvecoeur argues against immigrants' loyalty to their homelands by claiming that no one can feel real patriotism toward a nation in which he has experienced only poverty. Do students agree or disagree with this position? How might the last two hundred years of history have complicated this view? Crèvecoeur attributes Americans' economic opportunities to our government and our laws. Would we agree today?

Read carefully with the class the paragraphs in which Crèvecoeur outlines his theories on how the American landscape has influenced the American character. What do students make of this idea? Does Crèvecoeur seem to be speaking metaphorically, or is he theorizing about the physical world? How does the expression of these ideas reinforce the "farmer" persona? Ask the class whether similar ideas survive today. How scientific do they seem? Are they perhaps meant to be symbolically, rather than literally, true?

Crèvecoeur claims that American hospitality is far superior to that of Europe. If this statement were true, how would it support his other characterizations of American society? What is the American reputation for hospitality today? Ask the class whether they think this reputation is justified. What does a nation's attitude toward visitors reveal about the way in which its citizens view themselves?

In the letter, Crèvecoeur tells stories about poor men who came to America and made themselves rich by their own efforts. What seems to be his aim in telling these tales? What are the underlying assumptions in the stories? Does Crèvecoeur choose to overlook some factors contributing to economic success or failure? Discuss the conventions of rags-to-riches stories. How does this mythology survive today? What is its role in our society? Ask students to consider its incarnation in supermarket tabloids, tabloid television, movies, soap operas, and popular novels. How is the rags-to-riches story an expression of common social goals?

How would students sum up Crèvecoeur's characterization of America? How valid might it be today? Do they see the roots of our contemporary national mythology in this essay? How does our view of American character and society differ from Crèvecoeur's?

Additional Activities

Students interested in Crèvecoeur might want to read others of the *Letters from an American Farmer* and report on them to the class. How do Crèvecoeur's observations on specific aspects of American society challenge or support his presentation of American character?

You may want to bring in selections from other works of the era on America and Americans, or assign students to gather quotations on the topic from Crèvecoeur's contemporaries. What seems to be the consensus on the state of our nation in the late eighteenth and early nineteenth centuries? You might assign a short selection from H. H. Brackenridge's *Modern Chivalry* (College and University Press, 1965) to give the class a sample of the satirical attacks on the national spirit that Crèvecoeur celebrates.

Generating Writing

1. Ask students what, based on this essay, they feel Crèvecoeur would give as his blueprint for success. Would this model be adequate today? Does Crèvecoeur's description of American society fail to include their own experience? Do the many social changes of the last two hundred years explain the difference between Crèvecoeur's theories and their lives, or are there gaps in his social models?

2. Have the class imagine that they have just signed a contract to write a sequel to Crèvecoeur's work — *Letters from an American Student*. What persona would they adopt? Who would be the fictitious recipient of the letters? Ask them to write a brief draft of their own letter on the topic, "What is an American?"; what do they have to say about this subject? How does their own characterization differ from Crèvecoeur's?

Ishmael Reed

America: The Multinational Society

Teaching Strategies

It might be helpful to give students a little background on Ishmael Reed and his career. As a highly regarded African-American author, he is in the somewhat paradoxical position of having his work accepted and celebrated by the very establishment it challenges. A number of his works, such as *Mumbo Jumbo* co-opt and rewrite history, cliché, and stereotype to stretch American mythology, by force if necessary, until it includes the non-European.

Does this essay seem to be part of the same effort? Ask the class to analyze Reed's opening paragraph carefully. How does the element of surprise reinforce his point about the unexpected presence of diverse cultural groups in the most typically American setting? Why are we surprised by the mosques in Detroit, or the Navajo road signs in Arizona? How does the structure of Reed's opening mimic our encounters with our own culture? Does it encourage readers to reevaluate their attitudes and expectations?

The vignettes in this essay's first four paragraphs give different illustrations of our cultural cross-pollination. What do all the incidents Reed mentions have in common? How do they differ? How does his choice of presentation — the incidents are given briefly, in a kind of montage — parallel his characterization of our culture as a collage of perspectives?

Reed argues here against those forces in the educational and cultural world who advocate focusing on the study of Western civilization. What is your own college's or university's position on this issue? Are courses on Western and non-Western civilizations granted the same weight in your school's curriculum? Why or why not? What opinions do students have on this topic? What agitation or action has there been from each side of the issue? Ask the class to define Western civilization, as they see it. What vital parts of American society are excluded by that definition? How can the non-Western aspects of our culture best be included in our education?

How do students react to Reed's attempt to demystify the legacy of Puritanism? How valid do they find his critique of Puritan mythology? What influence does that mythology still have today? You may need to explain the concept of an Elect, and the history of that concept, to the class. How does Reed use the expression to describe a particular way of constructing the world? Ask students which current public figures might, in their opinion, think of themselves as belonging to the Elect. Does our society reinforce this way of thinking?

In his concluding paragraphs, Reed seems to equate an America that focuses solely on its Western heritage with "a world of robots with human attendants bereft of imagination, of culture." By implication, then, a multicultural America is a vital, imaginative society. How valid do students find Reed's critique to be? What might we gain by stressing the ideals of Western civilization? How would our culture's losses outweigh those gains? Ask students if their own lives would not be impoverished if all non-European contributions to American culture vanished tomorrow. Popular music as we know it — rock, rap, and jazz — would cease to exist; our fiction, from children's stories to the most avant garde novels, would become a much smaller and less various body of work, as would our poetry and even our history. Mathematics would grind to a halt, because so many of its basic concepts come from the Arab world; science, too, would be at a standstill without the many techniques and discoveries from non-Western nations. Even the food we eat would change drastically; ask students to turn back to the epigraph with which Reed opens his essay. Can we imagine an America without sushi, bagels, yams, curry, coffee, or chocolate?

Reed concludes with the statement, "The world is here." How does the class respond to this idea? Discuss it briefly; ask students to unearth the various meanings they find in it. Could Reed be accused of cultural imperialism? Is the world really "here?" Where, then, does that leave all the other places?

Additional Activities

You may want to teach this selection together with Chapter 6 on "Divided Identities." How might Noda, Rich, and Steele differ with Reed's view of the coexistence of cultures in today's America? How might they endorse his call for our educational system to adopt a multicultural focus?

Reed claims that interaction between cultures "is probably more prevalent than the sensational conflict between people of different backgrounds that is played up and often encouraged by the media." Do students find this statement to be true? An interesting class project might be to keep watch on newspapers, magazines, radio, and television for stories about interactions between Americans of different backgrounds. How many of these stories depict violence, clashes, and struggles? How many describe positive encounters? How does the coverage differ? Why might it be in the interest of the media to publicize and foster antagonism between people of different heritages?

Generating Writing

1. Have students keep a journal for one day, focusing on the influences of non-Western cultures in their lives. Ask them to write down their encounters with these cultures: they might be a television program on Gandhi, a friend's Africa medallion, a parent or grandparent's reminiscences of their native land. (Students who are themselves non-Westerners might want to focus on which other cultures they find represented here; what is their part in defining America?)

2. Ask the class to analyze Reed's essay closely. How does his style advance his argument? What rhetorical devices does he use to make and reinforce his points? How does the structure of the essay mirror his characterization of the structure of American society?

Mary Gordon

More than Just a Shrine:
Paying Homage to the Ghosts of Ellis Island

Teaching Strategies

One way to open class discussion of this essay might be to ask students what Ellis Island means to them. How familiar are they with the history of immigration to this country? How are the decades of Ellis Island's operation (1892–1924) representative of America's three hundred years of immigrants?

Ellis Island is the most recognizable symbol of American immigration. Whose experience does this symbolism overlook or exclude? Native Americans seem to be an obvious answer, but what about Latin Americans? African Americans? Those of us whose ancestors arrived more recently than the 1920s? Those whose ancestors came before the 1890s? Ask students how many of their ancestors may have been processed at Ellis Island. Do individuals' family histories affect their perception of the site as a national landmark? The Parks Service has recently thoroughly renovated Ellis Island, including a state-of-the-art multimedia exhibit on its history. Discuss this project with the class. What kind of statement does the government seem to be making with this action? What might the motivation behind the preservation effort have been? What effects might it have?

Why does Gordon begin her essay with a reminiscence about an encounter with a Russian in England? What point is she making about other nations' perceptions of American identity? Gordon says she told the Russian that Ellis Island was the one bond she could think of between people of diverse backgrounds? Talk about this statement with the class; how do they react to it? Do they feel included or excluded by it? How might they have responded to the Russian's request for information about their ethnic background?

Read closely Gordon's description of Ellis Island as "the only American landmark I'd ever visited." How do students respond to Gordon's characterizing other landmarks as alien to her experience? What are their own responses to historic sites and monuments? What might be some reasons for Gordon's distance from them?

How powerful do students find Gordon's "ghosts" metaphor? What might these ghosts symbolize for her? Do the ghosts have the same resonance for the class? Do students not descended from Ellis Island immigrants feel the pull of its history — is it a site for national remembrances, as well as personal ones? Do students think Gordon's differentiation of historic places into the distant and alien, like Civil War battlefields, and the personal and immediate Ellis Island, "the one place I can be sure my people are connected to," is a valid one? How much personal investment ought we to have in our country's history? Should we disassociate ourselves from those events in which our ancestors had no role? Which other Americans might oppose the preservation of Ellis Island, and on what grounds? How might Gordon respond to their objections?

How do students respond to Gordon's vivid evocation of the cruelty of the immigration procedures? What point is she making here? How does her description of the abuse of the hopeful immigrants change our view of Ellis Island and its meaning as a "shrine"? What does the class make of her conclusion, that Ellis Island is a place to feel her "differentness," and to champion "her people" against the Americans who gave them such a harsh welcome? Discuss this conclusion at length; ask students to consider each of the sentences in the essay's final paragraph. How do their own views and experiences differ from Gordon's?

Additional Activities

Some students might be interested in researching the history of American immigration. Gordon mentions some of the laws restricting and controlling immigration; what laws restrict immigration today? Whom do they benefit? Whom do they injure? What seems to be the motivation for our country's immigration policy, and how has it changed? You might want to ask a representative from your local Immigration and Naturalization Service office to speak briefly to the class on the INS and its role in American life.

How do our ancestors' experiences shape our view of a national identity? This selection, too, might be looked at, recalling students' work on Chapter 6 ("Divided Identities"). What critiques might Noda, Rich, and Steele offer on Gordon's essay? Does it adequately represent their places in American history and society?

Generating Writing

1. Have students write a brief personal essay describing a place that has special meaning for them because of its importance to an ancestor or ancestors. How would they pay homage to their own "ghosts," and how does society recognize this place? Is it a historic landmark? Why, or why not?

2. How would students describe Gordon's view of American history? How is it similar to, or different from, their own? With which historic places and events do they identify? From which do they feel excluded? Why?

WRITING ABOUT THE CHAPTER

1. Assign an essay discussing the melting-pot model of American society. Ask students to weigh the opposing claims of unity and diversity, drawing on the chapter selections and epigraphs for support, or choosing ideas from them to refute. How viable is the melting-pot idea today?

2. Ask students to compare and contrast Crèvecoeur's and Reed's views of American society. How does each writer evaluate the contributions made by different cultures? Which does each author see as more important, cultural diversity or national unity? Which of the differences between the authors are attributable to their different historical contexts? Which seem to be philosophical differences? What views do both writers share?

3. Have students write a personal essay about their own experience in reading this chapter. Where did they feel themselves to be situated in each selection? With which writer's views did they most identify? What aspects of their own vision of American identity were not represented in any of the selections? How has their work on the chapter changed their own opinion of our national character?

8

Bridging Distances

James Baldwin, Stranger in the Village

Jonathan Kozol, Distancing the Homeless

Sallie Tisdale, Neither Morons
nor Imbeciles nor Idiots: In the Company
of the Mentally Retarded

WORKING WITH THE CHAPTER

The metaphor of a social fabric suggests that we are all part of the same cloth, woven tightly together to form the texture af human society. Yet it is an inescapable fact that some of us are more closely knitted into this fabric than others. Separated by barriers of racial prejudice, economic status, political power, or differences in background, ability, and opportunity, many people are forced to live at the margins of society or — James Baldwin's powerful image — as strangers in the village. For Baldwin, his estrangement is inextricable from the "battle waged by Americans to maintain between themselves and black men a human separation which could not be bridged." Bridging human separation is also the subject in the essays by Jonathan Kozol and Sallie Tisdale. In portraying homeless people, Kozol worries that the psychological labels we assign to the destitute say "that they aren't quite like us — and, more important, that we could not be like them." By joining the company of the mentally retarded, Sallie Tisdale tries to overcome another human separation: "the difference between *them* and *us*," she once thought, "was a gulf that could not be bridged."

Teaching Strategies

Any society of course has numerous gaps dividing people from each other, creating worlds of insiders and outsiders. The following selections demonstrate three types of social distancing prevalent today, three ways in which we can he separated into "us and them." But before getting into the selections, you can start the discussion by examining the four epigraphs to the chapter.

Lewis Thomas's is the most straightforward; he warns that our society has not dealt properly with its outcasts and that we "must mend our ways." The other epigraphs, however, may require explication. Cherrie Moraga's point is an interesting one that most students will not have considered — the fact that an oppressor fears his victim's similarity more than his difference. If your students understand this comment they will be better prepared to handle the complexity of James Baldwin's classic essay. E. M. Forster's observation is from his essay "Tolerance." A very appropriate epigraph to the selections, it reminds us that our ability to understand "other" classes, races, and nations "entails imagination," in the sense that we have to put ourselves in someone else's place.

The R. D. Laing quotation is directly about the distance between "us" and "them." But it is difficult and deserves some class discussion. Invite students to interpret what Laing means by our creation of the "other." This passage can open up productive speculation about how distances between us and them are created in the first place.

Each of the selections depicts people who are placed, James Baldwin says, "at a certain human remove." A good way to connect all these selections is to focus on elements of language. You can concentrate discussion on these questions: How does each writer try to understand separation according to the labels we use to categorize the people who are being distanced? Why, for example, does James Baldwin argue that "the root function of language is to control the universe by describing it" (para. 12)? Or why does Jonathan Kozol argue that "the label of mental illness places the destitute outside the sphere of ordinary life" (para. 22)? Why are the difficulties in establishing a definition of "retardation" important to Sallie Tisdale's case about the abilities of the mentally retarded (para. 23–34).

Another way to connect these selections for class discussion is to examine the related ways in which each writer looks at "outsiders." As Lewis Thomas writes, how we deal with our disadvantaged says something about us. In other words, there's a reciprocity between "them" and "us" — no matter who those groups are — that makes it impossible to define either group in isolation. One definition depends on the other, as the epigraph from R. D. Laing indicates. Students may find that Laing's difficult observation is clearer after they've read the selections.

Each one of the selections also deals with problems of misconceptions. The way in which a society looks at its "strangers" — whether they are black, or destitute, or retarded — -is usually influenced by widespread popular misconceptions. You might want to focus on the respective misconception in each essay and ask students to concentrate on how the writer uses misconception as part of his or her argumentative strategy.

A Writing-before-Reading Exercise

People once had a convenient label for elderly destitute women who struggled to survive at the edges of towns — the distancing word was "witch." Today, some of these same women might be called "bag ladies." To make separations between ourselves and others, us and them, invariably requires some kind of label. That label might be an offensive racial epithet, a pejorative description, a slang expression, or an accepted euphemism. Think about a label that you commonly use to distance yourself from others or one that others use to do the same to you. After considering the word carefully, draft an essay in which you discuss the nature and extent of the distancing implied by the label and offer suggestions on how the distance can be bridged.

WORKING WITH THE SELECTIONS

James Baldwin

Stranger in the Village

Teaching Strategies

Because this is a classic American essay, you might want to provide some background here about Baldwin's life and career. Students might be interested in knowing that Baldwin

(1924–1987), one of our major writers, was born in Harlem to very religious parents. A precocious reader and writer, he became a preacher at age fourteen, but left the ministry three years later to write. His first novel, *Go Tell It on the Mountain* (1953), dealt with his religious experiences; the first of his four major collections of essays, *Notes of a Native Son* (1955), which included "Stranger in the Village," earned him a reputation as one of America's finest essayists (many of Baldwin's other works are listed in the biographical appendix). In the prefatory essay to *Notes of a Native Son*, Baldwin wrote: "One writes out of one thing only — one's own experience. . . . Everything depends on how relentlessly one forces from this experience the last drop, sweet or bitter, it can possibly give. This is the only real concern of the artist, to recreate out of the disorder of life that order which is art."

It will also help students better understand the essay if they realize that Baldwin spent much of his career in France (where he died) and that such essays as "Stranger in the Village" were written before the civil rights movement got underway. If students are surprised by his frequent use of the word "Negro," some historical context will help.

This essay may be difficult for students to follow for several reasons: (1) its language and syntax are complex; (2) its argument often depends on subtle distinctions and discriminations; and (3) its subject is not literally what the title suggests. But this is clearly an essay that is worth close classroom analysis.

You might begin by addressing the essay's ostensible subject. In what literal sense is Baldwin a "stranger in the village"? Of course, a real Swiss village is portrayed in the essay, and Baldwin describes it with precision and some affection. Make sure your students have a clear sense of what this village is like: of what significance, for example, is Baldwin's descriptive phrase, "a white wilderness"? How does Baldwin regard the people in the village, and how do they regard him?

But students should become aware of the larger implications of Baldwin's essay. He's writing about more than a Swiss village and his awkward position in it. It's essential for understanding the essay that students realize Baldwin is not speaking of being a foreigner in a European village but as a black in a white world. The village in effect represents the "West," a place where Baldwin is in many ways a "stranger." Baldwin's use of "stranger," however, is not easily pinned down (it is an excellent trope), and it may help if you ask students to discuss some of the ways in which the word changes during the essay.

Baldwin's essay, students should come to see, is not about being a foreigner but about being an American. As such, "Stranger in the Village," is part of an essay tradition that goes back to such classic statements on the theme as Crèvecoeur's "What Is an American?" (see Chapter 7). Yet what it means to be an American for Baldwin cannot be simply stated, for his definition wholly depends on the complexity of white–black relations in this country. For Baldwin, the problem of identity is so tangled by question of race that the identity of neither whites nor of blacks can be easily separated from each other, no matter how hard each group would like to try. The Swiss village, Baldwin concludes, is a model of simplicity that no longer exists in America. This is not, however, a simplicity that Baldwin longs for. Words for struggle, battle, and warfare have surfaced throughout this essay, and students should see that Baldwin's conclusion is on the side of complexity and challenge, not innocence and denial.

Another complex aspect of this essay deserves attention. The essay is not just intellectually challenging; it is emotionally challenging as well. Students may not be accustomed to the level of distinction and discrimination Baldwin brings to human emotion. You might want to look closely in class at a passage in which Baldwin deals with the complexity of emotion, such as his discussion of "rage" (para. 8). Try taking your students slowly through this paragraph, inviting them to explicate sentence by sentence Baldwin's point. They will begin to see that this is not an essay that can be reduced to clichés or simple summaries.

Additional Activities

As suggested earlier, you might want to teach Baldwin's essay in conjunction with Crèvecoeur's "What Is an American?" in Chapter 7. Both essayists try to define an American identity, but they depart in their approaches. Though both authors believe that our identities are shaped by society, and both see important comparisons to Europe and America, each writer proceeds with a different vision of America. You might want to discuss some of these similarities and differences in class, asking students whether they think the differences between the two writers can be attributed mainly to their different historical periods.

Generating Writing

"Stranger in the Village" offers a good opportunity to assign a critical paper. A number of images or terms recur throughout the essay that you might want to ask students to identify and explicate. Baldwin frequently alludes to wonder and astonishment, to battle and struggle, and he refers to the "devil" often enough to consider this image a deliberate pattern. Or you may have noticed other underlying patterns. You might ask students to (1) discover a recurring pattern on their own, or (2) give them one and ask them to identify and cluster related words and images. Either way they should show how the pattern they write about contributes to the overall meaning of the essay.

Jonathan Kozol

Distancing the Homeless

Teaching Strategies

Your students are undoubtedly aware that one of our society's most pressing problems is homelessness. If yours is an urban campus the condition may be visible every day on your doorstep. Yet, despite many studies of homelessness, we still know very little about homeless individuals — who they are and how they survive. And your students may have read very little on the subject outside of newspaper reports or columns. Before beginning Kozol's piece, you might want to survey the students' understanding of the problem. Who do they think the homeless are — vagrants? alcoholics? psychotics? Do they see them as people like themselves or as "strangers in the village"? An open discussion about the class's collective image of homelessness will provide a useful context in which to read Kozol's selection, because he builds his argument on misperceptions of the problem that he believes are general. "A misconception," Kozol maintains, "once it is implanted in the popular imagination, is not easy to uproot, particularly when it serves a useful social role." You might want to focus on this statement, asking your class to identify what he means by a "useful social role." What benefit does society gain by viewing the homeless as "largely psychotics who belong in institutions"?

Kozol makes his position clear from the start. He does not accept the view that homelessness is caused by mental illness, alcoholism, or related problems that put the burden of blame on the individual; rather, he believes it is caused by specific economic conditions and the lack of affordable housing. Students should understand an important part of Kozol's argument: the relation of cause to effect. Though it's often thought that some people are homeless because they're mentally ill, it's also possible, Kozol maintains, to argue that they're mentally ill because they're homeless. Much of Kozol's essay is devoted to dispelling the idea that homelessness has psychiatric roots.

You might ask your class to concentrate on paragraphs 34 to 36, where Kozol criticizes a *New York Times* item on a homeless woman. This passage will readily dramatize Kozol's position on mental illness. It will also allow you to point out in class a clash between two terminologies — the *Times* writer's psychological jargon versus Kozol's ordinary language. You can then discuss in class which vocabulary results in the greater "distancing." Then you can invite the class to find more examples of how our vocabulary (our labeling) establishes the kind of distances considered in this chapter.

Though Kozol argues eloquently for the homeless, his position — as he admits — is not a unanimous one. Many experts see the problem of homelessness differently. This divergence of opinion should not be left out of an open discussion. Your class itself may be divided on the topic. How convincing do your students find his argument? Do they take exception to parts of his essay? You might have them look closely at Kozol's interview with a homeless young man in Grand Central Station (para. 43). Have someone read this passage aloud. Do your students feel that the man's comments strengthen or weaken Kozol's argument? What questions would your students ask the man if they were conducting the interview? What information would they be looking for — and why?

Additional Activities

Much has been written about homelessness, and a great deal of material is available in most libraries. It is an issue that could stimulate productive class discussion. You might try dividing the class into four or five small groups. Ask each group to research the topic and find one essay or article that it believes offers the best explanation for the condition. Monitor the research so that no two groups select the same material. Each group should then summarize the main points and argument of its selection, being sure to indicate how their research supports or contradicts Kozol's position. After each group has presented its explanation, the entire class could discuss and debate the relative merits of each argument. It would be a good idea to see if the presentations affect previous attitudes and whether the class can arrive at any consensus.

Generating Writing

In E. M. Forster's epigraph to the chapter he says that it is a "desirable spiritual exercise" to put yourself in someone else's place. This is an exercise your class might try in an essay. Ask them to imagine that they suddenly have no money and no place to stay, and no "fall-back" position where they can get immediate assistance. What would they do tonight? Where would they go? How quickly could they learn the ropes of being homeless and destitute? Invite them to write a personal essay in which they attempt to depict their new situation and their response to it. (If some members of the class have already experienced these conditions, they might want to describe it from first-hand experience.) Students might also be interested in sharing these spiritual exercises with each other in class.

Sallie Tisdale

Neither Morons nor Imbeciles nor Idiots: In the Company of the Mentally Retarded .

Teaching Strategies

In this moving essay, Sallie Tisdale — a writer and nurse — explores another and all too common human separation — the gap between the normal and the mentally retarded. To bridge the gap, Tisdale seeks the company of retarded individuals and discovers possibilities in them — and in herself — that she was unaware of. She attends a dance sponsored by a Portland, Oregon, "People First" organization, visits a group home in Brooklyn, New York, a Los Angeles Parenting Program and sheltered workshop, and — in a final unforgettable vignette — she participates in a hilarious and loving basketball game in San Francisco. All these experiences are eye-openers. She learns that many of the individuals we label "retarded" are incredibly competent, and she also discovers that knowing, working, and playing with the retarded can immensely broaden the capacities of the nonretarded.

Like Baldwin and Kozol, Tisdale is sharply attuned to language and labels, matters that are critical in her essay. You can get students thinking about these matters by inviting them to discuss Tisdale's title. They should be able to understand why she has phrased it negatively and how the title alone introduces us right off to questions of language. What does your class think about words like *moron, imbecile,* and *idiot*? How do they use these words themselves? In what contexts? They should recognize that these words go far back into their own childhood. Have they ever been called these words? Do they have any sense of the more technical, psychological use of the words? Do they think these words are used today in clinical ways?

Examining the title will help move the class into more general considerations of language in the essay. You might discuss the word *retard* itself, which Tisdale brings up in paragraph 3 ("When I was a child there were few words more insulting than *retard*"). Ask your class about this expression: do they feel the same as Tisdale does? They might speculate, too, about why — if she feels this way — she nevertheless uses "mentally retarded" throughout. Why do they think she doesn't substitute another label? What others might she have used?

Tisdale introduces the issue of labeling directly in paragraph 23, where she moves away from concrete experience to general knowledge about retardation. This section holds the intellectual core of Tisdale's analysis and is worth looking at in class. At this stage in the discussion, your students should be sensitive to matters of language. Have them notice the many expressions in quotation marks and the professional interest in definition. Invite speculation about why definitions are important here. How do they matter to the psychologists? to Tisdale? to the retarded themselves? Notice that paragraph 23 also has some expository foreshadowing. The term "difference" will reappear dramatically in the essay's final paragraph; it has a key part in our understanding of the essay. Tisdale, and many of the people who work with the retarded, do not pretend that there are no differences between the retarded and nonretarded. The question is what we do with those differences.

After surveying the problems of definition, Tisdale examines a very interesting case history of a mentally retarded man who lived an extremely competent life (paras. 30–31). She discovered his story in one of the professional journals, a back issue of *The American Journal of Mental Deficiency*. You might examine this passage closely in class. Make sure students are aware that Tisdale introduces this example of professional literature to demonstrate the limits of the scholarly approach. They should notice, too, how language fits into her analysis. She criticizes the article not only for its topsy-turvy logic but also for its "arid lack of narrative." Invite your students to consider this criticism. How would narrative improve the scholarly article? How does Tisdale herself use narrative as an antidote to scholarly aridity? Students should soon see the conflict between professional or "official" language and "unofficial" language. The official language "distances"; the unofficial language "bridges."

A main element in unofficial language is narrative — the human story composed of real individuals and actual events, not statistics and abstractions. You might move your class into Tisdale's narrative here by focusing on the final section in her essay, the basketball game at the Recreation Center for the Handicapped in San Francisco. The high point of the essay, this lovely episode pulls together much of what Tisdale has learned about the retarded, but does so with dramatic narrative, not informed exposition. While engaged in this strange, unruly play — it's more play than it is game — she truly overcomes her fears of the retarded. She bridges the distance.

Additional Activities

The passage in which Tisdale examines a professional journal report (paras. 30–31) also offers an instructive comparison with Jonathan Kozol's critique of professional literature in "Distancing the Homeless" (paras. 13–15). Each writer displays a distinct conflict between "official" and "unofficial" language. You might want to juxtapose the Kozol and Tisdale passages in class (both are brief enough to cover quickly) so that students can see how Tisdale and Kozol are dealing with similar problems.

Generating Writing

As Tisdale points out more than once, fear of the retarded has much to do with creating distance. You might want to ask your class to consider this fear carefully. In what sense do people fear the mentally retarded? How valid are these fears? How does fear surface throughout Tisdale's encounters? On this subject, the epigraph by Cherrie Moraga can come in handy. Though she is addressing different circumstances, the quotation is quite applicable to Tisdale's piece. Invite your class to write an essay in which they examine the fears that the nonretarded have of the retarded. They should use the Moraga epigraph for context.

WRITING ABOUT THE CHAPTER

1. If you've used the Writing-before-Reading exercise, you can encourage students to revise their earlier draft by asking them to reconsider the problem of labels. They could revise their draft by reflecting on the misconceptions inherent in the label they chose to write about. How does the label — and the images or terminology associated with it — create a sense of distance between them and others? As they rewrite the paper, they should consider the use of alternative labels. Would the distancing they discussed be bridged if a misleading label were replaced by a better one?

2. As an alternate writing assignment, invite students to speculate on James Baldwin's comment: "What one's imagination makes of other people is dictated, of course, by the laws of one's own personality. . . ." They should consider James Baldwin's observation in the light of the light of this entire chapter. In an essay, they should discuss as cogently as they can the meaning of Baldwin's statement. By bringing in examples from each of the essays — as well as the epigraphs — they could show how Baldwin's comment applies to the distinctions we commonly make between "them and us."

9

Affirmations of Love

George Weinberg, The Madness and Myths of Homophobia

David Leavitt, Territory

Dorothy Allison, Don't Tell Me You Don't Know

WORKING WITH THE CHAPTER

We have designed it to call respectful attention to the ways in which various affirmations of love create — and sustain — a sense of individual dignity and community bonds. We have chosen to focus on gay and lesbian affirmations of love because we believe that they have been neglected much too long in American college and university curricula and, when addressed, too often either reduced, either through ignorance or malice, to stereotypes or subjected to caricature. The chapter provides instructors with the opportunity to examine individual and societal assumptions, beliefs, and attitudes about gay and lesbian life-styles; it also promotes dissemination of accurate information about, and encourages understanding of, these sexual orientations.

One of the insidious expressions of discrimination that mark daily life in the United States is that directed at gay men and lesbian citizens. Discrimination based on sexual preference remains, for one obvious example, official government policy. Gays and lesbians are automatically excluded from service in the military; they are also routinely, and often silently, disqualified from enjoying opportunities for employment and public service that are taken for granted by most heterosexuals. Endemic in these expressions of discrimination is the notion that these life-styles share an assumption about sexuality: that everyone is heterosexual until someone specifically declares, definitively, that he or she is not. Rose Weitz says in her epigraph that the word *lesbian* is used "not only to describe women who love other women but also to censure women who overstep the bounds of the traditional female role and to teach all women that such behavior will not be tolerated." Gay men and lesbians are widely regarded in the heterosexual world as threats to the social order, and increasing pressure is exerted on them to conform to the expectations identified with the sexual behavior associated with traditional gender roles. But as Sigmund Freud writes in the final epigraph, establishing what is "an average normal man" or woman is far more complicated than traditional societal standards seem to allow. (Freud was one of the first psychologists who spoke out early in support of gay men and lesbians; he argued that sexual preference did not affect one's capacity as a professional counselor. Freud also had much to say that remains incisive about bisexuality, an issue not examined in this chapter.)

Overstepping the sexual boundaries that many societies routinely draw leads a substantial portion of their citizenry to regard themselves as marginal, as people who, Michael Denneny reminds us in the epigraph from *Gay Politics* that leads this chapter, hate themselves "because we grew up and live in a society that hates us." We trust that by calling respectful attention to gay and lesbian affirmations of love we will reaffirm the dignity of the self, whatever its sexual orientations, and help create a broader and stronger sense of community, a community in which fear and hatred of the self are eliminated in favor of mutual respect and understanding. It is with these goals in mind that we offer these suggestions for teaching the selections.

Teaching Strategies

We urge instructors who choose to work with the material in this chapter to contact national and local gay and lesbian resource centers for useful instructional and contextual materials. The National Gay and Lesbian Alliance in Washington, D.C., is one such source. In addition, an ever-increasing number of gay and lesbian caucuses function within such professional organizations as the Conference on College Composition and Communication (CCCC) and the Modern Language Association. Members of these professional caucuses may be able to supply helpful instructional information and recommendations for teaching gay and lesbian material sensitively and respectfully.

There are also a great many published sources to draw on for useful instructional and contextual material. Cooper Thompson and members of the Campaign to End Homophobia have published *A Guide to Leading Introductory Workshops on Homophobia*. The *Guide* includes useful information and workshop activities on such issues as "What is Homophobia?" and "What Do You Know about Lesbian, Gay, and Bisexual People?" as well as incisive chapters on "The Connections Between Homophobia and Other Forms of Oppression" and "Responding to Everyday Examples of Homophobia." The *Guide* is available from the Campaign to End Homophobia, P.O. Box 819, Cambridge, MA 02139.

Another useful source of instructional and contextual material is *Opening Doors to Understanding and Acceptance: A Facilitator's Guide to Presenting Workshops on Lesbian and Gay Issues,* by Kathy Obear (available through The Human Advantage, Suite 125, 6 University Drive, Amherst, MA 01002, telephone number [413] 584–0812). This manual has materials for designing learning activities that challenge homophobic attitudes and behaviors, including step-by-step lesson plans and widely varied instructional activities, ready-to-use handouts, as well as articles and bibliographies to use as resources.

Many gay and lesbian groups on college campuses have prepared similar materials for combating homophobia as well as gay and lesbian stereotypes. One such example is *Workshops on Homophobia and Homosexuality for College Campuses,* prepared by students at Wesleyan, Brown, and Cornell universities.

A productive, and early, activity common to all these workshops is the effort to encourage greater sensitivity to the nature and extent of stereotyping gay men and lesbians. You might want to engage your students in just such an exercise, asking them to list the characteristics that serve as stereotypes as well as to identify traditional attitudes toward them. These attitudes hold that they are committing "crimes against nature," that they are immoral and to be pitied, that they can be identified by mannerisms or physical characteristics, and the like. You might want to follow through on this activity by asking your class to report on what they *know* about the lives and behavior of gay men and lesbians. Examining the extent to which their knowledge is formed by myths may help clear the air for a more informed discussion as well as create the prospect that they will leave those discussions with a more factual basis for their views.

Reading the material in this chapter may prompt someone in your class to realize that he is gay or she is a lesbian. We urge you to consider being helpful and supportive in such cases. You might want to refer the student(s) to an appropriate campus or local gay and lesbian support group, as well as to contact those groups yourself for useful advice on how to handle the situation as professionally and as supportively as possible.

You should also be aware that "out" and outspoken students may speak from experience about the issues addressed in this chapter. You ought to draw on the same skills you use in teaching effectively in a multicultural classroom.

A Writing-before-Reading-Exercise

One of the most effective ways to encourage students to examine carefully their own assumptions about, as well as their own stereotypes of and prejudices against, gay men and lesbians is to invite them to document and analyze those assumptions, prejudices, and stereotypes in more public forms. The media provide ample evidence of societal stereotypes and prejudices. You might want to ask your students to identify those prejudices and stereotypes, as well as the sexual and cultural assumptions that lurk behind them, in media treatment of gay men and lesbians. You could ask your students to focus on how the media treat the matter of love between adults of the same sex. With sensitivity? With respect? With good-natured humor? With ridicule? Some combination of these? In some other way?

Ask your students to prepare the first draft of an essay in which they summarize and characterize media portrayals of gay men and lesbians. What conclusions do they draw about media attitudes toward gay men and lesbians? What conclusions do they draw about their own attitudes?

WORKING WITH THE SELECTIONS

George Weinberg

The Madness and Myths of Homophobia

Teaching Strategies

Dr. George Weinberg's article explores the richness and complexity of the "affirmations of love" between people of the same sex. From the start, Weinberg seems intent on challenging the expectations of his readers, be they gay, lesbian, or heterosexual. You might have your students examine the opening paragraph of the essay in detail. Weinberg writes that "Most gay people in the United States imagine that they would receive better treatment in England than in their own country." He then upsets that expectation, commenting that "The assumption is dead wrong. In the States, gay people get the chance to present their case for decent treatment on television, even national television, and on radio regularly." You might then ask students to discuss the evidence he provides to support this assertion. (From most accounts of gay men and lesbians, their treatment in England has improved markedly in recent years.)

Weinberg next recounts an anecdote about his appearance on a Chicago television program, during which people called in either asking for his authorization to be a lesbian or summarizing seemingly threatening episodes from the past (para. 2). Your students should be able to discuss in fairly specific language, even at so early a stage in their talk about the essay, the function this anecdote serves in Weinberg's article. You might ask them to explain the terms Weinberg introduces to define lesbian and gay behavior. What issues, and what implications, are embedded in his identifying such preferences as "matters of taste"?

Weinberg reports that he was threatened by the man who said he was "forced into it" at the movie theater (para. 2). When Weinberg responded that "he must have thought at the time he would enjoy it," the man said "he would come down to the station and kill me." You might want to ask our students to consider the final line of this paragraph, which seems especially problematic. Weinberg closes: "A couple of tough women from the Chicago Gay Alliance provided me an escort back to my hotel." It might prove fruitful to explore with your students the question of audience implicit in the final sentence of paragraph 2. Ask your students how they read this line. Can it be read as yet another example of an offensive stereotype of lesbians? As Weinberg's expression of a "campy" sense of humor? As something else?

You might want to follow through on this question of Weinberg's audience by asking students to characterize the diction he uses throughout the article. Weinberg identifies himself as a psychologist, yet he seems eager to distance himself from "Fancy, Negative Psychology." You might explore with your students the extent to which Weinberg seems to allow himself to sound "technical" in the article. He announces that "My own field at one time was statistics, and I wrote a textbook on statistics that has been used by over a million students in the United States. . . ." Ask students to assess the extent to which Weinberg bases either his choice of diction or his conclusions on statistical evidence. You might also ask them to comment on whether his seeming resistance to technical language suggests that he aims his remarks at a general audience.

You might want to follow up on this discussion of Weinberg's diction by asking students to identify the function of the paragraph labeled "Fancy, Negative Psychology." Invite them to consider what Weinberg accomplishes by including this paragraph. What disadvantages does including it create for Weinberg? What distractions does it pose for his readers?

Weinberg takes on a leading issue in many heterosexual discussions of homosexuality: How do "people get to be" homosexual? He examines the unexamined assumptions as well as the unstated aims of many of these discussions: "the desire to stamp out the causes, to be sure that future generations do not produce homosexuals as the past ones have." You might ask your students to summarize the theories that account for the "cause" of homosexuality as well as to characterize Weinberg's attitudes toward these "explanations."

In his third and fourth sections, Weinberg summarizes the sufferings these people must endure in the popular mythology associated with their life styles and warns of "the harm done to a homosexual man or woman by the persons trying to convert" them to heterosexuality. He concludes with an exposition of "The Real Problem," which he defines as "homophobia": "the morbid and irrational fear of homosexuals [gay men and/or lesbians], and the hatred of them."

This is Weinberg's summation: "In sum, homophobia is a form of acute conventionality." Ask your students to compare and contrast Weinberg's conclusion with Rose Weitz's talk about "crossing boundaries" in the epigraph at the beginning of this chapter. Similarly, you might ask them to judge whether Weinberg's assertion at the end of the article is consistent with the development of his essay. How do your students view his talk about homophobia as an "acute form of conventionality" as a means for describing and judging behavior in society? Such a discussion can move your students closer to appreciating fully whether this definition clarifies — or obscures — the causes of discrimination. In this sense, your students will be better able to judge the reliability of the equation that posits that homosexuality equals illness, disease, and deviance.

In his final paragraphs, Weinberg presents additional prospects for productive conversation. You could ask your students to discuss the specific ways in which fear and hatred balance each other and whether they are inseparable in Weinberg's construct as well as in your students' own experience. In this sense, you might ask them to discuss the specific ways in which the word *heterosexism* serves better or worse for describing the discrimination aimed at gay men and lesbians.

Implicit in Weinberg's article is the belief that affirmations of love depend on affirmations of the self. Working against expressions of individual as well as societal fear and hatred, Weinberg's article is dedicated to that belief and provides a context within which to examine the short stories by David Leavitt and Dorothy Allison.

Additional Activities

George Weinberg's article supplies several opportunities for your students to engage in research projects, during which they can reasonably expect to learn a great deal about the lives of gay men and lesbian as well as about the mores and democratic assumptions that inform the behavior of those who live both within and outside those communities. In his opening paragraph, Weinberg announces that "forty-five of the fifty states still have laws according to which adult men and women who engage in consenting sexual acts in private may be imprisoned, in some states for as long as ten years, even for a first offense." Dr. Weinberg published this article in 1973. Since then, the number of states with such laws has been reduced to twenty-six, and the gay and lesbian communities have applied increasing political and ethical pressure to drop that number to zero.

You might ask your students to find out not only the position of their own state legislature on this issue but also the rationale (as expressed in public debate) that informs that legislative position. To summarize the substantive rationale for their state's position on this issue, your students might want to read the minutes of the appropriate legislative hearings, examine the pamphlets and publicity summarizing and characterizing both sides of the issue, and to interview, if possible, the public officials elected to represent their districts.

The summaries of these materials provide material for class discussion and debate on many issues, ranging from privacy, ethics, and morality to the rights of citizens, the effects of discrimination, and the political and social consequences of stereotypes. One aspect of these issues is the ways in which the mass media, both within and beyond the gay and lesbian communities, have presented these issues. Take the myths about homosexuality. Ask students to document the ways in which the media portray gay men and lesbians. Have them discuss the stereotypes the media seem to rely on in portraying such people. (You might want to ask them to validate their contentions by drawing specific examples from television situation comedies, from films, from cartoons, from newspaper reports, and the like.) You might then follow up with questions on the assumptions about sexuality embedded in media treatment. What definitions of *normal* and *deviant* sexual behavior are implicit (or explicit) in media treatment? What are the cultural and social effects of media treatment?

Weinberg's article is also an interesting gloss on the essays in Chapter 21, "Gender Roles and Stereotypes," and Chapter 22, "Resistance to Stereotypes."

Generating Writing

1. Weinberg's article is a compelling account of the kinds of discrimination directed against gay people. Ask them to draft an essay in which they discuss the specific ways in which homophobia can be compared and contrasted with such other forms of discrimination as sexism and racism. In what ways is homophobia like and unlike sexism and racism?

2. Ask your students to write an essay in which they compare and contrast the assumptions and implications embedded in the word *homophobia* with those of *heterosexism*.

David Leavitt

Territory

Teaching Strategies

David Leavitt's "Territory" is a provocative series of portraits and vignettes expressing the complexities woven into familial and romantic affirmations of love. Leavitt's story dramatically illustrates the difficulties a mother and son share in expressing both their affection for each other and their understanding of their fundamentally different life-styles. In Leavitt's story, the differences between Neil and his mother include but are not limited to their sexual preferences. They are quite unlike each other in the public personae they present. Mrs. Campbell is active in an array of political and social causes; Neil distances himself from these activities; he watches as much as he feels that he is being watched by people who simply do not understand his behavior and his needs. You might want to follow through by asking students to point to the scenes in the story where Neil senses, whether accurately or not, that he is being watched. Have them explore the implications of what Neil perceives to be forms of surveillance.

Leavitt returns frequently to this motif of the characters' being watched; his story is about the difficulties two male lovers face as they try to negotiate the daily difficulties of expressing and nurturing their affectionate relationship, from embracing and kissing in public to holding hands at a dinner table. Ask students to identify other, subtler forms of such anxiety as well as their consequences in the story. Have them discuss the cumulative effect of such surveillance on the characters as well as on their own reading of the story.

With prose that is often elegantly understated, Leavitt encourages his readers to reexamine their assumptions about the affirmations of love that bond mothers and children as well as lovers. Leavitt addresses the similarities and differences between homosexual *and* heterosexual relations without a trace of polemics. This short story will work well in class to exemplify many of the points outlined in Weinberg's essay.

"Territory" provides abundant evidence to illustrate Weinberg's contention that popular imaginings about gay lives and behavior are bounded by stereotypes. Your students should have little difficulty identifying the gender and sexual stereotypes that surface in Leavitt's story: the strong mother and the absent father are two obvious examples. Yet the traditional biased markings of homosexuality run more deeply in his story. Have students consider much of the vocabulary Neil uses. Neil talks about the "faggot son's sodomist." Ask students to explain their reaction to this pejorative expression. Then ask them to consider how the term works for the speaker, who is gay. What responses does Leavitt elicit from his readers by using such language? You might also ask your students to explore the consequences of Leavitt's having established an incongruity between the bland situation he describes and this kind of language, traditionally associated with deviance and sin.

You can readily follow through on Leavitt's use of homosexual stereotypes. Direct students to several other provocative moments in the story. Ask them to discuss Leavitt's treatment of the homosexual "underworld": "bathhouses and back rooms, enemas and poppers, wordless sex in alleyways." As a way to help students understand the implications of such moments, you might want to ask them to apply Weinberg's warnings about the dire dangers of homophobia.

The issue of homophobia is in many ways at the center of Leavitt's story. Neil and Wayne are afraid to kiss in the airport, feel awkward when they do so in the car, and feel anxious and uncomfortable when holding hands in public or at the dinner table. Yet Leavitt makes it clear in his final scene (on board the airplane to New York) that his characters have moved toward openness and a more relaxed sense of their own sexuality. You might ask students to demonstrate the progression toward that openness which Leavitt builds into his story. Have students identify earlier moments that prefigure the openness of the final scene on the plane.

You might want to extend your class's discussion of the moments in the story when Leavitt touches on what have traditionally been perceived as several other homosexual "types": people who present themselves as a "combination of [the] hypermasculinity and effeminacy which exemplifies faggotry," of "men in leather and denim . . . who habitually do violence to each other," of men who are "more likely to carry diseases," and of "a sticklike man wrapped in green satin. . . ." You might want to use this last example as an opportunity to press your students to study Leavitt's attitudes toward his own characters.

You might also want to call your students' attention to the issue of AIDS, which lurks behind the story and appears in the moments alluded to in the preceding paragraph. No doubt AIDS will surface in your class's discussion of the Leavitt story, probably in your discussion of the myths and stereotypes shrouding the lives of gay men. But Leavitt has kept his treatment of the issue of AIDS lurking in the background, without having given it a great deal of attention. The subject is kept at arm's length.

You can open such a discussion by asking students to identify the principal features of Mrs. Campbell's character and identity. Have them discuss her affirmations of love for Neil. Ask them to describe her complex relationship with Neil and Neil's response to her. Your students should be able to identify and understand Mrs. Campbell's views of her son and the lover he brings home to meet her. You might ask them to talk about the specific ways in which Mrs. Campbell tries to deal with her fears and anxieties about Neil's sexuality. They should be readily able to discuss the implications of her having become an activist, but you may need to work with students to help them understand her activism.

Exploring the assumptions in the expression "alternative life-styles" will lead students to better understand family issues in Leavitt's story. Sexuality most often marks the change into adulthood for young people and establishes (or intensifies) a new kind of tension for many families as the young members negotiate their own relationship to creating a new sense of family for themselves. Many parents in these circumstances find it difficult to let go of their children, to release them fully into their own sexual identities. Being gay or lesbian then *does* make a difference. Traditional expectations prevail: the heterosexual model of the family will be replicated. Mrs. Campbell, despite her best efforts to sensitize herself, still endorses this assumption and therefore judges Neil a failure. But it might be useful to ask students whether the failure is Mrs. Campbell's, whether her refusal, however tacit, to even question the validity of this assumption marks the boundary of her affirmation of love.

Additional Activities

An interesting point for productive speculation about Leavitt's story is to ask students to identify the readers he imagines for "Territory." Is there any internal evidence to suggest that Leavitt addresses his story to gay or straight readers? to male or female readers? to all these? Here's what Leavitt had to say on the subject of his readers in an interview: "I'm happy that I've managed to attract an audience that is not exclusively gay. My ideal reader is an intelligent reader interested in everything but with no particular sexuality. Writing has a sexuality, but I don't think reading does." You might ask your students to discuss Leavitt's observations here and to apply the principles he articulates to their reading of "Territory."

You could follow this talk about the audience for Leavitt's story by asking students to find evidence in the text and speculate about the ways in which gay male readers are likely to find many more points of connection to the story than either straight or lesbian readers. (Or, you might draw on the experience of gay men, lesbians, or straight students in your class.) Pursuing the point about the readers' distance from the story (their emotional connection or attachment to it) will help emphasize an important point: the sense of alienation gay and lesbian readers can feel when asked or forced to read stories in which heterosexual assumptions and behavior dominate the discourse. Extending this principle about alienation and reading beyond sexual preference and into ethnicity and class should make for a more understanding, respectful, and tolerant community of readers.

Generating Writing

At an especially provocative moment in Leavitt's story, one of the characters realizes that "Guilt goes with the territory." You might have your students write about this notion, as it applies to family relations. Ask them to prepare the first draft of an essay in which they recount a family incident that enables them to explore the complex connections between expectation and guilt, failure and blame. As they prepare this draft, you might want to encourage them to define the expectations set for the character they feature as well as to make sure that they have made it clear who sets the expectations, judges the failure, and assigns the blame. How does all this definition occur within the framework of affirmations of love? Are such affirmations complicated by a belief in the notion that guilt goes with the territory?

Dorothy Allison

Don't Tell Me You Don't Know

Teaching Strategies

Dorothy Allison's story provides us with a remarkably clear view of female affirmations of love within familial suffering, alienation, and commitment. But her story also celebrates the individual's ability to come to terms with the stereotypes that constrain one's ability to see experience for what it is, not for what it was hoped to be.

In ways akin to David Leavitt's "Territory," Allison presents characters struggling with the stereotypes that populate both sides of the borders separating sexual preference. You might open an extended discussion of her story by asking your students to identify the full range of stereotypes in it. Consider those associated with class. Your students should have no difficulty spotting the poor-white-trash image of Aunt Alma and of the speaker's extended family as well as exploring its dramatic implications for the story. Similarly, the males who appear in the story do so as the most invidious stereotypical extensions of the poor-white-trash image that prevails in the story. But you might follow up by asking students to comment on the dramatic effect of the speaker's saying that "All my uncles were drunks, and I was more like them than I had ever been like my aunts." Have your students explain the specific ways in which the speaker is "more like them than [she] had ever been like [her] aunts."

This line of questioning can readily be developed into a productive discussion of the speaker's character. Her anger is perhaps the most prominent way in which the speaker is "more like" her uncles than her aunts. She says: "It was my anger that my aunts thought queer, my wild raging temper they respected in a boy and discouraged in a girl." This line might also lead into a discussion of sexuality and, more specifically, the complexities of sexual preference that are unfolded with such dramatic power in Allison's story.

You might ask your students to identify and explore the implications of the sexual stereotypes in this story. The women at the pool table is one of the more obvious examples. They shouldn't have much difficulty pointing to and talking about the others. Such a conversation probably will lead to taking up the question of the speaker's rape and the assumptions about sexuality and sexual preference implicit in her account of this horrifying event. You might well want your students to grapple with the issue of whether a sense of causality is implied in the relation between the speaker's sexual preference and her father's incestuous abuse.

The issue of homophobia may also come up in such a discussion. Your students might notice that the speaker's lesbian sexuality doesn't seem to bother either Aunt Alma or the other women in the family on behalf of whom she speaks. Here you might have students examine the effects of the speaker's almost casual announcement: "That I slept with girls was curious, but not dangerous. That I slept with a knife under my pillow and refused to step aside for my uncles was more than queer. It was crazy." It is reasonable to infer from this passage that the men alluded to in this story might consider lesbian sexuality dangerous, if their voices had been heard.

The speaker's bedroom activity doesn't seem to bother the women; her nonconformity seems far more troubling to them. You might want to refer students back to George Weinberg's essay, and especially to the section in which he talks about the "dangers" in gay behavior as well as the final few paragraphs, where he talks about homophobia as an "acute form of conventionality." Ask students to point out examples of the speaker's nonconformity. (The "dirty" collective household is perhaps the clearest example.) You then might lead them to examine the "costs" of such nonconformity for the speaker.

Dorothy Allison gives engaging examples of the dramatic effects of asserting an adult identity by separating from one's family. Here is one expression of that sentiment: "I was a grown woman minding my own business. I had a right to look her in the eye, I told myself." Have students identify other examples of the speaker's defiance, her assertions about her individuality and dignity. You might compare and contrast Allison's expression of her speaker's independent identity with David Leavitt's handling of the same issue.

You might also direct students to another point for comparing and contrasting the Allison and Leavitt stories: the relative acceptance of family as constitutive of personal identity. Allison frames the issue thus: "If they were not mine, if I was not theirs, who was I?" Ask students to explore this moment in detail and then compare and contrast it to Leavitt's handling of the issue. Which do they prefer? Why?

Having students engage in such comparison-and-contrast exercises may lead them to discover the distinctive differences evident in treatments of the family in lesbian contexts. The speaker in Allison's story resists her family's insistence on child-rearing as the most important means for establishing one's identity and stabilizing and extending a sense of community. Allison's story makes painfully clear the "costs" of trying to establish a family structure independent of blood ties. "These girls might be close, might be important to you, but they're not family," Aunt Alma reminds the speaker. The story eloquently expresses the difficulties women face in trying to establish collective arrangements beyond the conventional boundaries of heterosexual society, affirmations of love that may well exist beyond the abuse and messiness of traditional familial experience summarized in the line, "Nothing was clean between us, especially not our love."

Additional Activities

A great deal of important new work in gay and lesbian studies has increased the respectful attention paid to a movement that surely can now be called that in university criticism and scholarship, a movement that recently has appreciably accelerated its progress. One of the most articulate voices in this new wave is Eve Kosofsky Sedgwick. Her *Epistemology of the Closet* (Berkeley: University of California Press) analyzes a strikingly simple but enormously consequential proposition: that sexual definitions lie at the center of modern thought and culture. Professor Sedgwick posits a new direction for theoretical and critical inquiry: she adds sexuality to race, class, and gender as crucial factors to be considered when engaging in cultural analysis. "There is no aspect of twentieth-century thought and culture that can be understood well without asking how it's intersected with issues of homosexual/heterosexual definition. . . . Wherever you go in this culture and ask these questions, things look different."

You could invite students to respond to Professor Sedgwick's challenge by *rereading* a work of literature and re-viewing it with the issue of sexuality in mind. Because of the limited time most students have, you might ask them to reread a poem they enjoy. If they don't have one in mind, provide a copy of one you might like to reread with them. The issue is to consider the ways in which issues of sexuality surface as important considerations in rereading the poem. Another source for discussion in this context would be one of the many outstanding poems and stories from the now widely circulated collections of gay literature.

(Or, you might ask your students to consider ethical and legal issues as they relate to gay men and lesbians. Consider the rights of gay and lesbian parents in adopting children.)

Generating Writing

The word *queer* is repeated several times in Dorothy Allison's story. You might use it as a way into a writing exercise for your students. First, ask them to consider how the word functions in Allison's story. For what dramatic purpose is the word invoked? With what effect(s)? You might then want to broaden their consideration of the social and political consequences of the word's use in contemporary American culture. Should you choose to move the discussion in this direction, you might find this information useful.

You might follow up this discussion of the label *queer* by asking students to do some research on the group called "Queer Nation." Ask them to find out the rationale for a group's calling itself "Queer Nation."

Or, consider another example. A group of faculty affiliated with a gay and lesbian research group at the University of California at Santa Cruz sponsored a conference with the title "Queer Theory." Professor Teresa de Lauretis, conference organizer, explained in an interview that the use of the term *queer* is "meant to incorporate the experiences of lesbians and gay men, and to give positive meaning to what had been a slur." She went on to explain the function of the conference: "to understand homosexuality not as a perversion or an inversion of normal sexual identity but as a sexual behavior and an identity on its own terms — as a cultural form in its own right."

Professor de Lauretis rejects the charge that gay and lesbian teachers are "inappropriately preaching to their students." She argues instead that traditional classroom discourse implicitly endorses heterosexual values. She observes, "The point would be to see heterosexuality as a choice, not as a constraint. . . . But you can only see it as a choice when you allow homosexuality to be a choice as well."

You might ask students to choose an aspect of contemporary American life that would exemplify de Lauretis's point that the traditional behavior associated with that aspect of life implicitly endorses heterosexual values. Ask them to write an essay proposing specific ways in which that aspect of contemporary American life could be reimagined or reconstituted to include homosexuality as a choice, with all the pleasurable dignity associated with heterosexual experience.

We have in mind here not endorsing either heterosexuality or homosexuality but rather the role that societal endorsement plays in prejudging the distinctive qualities of our experiences. We're encouraging students to understand the relationship between experiences undergone, apparently unreflectively, experiences that when thought about reveal a rich form of self-awareness and self-diagnosis. In the present context, invite students to imagine themselves in circumstances that may well have been heretofore alien; that is, to respect the experience for its own dignity, to imaginatively engage in the experience, and, at the same time, to reflect about it and its distinct qualities.

WRITING ABOUT THE CHAPTER

1. In "The Madness and Myths of Homophobia," George Weinberg asserts that "Most gay people in the United States imagine that they would receive better treatment in England than in their own country" (para. 1). He challenges the validity of that notion, observing that in the United States "gay people get the chance to present their case for decent treatment on television, even national television, and on radio regularly." Ask students to draft an essay in which they compare and contrast the legal or social treatment

of these people in the United States and one other nation. Or, you might want them to focus on comparing and contrasting such treatment in two states or cities in the United States. An even more tightly focused writing exercise might concentrate on comparing and contrasting the laws governing publication of literature that presents portraits of these lives.

2. One recent strategy used by political groups in the gay and lesbian communities to call attention to attitudes that they judge to be hypocritical of some public figures in American life has been the practice of *outing*, the declaration that a public figure is gay. Those who practice or support outing assert that it is a strategy used primarily to unmask the hypocrisy of a public figure, who is either gay or lesbian, but has spoken or acted in ways detrimental to the interests and welfare of those communities.

The issue of outing raises deep questions about the right of citizens to privacy. Consider this example: A reporter for, say, the university newspaper hears a rumor that a university president is gay. The reporter pursues the rumor and establishes in interviews with sexual partners of the president incontrovertible evidence that he or she is gay.

This same president has recently refused to respond to a request from the gay and lesbian student alliance on campus to provide either counseling services to gay men and lesbians or access to student housing for such couples. Should the reporter publish the information that the president is gay? To what extent should the reporter respect the president's right of privacy? Ask students to draft an essay in which they address the moral choices and legal issues that the reporter faces.

3. Provide students with an opportunity to reassess the assumptions and prejudices that they summarized — from both their own attitudes as well as from the media's treatment of gay men and lesbians — in the Writing-before-Reading exercise they drafted for this chapter. Ask them to prepare detailed notes about what they learned by reading Weinberg's article as well as Leavitt's and Allison's stories. Using these notes as a basis, they could write an essay in which they explain the insights they have gained into gay and lesbian "affirmations of love." In what specific ways has their understanding of such affirmations been enriched or complicated?

10

Crises of Adolescence

David Elkind, *From* Teenagers in Crisis

Joyce Carol Oates, Shopping

WORKING WITH THE CHAPTER

Adolescence can be a time of turbulence, for the adolescent *and* for his or her parents. Laurence Steinberg, in an epigraph to this chapter, attributes the conflict between adolescents and their parents to biological factors. Because the physical onset of puberty is inevitable, he suggests that parent–child conflict may be inevitable as well. Margaret Mead, however, in the epigraph from *Coming of Age in Samoa,* claims that the opposite is true: her studies of Samoan youths have convinced her that "physiological puberty need not produce conflict." She attributes the crises facing contemporary American adolescents to their social environment. David Elkind, in "Teenagers in Crisis," would agree with Mead's analysis. He, too, grounds his discussion in a specific time and place, emphasizing the historical and social changes that have created specific problems for today's teenagers.

Teaching Strategies

Many of your students will have vivid recent memories of the crises of adolescence. In fact, those of your students who have just left home for college may recognize their own experiences, which Gail Sheehy calls the "first round trips between family and a base of one's own." They will be in a good position to critique David Elkind's analysis of the causes of difficulty for today's teenagers, whom he sees as "unplaced," neither children nor adults. And to supplement the expertise they have gained by personal experience, they can read Joyce Carol Oates's story of seventeen-year-old Nola Dietrich, who is the convincing fictional embodiment of several of the abstract principles laid out in the essay by Elkind.

In the context of the epigraphs and the essay by David Elkind, the story by Joyce Carol Oates should not elicit an urge, among your students, to fix the blame for the Dietrich family conflict on one or both of the characters in the story. Encourage your students to examine and discuss adolescence as a cultural phenomenon. Much of the material in this chapter treats the conflict between parents and teenagers as a problem to be solved. But Margaret Mead makes it clear, in an analogy with language, that this conflict is so bound into our culture as to make talk of a solution nearly absurd: "the conditions that vex our adolescents are the flesh and bone of our society, no more subject to straightforward manipulation upon our part than is the language which we speak. We can alter a syllable here, a construction there; but the great and far-reaching changes in linguistic structure (as in all parts of culture) are the work of time, a work in which each individual plays an unconscious and inconsiderable part." Her epigraph in particular, and the unit as a whole, could spark a general discussion of the potential influence of any one individual on a culture as a whole. What *can* your students do to ease the period of adolescence for their own children, and what do they feel powerless to change? What is the role of education — reading and writing about adolescence, for instance — in social change?

You may also want to discuss the positive function of conflict between teenagers and their parents. When Mrs. Dietrich asks one of her friends, also the parent of a teenager, "how can you keep living with someone you don't know?" her friend answers, "Eventually you can't." Lead your class in discussing the separation of children from their parents, which is necessary if the child is to make a life for him- or herself. Discuss how conflict helps the teenager to define his or her world view in contradistinction to that of his or her parents.

A Writing-before-Reading Exercise

The authors of the epigraphs and selections that make up this chapter disagree about the causes of conflict between adolescents and their parents. Before your students read the chapter, they may profit by getting their own ideas about the sources of this conflict down on paper. Ask them to write a draft in which they explore possible answers to the question of whether conflict between teenagers and parents is inevitable. Ask those who have decided that such conflict is inevitable to explore some possible sources for that conflict, and ask those who believe that teenagers need not fight with their parents to explore some conditions that help make such conflicts unnecessary.

WORKING WITH THE SELECTIONS

David Elkind

From Teenagers in Crisis

Teaching Strategies

David Elkind has a thesis to prove, and he does a thorough and fairly convincing job of it. Your students may be bowled over by his evidence that today's teenagers face an unprecedented crisis, which did not exist "barely a decade ago." He bolsters his argument with statistics and with insights drawn from experts in psychoanalysis and social philosophy. After reading his essay, many of your students will agree with Elkind's assertions. Of course, you'll also want to give them the option, and the necessary strategies, to disagree. After all, Elkind himself, drawing on John Naisbitt, has characterized our culture as a "multiple-option society."

The Writing-before-Reading exercise for this chapter will allow your students to put their own opinions about adolescence in writing before they read Elkind's opinions so that they will be alert to differences between their views and his. If Elkind is right when he says that "Young people who have a self constructed by substitution are easily swayed and influenced by others," and if some of your students fit into that category — if indeed anyone fits neatly into such categories — they will welcome the chance to define and refine their own opinions before being put in a position to be swayed and influenced by his. Because this chapter does not include an argumentative essay from an opposing viewpoint, this is a perfect opportunity for your students to practice their skill in critical reading, and perhaps to write an opposing argument themselves.

You may want to guide your students in a critique of Elkind's historical claims. You can help them to find leverage for their critique by directing their attention to the quotation from *Steppenwolf.* You might also encourage them to analyze his statements about parental "ambivalence" and "confusion" (para. 25). If it is true that the parents of today's teenagers were granted a moratorium during which to construct a sense of personal identity when *they* were teenagers, then why can't they come to a satisfactory resolution when faced with conflicting value systems? The parents in his account often sound as if they are less well equipped than are their children to cope with today's pressures and choices.

You might ask your students if they think Elkind is objective. Draw their attention to paragraph 23, where he claims that the "important point here is not that one philosophy is good and the other is bad, but rather that we as adults and parents are caught in the crossfire of these two social philosophies." Can your students discover any basis from which to question his avowed impartiality? Does he really think of parents as the innocent victims suggested by his "crossfire" metaphor? Can your students characterize his attitude toward parents? toward teenagers? Can they tell where his sympathies lie? What else can they infer about Elkind's attitudes? Have them look at the paragraph in which he provides statistics on teenage sexual activity. Why does he focus on the sexual activity of teenage *girls* ? And why does he group statistics on sex among statistics on substance abuse, suicide, and crime? And why doesn't he mention birth control in that paragraph?

Although he never comes out and says how he thinks parents should raise their children, can your students infer Elkind's feelings about childrearing from what he says in the essay? Have them give evidence for their inferences. Can they think of any objections to Elkind's position? Would his method be effective in preventing the problems he outlines? To help focus this discussion, you might ask them to look at specific places in the text where Elkind describes a situation faced by a parent — the mom whose son watches X-rated movies, or the father whose daughter is living with a man. Can they tell what response to these situations Elkind advocates? Can they imagine the consequences if these parents were to follow his implicit advice?

Additional Activities

In the final section of his essay, David Elkind describes "Two Ways of Growing": growth by differentiation and integration, and growth by substitution. To enable your students to fully understand as well as critique his categories, you might try this classroom exercise. Divide the class into groups of three or four students. Ask each group to devise questions designed to determine whether the person answering the questions has grown by integration or by substitution. Have them look again at Elkind's final section to review his criteria for placing a person in each category. You might suggest that in composing their surveys they remember that sometimes a direct question, such as "Do you habitually succumb to peer pressure?," is series of indirect ones, such as "Do you sometimes drink to be sociable?" and "Are you comfortable expressing your opinion to your friends when it differs from theirs?" scattered throughout the survey. Let each group decide how its own survey will be set up: statements to be marked true/false or never/seldom/sometimes/usually, or questions to be answered yes/no or with more elaborate answers, for instance. Also let each group decide how the results of each survey will be calculated.

For homework, have them type up and duplicate their surveys. Provide them with an audience in one of two ways: have the other members of the class act as the audience for each group's survey, or have them administer the survey to friends outside the class. The disadvantage in surveying their own classmates will be that their audience, having read Elkind and composed their own questionnaires, will see through and hence be able to circumvent the intent of the questions, should they wish to do so. An outside audience will definitely be more innocent. But a possible advantage also lies in surveying their classmates: students who have responded to such a survey and been categorized accordingly will be able to speak about how it feels to be categorized, and whether they think Elkind's scheme is accurate enough to be useful.

Generating Writing

1. David Elkind is an expert on the topic of teenagers, a parent whom other parents approach for advice on how to deal with their adolescent offspring. Many of your freshmen are also experts on teenagers — they have been doing informal field research on teenagers for years, and they have been observing parental behavior even longer. It will no doubt be enlightening to tap their knowledge by assigning an essay in which they propose a scheme for childrearing, focusing particularly on ways in which parents can effectively deal with teenagers. Have them describe typical areas of conflict between adolescents and their parents, and then suggest methods for reestablishing domestic harmony. Also have them think about what parents can do when their children are still young to minimize problems in the teenage years. Such writing assignments give the students a sense of their own authority; by suggesting such a topic, you say to them, "Here is an area in which you know more than I do, about a topic that I consider very important." The strong sense of audience created by such an assignment comes from the genuine eagerness you will feel at the prospect of reading about the crises of adolescence from those with the most immediate experience of those crises.

2. You might similarly draw on their expertise by assigning an essay in which they design an advertising campaign that will persuade teenagers not to drink and drive, or not to use hard drugs. Have students think back to their own and their friends' experiences with substance abuse, and then come up with a message that might get through to teens who face similar situations. As part of their assignment, they should write a justification of the approach they have taken in their ad campaign, as if they are trying to sell their idea to a sponsor, for instance.

3. Elkind writes (para. 2) that the "media and merchandisers, too, no longer abide by the unwritten rule that teenagers are a privileged group who require special attention and nurturing. They now see teenagers as fair game for all the arts of persuasion and sexual innuendo once directed only to adult audiences and consumers." Have students test Elkind's assertion against a specific example they have chosen from the media — an advertisement, television show, or movie directed at a teen audience. Have them tease out the assumptions about teenagers that are woven into the texture of the advertisement or show they have selected. If you want to make this into a more challenging research assignment, and simultaneously give them an opportunity to test Elkind's historical assertion, you might assign an essay in which they compare and contrast an advertisement from the 1950s and one from the 1990s, or two movies or two television series, one from an earlier decade and one that is popular today. Remind them that their essays will be better focused and more effective if they choose two examples that are analogous — two ads for jeans, for example, rather than one for a car and one for a brassiere.

Joyce Carol Oates

Shopping

Teaching Strategies

You might begin a discussion of "Shopping" by directing students to the issue of point of view. Ask them whose perspective is represented in the story. They should notice that most if not all of the story is filtered through the consciousness of Mrs. Dietrich. Ask them to point to locutions that capture the nuances of Mrs. Dietrich's "interior voice." Ask if they can tell where the author stands in the text. Mrs. Dietrich's "interior voice" is described as "free of irony." Do your students sense irony in the text? Have them point to specific instances. Where does the ironic gap form in the examples they have chosen? Also ask how the point of view is limited. Have them speculate about why the reader never has access to Nola's mind. How would the story differ if we were told, for example, what a seventeen-year-old's laughter means (para. 6)?

You might also want to focus on the two main characters in this story, beginning with Mrs. Dietrich. What can students tell about her from reading this story? Which of these traits is she aware of, and which is she not aware of? Ask students to identify the specific ways in which Oates gives us insights into Mrs. Dietrich's character, working these insights in where Mrs. Dietrich herself will not notice them, even when the clues are embedded in her own thoughts. Do students sympathize with Mrs. Dietrich? If so, how does Oates create that sympathy? If not, why not? To what extent and for what reasons do they blame Mrs. Dietrich for her own predicament?

Next, have them analyze the character of Nola. What can we tell about her without overhearing her thoughts? Where do we get our clues to her character? Does Nola seem old for her age, or young for her age, or both in turn? What kind of childhood has she had? What are the pressures she faces as a teenager? Do your students feel sympathy toward Nola? If so, how does Oates create that sympathy? How does Oates's use of point of view affect the reader's reaction to the characters? Do students find that the inaccessibility of Nola's thoughts makes them more likely or less likely to give her the benefit of the doubt?

You will also want your students to discuss the relationship between Nola and her mother. What are the sources of the tension between them? Why does Mrs. Dietrich spend so much time trying to understand Nola? What keeps her from understanding what's really wrong? Does she spend any time trying to analyze her own role in the formation of Nola's character? Have your students characterize the love Mrs. Dietrich feels for Nola. Why does she consider the time Nola spent in the womb as the happiest they've spent together?

During your class discussion of the characters in this story, you might bring up the recurring image — and issue — of hunger. Mrs Dietrich "gets ravenously hungry, shopping at the Mall" (para. 17). What else besides its literal meaning could her hunger stand for? Some of your students may have noticed the clues that Nola has an eating disorder. Have them discuss the issue of food together with that of control. You might also bring up the suggestions of Mrs. Dietrich's to facilitate discussion of their family dynamic. Also ask your students to describe Mr. Dietrich's role in creating that dynamic.

Your students might also be interested in this excerpt from an interview with Joyce Carol Oates that appeared in the *Paris Review* in 1978. Oates was asked if her mood affected her ability to write. Her answer might be encouraging to those among your students who procrastinate, waiting for the right mood before they begin to draft an essay. She said, "One must be pitiless about this matter of 'mood.' In a sense the writing will *create* the mood. If art is, as I believe it to be, a genuinely transcendental function — a means by which we rise out of limited, parochial states of mind — then it should not matter very much what states of mind or emotion we are in. Generally I've found this to be true: I have forced myself to begin writing when I've been utterly exhausted, when I've felt my soul as thin as a playing card, when nothing has seemed worth enduring for another five minutes . . . and somehow the activity of writing changes everything. Or appears to do so. Joyce said of the underlying structure of *Ulysses* — the Odyssean parallel and parody — that he really didn't care whether it was plausible, so long as it served as a bridge to get his 'soldiers' across. Once they were across, what does it matter if the bridge collapses? One might say the same thing about the use of one's self as a means for the writing to get written. Once the soldiers get across the stream. . . ."

Additional Activities

The setting of this story is as important as the characters themselves. Ask students why it might be true for Nola and her mother that "At the Mall, in such crowds of shoppers, moments of intimacy are possible as they rarely are at home." Have them skim through the story, looking for each mention of the mall. What are the various analogies and associations connected with the mall? What is the significance of the mall's architecture, with its "buttressed glass domes"? Why are the mother and daughter drawn to La Crêperie? Why do they feel, upon entering the mall, as if they are "coming home" (para. 7)?

If you focus on the mall, you may want to teach this story along with the selections in Chapter 16, "Consumer Culture." The article by William Severini Kowinski, in particular, links the idea of the mall to issues of control, which are also significant in the Oates story.

Generating Writing

1. When Nola is in her mother's womb, Mrs. Dietrich knows that the baby will be a girl: "It would be herself again, reborn and this time perfect." This is not the only suggestion in "Shopping" that Nola and Mrs. Dietrich are being set up as doubles for each other. Of course, as with most doubles, the mirror is not perfectly smooth. You might assign an essay in which students explore the doubling motif in this story, focusing on the points of comparison between mother and daughter. What do these similarities and analogies signify?

2. An extension of the doubling motif appears in the homeless woman sitting outside Lord and Taylor's. Assign an essay in which your students explore the significance of this homeless woman. What is it about her that triggers Nola's tears at the end of the story? Have students seek the possible points of comparison between the homeless woman and the two Dietrich women.

WRITING ABOUT THE CHAPTER

1. Have your students revise the draft they read before reading the epigraphs and selections in the chapter. They should argue either that conflict is inevitable between adolescents and their parents or that it is not. They may want to limit their claim to the United States in the late twentieth century, or they may not. If some students have different ethnic backgrounds or the experience of living in another country, they may want to draw on their experience of other cultures to help them make their point about the universality or culture-specificity of parent–teenager conflict.

2. Your students may want to apply the insights they gained from reading David Elkind's essay to the situation described in Joyce Carol Oates's story. In what ways does "Shopping" provide a paradigm for the sources of conflict discussed in the Elkind article? What might Elkind say about Mrs. Dietrich's behavior toward her daughter? How might he assess Nola's situation?

3. The conflicts between teenagers and their parents have spawned a lot of humorous writing down through the ages. Fran Lebowitz and Erma Bombeck both poke fun at teenagers: Lebowitz suggests, "Think before you speak. Read before you speak. This will give you something to think about that you didn't make up yourself — a wise move at any age, but most especially at seventeen, when you are in the greatest danger of coming to annoying conclusions." Bombeck has said that a child "develops individuality long before he develops taste. I have seen my kind struggle into the kitchen in the morning with outfits that needed only one accessory: an empty gin bottle." Mark Twain directs his humor at himself as a teenager: "When I was a boy of fourteen, my father was so ignorant I could hardly stand to have the old man around. But when I got to be twenty-one, I was astonished to see how much he had learned in seven years." Assign a paper in which students write a humorous account of the teen years, from the point of view of either a parent or a teenager. Or they might choose to write a teenager's-eye view of parental foibles.

11

A National Obsession

Marie Winn, TV Addiction

Pete Hamill, Crack and the Box

WORKING WITH THE CHAPTER

Television is an inescapable part of our daily lives. We can choose not to watch it ourselves, but we cannot choose not to interact with a culture that is profoundly shaped by the ubiquitous medium. From the politics of sound bites to the new internationalism of a global village with satellite transmission of sitcoms and music videos, television has become a powerful force in shaping the modern world. Most of today's students are second-generation members of the television culture; it may be almost impossible for them to imagine a world without it.

Teaching Strategies

This chapter presents a number of arguments against television. Students may be uncomfortable with the orientation of the selections; one way to approach this issue might be to remind them that television has more than ample opportunity to make its case for itself. Their own viewing habits and understanding may provide the strongest argument against the chapter's antitelevision slant. Encourage the class to address the authors' complaints against television directly; how might they defend their favorite medium?

You may want to begin work on this chapter with a general discussion of television and its part in our lives. Some students may have parents who forbade or restricted television viewing. How do they feel this proscription influenced their childhood? Their emotional development? Their intellectual growth? Others may have spent the bulk of their childhood and adolescence in front of the small screen. How do they feel this exposure affected them? What limitations, if any, might students put on their own children's viewing?

Neil Postman's epigraph supplies interesting statistics that might serve as a foundation for class discussion. Are students surprised by his figures? How do they feel their own viewing time measures up to the national average?

Not everyone may be familiar with Huxley's *Brave New World* and with soma, the fictional drug with which the novel's repressive government maintains mental control over its citizens. Does the class find this metaphor to be valid? Postman also states that the power of television "is not to be taken as an attempt . . . to employ the age-old trick of distracting the masses with circuses." Do students catch the allusion to the classical era? Might they disagree with Postman here? He goes on to argue that the chief danger of television is its power of "transforming all serious public business into junk." Does the class think this is an accurate statement? Ask them to analyze some programs that deal with "serious public business" — news, political debates, roundtable discussions — applying Postman's characterization. Does his description seem apt? Why or why not? What forces might be inimical to serious televised discussion or reportage?

Pauline Kael's discussion of the regular television viewer is, of course, formed by her experience as a professional film critic. Students may be familiar with her work from *The New Yorker* or her numerous books of essays and reviews. Like most film critics, Kael sees movies as a powerful socializing force. Does she cast television as the enemy of socialization? How true to students' experience is her depiction of the television viewer? What do they make of her statement equating television with prison?

The Maurine Doerken epigraph deals with some potential conceptual problems the frequent television viewer may face. Like Postman, Doerken uses the metaphor of the drug, referring to television's "narcotizing aspect" and "its potential for . . . drugging people not to care." How does television make its viewers uncaring? You may want to discuss the example of television violence. Do students feel that their own exposure to hundreds or thousands of graphically depicted murders, accidents, beatings, rapes, and assaults has somehow hardened them to the realities of violence? Do they feel that television violence has helped make society as a whole more violent and more inured to human suffering?

Doerken also discusses confusion between fiction and reality as another possible effect of television viewing. Do students know or know of anyone for whom television actors, characters, and situations are more real than the persons or incidents in their own lives? Kael, too, claims that for the frequent viewer, the television world is the real world, and it is everyday existence that seems unreal. This accusation is most frequently leveled against soap-opera viewers. Might some genres be more susceptible to this sort of confusion than others? How do television programs maintain the illusion of reality? Why might they seek this vision?

The class may want to discuss one of the most interesting phenomena of conflated fact and fiction, the obsessed fan. Supermarket tabloids and tabloid television carry innumerable accounts of celebrities' difficulties with, and sometimes even danger from, fans who have incorporated performers and their roles into their own fantasy world. Students might choose one of these cases and analyze it, considering Doerken's and Kael's thoughts on frequent television viewing. How do these cases support the authors' ideas? What other forces might be at work here?

The Daniel Boorstin epigraph gives a social historian's view of how a television culture develops. Ask the class to read this epigraph closely. How accurately does it describe their own attitude? Do they feel political events, sports, and entertainment are stage-managed for television? Some of them might have had the experience of attending a game, concert, or meeting only to find that the audience's attention was focused more on the cameras and monitors covering the event than on the event itself. Do students agree with Boorstin that our culture has revised its "criteria for experience" to reflect television values?

The theme of television as drug is common to Postman, Doerken, Winn, and Hamill. Why would the authors select this metaphor? What significance do drugs have in our society? What is the symbolic value attached to them? How do the authors use the metaphor differently?

Might Winn and Kael agree on the problems frequent television watchers experience in making meaningful connections with others? What might Hamill say about this issue? How do the subjects Winn and Kael describe differ from the people Hamill talks about? Ask the class to discuss how class, race, status, and gender determine television viewing. Are some groups of people more likely to watch television than others? Are some groups more apt to have problems from extensive viewing? Which of the epigraph authors seems to share Hamill's perspective on television's dangers? Have students talk about the differences between Winn's and Hamill's agendas. Winn seems to focus on television as a detriment to creativity and connection with the world; her examples and references are about relatively well-educated and privileged people (the "college English instructor," for instance) and their activities (reading, crocheting, gardening). Hamill, on the other hand, believes that television's greatest failing is its tendency to discourage viewers from dealing with the challenges and complexities of life; his examples refer mostly to the disadvantaged ("those children in that welfare hotel"). On which group does television take a greater toll? One might argue that the poor, uneducated, and otherwise underprivileged are not offered a variety of opportunities to entertain themselves; most other cultural activities require money (the movies, concerts, plays) or education (reading, the arts) for participation in them. How might Hamill counter this argument?

A Writing-before-Reading Exercise

Ask students to take a few minutes to list the television programs they watch regularly. (They might want to make a week's schedule on the model of *TV Guide*.) Have them write a brief (one- or two-sentence) description of each program. When they have completed this passage, ask them to go through their viewing schedule and write one sentence explaining why they watch each program. Encourage honesty; they may watch some shows because they precede other shows, or because they have nothing else to do at that hour, or because others are watching the shows. What percentage of the shows do they watch because of real interest in the topic or presentation?

Have the class discuss their favorite programs. Ask each student to select one program, and make an argument for it. Why should class members watch it? What might it add to their lives? Encourage students to debate these questions.

WORKING WITH THE SELECTIONS

Marie Winn

TV Addiction

Teaching Strategies

This selection is from Winn's influential book, *The Plug-In Drug: Television, Children, and Family* (New York: Viking, 1985). What is the rhetorical power of Winn's title? Ask students to read Winn's opening paragraph closely. What does she make of claims that some activities might be described as addictive? Does she simplify the issue of addictions and the belief that some behaviors are substantially like addiction to drugs? We seem to see an ever-proliferating world of addictions and their cures: tabloids, magazines, and talk shows feature sex addicts, shopping addicts, gambling addicts, exercise addicts, and their stories of despair and redemption. Discuss this spread with the class. Why is the metaphor of addiction so powerful in our society? Winn refers to "the lighthearted category of cookie eating" (para. 2), yet food addictions are actually among the most serious of the dependency problems. What other techniques does Winn use to dismiss the claims of other potential addictions?

Ask students if they agree with Winn's description of addiction as essentially "a pursuit of pleasure" (para. 3). Are there other ways of approaching addiction that might be more descriptive? Is the class troubled by Winn's omitting data or references to other works of psychology and sociology to support her claims?

Winn distinguishes "serious addiction" from the "harmless pursuit of pleasure" by whether or not the addiction includes "destructive elements" (para. 5). What problems might there be with this definition? How might other forces than the addiction itself contribute to the addict's alienation from society? Winn's definition might also be taken as implying that if a heroin addict, for example, were able to keep jobs and relationships intact, the addiction would not be a social or personal problem. Is this a fair reading of her view? Ask students to discuss the social costs of addiction. Why do we, as a nation, oppose it so bitterly? What addictions are more acceptable in our society? Which are less acceptable? What are the differences between the two? Cigarette smoking is legal and accommodations are made for smokers in public places, and yet the cost to society in medical bills and lost productivity is greater for cigarette abuse than for any other drug. Heroin addiction, on the other hand, affects a very small percentage of the population, and shows no signs of increasing; and yet heroin addiction is the model for nightmare scenarios of drug abuse. Why does Winn compare the television addict to the heroin addict rather than the cigarette addict? What rhetorical advantage might she gain by likening familiar, middle-class television to frightening heroin, with its suggestion of crime and city streets? Winn's other chief metaphor for television addiction is alcoholism, a problem much more familiar to her readers. How is dependence on television like dependence on alcohol? How are they unlike?

Winn's calling television viewing potentially addictive rests on three assumptions; first, that television viewers use the medium as a way to "blot out the real world"; second, that they are unable to control or limit the time they spend watching television; and third, that television itself alters personal experience for the worse, by changing the ways in which we perceive the world around us. Are these assumptions valid? Discuss with the class. If these assumptions are valid in themselves, do Winn's conclusions follow naturally from them? What other conclusions might be reached from the same data?

The selection's final paragraph raises an interesting point, that television watching is a self-perpetuating act. The more television you watch, the more you become attuned to the conventions and structures of television, and the more you want to watch. Do students feel that is an accurate assessment of their experience? What motivations might there be to watch television other than a television-induced craving for itself? Why does the class watch? If some class members do not watch television, why do they choose not to? What positive aspects of television does Winn overlook? One argument against Winn's position might be that television addiction is closer to dependence on cookies than on heroin, for the medium itself is benign if not positive, but it does have the capacity for abuse by some individuals. We should not all stop eating just because many people have difficulty with food; we will not stop having intimate relationships because some are addicted to romance or sex. Must we stop watching television, then, because it is an experience some of us cannot handle?

Additional Activities

Interested students might want to read the rest of Winn's book and report on it to the class. Another work in the same vein is Jerry Mander's *Four Arguments for the Elimination of Television* (New York: Morrow, 1978), from which other students may want to present selections. Others may want to research studies in television by critics like David Marc and Andrew Ross, who treat the medium as an important part of our culture. You might also want to assign some students to read and present Marshall McLuhan's *Understanding Media: The Extensions of Man* (New York: McGraw-Hill, 1964). McLuhan was one of the first academics to understand the power of television in modern society. How do his conclusions differ from Winn's? Why might they differ?

Generating Writing

1. Ask students to keep a television journal for one week. In it, they should record all programs viewed and under what circumstances they were seen (alone, with friends, in a student lounge). Have them pay close attention to their mood and emotions before,

during, and after watching. Did television change the way they felt? Why did they watch? What were they expecting from the show? Were their expectations fulfilled?

2. Have the class write a brief essay analyzing Winn's argument in this selection. They might start by critiquing or defending her definitions of addiction; they should also try to evaluate how applicable these definitions are to the circumstances of television viewing. How does Winn's style help reinforce her position?

Pete Hamill

Crack and the Box

Teaching Strategies

As a newspaper and magazine journalist, Pete Hamill might be expected to have prejudices against television. This selection first appeared as a column in *Esquire* magazine. What self-interest might other media have in criticizing television? Must these conflicting interests be taken into account when reading these critiques? Why are newspapers and magazines considered more culturally respectable than television? What criteria do we use for deciding how serious the different media are?

What do students make of Hamill's tone? Discuss his style and self-presentation. How does he come across? What authority does his rhetoric give to his opinions? Read his second paragraph closely. Does he reinforce his own perceptions with a reference to his years of experience? How does Hamill's depiction of crowds of people with the same problems affect his description of those problems?

Ask the class to look carefully at Hamill's third paragraph. Once again, he appeals to the sheer volume of his experience with "hundreds of addicts," none of whom could provide "sensible" explanations for their addictions. What do students make of the explanations Hamill says they did give? Some of them seem to be rather cogent arguments in favor of a retreat from the world; what kind of explanation might it take to satisfy Hamill?

Hamill describes our country's drug policy as asking the wrong questions; rather than wondering why so many groups and nations are willing to sell us drugs, we might consider why we are so willing, even eager, to buy them. What does the class think of this argument? Why might it be in the government's interest to attack the supply side of the drug equation, rather than try to lessen society's demand?

The issues Hamill discusses here are not particularly new, but his explanation for our willingness to alter our consciousness is unusual. Do students agree with Hamill that television serves as an introduction to a life-style of escapism, which manifests itself most dangerously in drug abuse? Ask the class to analyze Hamill's argument connecting the two phenomena. Does his position seem to follow from cause and effect, or from the conjunction of two simultaneous and unrelated circumstances?

Is Hamill's argument from his own memory that drug abuse was not a problem in the pretelevision years valid? Might we want to see some data bearing this claim out? Is Hamill's statement true for all segments of American culture? Notice, too, that Hamill excludes alcoholism — higher, by many reports, in the 1950s than today — from his definition of "drug abuse." What might that omission suggest about the assumptions underlying his position?

Hamill's point about the constant presence of television being a completely new phenomenon in entertainment is an interesting one. His examples are persuasive, certainly; it's true that theater, books, and movies do not consume the time and attention television demands. On the other hand, Hamill leaves broadcast radio out of the picture. Between the 1920s and 1950s, radio provided a form of entertainment highly analogous to television today. Commercial radio broadcast soap operas, dramas, comedies, news programs, and talk shows, as well as musical entertainment and sporting events. Many American households structured their schedules around favorite programs, and the radio would be on in many homes from morning until night. A number of critics at the time, from Henry Ford to George Bernard Shaw, predicted that radio's popularity would have dire consequences for society. Why might Hamill have chosen not to discuss radio?

Do students find Hamill's differentiation between active perception of information, as in reading, and passive reception, valid? Some critics argue that television actually helps viewers comprehend new methods of information storage and technology. There certainly seems to be a correlation between computer skill and interest in video entertainment; might the perceptual abilities required and reinforced by television be as useful in an age of increasingly nonlinear information as the traditional abilities involved in reading printed matter?

Hamill also feels that we impose the structures of television drama on our own experience. How true do students find that to be in their own lives? In the past, some critics have held that other arts shape our perceptions of ourselves and others; Rachel Brownstein's *Becoming a Heroine* (New York: Penguin Books, 1984), for instance, argues that novels shape women's self-image, and art historian T. J. Clark describes, in *The Painting of Modern Life* (New York: Knopf, 1985), how the Impressionist movement changed Paris's view of itself. Is this influence necessarily bad? Discuss this question with the class. Hamill claims that the problem with television's conventions is that they are just too oversimplified to provide a useful perspective on real conflicts and challenges. Do students find this an accurate criticism?

Ask the class to talk about Hamill's recommendations for action. Do they think these are effective and positive counters to our culture's overdependence on television? How many of his suggestions might they implement for themselves?

Additional Activities

Ask students to list the conflicts presented in an average evening of television, and to discuss their resolution. How realistic were these resolutions? Did individual programs overlook difficulties and complications that could not be avoided if the same situations were to occur in real life?

Have the class return to their work on Chapter 3, "Moments of Recognition." Discuss the complexity cf the problems presented in the selections, the moral and ethical choices faced by the authors or protagonists, and the way in which the conflicts are resolved. Now ask students to imagine they are television writers and executives commissioned to drama-tize these selections for a new television series. What changes would be needed to make these pieces "good television"? What would be lost?

Generating Writing

1. Ask students to write a brief essay challenging or defending Hamill's argument. One place to start might be by questioning the validity of his cause-and-effect hypothesis: Might overdependence on television and dependence on drugs be the products of other social forces not cited by Hamill? Could they both be caused by such problems as crime, economic and social inequality, or lack of civic responsibility?

2. Students may also want to challenge or defend Hamill's statements about the lessons television teaches. Is television educational? How does it undermine efforts by parents, teachers, and institutions to instruct children about choices and values? How might the educational value of television be increased?

WRITING ABOUT THE CHAPTER

1. A traditional compare-and-contrast essay could certainly be assigned for this chapter. Ask students to read Hamill's and Winn's arguments closely, and compare them. What issues seem to be at stake for each author? Who are their audiences? Who are the subjects they discuss? What are their underlying assumptions? How do their aims seem to differ?

2. Have the class write a personal essay about a significant experience with television. This may be a program they found especially informative or enlightening, or perhaps an event they found frightening or horrifying when seen on video. Perhaps they want to protest against an offensive stereotype or attitude to which television has exposed them. They might also want to discuss the act of viewing itself; television may have been a welcome distraction in the hospital, for example, or at a time of family conflict. Ask them to consider how the medium shaped their encounter with it. Was this an experience unique to television?

12

Family Stories

Elizabeth Stone, Stories Make a Family

Judith Ortiz Cofer, *Casa:* A Partial Remembrance
of a Puerto Rican Childhood

Maxine Hong Kingston, No Name Woman

Itabari Njeri, Granddaddy

WORKING WITH THE CHAPTER

The urge to tell stories is surely a primitive one. Families and communities use stories to shape a collective version of reality: to describe their past, to define their present identity, and to instruct the younger generation, so that the future of the family or community will be continuous with the past. The child who listens to these stories discovers his or her own identity in learning to identify with his or her family. Clyde Edgerton writes in an epigraph to this chapter, "In defining my family's history, Uncle Bob was defining me." For many children, a sense of ethnic identity is crucial to a strong sense of personal identity: Alex Haley needed it as well as Judith Ortiz Cofer, who learned what it means to be a Puerto Rican woman from the stories her grandmother told.

Family stories not only bridge the generations but also reconcile other sources of discontinuity. William Kittredge describes storytelling as a way of "enclosing otherness." The epigraph by Leslie Marmon Silko suggests that this discontinuity, this "otherness," often stems from differing perspectives. The Pueblo people she writes about understand that stories change according to the teller's point of view. These people "sought a communal truth, not an absolute." For a writer such as Itabari Njeri, however, the communal truth is not acceptable, not when the community is as sorely divided as is the South. She is determined to break through the self-serving and bigoted stories told by a white community about her black grandfather's death, only to find a discouraging complicity even in her own family. She learns that which all the writers in this chapter learn: that she will never discover the whole truth.

Of course the whole truth is seldom the goal of family stories. Sometimes the listeners find themselves in the position of Maxine Hong Kingston, having to listen between the lines, revising the traditional story so that it will provide "ancestral help" that's appropriate to their immediate needs in a rapidly changing world. And Elizabeth Stone writes of the evolution in her family's stories, which helped them to combat racial stereotypes about Italians when they first arrived in the United States, and later helped them to assimilate to their new culture. In this way new stories grow from the old, allowing the family or community to grow with the times.

Teaching Strategies

Elizabeth Stone writes that "literal truth was never the point," and several other authors in this unit echo her sentiment. If literal truth is not the point in storytelling, what is? In what sense *are* these stories true, despite their sometimes loose renditions of the facts? Maxine Hong Kingston's essay is from *The Woman Warrior,* which her publishers label "autobiography." Do your students accept this label or not? Have them debate its appropriateness.

Ask students to describe the function of gossip in the selections in this chapter. Which of the stories recounted in the essays would they categorize as gossip and which as family stories? Is there any overlap between the two categories? What is the relation of truth value to gossip, compared with the truth value of family stories? What can your students say about the societal taboo against gossip? What is the purpose, for these writers, in speaking out despite forces that conspire to keep them silent?

A Writing-before-Reading Exercise

Every family tells stories about itself, perhaps at Thanksgiving dinner, when the extended family gathers, or perhaps, as in Judy Ortiz Cofer's home, when the women (or the men) of the family find themselves home alone. Invite your students to record one of their family's prized stories. If they wish, they can take on the persona of the family member who usually tells the story, capturing the nuances of his or her voice and narrative style.

WORKING WITH THE SELECTIONS

Elizabeth Stone

Stories Make a Family

Teaching Strategies

In this essay exploring family stories, Stone tells stories about her family that were as familiar to her as the tale of Cinderella. Her mention of Cinderella is not gratuitous: many of the family stories she relates have the style and structure of fairy tales. You might begin class discussion of this essay by having your students identify the fairy-tale elements of her family stories. Besides her diction and syntax, they might notice the fairy-tale plots underlying several stories. Encourage them to speculate about the pervasiveness of such plots. Why is the paternal obstacle to young love such a durable feature in such stories? Why is the story of a rich young woman falling in love with a poor but talented man told and retold, in various forms? What is it about symmetrical plots — in which "two brothers and a sister married two sisters and a brother and all came to live in the same house" — that makes them so appealing?

Your discussion of the forms and features of fairy tales may lead naturally to discussing the function of fairy tales. See if your students can draw analogies between the ways in which fairy tales serve a culture and how family stories serve a family. Stone explores several ways in which her family's stories shape and unite her family; can your students think of analogous functions fulfilled by the stories told by a culture about itself and its past? Stone also interprets some of the stories, making explicit the implicit morals of the family stories she heard in her childhood. Have your students brainstorm names of fairy tales, and then ask them to paraphrase the morals of these stories. To what degree and in what sense are fairy tales stories whose morals one might be expected to "live by"?

To analyze how a family or culture may choose the stories that will define it, you might ask your class what Stone means when she writes, "My grandfather, despite his surname, was not a true Bongiorno. . . . The true Bongiorno was my grandmother, the first Annunziata's last child." Ask them how she might define "Bongiorno." What are some of the family traits? How does Stone go about establishing the authenticity of these traits in her essay? Why does she define "Bongiorno" by these traits, rather than, say, by her grandfather's personality? Invite them to describe the role of storytelling in this family definition.

Each selection in this chapter emphasizes somewhat storytelling's special part in the homes of ethnic minorities. Stone writes that her "family stories often tried tacitly to counteract what the culture said about Italians." Ask students to list and discuss specific ways in which the stories she relates in this essay counteract ethnic stereotypes. She writes that the "process of assimilation" of her Italian family was accelerated by her mother's generation. How do the stories about the previous generations help these children, who "barely understood Italian," preserve their ethnic identity? You might choose to expand the discussion of storytelling's overall role in ethnic identity to the other selections in this chapter.

Additional Activities

Family stories can be fun to share, and the sharing can help break the ice in a reading and composition classroom. If you are using the Writing-before-Reading Exercise at the beginning of this unit, you might try assigning it as an in-class essay, allowing half the class period for your students to draft a family story of their own. Then ask students to form small groups, with perhaps three students per group, and to read their stories aloud to each other. After the students have listened to each story, have them jot down a line or two expressing its significance as they heard it. You might phrase the question in this way: "What did you learn about the writer's family from the story he or she just read to you?" The students can hand their interpretations to the writer at the end of the period, and the writer can use these observations when revising the draft. The revision question in "Working with the Chapter" asks that the student weave his or her interpretation into the family story, and this feedback from the other students might provide a jumping-off place for the writer's own interpretation. Sometimes we hear meanings in other people's family stories that the teller, who may be too close to the subject, cannot hear.

Stone's essay can also be used as part of a lesson on organization. Ask your class to identify the ordering principle behind the stories she records. Ask why she puts them in this order. How are the changes in her family history accounted for in the stories they tell about themselves? How do family stories evolve so as to remain useful for each successive generation? If you decide to discuss organization in class, check the Elements of Composition table of contents for the names of other essays that will provide different models of organization. By drawing their attention to several writers' choices and the effects of those choices, you help make students aware of ways in which form matches and reinforces the content of written works.

Generating Writing

1. Ask your students why Stone begins the essay by tracing her family line back to her great-grand*mother*. What other evidence does she give to support the observation that she conceives of her family as matrilinear? How does the focus on storytelling determine this matrilineal slant? (To help students articulate an answer to this question you might ask them what kinds of essays one could write about one's family that would emphasize the male line.) You can also suggest that they look at Kingston's "No Name Woman" and Cofer's

"Casa," which also appear in this chapter, to build an argument about the connection between women and family stories.

2. Ask students to write an essay exploring the specific ways in which Stone's family stories resemble fairy tales. Have them consider such elements as style, plot, character development, structure, motifs, and the moral of the story. What is the effect of the several analogies between her family stories and fairy tales? Have them draw larger comparisons and contrasts between the two genres, based on the features they have examined.

Judith Ortiz Cofer

Casa: A Partial Remembrance of a Puerto Rican Childhood

Teaching Strategies

Like Elizabeth Stone, Judith Ortiz Cofer lets the reader overhear several family stories, but in Cofer's piece the impression of eavesdropping is more pronounced. This impression comes from the carefully detailed context Cofer provides for the stories: we see the furnishings of the room, we see the storyteller and her audience, and this context becomes at least as important as the content of the stories. You might begin by asking students to comment on the importance of the setting in Cofer's essay. Why is the description of the room significant? You might also mention the timing of the stories: Why does the grandmother tell this story at this time? What would Cofer sacrifice if she were to omit details about time and place?

Cofer characterizes her grandmother's stories as "cautionary tales." Ask students to identify what she cautions her daughters and granddaughters against. Have them para-phrase the moral of the story about Maria la Loca. What preconceptions about gender roles are implicit in the moral? How would they characterize relations between the genders as portrayed in the grandmother's tales?

Cofer says she used the stories of Maria and the other crazy people in her village as "a measuring stick" in her "serious quest for a definition of normal." Have students discuss her possible reasons for seeking such a definition. Ask them what factors might have contributed to her uncertainty about normalcy. How do the family stories she hears at her grandmother's house help her define normalcy? How do people in general arrive at definitions of normalcy? How do stories in general contribute to a society's definition?

Additional Activities

If you'd like to teach Cofer's essay in conjunction with essays in other chapters, here are some options. Like Alice Walker and Gloria Steinem, in Chapter 19 on "Mothers," Cofer gives credit to the women in her family for inspiring her own written work. Although many of your students probably do not identify themselves as writers, they may have been inspired in other ways by their parents' lives. These essays might spark a discussion of the ways in which our role models become "a part of [our] subconscious" mind, and of the ways in which they "later surface."

Cofer's essay, as well those by Stone and Kingston, would also work well with the essays in Chapter 6, "Divided Identities." You might speculate on the special significance of family stories for children of mixed heritage, or children whose families are engaged in assimila-tion.

Generating Writing

1. The world Cofer re-creates in her essay is dominated by women. You might want to assign a paper in which your students explore the implications of this observation. What are the sources of the women's authority in this selection? What are the limits of their authority? How does a woman in the culture Cofer describes define her own identity? Suggest that students examine the images of women in the stories told by the women of Cofer's family. To what extent can these women be seen as female stereotypes? What is the function of these stereotypes? What might the "infectious joke of our lives" refer to?

2. Throughout the essay, the act of telling a story is linked to that of braiding hair. Assign an essay in which the students explore the significance of this running analogy. On what similarities is this analogy based? Can students think of other images often called up to represent women's creativity? What do these images imply about our culture's way of viewing female creativity, compared and contrasted to male creativity?

Maxine Hong Kingston

No Name Woman

Teaching Strategies

"No Name Woman" blends fact and fantasy in a way that can be dizzying to the reader encountering Kingston's prose for the first time. For this reason, we've found it works best to start by making sure that students understand the essay's overall structure. Have them tell you where Maxine's mother's story ends and Maxine's versions start. Also see if they can identify the versions of her aunt's story that Maxine considers in her attempt to understand the truth.

The truth, always problematic in such autobiographical narratives, is especially tricky in "No Name Woman." Make sure your students don't fall into the error of referring to the mother's account as "the truth" and Maxine's account as "fantasy," just because Maxine is open about the speculativeness of her contributions to this family story. Encourage students to question the mother's veracity. It might be easiest if they start by recalling the doubts that Maxine raises about her mother's story. Then, if they can't think of further doubts to raise, you might lead them to think about the mother's motive for telling this story. Because she tells Maxine the family secret as a cautionary tale, timed to coincide with Maxine's first menses, she may have altered the story so as to make its cautionary effect more powerful. And a tale whose moral is the consequences of one's actions works best when the consequences follow directly upon the actions. How else could one explain these improbable lines, spoken by the mother and unblinkingly accepted by Maxine: "The village had also been counting. On the night the baby was to be born the villagers raided our house"? (You might point out — or one of your students may notice — the similarity between the mother's technique and the villagers': both can be charged with "speeding up the circling of events" to make their message clearer.)

Alternatively, students may consider the mother's story more suspect than Maxine's versions. After all, the mother has an ulterior motive for the tale she tells, whereas Maxine seems to be genuinely searching for the truth, using every bit of data on Chinese culture she can find to help her reconstruct what really happened. And Maxine characterizes the two generations — her mother's and her own — in this way: "They must try to confuse their offspring as well, who, I suppose, threaten them in similar ways — always trying to get things straight, always trying to name the unspeakable." Still, it's not accurate to draw a sharp line between Maxine's mother, as an inscrutable, superstitious Chinese woman, and Maxine, as the American-born child who sheds the objective light of truth on her mother's confusing stories. Maxine is neither Chinese nor American, but rather Chinese-American, and both traditions have shaped her identity and outlook. You might have your students identify elements in her stories which non-Chinese people might consider superstitions, but which Maxine doesn't question. In short, do everything you can during class discussion to make sure that they don't construct neat little boxes for their ideas about this complex and rewarding text.

Additional Activities

During class discussion you might find it useful to ask what Kingston means when she writes that her mother's stories "tested our strength to establish realities." Ask them how her mother would have meant that statement, if, indeed, one can attribute its sentiment to her. Then ask what else it might mean, in the context of the story she tells in "No Name Woman." How else does that story function? For Maxine? For her mother? How closely would their explanations of the function of stories coincide? On what points would they disagree?

Gender is a primary motif in "No Name Woman." Judging from the evidence in this piece, how would your students characterize Chinese expectations of men? of women? How much do these gender stereotypes determine the events of the story about Maxine's aunt? Have students describe the double bind that these stereotypes create for Maxine. Have them describe the double bind that Maxine imagines them to create for her aunt.

Kingston donated her typescript for *The Woman Warrior* to the Bancroft Library, which houses the rare-book collection of the University of California, Berkeley. Kingston and her editor carry on a handwritten dialogue in the margins of this typescript. Some of Kingston's justifications for keeping words and phrases that her editor wanted to change provide evidence countering the common student argument that the author couldn't possibly have meant all those things that English instructors so cleverly find in their texts.

In the paragraph in "No Name Woman" describing the raid on the house where her aunt lived, Kingston writes about the "broken bunds." Her editor objects to *bund* as unfamiliar, apparently suggesting, in an emendation erased by Kingston, that the *dikes* be used instead of *bunds,* "to clarify" the meaning. Kingston writes in the margin, "I'd rather use 'bund' because it's from Hindu and specifically refers to Japan, China, India, whereas 'dike' is Anglo-Saxon and French in origin."

In the paragraph in which Kingston thinks about her aunt's fear, she writes "But women at sex hazarded birth and hence lifetimes." Her editor questions the phrase *women at sex,* which Kingston defends in this way: "I like 'women at sex' because it recalls 'guests at table,' 'hard at work,' 'lions at meat,' 'men at war.' Women at sex hazarded birth . . . ('Germans at meat . . .' Katherine Porter)." When we spoke with Kingston (see the treatment of "A Song for a Barbarian Reed Pipe" (see Chapter 30) in this manual for further details from that interview), she said that her first editor tried to make her "sound like anyone else." That editor was replaced by the one whose handwriting we see in the margins, and Kingston was never even shown the disastrous results of her first editor's work. Still, there's the danger that readers will think that this Chinese-American girl doesn't speak flawless English. This marginal comment from Kingston proves that she is very aware of the connotations of her phrases, that her nonhomogenized English is no accident.

Midway through the typescript, Kingston writes "On a farm near the sea, a woman who tended her appearance reaped a reputation for eccentricity." To her editor's suggestion that she change her phrasing, Kingston asks, "Isn't the sowing and reaping farm metaphor clear here? I'd like to keep it." And at the end of the chapter, when she is describing the origami figures, she defends part of her list in this way: "How about leaving paper cars? I enjoy so much seeing how Chinese update the myths. Maybe 'paper automobiles' would be even better. (p. 82 has a Ford.)" These and other marginal comments provide a glimpse into the workings of the creative mind — a glimpse that most student writers, who are struggling with their own stylistic choices, may really appreciate.

Generating Writing

1. Call your students' attention to the opening line of "No Name Woman": "'You must not tell anyone,' my mother said, 'what I am about to tell you.'" Help them unfold the implications of that tantalizing opening. Among all the other observations and inferences they might mention upon reading that sentence, they should notice that it sets up two doubles for Maxine: her aunt, whose act of rebellion is mirrored in the disobedience necessary to writing "No Name Woman"; and her mother, who, like Maxine, gives voice to the family secret. Have your students write an essay in which they pursue this doubling motif throughout the essay.

2. Kingston identifies her aunt's sin as that of individuality: "Children and lovers have no singularity here, but my aunt used a secret voice, a separate attentiveness." Have students write an essay exploring the tension between the individual and the community, also figured as a tension between individualism and duty to one's family, in Kingston's piece. Among the many passages to which you'll want to direct attention on this issue is the birth scene.

Itabari Njeri

Granddaddy

Teaching Strategies

Njeri's essay is similar in several points to detective fiction. As in a murder mystery, the crime occurs early in the text, and the remainder of the story is taken up with identifying the perpetrator. Njeri herself fulfills the detective function. As a journalist, she stands, like the detective, in a space midway between the public, with its right to know, and the criminal, with his desire to preserve the mystery. She picks up clues, interrogates witnesses, makes educated guesses, and even disguises her identity in her search for the truth. And, like all good fictional detectives, she does discover the murderer's identity. But the resemblance to fiction ends here because, unlike a mystery novel, the murderer is not an aberrant individual whom the detective can place in quarantine, so that the good, innocent members of normal society will not risk contamination. When Njeri asks who is to blame, she comes to realize "how insidious was the impersonal social system that had coldly denied opportunity to blacks, and seemingly left no one to blame, as if systems do not bear the marks of their creators." She is frustrated in her search for the truth, finding after all her detective work that "nothing was resolved, nothing was settled." As long as societies are pervaded by racism, no neat novelistic resolution will be available to writers such as Njeri.

Of course, Njeri reveals her divergence from the detective model long before the end of her essay. Despite "the trappings of the dispassionate journalist," her love for her grandfather makes it impossible for her to achieve the detective's ideal of distance. And unlike most detectives, she herself has a family story to hide: the story of her father, who turned to alcohol because he couldn't tolerate the realities of racism. History is embedded in that of her grandfather, who fought racism every day of his life, only to be defeated by it after death. Her personal stake in the results of her research makes her a less than ideal detective, but it enhances her essay by forcefully reminding us of the real pain and sorrow informing the abstract word *racism*.

Additional Activities

Racism appears in many guises in this essay, from "men who killed a black man and laughed" to "men who, without malice, killed a black man and sighed, knowing it ultimately did not matter"; from the doctor who openly expressed racist viewpoints to the police chief who praised Njeri's grandfather but neglected to shake her hand. Leslie Simon, who teaches at the University of California at Berkeley, has an effective classroom exercise to help open up the discussion of racism. She draws three overlapping circles on the board. Inside the first she writes "blatant racism," in the second, "covert racism," and in the third, "recovering racism." When she tells her students that all white people are racist, they do not immediately reject her statement: those who are reluctant to admit to even the slightest tinge of racism are more likely to be open to discussing the inescapability of racism if they can think of themselves as "recovering." And of course, if they so think of themselves, they may begin to take the kinds of actions suggested by the recovery model. Some of your students may protest that blacks and other ethnic groups are also racist. You might draw on a useful distinction articulated by Opal Palmer Adisa, also of the University of California at Berkeley. Adisa reminds us that only people in power can be "racist"; people who have no power to force their biases on others are merely "prejudiced." In your discussion of racism, you may want to show Spike Lee's film *Do the Right Thing*, which is available at video rental stores.

Generating Writing

1. "Granddaddy" can be profitably compared with "No Name Woman." Both writers run into a conspiracy of silence in their own families, a silence that turns out to be hurtful. You might wish to assign a paper in which students explore the role of silence in these two selections about family stories.

2. Names are significant in "Granddaddy," particularly Njeri's own name and that of her grandfather, as it is written on his headstone. If you are teaching Chapter 5, "The Power of Names," you might have students write a paper on the significance of names, drawing on insights gained from the unit on names and applying those to the essays by Njeri, Stone, Cofer, and Kingston. Or, you might have students write a family story that hinges upon their family name, or tell the story of how someone in their family got his or her name, if such a story is in their fund of family legends.

WRITING ABOUT THE CHAPTER

1. Invite your students to revise the draft they wrote before reading the selections that make up this chapter. Encourage them to follow the lead of Kingston, Cofer, and Stone, and weave their own interpretations among the details of the family story narrated in their first draft. Ask them to speculate about why their family would choose, consciously or unconsciously, to repeat these incidents, in these forms, among all the countless incidents and forms they could have chosen. What lessons — about themselves, their families, and their cultures — have they derived from hearing these stories? What are the specific sites of tension between their lives and the traditions embodied in these family stories? Have they been able to adapt these stories to their needs, both as members of their families and cultures and as individuals?

2. In "No Name Woman" and "Granddaddy," the stories which are not told matter at least as much as those which are. Both Kingston and Njeri try to reconstruct the stories that lie behind their families' silences. If any of your students know of a mystery, large or small, in their family's past, they might want to do some reconstruction work of their own. Have them choose the model provided by Njeri, the reporter, interviewing anyone connected with the incident and conducting research into records of the period, or the model provided by Kingston, the storyteller, embroidering possibilities to fill in the blanks of a spare narrative.

3. Cofer writes that her grandmother told stories to teach her cousin and her "what it was like to be a woman." Ask students to compose an essay exploring the messages about

gender roles embedded in the stories in this chapter. They might want to focus their essays by comparing and contrasting two of the selections, or by comparing and contrasting male and female gender roles within one selection.

Everyday Life

13

Anxieties of Appearance

Alice Walker, Beauty: When the Other Dancer
Is the Self

Nora Ephron, A Few Words about Breasts

John Updike, At War with My Skin

WORKING WITH THE CHAPTER

As the epigraph from a recent Louis Harris opinion poll shows, nearly all Americans are, for one reason or another, "close to being obsessed with their physical appearance." This obsession is often grounded in dissatisfaction with one's looks. In fact, a 1990 poll published in the *New York Times* indicated that dissatisfaction with physical appearance is one of the leading causes of adolescent depression. Surely, this is one topic about which students will have plenty to say.

Teaching Strategies

To get discussion going, you might see how many in class agree with Louis Harris about our preoccupation with how we look. You might, too, ask them to read the epigraphs by Nellie Wong and the philosopher Arthur Schopenhauer. Wong introduces the theme of dissatisfaction and concealment, which appears in each essay. Though students will probably disagree with Schopenhauer's claim for physiognomy (now, of course, a discredited "science"), it is instructive to see how many people still judge others by appearance alone.

In this chapter, three prominent American writers remember how their childhoods were shaped by a preoccupation with their physical appearance. Recalling a severe childhood injury, Alice Walker claims that her medical condition was less disturbing to her than disfigurement: "it is really how I look that bothers me most. Where the BB pellet struck there is a glob of whitish scar tissue, a hideous cataract, on my eye." The scar leaves her with "feelings of shame and ugliness" that persist into adulthood. These feelings are shared by another prominent novelist, John Updike, whose bouts with a skin disease turned him into a brooding, painfully self-conscious teenager. Updike recalls how he longed to be normal: "An overvaluation of the normal went with my ailment, a certain idealization of everyone who was not, as I felt myself to be, a monster." But one needn't be the victim of injury or disease to feel physically abnormal. The novelist and screenwriter Nora Ephron vividly evokes an adolescence tormented by her lack of "development" — "I knew that no one would ever want to marry me. I had no breasts. I would never have breasts."

In combining these three selections for class discussion, you may want to mention how each writer perceives his or her condition as it affects personal identity: Alice Walker's final image is a dance that merges two selves; one of Nora Ephron's main themes is androgyny; and John Updike believes that his skin disease has made him what he is.

A Writing-before-Reading Exercise

Interpreting one of his recent opinion polls, Louis Harris claimed that the fear of not being physically "acceptable" may be one of the dominant worries of young people in our time. You might invite students to consider this remark in thinking about their own lives. They might address some of these questions in an essay: How accurate do they think Harris is? How worried are they about own their appearance? Do they regard good looks as a big advantage in life? Would they rather not worry about looks and yet do they feel pressured to do so by their social environment? How do the media — especially advertising — affect their self-image? Finally, do males and females have the same or different worries?

WORKING WITH THE SELECTIONS

Alice Walker

Beauty: When the Other Dancer Is the Self

Teaching Strategies

This essay is rich in literary technique, and you may want to make sure students follow Alice Walker's narrative structure and imagery. If they read and reread this essay, they should see how nonfiction can weave together strands of imagery like poetry or fiction. Recognizing these strands, however, will require a second reading. Students should reread the essay to see that Walker's casual comment about her father's "beautiful eyes" in the opening paragraph is not accidentally thrown in to fill out description. They should see, too, in the opening paragraph that the suggestion of pain as she has her hair combed is the first of many painful and violent details in the essay.

It would be worthwhile to have students closely examine this intricate network of imagery. Nearly every image finds a parallel image elsewhere. The Easter-lily poem Walker recites (para. 4) is echoed later in the "lily leaves" her father uses right after her injury (para. 12). The image of a tree that appears as the last image (literally) that her right eye sees (para. 11) will resurface later in her poem about the desert. These are only a few parallels; your students will find others.

Walker's essay moves through abrupt shifts in time, taking her through moments in her life from age two and a half to her late thirties. That she doesn't move in a continuous narrative may confuse students at first. You might invite speculation about her narrative technique. What advantages do these "jumps" in time offer her? You may also want to point out her use of the present tense throughout, which also helps establish dramatic immediacy and focus. Another structural technique is Walker's use of italicized questions and comments, which seem to be directed not to the reader but to herself. This self-commentary also establishes a voice outside the time frame of the essay so that the drama is not entirely in the present tense.

Aside from the main incident, the "accident" to Walker's right eye (you might want to ask why she encloses the word *accident* in quotation marks), the essay is interlaced with references to violence and torture. Ask students to identify some of these incidents. In this way they will see how much detail in the essay reinforces a world of pain and violence: the childhood cowboy-Indian games (para. 8); the penitentiary and electric chair (paras. 16–19); mother's illness (para. 27); and her high-school classmate who was shot to death (para. 32).

But this is not only an essay about pain; it is about beauty, as its title indicates, *and* about seeing. Ask students to pay attention to two quotations: the doctor warns that "Eyes are sympathetic" (para. 12), and Walker's child, who exclaims "Mommy, there's a *world* in your eye (para. 44). Students should closely examine the language here. Both quotations have literal and figurative meanings, and they should be able to explain each meaning, and see how Walker uses the figurative meaning of each expression as a source of inspiration.

Additional Activities

If you want to take the literary attributes of Alice Walker's finely crafted essay further, you might explore in class its imagistic connections with the famous last stanza of William Butler Yeats's "Among School Children," with some of the twentieth century's most memorable poetic lines. Students should be able to recognize many images concentrated in this stanza that they have seen throughout Walker's essay.

Generating Writing

For a writing exercise, ask your students to consider carefully what Alice Walker means when she says "There *was* a world in my eye." What are the origins of this image? In what ways is the image appropriate? How does she transform its meaning? Invite the class to write an essay in which they explain this image in the context of the entire essay. They should describe, too, how the image enables her to deal emotionally with her injury.

Nora Ephron

A Few Words about Breasts

Teaching Strategies

This frequently anthologized confessional essay has its amusing and bitter sides. Your students may be surprised (and some may even feel embarrassed) to read a candid account of a woman's anxiety over the size of her breasts, and so you may need to begin by asking if the topic makes anyone uncomfortable, and then open discussion on that front first. Ephron knows she's dealing with a delicate topic, and she confronts it as honestly as she can. Her honesty is at times funny, at times, caustic.

Much of the essay is about gender distinctions, and so you may want to ask why Ephron herself feels obliged to start with the subject of "androgyny." The class should realize that Ephron is anxious not merely about physical appearance (though that's certainly part of it) but her story has much to do with insecurity about her identity as a woman. For Ephron, breast size is more closely related to being female than to being physically attractive. She's quite explicit: draw students' attention paragraphs 3 and 4, where she claims that breasts are more important to the coming of adolescence than menstruation. The essay's main issue is not unattractiveness but inadequacy.

Invite students first to see the amusing side of the essay. Much of Ephron's humor is directed against herself and her own childish naiveté. Writing from an older perspective, she can make fun of herself as an obsessive teenager trying to look grown-up in padded bras and bathing suits. But this essay is surprising in that it does not take an expected turn.

We expect that as she matures, Ephron will outgrow this anxiety and come to terms with her physical appearance. Ask students how she might have ended her essay.

Ephron, however, doesn't overcome a handicap, so to speak, but instead confesses to still being "obsessed by breasts" (para. 31). Her tone begins to change from amusement to anger with the italicized passage (paras. 21–27) describing her confrontation with a fiancé's mother. You might look closely at this passage in class, asking students why they think Ephron put the moment into italics and how her tone differs here from earlier in the essay. They should see that the issue, far from being a girl's silly anxiety, is becoming more serious. This moment introduces the issue that will be the main theme in the essay's conclusion and the cause for Ephron's bitterness — female competitiveness.

The fiancé's mother, who points out that her "bust is very large," was, Ephron says, "only the first of what seems to me to be a never-ending string of women who have made competitive remarks to me about breast size." Though Ephron can make fun of her childhood anxieties, she apparently has a harder time seeing her current anxieties as comic. The final paragraphs in the essay are increasingly confessional and bitter, as she recalls unpleasant encounters with other women. If you want to demonstrate her attitude to your class, ask someone to read aloud paragraph 31, making sure he or she gets the intonations correct.

You might also discuss another movement in the essay: Ephron's nervousness that she is beginning to sound too peculiar to be taken seriously. Ask the class to notice how in paragraph 28 she insists that what she is writing is "true." Why do students think that Ephron is worried that readers won't believe her? Ask them to notice, too, in paragraph 31, a similar worry that is addressed directly to the reader: "you probably think I'm crazy to go on like this: here I have set out to write a confession that is meant to hit you with the shock of recognition, and instead you are sitting there thinking I am thoroughly warped." This statement will bear some interesting close analysis in class. What does Ephron mean by a "shock: of recognition?" In what way was achieving this shock her intention in writing the essay? Do students think she seems "thoroughly warped"? Do they find her honest and candid in acknowledging this possibility?

The possibility is strong that students will have a mixed response to this essay: many may find the first part of the essay dealing with her adolescence more satisfying than the second. You may want to explore these responses in class. How much are they bothered by Ephron's refusal to turn her experiences into some positive form, to give her essay a more acceptable and conventional conclusion, the kind that usually sounds something like: "Thus, looking back, I can see now that. . . ." That she takes no comfortable way out of her anxiety (how does your class interpret the tone of her final sentence?) may ultimately prove more uncomfortable to your class than her delicate topic itself.

Additional Activities

You might productively compare Ephron's essay with either of two others in this collection. To contrast two personalities coping with a girl's "coming of age," you could assign Ephron's piece in conjunction with Mary McCarthy's "Names" in Chapter 5, "The Power of Names." Another interesting comparison to Ephron's essay is the excerpt from Plato's *Symposium* on androgyny in Chapter 38, "Origins." You could first introduce androgyny as a main theme in Ephron, and then use the passage from Plato to broaden the discussion.

Generating Writing

Ephron's essay might offer some of your female students a "shock of recognition"; others may find themselves disagreeing with Ephron. And what about males? Do they have similar anxieties about appearance? You might ask students to write personal essays in which they identify a childhood or adolescent anxiety about physical appearance and describe how they coped with it. Using Ephron as a model, they should be as honest as they can about their anxiety and how they overcame it — if they did.

John Updike
At War with My Skin

Teaching Strategies

Like Alice Walker and Nora Ephron, Updike confesses to acute feelings of abnormality as an adolescent. A skin disease (psoriasis) left him painfully self-conscious about his appearance, resulting in a desire for privacy and concealment that led directly to his chosen vocation.

As a novelist Updike is often praised for evocation of sensuous detail. You might ask your students to notice how often Updike appeals to the senses in this brief excerpt from his autobiography, appropriately called, *Self-Consciousness*. In the first three paragraphs Updike makes us aware of smell (the odor of Siroil), touch (the fuzzy towels), sight (photographs of his childhood), taste (the foods he abstained from), and sound (the noises he heard while lying half-awake in the sun). These are only a few examples; Updike's prose is full of details that evoke all the senses.

These details are not evoked in isolation but are so closely linked to his condition that all become part of the same experience: the smell, texture, and color of his childhood medicine become "deeply involved with [his] embarrassment" (para. 1). The scent of Siroil even tells him who he is, so intimately does it merge with his own sense of identity. In fact, students should observe how closely related is Updike's preoccupation with his skin and his personal identity. You might want to examine this connection carefully in class. Updike sometimes seems to identify himself entirely with his condition (he is a "monster"); at other times, he can detach himself from that condition ("it was temporary and . . . illusionary"). How serious is he about his condition? students may want to know. Is he exaggerating, or did his skin disease affect him even more than he admits? There's no answer here — Updike himself seems divided about it — and so these questions might work well for open discussion and speculation. Updike's ambivalence toward the disease can be discussed more fully by looking in class at paragraph 5. Here psoriasis is connected to strategies of thinking and self-examination. Students should notice how Updike enlarges the scope of discourse in this passage, turning his condition into a great conflict between Nature and Self.

Like Walker, but unlike Ephron, Updike finds some consolation in his disease. It has encouraged him to be courageous and original, and much of this consolation seems tied to his identity and career. As you discuss the conclusion of the selection (reminding students that this is an excerpt and not an essay), you might want to invite comments about how persuasive Updike seems here. Are they convinced by his list of explanations about how psoriasis altered his life?

Additional Activities

You could use this autobiographical episode in class to see what connections your students can make between a writer's life and his art. Ask your class to read Updike's "A & P" (in Chapter 3, "Moments of Recognition") in conjunction with this selection. They should be prepared to discuss in class the relationship they find between Updike's personal preoccupations and the short story's narrator. The connection, of course, will have nothing to do with psoriasis; but they will discover other, subtler, resemblances.

Generating Writing

After considering the connections Updike makes between himself and his "condition," students should be able to write a similar essay in which they describe how an illness (or disease, injury, and so on) from their own childhoods helped shape their identity and ultimately determined important decisions in their lives.

WRITING ABOUT THE CHAPTER

1. Having read the selections, your students might want to go back and revise their Writing-before-Reading draft. The selections in this chapter have introduced them to several sophisticated literary techniques: patterns of imagery, tonal shifts, resistance to expectation, and the use of sensuous detail. You might encourage students to choose the technique they find most suitable to their topic and to rewrite their essay using their new technique.

2. All these selections showed that acute self-consciousness can accompany feelings of physical unattractiveness, especially in young people. If, instead of a personal essay, you'd like to have students write about the selections, you could address this issue of self-consciousness. Can they identify ways in which self-consciousness is manifested in style and imagery (Updike equates it with concealment)? Can they discuss how self-consciousness plays a part in each person's development as a writer?

14

Public Space

Desmond Morris, Territorial Behavior
Susan Jacoby, Unfair Game
Brent Staples, Just Walk on By: A Black Man
Ponders His Power to Alter Public Space

WORKING WITH THE CHAPTER

According to anthropologist Desmond Morris, "we with us, everywhere we go, a portable territory called a Personal Space." A large part of our everyday behavior consists of the countless adjustments we make in maintaining this space in public — a crowded bus, a college classroom, a city sidewalk, a busy restaurant. But, as your students will be aware, this personal space is precarious. Sometimes, Susan Jacoby makes clear, a woman's space is invaded by "the unwanted approaches of strange men" who fail to acknowledge her "right to sit at a table in a public place without being drawn into a sexual flirtation." And our personal space may be affected even when we are not the victims of other people's invasiveness. Brent Staples gives a twist to what public space means by showing how — as a black man walking at night — his mere presence automatically threatens other pedestrians, especially women. As a young Chicago journalist, Staples soon learned that "being perceived as dangerous is a hazard in itself."

The way in which others respond to our territorial adjustments can often cause feelings of annoyance, hostility, or personal rejection. Though our sense of personal territory seems instinctive, much of it is nevertheless shaped by social and cultural factors. Different nations and regions display widely divergent attitudes toward personal space, as do groups within a society.

Teaching Strategies

In this chapter, students are invited to consider, in the context of Desmond Morris's general remarks, how human territory is specifically affected by differences in race and gender. But first, you might want to get thinking started about different ways in which we can view public space. The topic, of course, affects everyone, but you'll probably discover that few students have carefully considered it and fewer still have developed a vocabulary for discussing it. Like the air we breathe, our public space is so much a part of everyday life that it is invisible, is taken as an aspect of nature itself. Therefore, it would be useful to begin by examining the four epigraphs in class. These cover a lot of ground, and serve up some preliminary ideas out of which class discussion can evolve.

You can start with the comment on city sidewalks by the well-known author and urban planner, Jane Jacobs. She introduces the idea that the quality of streets and sidewalks is important to successful neighborhoods, especially in their equipment for handling strangers. The "strangers" issue has a big part in all the selections. A public space is almost by definition a place in which strangers gather. As the selections show, strangers can mean discomfort and irritation or vitality and diversity. Success in a public space depends primarily on how well strangers can function together there.

This idea of successful public places is taken up by sociologist Richard Sennett in his historical observation about public life in America. While participating in a forum on the disappearance of the public square, Sennett remarked that public life in America is no longer politically educative and that both men and women have been forced into isolated and silent realms. His emphasis on women's historical relation to public space is intriguing and later dovetails perfectly with Susan Jacoby's essay on the difficulties that many women experience in public places.

The observation of the Asian writer Liu Binyan introduces students to another aspect of public space — its cultural relativity, a topic that they will find again in Desmond Morris's examination of human territoriality. Binyan's comment reminds students that their relationship to public space is not a natural function, but is often a subtle aspect of their culture. With a greater national tradition of open space, Americans are probably less tolerant of crowded conditions than people from nations in which space is at a premium. But these cultural differences apply not only to nations and cultures but also to individual backgrounds and customs. If your campus houses students, you might ask students if those from suburban homes who had their own rooms (and some, private baths) have a tougher time adjusting to college life than those coming from city apartments.

Finally, satirist and humorist Fran Lebowitz brings up a matter that nearly all discussions of public space eventually touch upon — music. You can generate conversation by asking students to expand the list of places Lebowitz cites as guilty of piping in unwanted music. You might also encourage them to consider why music has become an integral part of the public environment. Invite them to consider this question, keeping in mind Richard Sennett's observation.

In linking the three selections you might begin by asking students to discuss how Morris's anthropological explanations apply to the personal experiences of Jacoby and Staples. For example, Desmond Morris claims that people can defend their personal space with "a minimum of open hostility" by means of "signals." In what ways are his observations borne out by Jacoby and Staples? Your class should be able to describe the signals these writers use and how effective they are. But the Jacoby and Staples selections introduce another issue not explicitly covered by Morris; namely, to what extent does territorial behavior explain racism and sexism? Does your class think that Morris's explanation can be made to cover these issues, or do they think his point of view is too restricted?

A Writing-before-Reading Exercise

Desmond Morris argues that "no one can ever become completely immune to invasions of Personal Space." Ask your class before they read the selections to consider his statement, recalling their own experiences. How tolerant are they about such invasions of space and privacy? Do they find that some invasions are far worse than others? They could draft an essay based on personal experience, discussing what they believe is the worst violation of personal space.

WORKING WITH THE SELECTIONS

Desmond Morris

Territorial Behavior

Teaching Strategies

In this excerpt from Desmond Morris's popular anthropological study, *Manwatching: A Field Guide to Human Behavior* (1977), he systematically summarizes what people generally mean by public and personal space. For those who want to introduce students to rhetorical arrangement, the author proceeds in a highly organized format, demonstrating an easily observable use of definition, classification, and illustration.

Two main features of the selection are worth mentioning in class. First, territoriality as Morris uses it is linked by definition to defense; a territory is space we defend — it is not merely a vaguely defined area. Thus, throughout the selection we feel an image or metaphor of war, competition, hostility, and struggle. Students should be able to see and discuss this definitional aspect of defense. They should speculate on whether there are alternative ways of defining human territory.

A second feature of Morris's selection is its generality. Students should be aware that Morris sets out to define territoriality broadly enough to explain many kinds of behavior. You can point this plan out clearly by examining paragraph 2. The idea of an "invasion" (make sure students are aware of the many military expressions) is such a generalization: Morris wants it to cover military action, gang activity, trespassing, and burglary; it includes the bully who pushes to the front of a line and the driver who steals a parking space. You might discuss Morris's generalizing task here. Students should see that it is intentional and that it is essential in his writing. Though nothing is wrong with generalizing in itself, students should be aware of its dangers, especially when it's based on only a few examples. The topic of public space will attract many such generalizations in class and you may want to encourage students to discriminate between those which seem valid and those which seem like mere exaggerations.

Morris's organization proceeds through larger to smaller territories: the tribal, the family, and the personal. Class discussion is most likely to focus on Morris's examination of personal space, a topic with which students can readily identify. You might direct discussion here by asking students to respond to Morris's examples. All are based on behavior that students see every day. Point them to the passage describing how people seat themselves in public waiting rooms or behave in elevators (para. 15). Have they too observed these things? Can they come up with additional examples? What about your classroom? Unless you have a seating plan, invite speculation about how students spatially arrange themselves.

Morris concludes by examining "body territories." Again, this idea will hit close to home with students who regularly deal with crowding — in dormitories, lounges, reading rooms, and so on. Students will readily see their own behavior reflected in Morris's well-chosen examples. Many will recognize "cocooning," or "favored object," or personal "markers." But how many are aware that this behavior is something studied and labeled? You might here bring up the topic of awareness: do they feel that in the future they will be more conscious of public behavior and more observant of the ways in which people use public space?

Additional Activities

Personal essays and fiction often use private and public space for drama, characterization, atmosphere, metaphor, and so on. It might prove instructive in class to apply some of Morris's observations to one or more of the personal essays or short stories in this collection. Several that would work especially well are: George Orwell's "Shooting an Elephant," in Chapter 3 (an individual's relation to a crowd and the clash of cultural differences); David Bradley's "Ringgold Street," in Chapter 4 (a detailed description of one man's relation to private and public space in a big city); or Joyce Carol Oates's "Shopping," in Chapter 10 (a modern shopping mall as a location for a moment of privacy).

Generating Writing

Using Morris's examples of "body territory" as a model, invite students to make a first-hand observation of behavior not mentioned by Morris. They could make such observations in a cafeteria, dormitory, classroom, parking lot — just about anywhere. They should use these observations in an essay in which they demonstrate Morris's point about how people try to create privacy in public places.

Susan Jacoby

Unfair Game

Teaching Strategies

This short essay originally ran in the *New York Times* "Hers" column in 1978. She deals directly with one aspect of this chapter's topic: our need for private space. The issue here specifically is a woman's right to be left alone in public. An effective way into discussing this essay is to ask about the title: What does it suggest? What is the pun? Students should see that Jacoby's wordplay extends two ways — an allusion to the "fair game" of hunting and to the "game" of picking up dates.

Call your class's attention to Jacoby's tone in this essay, especially her irony. You might ask students how she responds to the man at the Plaza who tries to pick her up with a "snappy" opening line. What does she mean by "snappy"? What does she mean by "bright social patter" in paragraph 3? As a way of getting closer to her tone, try dramatizing the pickup situation in class by asking various male-female pairs to act out the dialogue. Different pairs may give different intonations to the lines, which may make for interesting class discussion.

Notice that the first part of the essay is entirely based on a concrete incident that's narrated in the present tense. You might discuss the effect of beginning with a specific instance rather than a general observation. Not until paragraph 6 does Jacoby introduce her general point about women in public without male escorts. Ask the class to reverse Jacoby's presentation to see what happens: if they revise the opening of paragraph 6 — the general observation — and start the essay with it, what happens?

You might also discuss the quality of the generalization itself. Does the class feel it's valid? Do they believe that it's justified by her experiences and their own? As mentioned earlier, one of the problems in such discussions is the legitimacy of our generalizations. Jacoby's essay is perfect for discussing this important topic that is at the heart of many first-year compositional problems.

This essay has proved controversial in class. Though some students agree with Jacoby, a surprising number (women included) are not sympathetic to her predicament. Some are put off by her "elitism" — her tony bars and professional jet travel — and have difficulty identifying with her problem. Others think she is "dated" — someone from another generation of women who are needlessly "sensitive." And still others think she is trying to have things both ways — she deliberately puts herself in situations (that is, big-city bars) where she invites men's advances only to have the satisfaction of rejecting them. These are a few of the viewpoints students report on, regarding an essay that clearly evokes strong feelings.

Additional Activities

Jacoby's remark about a "code of feminine politeness, instilled in girlhood" can be used to introduce historical ideas on the topic of women and public space. Besides the Richard Sennett epigraph opening the chapter, you may want to invite students to read a passage from Anthony Trollope's *North America* (1862). While traveling in the United States early in the 1860s, Trollope observed American culture and behavior from the point of view of a Victorian Englishman. His observations on American women in public (reprinted here) offer an unsympathetic male's perspective on female "private space" as well as an example of one culture looking at another culture's public behavior. Your class may want to examine (1) why Trollope is appalled to find that American women ignore men in public, and (2) what "signals" Trollope might be missing.

The street cars are manned with conductors and therefore are free from many of the perils of the omnibus, but they have perils of their own. They are always quite full. By that I mean that every seat is crowded, that there is a double row of men and women standing down the centre, and that the driver's platform in front is full, and also the conductor's platform behind.

I soon gave up all attempts at keeping a seat in one of these cars. It became my practice to sit down on the outside iron rail behind, and as the conductor generally sat in my lap I was in a measure protected. As for the inside of these vehicles, the women of New York were, I must confess, too much for me. I would no sooner place myself on a seat, than I would be called on by a mute, unexpressive, but still impressive stare into my face, to surrender my place. From cowardice if not from gallantry I would always obey; and as this led to discomfort and an irritated spirit, I preferred nursing the conductor on the hard bar in the rear.

And here if I seem to say a word against women in America, I beg that it may be understood that I say that word only against a certain class; and even as to that class I admit that they are respectable, intelligent, and, as I believe, industrious. Their manners, however, are to me more odious than those of any other human beings that I ever met elsewhere. Nor can I go on with that which I have to say without carrying my apology further, lest perchance I should be misunderstood by some American women whom I would not only exclude from my censure, but would include in the very warmest eulogium which words of mine could express as to those of the female sex whom I love and admire the most.

The happy privileges with which women are at present blessed, have come to them from the spirit of chivalry. That spirit has taught men to endure in order that women may be at their ease; and has generally taught women to accept the ease bestowed on them with grace and thankfulness. But in America the spirit of chivalry has sunk deeper among men than it has among women. It must be borne in mind that in that country material well-being and education are more extended than with us and that, therefore, men there have learned to be chivalrous who with us have hardly progressed so far.

The conduct of men to women throughout the States is always gracious. They have learned the lesson. But it seems to me that the women have not advanced as far as the men have done. They have acquired a sufficient perception of the privileges which chivalry gives them, but no perception of that return which chivalry demands from them. I have heard young Americans complain of it, swearing that they must change the whole tenor of their habits towards women.

In no position of life does an unfortunate man become more liable to anti-feminine atrocities than in the centre of one of these street cars. The woman, as she enters, drags after her a misshapen, dirty mass of battered wirework, which she calls her crinoline, and which adds as much to her grace and comfort as a log of wood does to a donkey when tied to the animal's leg in a paddock. Of this she takes much heed, not managing it so that it may be conveyed up the carriage with some decency, but striking it about against men's legs, and heaving it with violence over people's knees. The touch of a real woman's dress is in itself delicate but these blows from a harpy's fins are loathsome. If there be two of them they talk loudly together, having a theory that modesty has been put out of Court by women's rights.

But, though not modest, the woman I describe is ferocious in her propriety. She ignores the whole world around her, and as she sits with a raised chin and face flattened by affectation, she pretends to declare aloud that she is positively not aware that any man is even near her. She speaks as though to her, in her womanhood, the neighbourhood of men was the same as that of dogs or cats. They are there, but she does not hear them, see them, or even acknowledge them by any courtesy of motion.

You will meet these women daily, hourly, everywhere in the streets. Now and again you will find them in society, making themselves even more odious there than elsewhere. Who they are, whence they come and why they are so unlike that other race of women of which I have spoken, you will settle for yourself. Do we not all say of our chance acquaintances after half an hour's conversation — nay, after half an hour spent in the same room without conversation — that this woman is a lady, and that that other woman is not? They jostle each other even among us, but never seem to mix. They are closely allied; but neither imbues the other with her attributes. Both shall be equally well-born, or both shall be equally ill-born; but still it is so. The contrast exists in England, but in America it is much stronger. In England women become ladylike or vulgar. In the States they are either charming or odious.

— Anthony Trollope

Generating Writing

Jacoby makes it clear that she is not "necessarily against men and women picking each other up in public places" (para. 18). The issue, as she describes it, is mainly one of sensitivity and courtesy. You might want to ask your students how they think males and females who are strangers to each other can best meet in public. What do they think are the best places, and why? What are the "signals"? Who should speak first? Is an "opening line" important? They could write an essay in which they describe their idea of a successful "approach."

Brent Staples

Just Walk on By: A Black Man Ponders His Power to Alter Public Space

Teaching Strategies

Like Susan Jacoby's essay, this one begins with an immediate, concrete incident instead of a generalized statement. Students should be aware of such openings and notice how effective they can be in an essay. Too often, introductory students see essays as a string of expository statements that offer very little possibility for narrative or dramatic action. It would be worth the time to work closely with Staples's opening paragraph in class, observing how he sets up a scenario that at first makes it appear he is in fact a threat (ask students to explain how he achieves this effect).

The opening paragraph also introduces a shift in point of view that is significant in the essay and essential in understanding Staples's attitude. There's a complexity in this essay that could easily be missed. In the middle of the first paragraph he suddenly assumes the young woman's viewpoint — "To her, the youngish black man. . . ." Students should see that this movement in point of view supplies more than drama; throughout the essay Staples shows a remarkable capacity to see himself as others might see him. Students must be aware that Staples is not blaming the woman for being afraid — in a sense, she really is a "victim." Instead of proclaiming his innocence and wondering why he is frightening to people; Staples himself assumes the burden of making himself "less threatening."

Staples's attitude is complex because of his double awareness: he realizes that the danger women perceive is real but he also is aware of the alienating power of their fear, which turns him into a suspect, "a fearsome entity" (para. 6). Invite the class to discuss how this double awareness is related to Staples's own background (paras. 7–9). For example, why does Staples not take any satisfaction in his "power to intimidate"? Notice how his images of "manly" intimidation show that he sees this power as infantile.

Staples's double awareness — that he is both victim and victimizer — is not without struggle. Make sure the class sees that Staples has "learned to smother the rage" he feels at being "taken for a criminal" (para. 12). Instead of giving in to this anger and becoming paranoid, he deliberately takes precautions that will relieve the fear and anxiety his presence often produces. All these precautions, your students should know, relate to his behavior in public spaces. The final paragraph invites interesting discussion. You might ask why whistling classical melodies works so well: what does this "tension-reducing measure" tell us about Staples — and about people's fears? Students should pay close attention to the last sentence. It's a wonderful analogy and they might discuss how it summarizes the essay.

Additional Activities

If you can spare the class time and have access to a VCR, you can link discussion of public space and racial discrimination to several easily available films that students will find both entertaining and instructive. John Sayles's *The Brother from Another Planet* (1984) or Spike Lee's *Do The Right Thing* (1989), or both, deal with street life and alienation. These films lend themselves directly to a discussion of public and private space, for this issue is vital — both visually and thematically — for both directors. Discussion will be enhanced if students are encouraged to watch either or both of these films specifically watching the "space" theme.

Generating Writing

Staples's essay is a suitable model for a similar student writing topic. Ask students to ponder their own ability to alter public space. They might consider these questions: In what ways have they achieved such alteration? Have their experiences been negative or positive? Did they ever feel — like Staples — that they had to assume the burden of behavioral change? Did their ability to alter public space also change their self-perception?

WRITING ABOUT THE CHAPTER

1. If your students attempted the Writing-before-Reading exercise, you can now ask them to rewrite their drafts with the selections in mind. They should notice how Jacoby and Staples made their point by concrete illustrations and specific details. Why are these examples necessary? After considering how detailed examples influence their essays, they could return to their draft and check it for concreteness and specificity. As they revise their essays they should ask themselves two questions: (1) Have I provided clear and sufficient examples to make my case? and (2) Have I kept my essay from sounding like a trivial complaint?

2. Invite your class to select a specific "territory" on campus — a classroom, hangout, library, cafeteria, vending machine area, or parking lot — and observe how people handle the necessary adjustments between personal and public space. How close together do people come? What distances are maintained? Who are the dominant groups? How is hostility controlled or heightened? How do individuals and groups "mark" their territory? After careful observation and notetaking, students could write an essay in which they describe the territory and the territorial behavior as objectively as they can.

On Holidays

Russell Baker, Happy New Year?

Michael Arlen, Ode to Thanksgiving

Nikki Giovanni, On Holidays and
How to Make Them Work

WORKING WITH THE CHAPTER

All societies have holidays — periods set aside for special observances. The earliest holidays (the word derives from *holy days)* were for seasonal myths and religious festivals, many of which have survived into modern times. Christmas, though it celebrates the birth of Christ, has deep roots in pagan commemorations of the winter solstice. On the other hand, some religious holidays such as Mardi Gras (Shrove Tuesday, the day before Lent) and Halloween (All Hallow's Eve) have been almost completely transformed into secular celebrations.

Clearly, modern holidays have become more than religious holy days. They commemorate historical events (Independence Day, Memorial Day), birthdays of public figures (George Washington, Martin Luther King, Jr.), and national ideals (Thanksgiving). We have holidays to show affection for loved ones (Mother's Day, Father's Day, Valentine's Day). Individuals and groups celebrate privately designated holidays (birthdays, reunions). Even some annually observed recreational occasions have been elevated to the status of an informal holiday — football's Superbowl is celebrated on Super-Sunday with get-togethers all over the country.

Teaching Strategies

You might want to discuss with your class how holidays are commonly associated with specific emotions: we anticipate a "merry" Christmas, "happy" New Year, a "festive" Fourth. We are expected to feel loving on Valentine's Day, grateful on Thanksgiving, horrified on Halloween, appreciative on Mother's Day, and — if the television commercials are any indication — inebriated on Super-Bowl Sunday. So expected are these emotions that holidays can easily become disappointingly mechanical and trivial, as celebration deteriorates into convention and ritual into routine. Russell Baker points this descent out: "Humans treat time as a map and always know where they are located on it and respond with the appropriate emotion. If it's the Fourth of July we are happy to eat hot dogs, and if it's Thanksgiving we are unhappy to eat hot dogs." But Baker is easy on New Year's Eve compared to Michael Arlen's all-out attack on Thanksgiving. Arlen is so soured by the routinized celebration of Thanksgiving that he certainly would prefer hot dogs to the traditional turkey. Nikki Giovanni, too, notices how easily holidays in America lose their purpose: "I really love a good holiday," she says satirically, "it takes the people off the streets and puts them safely in the shopping malls."

Because they are so deeply embedded in our individual lives and cultural traditions, holidays are a favorite theme for writers to explore — they not only present an occasion to write, but also an opportunity to write about an occasion. You might point out to students that during holidays writers often feel a greater sense of community and also more urgency to communicate. But ask how many continue to satisfy that urgency with greeting cards, which — as we are well aware — have an unending supply of stock sentiments for every occasion. However festive or contemplative holidays may make us feel, they pose a special problem for the writer who wants to share the occasion not only in feelings but in words. Major holidays elicit so many standardized images that when we begin to write about them we may automatically resort to formula and cliché. The writers in this chapter show convincingly that the strength of a tradition is often sapped by the utter conventionality with which we perceive it.

Greeting cards are one conventional way in which we share the occasion of a holiday. But holidays, of course, engender more than conventional sentiment, as this chapter is designed to show. To get your students thinking about conventional and unconventional attitudes toward holidays, invite them to consider the three epigraphs, with very different points of view about Christmas. The first, from Charles Dickens's essay "A Christmas Dinner" (in *Sketches by Boz* [1834–1836]), presents the traditional image of a "merry" Christmas. Dickens, students may be interested to know, was instrumental in the "invention" of Christmas as one of our major holidays. His sentiments about the day, as this passage clearly shows, have become, through decades of media reinforcement, practically a national ideal. You might point out that these Dickensian sentiments are directly behind the American family's expectations vividly described by Jeijun; her Asian perspective not only gives another view of the holiday but poignantly shows the discrepancy between the "ideal" Christmas and an actual family celebration. For Gwendolyn Brooks the typical Christmas-card ideals could never suggest the complexity of her emotion toward a holiday whose ordinary repertoire of words and images does not adequately include black Americans. Here she proposes another kind of Christmas — a celebration that would merge the day with a traditional African holiday. But her festive ideals have a Dickensian ring.

These three descriptions of Christmas can introduce your students to some of the ways in which they can think about holidays in general. As they read the selections they should be thinking about how holidays so often confront us with a clash between traditional values and contemporary realities. They should be prepared to see how writers react to holidays with caution, resisting conventional sentiment. In the selections, three writers display their reluctance to fall into the ready-made language through which people ordinarily share these occasions.

A Writing-before-Reading Exercise

Before they begin reading, invite students to think of the one annual holiday that they like least. They should consider their reasons for disliking it: Do they find it difficult to share the mood? Do they disagree with the cultural or political ideals of the occasion? Do they feel excluded from the occasion? After they've thought about why a holiday doesn't appeal to them, they should draft an essay in which they describe their behavior on that day.

WORKING WITH THE SELECTIONS

Russell Baker

Happy New Year?

Teaching Strategies

You might begin discussion by asking students to think about the aspects of New Year's Day that best lend themselves to humor and satire. They could then see how many of these Russell Baker covers. For example, many of us joke about our own and other people's New Year's resolutions. But does he omit humorous issues? He claims that New Year's Day "is always a depressing holiday," yet he doesn't mention anything about hangovers, a most likely reason for depression on that day. It would be a good idea to ask students why he focuses on only four "horrors" of the holiday.

Because depression is the dominant mood in Baker's comic meditation (he's writing a humorous essay about depression), you will want to make sure students understand the larger theme of the essay — that this piece is not so much about Baker's own mood but about our relation to time and how it affects our emotions. You might ask your class to identify all Baker's references to time (some are specific details, others are general). They should see, then, that the anecdote about his cat has a serious implication. Human beings think themselves superior to other animals, but Baker wonders if his cat's ignorance of time gives it an emotional edge. Your students ought to be aware of the shifts between comedy and seriousness in this essay. For example, Baker's account of his fingernail clipping (para. 6) is intended to be absurd; but his comment about our "calendar-ridden minds" (para. 4) and his remark that "Humans treat time as a map" (para. 14) definitely have a sober side. His metaphor comparing time and maps, though casual, is a rich one, and you might analyze it in class discussion.

Students should see that Baker exaggerates throughout the essay. You might ask students to locate sentences they believe are exaggerated and to describe their humorous effect. But they should also see that his exaggerations serve a philosophical purpose. Analyzing the last three paragraphs will bring out both the meditative and comic aspects of Baker's mind. It should be clear to students that Baker is also poking fun at our conventional responses to holidays. Ask whether or not Baker himself shows unwillingness to indulge in the "appropriate emotion." What do they think that emotion is for New Year's Day?

Additional Activities

Russell Baker is considered one of America's leading contemporary humorists. He also writes on many major social and political issues, often blending seriousness with satire. For class discussion you might ask students to read the episode "Gumption" from Baker's autobiography (in Chapter 2). Or you might ask students to locate a few of Baker's recent columns in the *New York Times*. Use this occasion to encourage students to compare two works by the same writer. Discussion could cover Baker's use of humor and satire for serious purposes.

Generating Writing

Oddly, Baker doesn't mention New Year's Eve in his essay. You might invite the class to write an essay similar to Baker's but focusing instead on how they (or their family and friends) typically spend the night before. Students should describe their celebration and consider both the serious and humorous aspects of the holiday.

Michael Arlen
Ode to Thanksgiving

Teaching Strategies

Here is an essay that goes right to the heart of conventional holiday expression. Students, however, may have difficulty with Arlen's literary tone, deliberately low-keyed sarcasm, and irreverence for a holiday some of them may consider nationally sacred.

You might begin discussion by asking about Arlen's title. Does your class know what an ode is? Do they understand that the ode is ordinarily poetry, not prose, and usually pertains to a lofty topic expressed in a dignified tone? They should see that Arlen is using the label humorously, that he is *not* paying a lofty tribute to Thanksgiving.

Remind the class that humor often works by defying the reader's conventional expectations or assumptions. Point out Arlen's opening sentence: What assumptions is he making about his audience's attitude toward the holiday? What sort of things does he think readers will expect to hear? Ask students to list the items and props of a typical Thanksgiving.

If you point to the end of Arlen's essay, to his comment about "unrealistic expectations," students will more readily see what is going on in the essay. Though Arlen here refers to Christmas, it's clear that his remark about expectations is meant to include our reactions to holidays in general. You might want to move from this concluding remark back to the middle portions of the essay, asking how Arlen's comment applies to the essay as a whole. What holiday expectations specifically is he satirizing?

And who are the characters in this essay — Aunt Bertha, Uncle Jasper, Auntie Em, Cousin May, and the rest? Do your students recognize them? Do they understand their function? You might want your class to discuss Arlen's technique here of using specific characters in a representational way. Ask the class who these people are meant to suggest? Can students identify with them? In what sense do they seem like actual people? In what sense are they caricatures? How does the occasion deteriorate? Their routine attitudes and behavior clearly reinforce a world of expected responses.

Finally, you might direct discussion toward the main point of Arlen's satirical view of Thanksgiving. What is it about the holiday that he mainly dislikes? Granted, he sees nothing good about Thanksgiving ("What is the good side of Thanksgiving, you ask. There is always a good side to everything. Not to Thanksgiving. There is only a bad side and then a worse side," para. 4). But ask the class for their opinion about what Arlen finds *most* disappointing. To get discussion going, you could ask that they consider how Arlen might enjoy the day. Can they make some inferences about what Arlen *would* like, knowing what he clearly doesn't like?

Additional Activities

If you can locate a copy of Norman Rockwell's famous 1943 illustration of a Thanksgiving dinner, "Freedom from Want," you might use it to show exactly what Arlen objects to about the holiday. The illustration is available in Rockwell collections in many libraries. You could also ask students themselves to find typical depictions that they could bring to class. Discussion could be concentrated on the images of Thanksgiving portrayed in advertising and the media.

Generating Writing

If some of your students find Arlen's essay offensive or "too negative," you might invite them to write a rebuttal in the form of a positive view of the holiday (can they do it and avoid the clichés Arlen pokes fun at?) If some enjoy Arlen's essay — and agree with him — then invite those students to choose another holiday and write a similar "ode," attacking its "unrealistic expectations."

Nikki Giovanni

On Holidays and How to Make Them Work

Teaching Strategies

In this very short essay, the black poet and essayist reminds us that holidays have reflective and celebratory purposes that American society seems to overlook. She runs through a number of holidays — Labor Day, Christmas, Memorial Day, July 4, President's Day, and, most important from her point of view, Martin Luther King Day — to show how slight the connection is between the occasion and the manner in which it is honored.

You might begin discussion by asking her objection to the American way of celebrating the major holidays. Students should see that her biggest complaint is the way in which holidays become associated with consumption. She starts with Labor Day, claiming that on a day that is supposed to honor workers with a day off, people flock to stores where other people are forced to work. This reflection leads her to reflect satirically on "the American way," which makes all holidays into shopping opportunities.

You might want to report that her essay was written just as Martin Luther King Day was first celebrated; she uses the occasion for an ironic preview of what its celebration might mean in her town (thus the allusions to local streets and stores). Paragraph 3 contains the most satirical part of her essay, as she demonstrates how King's Day is most likely to be honored — with rampant commercialism and exploitation. You might want to ask about her audience here; what advantage does she see white Americans taking of this day? Why will they get behind the day? Ask the class to notice the distinction she makes between "Black" and "colored." Why does she introduce this distinction?

To get students to see Giovanni's satirical viewpoint in the essay, you might ask them to discuss her title. What does she mean by making holidays "work"? Ask students about her pun; she is using the word *work* in two senses — as labor and as performance. She clearly doesn't approve of turning holidays into a time of labor and consumption, but you could invite students to speculate about what she doesn't say: how should we celebrate such holidays as Martin Luther King Day?

Additional Activities

Nikki Giovanni's connection between holidays and work can lead to some interesting class discussion. An essay in the March 17, 1986, issue of *The New Republic* suggested that Americans have too many holidays and that these are part of a great loss of productivity. You might introduce this passage in class and invite students to debate the topic. The passage is especially relevant to Martin Luther King Day and to any proposal for new national holidays.

> The cost of a holiday isn't piddling. The Chamber of Commerce's numbers, cited in the [Martin Luther] King Day debate, put it at more than five billion dollars in lost productivity. More than that, however, is the symbolic effect of rewarding ourselves with more time off. I say let's cut back. We would not demean those who have fought and died for our nation if

we observed Memorial and Veterans days together. New Year's is celebrated around the world, but what reflective significance does it really have? And, though you don't have to be Leif Eriksson to wonder why we should have a Columbus Day if not a multitude of other ethnic holidays, the compromise offered by Senators David Boren and Sam Nunn during the King holiday debate back in October 1983 still makes sense to me when it comes to personages: celebrate King, Washington, and Columbus on their appropriate days, whenever they fall, and not as the Monday leg of a three-day bender. Most years at least one would fall on a weekend, so we would lose only two work days a year while preserving the ceremonial significance of three holidays.

— Tim W. Ferguson, "Too Many Holidays"

Generating Writing

Ask your students to write an essay in which they show how to make a holiday work. They should select a holiday that they feel has lost its true meaning in America. What would they do to restore that meaning? How do they propose that the holiday be celebrated? They should make their proposal as practical as possible.

WRITING ABOUT THE CHAPTER

1. If you asked students to write a draft before reading the selections, ask them now to go back through the essays and locate passages in which the writers made them aware of the deeper implications of holidays. They could then revise their essays about their least-favorite holiday so that readers will see the larger issues behind their personal opinion.

2. Invite students to try proposing a new holiday. They could choose a personality or event that they believe deserves a national holiday. In an essay, they should give the day an official name, explain why they think the day deserves to be celebrated nationally, and describe what they think the celebration should be like.

3. According to Nikki Giovanni, "A proper holiday . . . is supposed to be a time of reflection on great men, great deeds, great people." Why does she feel that this notion of holidays didn't "catch on" in America? Ask students to write an essay addressing this question. How do the essays by Baker and Arlen support Giovanni's view? What attitude about holidays links all these essays?

4. Though each writer is satirical about the subject of holidays, each essay has a serious theme beneath the exaggerated tone. Ask students to identify the serious side of each essay. How does each writer suggest that his or her antiholiday attitude is not just a matter of personal crankiness but is based on larger social or communal issues? Which essay seems most serious, and why?

16

Consumer Culture

William Severini Kowinski, Kids in the Mall:
Growing Up Controlled

Phyllis Rose, Shopping and Other Spiritual Adventures
in America Today

Toni Cade Bambara, The Lesson

WORKING WITH THE CHAPTER

College students should be well aware of the pressures theat consumerism exerts on every one of us. Most of them are members of the eighteen to twenty-four age group beloved and targeted by advertisers and manufacturers; older students may just be realizing how advertisers exploit insecurities and fears of aging, or perhaps they are beginning to have to resist children's demands for bigger, better, new, and improved toys, cereals, games and anything else their favorite cartoon characters think they need. Even our cats, television tells us, will suffer if we give them inferior or unfashionable food and litter. What's a responsible consumer to do?

Teaching Strategies

This chapter gives varied perspectives on our increasingly consumer-oriented way of life. Students should respond enthusiastically, for the issues raised in the selections and epigraphs are close to their everyday experience. The chapter's topic gives an excellent opportunity for first-person writing; every student has a story to tell about the drive to consume.

Ellen Willis's epigraph epitomizes the paradox of cheap luxuries; the consumer culture in whose service we labor is also the reward we receive for our work. Ask students to read the passage carefully. Do they agree with Willis that our high material standard of living is a bribe? From whom? Willis states that "buying is the one pleasurable activity not only permitted but actively encouraged by our rulers." Who is meant by the phrase "our rulers?" Who is the "us" to which Willis refers? What are the assumptions behind this description?

How might Willis's view be challenged? What recreations and pleasures do we as a society enjoy that are not bound up with manufacture, sale, and consumption? Television, for example, is many people's favorite recreation; yet it is in a very real way an extension of the shopping mall — advertising abounds, new products and styles are showcased, brand names are ubiquitous. Television sells more than goods, too. Its primary function may be to sell life-styles, all of which require accessories. Acquiring these accessories means we must work harder; more work means more goods are produced, which need to be sold; a desire is created for the new goods, which means more work to acquire them, which means more production, and the cycle repeats itself infinitely. Is this a valid description of our economic system? How is it misrepresentative or simplistic?

The epigraph from Veblen's *Theory of the Leisure Class* seems as apt today as it must have in 1899, when it was written. Tell students about Veblen and his pioneering in the development of American economics. You may need to read the passage carefully in class; ask students to look up unfamiliar words. How accurately do they feel Veblen's model describes their experience? Are they motivated to consume by peer pressure and a drive to achieve status? No one wants to admit they are; ask students if they feel these motivations are at work in society at large. What social forces help keep this system of ever-growing demands going?

The passage from More's *Utopia* may be the most difficult of the epigraphs. Students will probably be familiar with the word "utopia," but not realize its origin in More's fantasy about an ideal society. Remind the class that More was writing in the sixteenth century — how would today's ideal society differ? Do students agree that in a perfect world, no one's material desires would exceed their needs? Is More correct in explaining acquisitiveness as the product either of fear or of pride? Which of these drives seems to be the prime motivator in today's consumer culture?

How might Veblen's view on the perpetuation of material wants apply to Kowinski's researches in teenage mall culture? Does Veblen's phrase, "race for reputability," seem to describe the interactions between teenagers heavily involved in the mall world? How do Kowinski's subjects seem trapped in a value system based on acquisition? How might More react to the Greengate Mall and its inhabitants if he were transported there in a time machine?

How does Rose's view of the ritual of shopping differ from Kowinski's? Would the two authors disagree on facts, or interpretations? Return to Willis's epigraph; whose view does she share more closely, Rose's or Kowinski's? How are both writers more optimistic — or at least more sanguine — about growing consumerism than Willis is? Discuss the differences in the three authors' tone and approach. How do their assumptions seem to differ? Ask students whose ideas most closely resemble their own.

Invite the class to imagine an encounter between Kowinski's subjects and the characters in Toni Cade Bambara's short story. What common ground could these people find? How are their experiences different? What might their reactions to each other be? How might the processes of wanting, shopping, and buying differ for the two groups? Talk about people's varying motivations for owning things and wanting to own things. What might Willis have to add to the discussion?

A Writing-before-Reading Exercise

Ask students to list all the encounters they have had with the culture of consumption since they got up in the morning. Were they aware of the brand of toothpaste they used? What choices of soap and shampoo did they make? Did they choose clothes advertising a product, life-style, or entertainment personality? What have they bought so far today? What have they wanted to buy? What have people tried to sell them?

Once students have compiled this list, ask them to write a brief paragraph assessing how these encounters have affected them. How do they feel their product choices influence others' opinions of them? How do others' product choices influence their own opinions? What moments of pride or anxiety have material things caused them today?

WORKING WITH THE SELECTIONS

William Severini Kowinski

Kids in the Mall: Growing Up Controlled

Teaching Strategies

Encourage the class to read Kowinski's essay closely. Their first impulse may be to reject his characterization of teenagers as products of a mall culture, or to try to distance themselves from it. Ask the class to think about the role malls play in their lives. You might want to do a "reading" of the campus bookstore or student center as a miniature mall. Are the retail areas laid out in familiar, mall-like configurations? What might be the reasoning behind this plan?

Kowinski cites a number of sources as support for his statements about mall culture and his generalizations about the culture at large. How do students evaluate these sources? What do they make of Kowinski's unsupported claims, such as, "Teenagers in America now spend more time in the mall than anywhere else but home and school?" This has the ring of a statistic, yet Kowinski provides no source or data to back it up. What kind of rhetorical strategy is this?

Kowinski also relies heavily on anecdotal evidence to support his points. How effective do students find this tactic? How is this approach in tune with mall culture, which seems to bring out the same kind of gossip and oral history traditionally associated with the small town? How is a mall like a small town? How do they differ? Does the fact that a mall's primary and sole focus is the buying and selling of merchandise shape the kinds of interactions that go on inside it? How? How might the structure of a mall community differ from that of other groups? What other groups is a mall crowd like?

Do students find their own experience bears out the conclusions drawn in the International Council of Shopping Centers study? For example, Kowinski cites the study as stating that teens "congregate in groups of two to four and predominantly at locations selected by them rather than management." Does this statement seem true? Discuss the idea of the study with the class; what does it mean that there is an organization called the International Council of Shopping Centers? What does that say about malls' power and interests? Why might they have commissioned a study on teenage mall behavior? How do students respond to the idea that their generation's behavior is of such interest to mall proprietors that they will pay for studies and observations of their teen clientele? Does your class find this notion discomfiting?

The mall study's conclusion, Kowinski reports, was that teenage customers were to be welcomed because they shared "the same set of values" with mall management. Does the class agree or disagree with this statement? Do merchants and customers really share values, or are their values complementary? Certainly, the woman behind the counter at the card shop may want to run across to the shoe store on her lunch hour, just as the shoe salesman may want to head for the video arcade. These people aren't the ones who commissioned the study, however. Discuss this question with students: do they imagine the owners of malls shopping at the malls they own? Or would a cut-rate mall owner shop at a medium-priced mall, a medium-priced mall owner shop at a high-priced mall, and the owner of the high-priced mall shop in New York or Paris? How might this social structure influence the relationship between management and customers? Similarly, how do the values of an adult store owner conflict with those of her teenage employees and clientele?

What opinion do students have of Kowinski's assertion that the culture of consumption increases stress in young people's lives? How do merchandising and advertising urge teens to grow up and become sophisticated? How does the class feel these pressures have affected their own development? How does a commitment to an after-school or summertime job add stress to high schoolers' lives? Does the mall economy perpetuate itself through teen employment and teen consumption?

Ask students who may not have been exposed to mall culture — rural students, urban students, older or foreign students — their thoughts about Kowinski's article. Do they feel they have been left out of anything? How does the class react to Kowinski's attempt to praise mall culture? Do students agree that the mall is a microcosm of a future of controlled environments and interactions? For what do they feel the mall is a preparation?

Additional Activities

If circumstances permit, a field trip to a local mall might make an interesting class or individual research project. Ask students to conduct brief interviews with teenagers in the mall. (The class could discuss or formulate possible interview questions beforehand — what kinds of things would students like to ask? How do they think subjects might respond?) The class could draw up a group report, or students could present their own research to the class in a seminar format.

This selection might be looked at together with Chapter 4, on "Places in the Heart." How might a mall be a significant place in someone's development? How might it be a poor substitute for a neighborhood or a place in nature?

Generating Writing

1. Ask students to write a personal essay challenging Kowinski's view of the mall as the central location in American adolescent life. What other places were vital parts of students' development? How did these places teach other lessons than those which are to be learned at the mall?

2. Have students briefly dig out some of the assumptions in Kowinski's argument. How materialistic does he seem to find American culture? What prejudices and preconceptions does he have about adolescents? What kinds of personal and social development does he present as inevitable? How does he take the mall, as an institution, for granted?

Phyllis Rose

Shopping and Other Spiritual Adventures in America Today

Teaching Strategies

Discuss this essay's title with the class. Just how ironic is it? How did students take it before reading the piece? After finishing the essay, did their opinion of the title's irony change? Is shopping a "spiritual adventure?" In what ways?

This piece first appeared in the "Hers" column of the *New York Times*, a column that (as the name implies) presents women's perspectives on various issues. How does Rose's view of shopping seem specifically feminine? What might a "masculine" view of shopping be? Does society give women a freedom to discuss consumer issues that it denies to men? Around which gender role is the stereotype of the shopper constructed?

Talk about sex differences in shopping. How do men and women shop? What kinds of satisfaction do they expect from shopping and buying? For what kinds of goods is it acceptable for men to shop? What things are women encouraged to shop for? How do the conventions of advertising reflect these views? What does the division of shopping by sex say about our society's view of gender? For example, most ads for household products are directed exclusively at women; obviously, men buy cleaners and detergents also, but the world of advertising doesn't applaud them for it. Similarly, beer advertising seems to address men only; how are women to feel about their own purchases of beer? What do these conventions reveal about gender expectations and their social rewards?

What does the class make of Rose's almost incantatory use of the names of stores, lists of the goods available there, and their trademarks? Have someone read the opening paragraph out loud. Does Rose's tone here seem almost a parody of prayer? How does this tone foreshadow the essay's closing line, "Caldor, Waldbaum's, Bob's Surplus — these, perhaps, are our cathedrals"? How do students interpret this line? It is meant to be funny, certainly, but how serious is it? Cathedrals were the expression of shared social values in medieval Europe; communities would devote their surplus wealth and human energy to the construction of monuments to organized religion. Are stores, malls, advertising, billboards an expression of contemporary American values? How is our consumer culture a monument to our way of life? To what religious ideals do secular aims like comfort and security correspond? Is Rose's article a critique of this point of view or a celebration of it?

Additional Activities

One group project the class might enjoy would be to collect circulars, publications, and brochures from local stores and read them closely. What common themes do store copywriters use? To what desires and fears do they appeal? Do favorite images or metaphors appear again and again? What kinds of life-styles are the stores selling? How do they encourage customers to think about themselves? What kind of identity does a store offer its clients?

This selection seems to epitomize the logical development of Crèvecoeur's Americanism. Ask students to look back at Chapter 7, "What Is an American?" How might Crèvecoeur applaud Rose's defense of self-actualization through shopping? How are Americans defined by what they do buy, and *can* buy?

Generating Writing

1. Ask students to write a brief description of what shopping means to them. How do their views differ from Rose's? How do they agree? What, for them, are the spiritual dimensions of shopping?

2. How do consumer goods work as social equalizers? (It was indeed Andy Warhol — or his staff — who said, in his book *America* (Harper & Row, 1985), that you can have the same Tab as Jackie Onassis.) Invite students to comment from their own experience. What critique of this idea might Ellen Willis offer?

Toni Cade Bambara

The Lesson

Teaching Strategies

It is probably best to make sure students realize that the story's narrator, and most of the other characters in it, are African-Americans. The class may not be familiar with Bambara's work; she is one of our most noted writers of color. Her writing is generally focused on the urban experience and her protagonists are usually women. What is the perspective of urban women of color on this culture of consumption? What place does that culture accord them? Discuss this issue with the class. What are the differences in entitlement that advertising and merchandising make clear? How do stores treat minority and white patrons differently? How are advertising campaigns geared to different markets?

Ask the class to characterize Bambara's narrator. What seems to be her dominant trait? Why does she react as she does to Miss Moore? (Do students think that name is symbolic?) What does she object to about Miss Moore and her plans for the neighborhood children? How does she express her disapproval? She calls Miss Moore a "nappy-headed bitch" (para. 2) and describes her as "black as hell" (para. 1). Why does the narrator use the same abusive labels as a white racist might? How does she insist on identifying herself with majority culture? One thing she dislikes about Miss Moore is that Moore often talks about how "we all poor and live in the slums, which I don't feature" (para. 3). Why does the narrator reject the labels "poor" and "slum" for her life? Is this a courageous act or a thoughtless one?

What does the goal of Miss Moore's field trip to F. A. O. Schwarz seem to have been? Why is the narrator resistant to the trip and Moore's talk about economic justice? When her friend Sugar enters the discussion, the narrator perceives this as a betrayal. Why? What might she gain by refusing to consider the ways in which society has limited her options? Read the story's last paragraph closely. What does the narrator mean when she says, "She can run if she want to and even run faster. But ain't nobody gonna beat me at nothing." (para. 58)? How does the narrator opt out of contests that are stacked against her? What does Bambara's attitude toward the narrator's choice seem to be? Do we sympathize with this proud and angry girl?

Additional Activities

This selection might well be looked at in conjunction with Shelby Steele's "On Being Black and Middle Class" (see Chapter 6, "Divided Identities"). How might Bambara's narrator respond to an encounter with Steele? What might Steele's view of this story be? How do minority cultures encourage insularity and a lowered horizon of expectations? Why is it in the interest of the dominant culture to reinforce this kind of thinking? What might be the result for society be if more economically disadvantaged people started frequenting F. A. O. Schwarz, and Tiffany's, and Neiman Marcus, and wondering why none of these goods and opportunities were available to them?

A class project on advertising may help some students understand Bambara's story more fully. Choose a period — perhaps three months — and collate advertising from newspapers and magazines from that period. Once the class has gathered a number of ads, ask the group to analyze them, keeping their intended audience in mind. At whom is each ad directed? Do advertisers target different ethnic, racial, economic, and social groups for different products? Try to find ads for the same product that are obviously aiming at different audiences; for example, many household products run ads in Spanish-language newspapers, and some beers conduct simultaneous ad campaigns for whites and for African-Americans. How do the ads differ? Which aspects of the product do they stress? How does audience makeup affect the tone and approach of an advertising campaign?

Generating Writing

1. What is the meaning of the story's title? Assign a brief essay on this topic. Students may want to consider some of these questions: What lesson did Miss Moore want to teach the neighborhood children? What lesson did the narrator want to teach Miss Moore? What lesson did the narrator herself learn?

2. Ask students to write a personal essay about the horizon of expectations. When, in their own experience, have students been forced to confront society's limitation of their desires or aspirations? What factors combined against them? How did the restrictions make them feel?

WRITING ABOUT THE CHAPTER

1. Have the class choose any two of the selections and compare and contrast the authors' views of consumer culture. How critical are the authors of our society's focus on material goods? Which factors do the authors think are most important in evaluating the pressures placed on individuals by our national patterns of consumption?

2. Ask students to write an essay evaluating their own experiences as consumers, thinking back about their work on this chapter. How have the chapter selections and epigraphs inspired them to reevaluate their opinion of consumer mentality? With which of the authors are they most sympathetic? Least sympathetic? What questions did the chapter leave unanswered? Unasked?

3. Bambara's story complicates the issue of consumer culture by introducing the variables race, class, and gender. How do Rose and Kowinski overlook these variables? How do status, sex, and origin affect an individual's place in the world of consumption? Students may draw on their own lives for illustration. How do production, distribution, and consumption reinforce preexisting social distinctions?

17

The National Pastime

Gerald Early, Baseball: The Ineffable National Pastime

Doris Kearns Goodwin, From Father, with Love

Philip Roth, My Baseball Years

WORKING WITH THE CHAPTER

The prodigious number of books and articles published about baseball over the past few years is a good indication that the sport has truly captured a sizable portion of the American consciousness. Many are statistical, to be sure, but in many bookstores you can now find entire sections devoted to baseball — its history, its biographies and autobiographies, its legends and myths, its art and science. And the game has attracted the attention of many literary figures and intellectuals. Open up the *New York Review of Books* or *Natural History* and you're likely to find an essay by Harvard paleontologist, Stephen Jay Gould, on Joe DiMaggio's famous hitting streak or the Abner Doubleday controversy. *New Yorker* writer Roger Angell has been covering the game for that magazine for years, and prominent poet Donald Hall has written many literary essays on the subject. When a Harvard graduate student discovered the earliest known box score while researching mid–nineteenth-century newspapers for his dissertation, the story made the front page of the *New York Times*. In this climate, it is hardly news that the late baseball commissioner, A. Bartlett Giamatti, was a Renaissance scholar and former president of Yale University.

Teaching Strategies

Many of your students, though, may think of baseball only as reflected in sports writing in the local paper or broadcasting language of television commentators. In this chapter they read about the game at a different level of articulation than they may be accustomed to. You can introduce this literary level by asking the class to examine the epigraphs. The first, by Los Angeles writer Eve Babitz, would be hard to find on any sports page: it is a lyrical view of a baseball field as seen by someone for the first time, someone who doesn't even understand how the game is played. For Babitz there's a romantic, breathtaking beauty to Dodger Stadium itself, which — your class should notice — she describes with artistic images. Her panoramic view provides an interesting opening to the chapter; one doesn't need to know anything about the game to begin to appreciate it aesthetically.

With Roger Angell, students can see how the game of baseball can be elevated almost to an aesthetic philosophy. Angell, too, looks at the game from an elemental level — a ball going through its physical motions. This brief though elegantly written passage (you might invite someone to read it aloud), can open up interesting discussion about why baseball is satisfying not only to the senses but to the mind. Students should be able to discuss the essential human conflicts that Angell finds in the game — safety versus danger (the players "police" the field), constraint versus energy, rules versus freedom.

The intellectual attractions of baseball are taken a step further in the next epigraph. An emeritus professor of the history of technology at Massachusetts Institute of Technology, Elting E. Morison had always wanted to teach a college course on baseball. In this passage from an article he wrote for *American Heritage,* Morison describes how that course might have proceeded. He asks a tricky question that your class also might reflect on to get discussion moving: What did Reggie Jackson mean when he said, "The country is as American as baseball"? In this epigraph Morison also mentions how deeply baseball has permeated the American language. He offers several examples. Can your class think of others?

Having moved into the subject of language, you can ask the class to look at an excerpt from one of the most successful stand-up comic routines in the history of American entertainment — Abbott and Costello's "Who's on First?" Along with Ernest Lawrence Thayer's poem "Casey at the Bat," it's one of the classics in the language of baseball. If you can find a record or tape of the skit (several are available) it might be fun to play it in class and discuss the source of humor and reasons for its popularity. Incidentally, the skit wasn't written by Abbott and Costello; it had long been a popular vaudeville routine. The sample here is from the transcript of their 1945 film *The Gay Nineties.*

With these four epigraphs you should be able to get your class thinking how baseball pervades our language and culture. This opening will prepare them for the selections, which show how important baseball is in the childhood of these writers with widely divergent backgrounds: a black poet and essayist who grew up in Philadelphia and went to Phillies games with his grandfather, a native of the Bahamas; a noted biographer from Brooklyn who shows that women's lives, too, can be inextricably caught up in the sport; and a prominent novelist from Newark, New Jersey, who reminisces about his boyhood obsession with the game. This range of essays goes a long way in proving that baseball is truly the *national* pastime.

But the selections, your students will discover, are not only about baseball. Though he talks about players and the game, Gerald Early brings varied cultural material to bear on his discussion of the sport. "There is little here about the sport itself," he says in his opening paragraph. "The examination is centered on baseball's political, social, and cultural meaning." Doris Kearns Goodwin also sees more than a game; she sees a linkage of people with each other and with history. And for Philip Roth, the love of baseball is intimately connected with the love of literature. With this chapter, you can move from a popular topic like baseball to Fitzgerald and Hemingway, Orwell and Conrad.

A Writing-before-Reading Exercise

Before they read the personal accounts in this chapter, invite students to consider how sports influenced their own childhood. They could then draft an essay on the topic. The essay could be about participating in sports and how that affected their development, but it could also be about sports in their life and culture, even if they didn't play or care for sports.

WORKING WITH THE SELECTIONS

Gerald Early

Baseball: The Ineffable National Pastime

Teaching Strategies

If you begin this selection (it's the first part of a longer essay published in its entirety in *Openings: Original Essays by Contemporary Soviet and American Writers,* edited by Robert Atwan and Valeri Vinokurov [University of Washington Press, 1990]) by discussing the word *ineffable,* your students will see from the start that Gerald Early's subject here is not so much baseball as the connection between baseball and language. Chances are, few students will be sure about the meaning of *ineffable,* and so it might be a good idea to go over it in class and consider not just the dictionary definition but the range of connotations (the word is, of course, often used in a religious context to signify that which is inexpressible). It's a fancy label to put next to baseball, but Early uses it deliberately. He ends his essay with the question: "What is there to say about games anyway?"

Early's question goes to the heart of sports in America. Your students will soon see that Early doesn't spend much time in this selection describing baseball or events; most of it is about the relation of baseball to discourse. He finds it ironic that "athletic endeavor, such a speechless act, should generate such need for narrative, for language, for story" (para. 2), and he lists the "varieties of discourse" to which sports are subjected. This tendency to verbalize the sports experience, in which discourse "displaces the event," both fascinates and disturbs Early. Many of your students who are caught up in sports talk (some may listen regularly to all-sports radio stations or watch nonstop sports events on cable television) will recognize what Early means.

Early doesn't disassociate himself from these conversations; he doesn't write as a detached observer or an uninterested academic who finds sports curious. He makes it clear that he himself is a sports fan, knows several sports intimately, and can talk about them in varied ways; he shows us his knowledge in paragraphs 4 and 5, where he imitates the sports chatter of his boyhood. Though many of the names he runs through will probably not be familiar to younger readers, that isn't the point — invite students to reconstruct some of the list by replacing the names with the names of today's players. Sports talk hasn't changed much; if anything, with increased media coverage and daily call-in radio shows, it has become even more prevalent.

Early's identification of baseball (and sports in general) with "varieties of discourse" carries over into literature. "It did not occur to me," he says, "until I taught *The Great Gatsby* and Hemingway's *The Sun Also Rises* in a freshman English class that the connection between sports and literature is central to understanding what sports are and why they exist" (para. 12). Early's explanation for this connection is vital to his essay but difficult, and so you might want to walk your class through paragraphs 12 and 13. Invite class discussion on the point Early makes in paragraph 13 about the relation of our lives to the narratives of sports. Can students find any personal application to this idea?

Throughout the selection, Early makes it clear that he, too, is caught up in the "metalanguage" of sports. Toward the end of the selection, he recalls the number of baseball books he read and how these satisfied not only a hunger for baseball lore but also a need for narrative and story. Furthermore, these popular biographies and autobiographies provided him with dominant American myths, especially male myths of success and heroism. You might ask your students to discuss their own relation to such books (how many know similar books and read them, if not about sports figures then about other celebrities?). Do they also feel as Early does that these books provide them with "an orientation toward the culture" (para. 13)? You might ask, too, if students think that males, as Early suggests, derive far more of their cultural orientation and mythology from such discourse than do females.

You could wrap discussion up by returning to the "ineffable." Have the class examine closely Early's final paragraph, where he reintroduces his silent grandfather. Ask about this character and why he has an important part in this essay. Ask them to imagine the essay without the grandfather; what would be missing? Invite the class to discuss the significance of the last paragraph. How does Early present himself here? Why does he start talking about baseball? What is the significance of his grandfather's comment, "Oh, I don't know"? Make sure your class understands that this final paragraph is self-criticism, not criticism of the grandfather. Are your students aware of Early's reasons for being self-critical here? Invite your class to consider the final question: "What is there to say about games anyway?" Is the question merely rhetorical? Are some things worth saying and others not worth saying? Do students feel that despite his scepticism Early has said quite a bit about games and sports?

Additional Activities

Early's connections between baseball and narrative discourse can illuminate one of America's most popular poems, Ernest Lawrence Thayer's "Casey at the Bat," published in 1888. You might want to use this text in class to discuss some of Early's points about baseball language, narrative, and American myths of success and heroism, all of which come together in this poem. Invite the class to read the poem aloud — a different student could read each stanza and then interpret it, referring to Early's essay. You might ask students to speculate about the poem's popularity: what does it say about the American character?

Casey at the Bat

The outlook wasn't brilliant for the Mudville nine that day:
The score stood four to two with but one inning more to play.
And then when Cooney died at first, and Barrows did the same,
A sickly silence fell upon the patrons of the game.

A straggling few got up to go in deep despair. The rest
Clung to that hope which springs eternal in the human breast;
They thought if only Casey could but get a whack at that —
We'd put up even money now with Casey at the bat.

But Flynn preceded Casey, as did also Jimmy Blake,
And the former was a lulu and the latter was a cake;
So upon that stricken multitude grim melancholy sat,
For there seemed but little chance of Casey's getting to the bat.

But Flynn let drive a single, to the wonderment of all,
And Blake, the much despis-ed, tore the cover off the ball;
And when the dust had lifted, and the men saw what had occurred,
There was Jimmy safe at second and Flynn a-hugging third.

Then from 5,000 throats and more there rose a lusty yell;
It rumbled through the valley, it rattled in the dell;
It knocked upon the mountain and recoiled upon the flat,
For Casey, mighty Casey, was advancing to the bat.

There was ease in Casey's manner as he stepped into his place;
There was pride in Casey's bearing and a smile on Casey's face.
And when, responding to the cheers, he lightly doffed his hat,
No stranger in the crowd could doubt 'twas Casey at the bat.

Ten thousand eyes were on him as he rubbed his hands with dirt;
Five thousand tongues applauded when he wiped them on his shirt.
Then while the writhing pitcher ground the ball into his hip,
Defiance gleamed in Casey's eye, a sneer curled Casey's lip.

And now the leather-covered sphere came hurtling through the air.
And Casey stood a-watching it in haughty grandeur there.
Close by the sturdy batsman the ball unheeded sped —
"That ain't my style," said Casey. "Strike one," the umpire said.

From the benches back with people, there went up a muffled roar,
Like the beating of the storm-waves on a stern and distant shore,
"Kill him! Kill the umpire!" shouted some one on the stand;
And it's likely they'd have killed him had not Casey raised his hand.

With a smile of Christian charity great Casey's visage shone;
He stilled the rising tumult; he bade the game go on;
He signaled to the pitcher, and once more the spheroid flew;
But Casey still ignored it, and the umpire said, "Strike two."

"Fraud!" cried the maddened thousands, and echo answered fraud;
But one scornful look from Casey and the audience was awed.
They saw his face grow stern and cold, they saw his muscles strain,
And they knew that Casey wouldn't let that ball go by again.

The sneer is gone from Casey's lip, his teeth are clenched in hate;
He pounds with cruel violence his bat upon the plate.
And now the pitcher holds the ball, and now he lets it go,
And now the air is shattered by the force of Casey's blow.

Oh, somewhere in this favored land the sun is shining bright;
The band is playing somewhere, and somewhere hearts are light,
And somewhere men are laughing, and somewhere children shout;
But there is no joy in Mudville — mighty Casey has struck out.

— Ernest Lawrence Thayer

Generating Writing

As an interesting research assignment for a longer paper you might ask students to read Fitzgerald's *The Great Gatsby* (the book Early assigned his freshman English class to read) or Hemingway's *The Sun Also Rises,* with Early's essay in mind. Or you or your students could choose more recent novels dealing with sports — Richard Ford's *The Sportswriter,* Frederick Exley's *A Fan's Notes,* or others. Students could focus on sports in such books and discuss how sports are used as cultural orientation and national myth.

Doris Kearns Goodwin

From Father, with Love

Teaching Strategies

In this brief personal essay, a prominent scholar and prize-winning biographer demonstrates baseball's remarkable ability to link individuals and generations in a way that magically seems to dissolve time. You might begin discussion by drawing your class's attention to the word *linked* in the opening sentence; it is the essay's key word, and it appears throughout.

For Doris Kearns Goodwin, baseball means a world of associations — with her father, her childhood, her women colleagues, her children. In reliving memories of baseball, and she has many, she discovers bonds that link her with both the past and present. Baseball thus becomes more than a physical sport, for it has the spiritual power to alter our relation to time. Moments like Bobby Thompson's ninth inning home run in 1951 to beat the Dodgers in one of baseball's most famous games not only live in her memory as part of baseball history; they are also part of her personal and family history. You could ask your class if anyone has heard of that event. Is it part of their family history as well?

Ask students how her father influenced development of her interest in the game. What did her scorebook mean to her? Why did it matter that her father didn't tell her about box scores? How is this fact pertinent to their relationship?

Another question to ask is about her meeting with Red Sox catcher Carlton Fisk. How does that meeting illustrate her connection with the game? Are students surprised that she finds herself more awestruck at meeting Fisk than in meeting U.S. presidents? Would they feel the same way about baseball stars today?

The essay ends with a magical moment at Boston's Fenway Park. Invite the class to look closely at the last paragraph. Notice that her connection to the game at the moment is not to the play-by-play or the pennant race or to anything specific about baseball. Ask if they can describe what it is that attracts her to baseball. Why does she call the game "the most timeless of all sports"?

Additional Activities

Goodwin uses the words *mystical* and *magical* to describe baseball. In conjunction with this essay, you might want to use one of several recent films exploring this side of the game, such as *The Natural* or *Field of Dreams,* both of which are readily available on videotape. You can use either of these films (or, if you prefer, the books they are based on) to invite students to see how baseball lends itself to realistic presentation. Your class may want to discuss this aspect of baseball. Is there anything about the game itself that inspires this treatment?

Generating Writing

Your students might consider whether baseball (or any other sports or games) led to the kind of rituals that Goodwin describes in her essay. Invite the class to describe such rituals (softball outings, Superbowl parties, and so on) and explain how they created bonds between individuals and generations.

Philip Roth

My Baseball Years

Teaching Strategies

Philip Roth sees baseball as touching almost every aspect of American culture — myth, geography, careers, patriotism, aesthetics, history, and so on. You might want to start discussion here by asking about the connection Roth makes between baseball and education in his opening paragraph. This connection holds throughout the essay, as Roth makes it clear how much baseball has taught him. Many of the things it taught him, though, were things we expect to learn not from baseball but from school.

Your students should be able to identify some of the things Roth learned, such as American geography and its cities. But baseball mainly taught him about larger matters, including myth and aesthetics, which would lead directly to his interest in literature and writing. The "mythic and aesthetic dimension" (para. 3) of baseball, your students should see, was important also because it helped root Americans in their culture and bind them in "common concerns, loyalties, rituals, enthusiasms, and antagonisms" (para. 3). Invite discussion on this issue: do your students think that baseball still serves this "patriotic" function? Do they think baseball is helping to root new immigrant groups in the culture?

The main connection Roth makes in this essay is between baseball and literature. Students should notice that it is no accident he begins an essay on baseball with a reference to George Orwell. Like Gerald Early, Roth sees baseball as helping to develop an aesthetic and narrative sense that can lead to an appreciation of literary works. But the connections here are not obvious, and may need to be worked out in class. Ask students to concentrate on paragraphs 7 to 9, where Roth explains the basis for his comparison. They should notice especially the long last sentence in paragraph 7 beginning, "Or, more accurately perhaps. . . ." You might discuss this list of similarities in detail, asking what each item ("lore and legends," and so on) has to do with both baseball and literature. Then move to the next two paragraphs and ask what other connections Roth finds. Why, for example, was the account of a pitcher's having eaten a hot dog before a no-hitter significant in the context of a developing literary sensibility? If your students can catch on to this connection, they've come a long way in the chapter.

Once you've established Roth's connection between baseball and literature, you might ask your students to go back and examine the essay, thinking how Roth has used what he learned. We see right away that he brings in George Orwell. But students should notice, too, that in the opening paragraph he talks about his baseball "style." Invite students to discuss if Roth's style of writing bears any similarity to his style of play.

Additional Activities

Is baseball special — is it truly the *national* pastime — or are writers like Roth exaggerating its significance? Invite the class to suggest connections between American culture and other sports. Could Roth have written a similar essay using football? What about that great urban sport, basketball? Could any students in the class use basketball to make the same case Roth makes? This shift could lead to interesting class debate and also provide a useful exercise in analogy.

Generating Writing

Ask your class to consider the connection Roth makes between baseball and education. They might then write an essay in which they describe a favorite childhood sport or game and show how it helped them develop educational skills for later in life.

WRITING ABOUT THE CHAPTER

1. If you asked your class to try the Writing-before-Reading exercise, they could now go back to it and rewrite their essay with the selections in mind. They should pay special attention to each writer's way of demonstrating the influence baseball (or sports in general) had on his or her life, either emotionally or intellectually. Not everyone plays baseball or participates in sports, and we need to remind students that in none of these essays does playing ball well really matter. What matters is the meaning of sports in the individual life.

2. Ask your class to go back and reread the remark by Elting E. Morison in the epigraphs. Though he never did so, Morison imagines developing a college course on baseball. He doesn't mean a course coaching skills and rules, but one examining baseball as an integral part of American studies. Invite students to suppose they were asked by one of the college deans to design such a course (using baseball or a sport you find more important). They should write an essay (it could be an interesting group assignment) outlining their course's content, texts they'd use, and their intellectual objectives.

Perspectives on Gender

The Feminist Movement Today

Vivian Gornick, Who Says We Haven't Made
a Revolution?: A Feminist Takes Stock

bell hooks, Feminism: A Transformational Politic

Nancy Mairs, A Letter to Matthew

WORKING WITH THE CHAPTER

The selections and epigraphs in this chapter provide an opportunity for you and your students to discuss the successes of the feminist movement, and to look ahead to the challenges that remain. Vivian Gornick, in "Who Says We Haven't Made a Revolution?," finds that feminism "has changed forever the way we think about ourselves" (para. 17). She gives several examples from everyday life to support her assertion that the basic concepts of feminism have entered the collective unconscious of contemporary America. Of course, as Gornick realizes, the mere fact that more men "pay lip service to feminism" does not mean that the revolution has been won. Nancy Mairs points out in "A Letter to Matthew" that the criticisms of patriarchy Virginia Woolf made in 1938 are still painfully relevant today. Mairs, like Gornick, draws her support from everyday life. But the example of Aunt Helen and Uncle Ted illustrates the insidious presence of sexism in seemingly benign situations.

Both Gornick and Mairs are college professors. Their pieces represent the perspective of feminists within the academy. But an equally long tradition of feminism lies outside the academy, and recognizing these other voices is a vital part of the feminist movement today. Barbara Ehrenreich sees the "next great wave of feminism" rising from "the pink-collar ghettos and the blue-collar suburbs, the housing developments and the trailer parks." These feminists — lower-class women and women of color — bring to the feminist movement a message whose time has come. The feminist movement can no longer afford to remain, Esther Ngan-Ling Chow writes, "predominantly white and middle class." The domination of the feminist movement by these women can be seen as a repetition of patriarchal patterns of oppression, Audre Lorde points out in an epigraph to this unit. It is often true, the article by bell hooks makes clear, that "oppressed and oppressor share the same gender."

The intent of the new wave of feminists is not to cast blame, but rather to recast feminism in a new and more productive mold. When feminists communicate only with others who share their perspective and experiences, the possibilities for growth are limited. bell hooks proposes an end to the "separation of grass-roots ways of sharing feminist thinking across kitchen tables from the sphere where much of that thinking is generated, the academy." Direct contact between women of many life experiences helps to keep fresh the realization that oppression isn't just something external to fight against but also something within ourselves. Or, Rosario Morales says in her essay "We're All in the Same Boat," "I'm saying that the basis of our unity is that in the most important way we are all in the same boat   all subjected to the violent pernicious ideas we have learned to hate that we must all   struggle against them and exchange ways and means hints and how tos that only some of us are victims of sexism only some of us are victims of racism   of the directed arrows of oppression   but all of us are   sexist   racist   all of us." (Reprinted in *This Bridge Called My Back: Writings by Radical Women of Color,* edited by Cherríe Moraga and Gloria Anzaldua, published by Women of Color Press [1983].)

Teaching Strategies

Because the topic of feminism can raise a lot of defenses, it is often best not to come on too strong right at first when teaching such a chapter. You will have to decide for yourself, of course, where you stand on the issue, and whether or not you want to make that position clear from the beginning. But your stance is obviously not the only one to consider here. Often in discussions of potentially divisive topics such as feminism a few very vocal students will dominate the discussion, and everyone else will just watch, maybe at most nodding encouragement when someone else voices their opinion for them. Unfortunately, some of the subtlest and most insightful thoughts go unvoiced once such a dynamic gets established in the classroom. For this reason, it's a good idea to use any tricks you have up your sleeve to hear as many voices as possible in every class period devoted to feminism. The technique described at the beginning of Working with the Selections before the Vivian Gornick selection is one way to get their voice boxes warmed up right away. Another technique you might try as soon as you notice that a few students are beginning to dominate the discussion is to stop the discussion in midstream and instruct everyone to get out a pen and paper and freewrite a response to a question that you have drawn from the interrupted discussion. This technique will give everyone a chance to voice an individual opinion, at least on paper, and you can call on a few of the quiet ones whose eyes have been speaking volumes while their mouths remained shut to read theirs out loud to the class.

A Writing-before-Reading Exercise

Before your students read the epigraphs and selections in this chapter, it might be a good idea to provide an opportunity for them to think of their own evidence for and against the idea that the feminist movement's issues are outmoded. Many students believe, for instance, that because women have the vote the feminist revolution has accomplished its aims, and that feminists should quit complaining. Even Vivian Gornick, in her youth, considered women's rights an issue that was "over and done with." Others, particularly female students, will claim, quite sincerely, that *they* have never been discriminated against because of their gender. Even Nancy Mairs admits that "for many years I held back from calling myself a feminist because I couldn't conceive problems I hadn't experienced." This writing exercise should get them started thinking about areas where improvement is long overdue.

Ask your students to write a draft of an essay in which they explore answers to the question, "Has the feminist movement outlived its usefulness?" To answer this question, your student writers will have to decide what the aims of such a movement might be. Then they will have to decide, from personal knowledge, whether these aims have been accomplished. You might want to remind them to consider all spheres of their lives. The family circle: What does their family expect from the brothers? from the sisters? What is the mother's role? the father's? The workplace: Have they ever experienced discrimination on the job? Does the boss, or do the customers, treat male and female employees differently? Have they noticed discrimination in places where they do business? Have they noticed that some restaurants hire mostly waitresses and other restaurants mostly waiters? Why? School: Who does most of the talking in their classes? How do their instructors respond to comments by male students? by female students? Are there any classes in which members of one gender or the other feel out of place? What causes this feeling? And the social sphere: How do women show men that they are interested in them? How do men show women the same thing? What are the unwritten rules about who calls whom? Who does most of the talking on dates? Have they encountered a double standard in sexual intimacy? You might also ask them to consider data they have picked up in the news about such things as equal pay for equal work, rape and its legal ramifications, domestic violence, and so on. Let this be an opportunity for them to explore, individually and in writing, as many avenues as possible to answer the initial question in a way that is satisfactory to them — at least until they read the selections and discuss them in class.

WORKING WITH THE SELECTIONS

Vivian Gornick

Who Says We Haven't Made a Revolution?: A Feminist Takes Stock

Teaching Strategies

You might want to start your discussion of Vivian Gornick's essay by taking the roll; ask your students to give an adjective describing that essay when their name is called. No one is to offer an adjective that has already been said. We learned this opening gambit from Victor Squitieri, who teaches at the University of California at Berkeley. It is particularly effective with pieces such as this one by Vivian Gornick, which are likely to produce widely varied responses. You may find that many of your students' responses contradict each other. One might say "optimistic" and another "pessimistic." One might say "naive" and another "realistic." Although Vivian Gornick's prose is fairly accessible, students might have a hard time pinning down her main point. Or perhaps they will identify their difficulty as a matter of tone.

If it turns out that many of their responses contradict each other, you may want to ask the class to trace the essay's progression. As you go through the essay, marking shifts, say, between the thrill of the 1970s and the sobering 1980s, or between despair at the resistance to change and faith in the possibility of change, your students may start to get a handle on what's unusual about this essay. The progression here is not one of ideas. She gives what she considers the main idea of feminism, in plain English, early in the essay: "It was so simple, really: the idea that men by nature take their brains seriously, and women by nature do not, is a learned one; it serves the culture; from that central piece of information all else follows." Whereas the other authors in this chapter are thinking in writing about patriarchal structure and its implications, the mechanism of oppression, and other weighty ideas, Gornick takes the *ideas* for granted. It's the progression in the *response* to those ideas that she traces.

Of course, you don't want your students to take this as a criticism of Gornick, as if she had tried to do what the others were doing but failed. Ask the students to identify Gornick's purpose in writing this essay in this way: What explanation can they find in the essay that might tell them why she chose to trace the response rather than the ideas? Your students should notice that Gornick emphasizes the repetition of the same ideas through history: the same ideas can find a fresh response over and over, among new generations of people. You or some of your students may want to question her feeling about recycled ideas — to present a history of feminism as an evolution rather than a sort of whirlpool. This is certainly one point on which Gornick can be challenged. But if one accepts her premise, then the other decisions she made while composing her essay do follow logically.

Once your class comes to realize Gornick's guiding principle, you might want to ask them *whose* response she is tracing. She describes a changing social climate, but at the same time she traces changes inside herself. Ask students to explain the relationship between Gornick's moods and those of the feminist movement as a whole. What in her essay justifies an identification between the individual and the movement as a whole? You might want to point out the significant shift in the personal pronoun from her first title (for her *Village Voice* article, "The Next Great Moment in History Is Theirs") to her present title ("Who Says We Haven't Made a Revolution?: A Feminist Takes Stock"). You may also want to encourage them to discuss the connection between the groups of women that Gornick finds so essential and the "social explanation of how their lives have taken shape" that provides the content of their discussions.

You will probably also want to spend class time reviewing the anecdotes Gornick supplies as evidence of the movement's success. Can they think of any other pieces of evidence that feminism has altered the general public's way of thinking? How do the examples supplied by Gornick and your students jibe with the idea of the circular pattern of the feminist movement? Don't these examples suggest a sense of forward progression instead? You might want to direct your students' attention to the principle she mentions in paragraph 42: "two steps forward, one step back." Do they find this metaphor more or less useful than the recycling metaphor to describe the feminist movement? to describe the structure of her essay? In this context, you might also want to encourage them to critique the anecdotes she cites as evidence of progress. Do they see evidence in the anecdotes themselves that progress is not the only principle being illustrated?

Additional Activities

In discussing the movie *All About Eve*, Gornick writes that it would be "inconceivable" that a speech such as the one delivered by Margo Channing "would be written into an American movie today." You may want to rent *All About Eve* and show it to your students some evening when you can reserve a room with a VCR. After the film, ask students to discuss their reactions to the scene in question. Then have them brainstorm titles of more contemporary films with sexist scenes, speeches, or premises. These should not be hard to come up with. This activity could lead naturally into a writing assignment, in which students choose a recent movie and analyze it as part of an effort to test Gornick's assertion about the feminist movement's effect on the film industry.

To test Gornick's assertion that Elizabeth Cady Stanton said one hundred years ago what modern feminists are now saying, you might want to teach Stanton's "Declaration of Sentiments and Resolutions" along with the feminist essays in this chapter.

Vivian Gornick also speaks about the power of language. She writes that feminism has released generations of women from "a collective lifetime of silence." Throughout the essay Gornick emphasizes talk shared by groups of women engaged in exploring a social explanation of their treatment and self-image as women. Gornick's essay would work well together with the unit on Language and Politics.

Generating Writing

1. You might want to assign an essay in which students explore Gornick's extended metaphor drawn from psychoanalysis. How and for what reasons is this metaphor effective and appropriate? Instruct them to apply the insights gained from the metaphor to the essay as a whole.

2. Gornick opens her essay with an example of role reversal, which she attributes to the feminist movement: she and a male colleague find themselves ardently supporting

values that are traditionally supported by members of the other gender. Much later in the essay, she quotes a friend as saying, "Reversed positions is not what I've been working for." Ask students to write an essay exploring the usefulness of role reversal, as a concept, as a goal, and so on. What *is* Gornick's position on role reversal? Have students take their own position on role reversal as well, rather than limiting themselves to discovering and explaining Gornick's belief.

bell hooks

Feminism: A Transformational Politic

Teaching Strategies

Although bell hooks is more radical than Vivian Gornick, your class may be more receptive to her essay than they were to Gornick's — or at least some members of your class will be. Her strategy of focusing on the overall structure of domination rather than on patriarchal domination will give everyone a way of participating in the discussion. Groups — such as women of color — who have traditionally felt ignored by the feminist movement, and groups, such as men, who have traditionally felt under attack by the feminist movement, should be able to discover a common goal in the ideas expressed in her essay. The ensuing class discussion, in which everyone has a stake and a voice, can contribute to the kind of transformation that hooks proposes.

This is not to say that reading and discussing this selection is easy. Despite hooks's declared "emphasis on communicating feminist thinking, feminist theory, in a way that can be easily understood," it is sometimes difficult to follow her argument. Sometimes she advocates attention to the large and complex structure of domination, and at other times she advocates the time-honored feminist focus on sexism. Ask students to identify what it is about feminism that hooks wants to keep, and what she'd like to see changed. You may want to write their suggestions on the chalkboard, reserving half for the feminist ideas that hooks would like to preserve, and half for the ways in which she'd like to transform feminism. When you have recorded several suggestions, ask students to make more general statements about the ideas on each side of the blackboard. They may notice that hooks wishes to keep the method of feminism while transforming the content. Consciousness-raising, for example, has always been counted among the strengths of the feminist movement, and hooks *does* advocate "the work of education for critical consciousness (usually called consciousness-raising)." She adds, however, that this education must not be limited to "identifying the ways men oppress and exploit women." The content of the education must be expanded, and hooks outlines the areas that still need attention. Your students must understand that hooks is not trying "to dissuade people of color from being engaged in the feminist movement," but rather that she believes that transforming ourselves and society depends on recognizing larger paradigms of domination.

You may want to initiate a discussion, in which your students draw on the observations by bell hooks and their own experience, of the many and varied forms of oppression that are encountered in everyday life. Why would hooks say that sexism is the "form of domination we are most likely to encounter in an ongoing way in everyday life"? Do your students agree? If women of color are in your class, do they find that they encounter racism or sexism most often? Which is more blatant? What is it about our culture's stereotypes about women and, say, blacks, which might make one form of bigotry more or less noticeable than the other? Does "not noticeable" equal "not present"? Which forms of oppression seem most insidious to them?

bell hooks draws our attention several times in the essay to the home environment. Ask students to identify some reasons for her focus on the home and family. In addition to the insights provided by hooks on this subject, and the insights the students bring from their own experience, you might want to direct them to "A Question of Language," by Gloria Naylor (see Chapter 34). This essay might help bring out an idea that is only implied in the essay by hooks, that the members of a family share an ethnic identity, so that children often do not encounter ethnic difference and ethnic discrimination until they leave the home. Sometimes, as with Naylor, the moment of recognition of racial difference does not come until as late as the third grade. Because most families have both male and female members, however, recognition of gender difference and discrimination usually occurs much earlier in a child's life. You might ask your students if they remember the moment when they first realized their gender or their race. Have them recount the experience. You might also ask them what other differences between racism and sexism stem from the fact that people of the same race but different genders share the same home. Hooks brings up the idea that caring and connection coexist with domination in the home: what are the implications of this insight when coupled with the discoveries your class has made about the differences between racial and gender oppression?

Additional Activities

It would be productive to have your students compare and contrast the guiding principles of the essays by Vivian Gornick and bell hooks. What does each see as the "basis for our coming together"? How does each author define the role of men in the feminist movement? What is the connection between the individual and the group, the personal and the social, in each essay? How does the hooks essay bring to the surface, and question, some of the assumptions that underlie Gornick's essay?

Generating Writing

1. In paragraph 19, hooks puts these clauses together in apposition: "we must first learn how to be in solidarity, how to struggle with one another." Direct your students to this sentence, and ask them to think about how these two seemingly opposite thoughts can be yoked in this way and, more important, *why* they are brought together in this way. Have them find other seeming contradictions or opposing forces at work in this selection, and write an essay exploring the function of these contradictions. How does the fact that such sentiments struggle with each other on the page work with hooks's ideas about the path to transformation?

2. Suggest that your students analyze all the structures of dominance in which they play a part. Of course, structures of dominance are very complex and far-reaching, and many seem so natural that we no longer even notice them. But encourage those who choose to take on this analysis to be as thorough as possible. Make sure that they consider race, class, and gender, and that they think about their family of origin (as well as their own family, if they are married or have children or both), and about their work, school, sports, friendships, and intimate relationships. You might adapt an idea from bell hooks and extend this assignment into a collaborative writing project, in which students from diverse backgrounds "concentrate on working out their status in terms of sex, race, and class," using the material generated from their small-group discussion to collaborate on an essay exploring patterns of domination.

Nancy Mairs

A Letter to Matthew

Teaching Strategies

Nancy Mairs' letter to her fourteen-year-old son makes several of the leading concepts in this chapter quite clear-and accessible. She talks about the evils of sexism in personal everyday language, but also explores the larger reasons that make everyday sexism so evil. Your students may have mixed reactions to her tone. She's equally open with her praise and her censure, which some students might find surprisingly harsh, but others will find refreshing. However they respond to her tone, though, they will have a hard time missing the implications of her words.

Start, perhaps, with Mairs's explanation of when and why she dislikes her son, for Mairs herself covers the censure before the praise. Make sure students understand that she does not dislike his cockiness and quickness to pronounce judgments merely because they are traits traditionally designated male. Have them explain the larger consequences of such traits, as Mairs sees them. How does Mairs move from "Calculus is a waste of time" to the tension between America and the Soviet Union? Where else in the essay does Mairs accomplish similar transitions from individual men to crises of global scope? How, for instance, does Mairs place the blame for Vietnam and Central America on patriarchy?

You might use this opening as a way into discussing the juncture of the personal and the political in this essay. The very form of the essay — a letter — points to its grounding in the personal realm. Mairs hopes to effect a transformation in one man — her son — as a small but significant part of a transformation of the world. Have students discuss the ways in which personal perceptions and decisions determine the larger structures of society. Have them discuss how each realm — the individual and the social — functions in this essay. Her examples are mostly individual: she writes at great length about the relationship between Aunt Helen and Uncle Ted. But she also reminds readers that their relationship is not unique: millions of other couples play out the same basic interactions. She doesn't blame the individual — Matthew's aunt and uncle — but she does believe in the efficacy of individual action; otherwise, she wouldn't be writing this letter to her son.

This essay gains its effect partly from dealing with attitudes that are usually considered benign forms of sexism: when men put women on a pedestal or show that they feel protective toward women, students often don't recognize these acts as symptoms of sexism. And although Mairs mentions rape and domestic violence, she focuses mainly on these seemingly innocent "behaviors and attitudes which suggest that [the men who think and behave in these ways] share a set of cultural assumptions about male power and rights which devalue women's lives." This focus might help to enlighten students who still believe, even after having read Gornick and hooks, that the feminist movement is an anachronism.

Additional Activities

Many fertile connections tie Nancy Mairs's letter to her son to other selections in *The Winchester Reader*. Her letter helps reveal the mechanism behind "us-and-them" thinking, making this a good piece to teach together with the selections in Chapter 8, "Bridging Distances." Her discussion of Aunt Helen's daily life makes a nice counterpoint to Thomas Edison's view of "women's work" in "The Woman of the Future" (see Chapter 21). Because Mairs insists on the timeliness of Virginia Woolf's insights on sexism, her letter to Matthew might be used to ward off possible attacks on Woolf when your class reads "Thoughts on Peace in an Air Raid" (see Chapter 22). Mairs's letter to her son, in whom she has so much faith, also interacts beautifully with "Mothers and Sons," by Barbara Lazear Ascher (see Chapter 19). Finally, you might want to teach Opal Palmer Adisa's poem "I Will Not Let

Them Take You" — which is addressed to Adisa's son Jawara — in conjunction with Mairs's letter to her son. Both mothers demonstrate love and fierceness, and both look forward to a future that will be better than the present time in which they and their sons are living. In class, you might want to ask what different race (not an issue to Mairs) makes in the poem. How does the fact that Adisa's son is black affect the tone of the poem? You might also want to address questions of genre; what are the different constraints and possibilities of the letter and the poem as formal structures?

I Will Not Let Them Take You
(for Jawara)

tell them
tell them loud and clear
i will not let them
take you

tell them
tell them your mother is
a crazy jamaican woman
who will wage war
for her children
so tell them
tell them now
i will not surrender
you to the streets
i will not give you over
to dope dealers
i will not relinquish
you to the cops
who target you because
you are black and male
i will not let
you slip through
the school system
which acts as if
you are unteachable

so tell them
tell them
you have a mother
who remembers
all the fears
all the pain
all the discomfort
she endured in getting
you here
and she will not give you up
will not give you up
to no one
but the love of life
and to help shape
the dreams
of our people
tell them
tell them
now

— Opal Palmer Adisa

Generating Writing

1. Mairs ironically suggests that "one answer to Mr. Buckley's question might be that women have it better than men." Of course, she hastens to explain that although women may be better off psychologically, they are at a disadvantage politically, legally, financially, and so on. Suggest that students keep in mind this important caveat if they choose this essay assignment: Have them write an essay in which they describe some advantages of being a woman in contemporary America. Have them remember Mairs's arguments against the idea that being placed on a pedestal or protected by men is an advantage. Instruct them to scrutinize any possible advantages they can come up with before concluding that they are indeed advantages.

2. Some students might like to try their hand at writing a letter to a Matthew in their own lives — one of their own children, a child they may have some day, or a younger sibling or other relative. Have them draw on the techniques Mairs uses, such as supporting details for her assertions, and a tone that's appropriate to the genre and audience. Ask them to replicate if they can the connection between personal action and social consequences.

WRITING ABOUT THE CHAPTER

1. bell hooks ends her essay by discussing love as a catalyst, a powerful force against domination. Suggest to students that they write an essay exploring the connection between the selections by bell hooks and Nancy Mairs, focusing on the idea of the power of love. How does this idea tie in with the idea, repeated or implied in all three essays in this unit, that transforming society requires transforming ourselves?

2. Both bell hooks and Nancy Mairs suggest a connection between women and children, hooks to illustrate the structure of dominance and Mairs to help her son imagine what it's like to be a woman. Have students draw on childhood memories of powerlessness to tap into a gut-level understanding of the structure of oppression. Suggest that they write an essay on domination, focusing on a particularly vivid and appropriate childhood memory as the primary evidence for their assertion about domination.

3. Now that they have read the entire chapter, have students revise (or, as hooks would say, "revision," rethink, reexamine) the draft they wrote before reading the chapter. If they did as they were instructed, exploring all possible avenues in their draft, and if they thought about the points made by the authors in this chapter, they should now have a lot of raw material from which to draw for a polished essay on the timeliness of the feminist movement. At this stage in composing, they may wish to refocus their essay around an answer to the question of what ideas and actions are necessary at this time.

19

Mothers

Gloria Steinem, Ruth's Song (Because She Could Not Sing It)
Alice Walker, In Search of Our Mothers' Gardens
Barbara Lazear Ascher, Mothers and Sons

WORKING WITH THE CHAPTER

The initial miracle of creation is just the first of countless acts of creation performed by each and every mother. In Marguerite Duras's graphic account of bearing and nurturing children, the physical body of the mother becomes the matter from which children are created: "Motherhood means that a woman gives her body over to her child, her children; they're on her as they might be on a hill, in a garden; they devour her, hit her, sleep on her; and she lets herself be devoured." Our mothers also help to create our personalities. To some extent we all define ourselves according to and against the models provided by our mothers as we were growing up.

And our mothers play a large part, for better or worse, in creating our futures. As Marilyn French writes, "Women, not men, are considered responsible for the children of Western society and are blamed for our children's fates." Gloria Steinem's mother and Alice Walker's mother worked against almost insuperable odds to ensure a better life for their children than they themselves had had. For their mothers, as for Russell Baker's mother, life was indeed "combat," and each was "a formidable woman" in her own way. In a larger sense mothers also create the future of humanity. Barbara Lazear Ascher argues that mothers have it in their power either to perpetuate or to eradicate sexism, depending on the ways in which they choose to raise their sons.

Each of the selections in this chapter represents a woman's attempt to give voice to the messages of mothers — whether their own or others' — who have been silenced by society. In this respect the essays in this chapter are arranged from the most personal to the most general. Gloria Steinem unravels the mystery of her own mother's life; she uses Ruth's life as the main exhibit in a case against society's treatment of women. Alice Walker focuses primarily on black women artists — of her mother's, grandmother's, and great-grandmother's generations — in her search for signs of the creative spirit that was beaten and smothered but not killed. The story of her own mother's life is told as one thread among the many that make up the tapestry of women's creativity. Like Steinem's, Walker's essay is a "personal account that is yet shared." Although Steinem and Walker celebrate mothers and Barbara Lazear Ascher mainly attacks them, Ascher's ultimate goal is a world in which mothers, and all women, will be able to speak their minds and express their needs. Her final paragraph implies that the men who "feign ignorance and declare that they just don't know what women want" do so because they have been led to believe that women don't want anything.

Ascher writes her essay on behalf of "all of our daughters and daughters-in-law." You might initiate a discussion of the topic of daughters in these selections about mothers. What do the daughters receive from their explorations of their mothers' lives? How do their own lives at once mirror and surpass the lives of their mothers? In a sense all three authors trace a matrilineal line of descent. What are some of the concerns, themes, and tropes, which might be alien to a patriarchal account, that distinguish their essays?

A Writing-before-Reading Exercise

Ask students to write an exploratory draft in which each of them tries to come to an understanding of his or her mother as a person. To do this each student may want to reconstruct a sense of what his or her mother's life was like before any of her children were born. Have them include any anecdotes they might have heard about her youth. Have them consider the following questions: How does her life seem to have changed since her children were born? What were her youthful aspirations? How have those aspirations changed over the years? Have them sort through their personal memories of their mother as they were growing up. Which of these would they tell to someone if they were trying to capture the essence of their mother's identity?

WORKING WITH THE SELECTIONS

Gloria Steinem

Ruth's Song (Because She Could Not Sing It)

Teaching Strategies

In "Ruth's Song," Gloria Steinem writes the story of her mother's life. When students read the anecdotes about eight-year-old Gloria providing meals of "bologna sandwiches and dime pies," or twelve-year-old Gloria spending Thanksgiving protecting her mother from her own hallucinations, they may feel that Steinem's childhood was horrifying but unique. By the time they finish the essay, however, they should realize that Steinem is writing here about "patterns women share." You might start by asking what Steinem learns in the course of this essay. Students should notice, and be able to discuss, Steinem's revelations about our society's treatment of women, about her mother as a person and about herself.

If students are not noticing the importance of social analysis in this essay, you might prompt them to do so by asking why Steinem opens the essay with the mystery of her uncle who suddenly changed. How is this story set up in relation to the main story of her mother's transformation? What are the points of similarity and difference between the two stories? Do students see the implications of the fact that "exterior events were never suggested as reason enough" for her mother's problems? Ask students to analyze the causes of Ruth's breakdown and subsequent mental problems, drawing on what Steinem both says and implies about her mother and the society at large. Ask them which parts of Ruth's story are not merely "personal or accidental." Can they name other women who have given up their own careers for their husbands or children? Help them to see, if they do not already know, how pervasive are the assumptions of patriarchy: even a seemingly objective field such as medical science will pronounce a woman such as Ruth "recovered" if "she was able to take care of my sister again, to move away from the city and the job she loved, and to work with my father at an isolated rural lake in Michigan." Of what does such a "recovery" consist?

To understand the patterns women share, Steinem must also understand her mother "as a person." She does some detective work and pieces together the facts of her mother's life. Some of these episodes of her mother's life are presented *as* pieces: Steinem lists them but doesn't explicitly synthesize them. Draw students' attention to the three lists of anecdotes in this essay: the list of brief memories from Gloria's childhood living alone with her mother; the list of verbal snapshots of the former Ruth, the woman Steinem "had never known"; and the list of "moments of spirit or humor." Have students come up with statements that generalize from the particulars provided in each list. A development of these generalizations would also make a good essay topic.

There is a series of paragraphs beginning with the word *I.* You will probably want to spend some class time tracing the evolution in Steinem's feelings toward her mother as expressed in this essay. Look at the shift in emphasis expressed in the following brief paragraph: "I'm no longer obsessed, as I was for many years, with the fear that I would end up in a house like that one in Toledo. Now, I'm obsessed instead with the things I could have done for my mother while she was alive, or the things I should have said." How does she come to understand and sympathize with her mother? What are the similarities between mother and daughter? What does Steinem learn about herself in the process of exploring her mother's story?

Additional Activities

As a journal assignment or freewriting topic, you might want to pose the following question: Why does Steinem refer to her mother sometimes as "Ruth" and at other times as "my mother"? See if students can find a pattern in her ways of referring to her mother, and a reason for the pattern.

"Ruth's Song" could be taught with good results along with "No Name Woman," by Maxine Hong Kingston, and "Granddaddy," by Itabari Njeri (both selections are in Chapter 12, "Family Stories"). All three essayists attempt to unravel a family secret, and all three discover truths not only about their families but also about their cultures.

Generating Writing

1. The subtitle of this essay is "Because She Could Not Sing It." For the most part it is true that Steinem speaks for her mother, who died before the essay was written, in "Ruth's Song." There is one passage, however, set off from the text but embedded in it, in which Ruth speaks in the first person. Have students write an essay exploring the significance of this story *in this form.* Why, among all of the anecdotes from her mother's life, does Steinem decide to quote her mother directly on this one? Students may also like to look at the short episode in which Ruth fills in both her own and her daughter's answers to a quiz that was composed by Steinem. What is the significance of this anecdote? Do they hear Ruth's own voice, or see her own handwriting, anywhere else in the essay? To what extent and in what ways does Ruth assert herself despite the subtitle?

2. Steinem writes that she "did not blame" her father for leaving her mother when Steinem was only eight years old. Have students reread the essay in search of clues to the father's personality, and Steinem's feelings toward him. In the context of her critique of patriarchy, how are we to take her claim that she doesn't blame her father? Suggest that they also consider the clues about Steinem's paternal grandmother, Pauline. How might her father's upbringing have shaped his personality? In this context, students might want to consider insights from "Mothers and Sons," by Barbara Lazear Ascher.

Alice Walker

In Search of Our Mothers' Gardens

Teaching Strategies

Before Alice Walker's own voice is heard in her essay, she quotes not only Marilou Awiakta but also Jean Toomer. Because Awiakta's poem "Motheroot" might just as easily serve as an epigraph to "Ruth's Song," you may want to treat it in the context of a discussion of the similarities between the essays by Steinem and Walker. But you will probably want to begin your discussion of Walker's essay by considering the material by and about Toomer, because this material might be a stumbling block to students' understanding of "In Search of Our Mothers' Gardens."

Toomer has no trouble speaking in the first person, talking, by his own estimate, "beautifully" about the "nature and temperament" of a black prostitute who is asleep in his lap. Walker, on the other hand, is less direct. She more or less backs into her essay. Students might be a little confused by the beginning of her essay: they may not understand, for instance, that Walker rejects the label of "Saints" as it was applied to suffering women such as the women Toomer met on his travels. Help them to understand the significance of the fact that it is "men" who "lit candles to celebrate the emptiness that remained, as people do who enter a beautiful but vacant space to resurrect a God." Help them to understand that Walker sets up Toomer's interpretation of these women, whom she identifies as "our mothers and grandmothers," in order to critique it, and to substitute a reading by which these women are seen not as "Saints" but as "Artists."

Walker paints a vivid picture of the obstacles faced by creative black women in her grandmother's time. But she believes that instead of killing their artistic spirit outright, the overseers and legislators only forced that spirit to take a more circuitous route to reach the light. Have students list some of the forms taken by these women's "living creativity" in their own lifetimes. And have them explore the legacy these women passed on to their daughters. What, precisely, can a woman who is not allowed to own property, or a woman who hasn't a moment "to unravel her private thoughts," leave to her children?

You may want to use the Walker essay as the jumping-off point for a discussion of high and low culture. After all, Walker writes that in our search for evidence of our mothers' creativity "we have constantly looked high, when we should have looked high — and low." What genres would students characterize as "low culture"? How many of these genres are traditionally characterized as feminine? Certainly the quilt and the flowers mentioned by Walker fit into a realm traditionally relegated to women. In fact, neither sewing nor gardening is conventionally considered in the category of art at all. What are the artistic fields in which women can be said to dominate?

Of course, you will not want students to come away from this essay with the impression that it is merely, or even mostly, an attack on patriarchy. It is also an expression of respect and gratitude toward the women who have come before us, women who "knew what we / Must know / Without knowing a page / Of it / Themselves." Alice Walker celebrates the persistent spirit of such women, whose legacy has empowered writers such as Walker herself.

Additional Activities

Walker's discussion of Phillis Wheatley provides a good interconnection with Chapter 23, "Conflicting Loyalties." She draws on Virginia Woolf's *A Room of One's Own* to explain why female writers such as Wheatley, Zora Neale Hurston, and Nella Larsen might be affected by "contrary instincts." You and your students may find signs of internal struggle or ambivalence in many of the selections written by people of color in this manual. If so, you might want to encourage students to be sensitive to the cultural sources of this conflict.

In this essay Walker is working against several dominant stereotypes concerning women's creativity. According to one stereotype, men produce, whereas women merely reproduce. Walker challenges this stereotype in her closing line: "Perhaps in more than Phillis Wheatley's biological life is her mother's signature made clear." Another popular stereotype casts men in the role of artists and women as works of art. When Jean Toomer describes the prostitute as she lies asleep and therefore is incapable of speaking for herself, she creates her in an image that may very well clash with her own unheard account of herself. The images she chooses — the vacant space that suggests a receptacle and the "vacant and fallow field" that lies ready to be plowed — suggest a male fantasy about female passivity. In the context of your discussion of the male artist defining the passive female, you might want to teach the poem "Jenny," by Dante Gabriel Rossetti, included here in the manual. The narrator of this poem, like Toomer, is talking to a prostitute who lies asleep in his lap. Also like Toomer, he attributes his own thoughts and feelings about Jenny to Jenny herself.

Jenny

"Vengeance of Jenny's case! Fie on her! Never name her, child!" — (Mrs. Quickly)

LAZY laughing languid Jenny,
Fond of a kiss and fond of a guinea,
Whose head upon my knee to-night
Rests for a while, as if grown light
With all our dances and the sound
To which the wild tunes spun you round:
Fair Jenny mine, the thoughtless queen
Of kisses which the blush between
Could hardly make much daintier;
Whose eyes are as blue skies, whose hair   10
Is countless gold incomparable:
Fresh flower, scarce touched with signs that tell
Of Love's exuberant hotbed: — Nay,
Poor flower left torn since yesterday
Until to-morrow leave you bare;
Poor handful of bright spring-water
Flung in the whirlpool's shrieking face;
Poor shameful Jenny, full of grace
Thus with your head upon my knee; —
Whose person or whose purse may be   20
The lodestar of your reverie?

This room of yours, my Jenny, looks
A change from mine so full of books,
Whose serried ranks hold fast, forsooth,
So many captive hours of youth, —
The hours they thieve from day and night
To make one's cherished work come right,
And leave it wrong for all their theft,
Even as to-night my work was left:
Until I vowed that since my brain   30
And eyes of dancing seemed so fain,
My feet should have some dancing too: —
And thus it was I met with you.
Well, I suppose 'twas hard to part,
For here I am. And now, sweetheart,
You seem too tired to get to bed.

It was a careless life I led
When rooms like this were scarce so strange
Not long ago. What breeds the change, —
The many aims or the few years?   40

Because to-night it all appears
Something I do not know again.

The cloud's not danced out of my brain —
The cloud that made it turn and swim
While hour by hour the books grew dim.
Why, Jenny, as I watch you there, —
For all your wealth of loosened hair,
Your silk ungirdled and unlac'd
And warm sweets open to the waist,
All golden in the lamplight's gleam, —   50
You know not what a book you seem,
Half-read by lightning in a dream!
How should you know, my Jenny? Nay,
And I should be ashamed to say: —
Poor beauty, so well worth a kiss!
But while my thought runs on like this
With wasteful whims more than enough,
I wonder what you're thinking of.

If of myself you think at all,
What is the thought? — conjectural   60
On sorry matters best unsolved? —

Or inly is each grace resolved
To fit me with a lure? — or (sad
To think!) perhaps you're merely glad
That I'm not drunk or ruffianly
And let you rest upon my knee.

For sometimes, were the truth confess'd,
You're thankful for a little rest, —
Glad from the crush to rest within,
From the heart-sickness and the din   70
Where envy's voice at virtue's pitch
Mocks you because your gown is rich;
And from the pale girl's dumb rebuke,
Whose ill-clad grace and toil-worn look
Proclaim the strength that keeps her weak
And other nights than yours bespeak;
And from the wise unchildish elf,
To schoolmate lesser than himself,
Pointing you out, what thing you are: —
Yes, from the daily jeer and jar,   80
From shame and shame's outbraving too,
Is rest not sometimes sweet to you? —
But most from the hatefulness of man
Who spares not to end what he began,
Whose acts are ill and his speech ill,
Who, having used you at his will,
Thrusts you aside, as when I dine
I serve the dishes and the wine.

Well, handsome Jenny mine, sit up:
I've filled our glasses, let us sup,   90
And do not let me think of you,
Lest shame of yours suffice for two.
What, still so tired? Well, well then, keep
Your head there, so you do not sleep;
But that the weariness may pass
And leave you merry, take this glass.
Ah! lazy lily hand, more bless'd

If ne'er in rings it had been dress'd
Nor ever by a glove conceal'd!

Behold the lilies of the field,   100
They toil not neither do they spin;
(So doth the ancient text begin, —
Not of such rest as one of these
Can share.) Another rest and ease
Along each summer-sated path
From its new lord the garden hath,
Than that whose spring in blessings ran
Which praised the bounteous husbandman,
Ere yet, in days of hankering breath,
The lilies sickened unto death.   110

What, Jenny, are your lilies dead?
Aye, and the snow-white leaves are spread
Like winter on the garden-bed.
But you had roses left in May, —
They were not gone too. Jenny, nay,
But must your roses die, and those
Their purfled buds that should unclose?
Even so; the leaves are curled apart,
Still red as from the broken heart,
And here's the naked stem of thorns.   120

Nay, nay, mere words. Here nothing warns
As yet of winter. Sickness here
Or want alone could waken fear, —
Nothing but passion wrings a tear.
Except when there may rise unsought
Haply at times a passing thought
Of the old days which seem to be
Much older than any history
That is written in any book;
When she would lie in fields and look   130
Along the ground through the blown grass,
And wonder where the city was.
Far out of sight, whose broil and bale
They told her then for a child's tale.

Jenny, you know the city now.
A child can tell the tale there, how
Some things which are not yet enroll'd
In market-lists are bought and sold
Even till the early Sunday light,
When Saturday night is market-night   140
Everywhere, be it dry or wet,
And market-night in the Haymarket.
Our learned London children know
Poor Jenny, all your pride and woe,
Have seen your lifted silken skirt
Advertise dainties through the dirt;
Have seen your coach-wheels splash rebuke
On virtue; and have learned your look
When, wealth and health slipped past, you stare
Along the streets alone, and there,   150
Round the long park, across the bridge,
The cold lamps at the pavement's edge
Wind on together and apart,
A fiery serpent for your heart.

Let the thoughts pass, an empty cloud!
Suppose I were to think aloud, —
What if to her all this were said?
Why, as a volume seldom read
Being opened halfway shuts again,
So might the pages of her brain   160
Be parted at such words, and thence
Close back upon the dusty sense.
For is there hue or shape defin'd
In Jenny's desecrated mind,
Where all contagious currents meet,
A Lethe of the middle street?
Nay, it reflects not any face,
Nor sound is in its sluggish pace,
But as they coil those eddies clot,
And night and day remember not.   170

Why, Jenny, you're asleep at last! —
Asleep, poor Jenny, hard and fast, —
So young and soft and tired; so fair,
With chin thus nestled in your hair,
Mouth quiet, eyelids almost blue
As if some sky of dreams shone through!

Just as another woman sleeps!
Enough to throw one's thoughts in heaps
Of doubt and horror, — what to say
Or think, — this awful secret sway,   180
The potter's power over the clay!
Of the same lump (it has been said)
For honour and dishonour made,
Two sister vessels. Here is one.

My cousin Nell is fond of fun,
And fond of dress, and change, and praise.
So mere a woman in her ways:
And if her sweet eyes rich in youth
Are like her lips that tell the truth,
My cousin Nell is fond of love.   190
And she's the girl I'm proudest of.
Who does not prize her, guard her well?
The love of change, in cousin Nell,
Shall find the best and hold it dear;
The unconquered mirth turn quieter
Not through her own, through others' woe:
The conscious pride of beauty glow
Beside another's pride in her,
One little part of all they share.
For Love himself shall ripen these   200
In a kind soil to just increase
Through years of fertilizing peace.

Of the same lump (as it is said)
For honour and dishonour made,
Two sister vessels. Here is one.

It makes a goblin of the sun.

So pure, — so fall'n! How dare to think
Of the first common kindred link?
Yet, Jenny, till the world shall burn
It seems that all things take their turn;   210
And who shall say but this fair tree
May need, in changes that may be,

Your children's children's charity?
Scorned then, no doubt, as you are scorn'd!
Shall no man hold his pride forewarn'd
Till in the end, the Day of Days,
At Judgment, one of his own race,
As frail and lost as you, shall rise, —
His daughter, with his mother's eyes?

   How Jenny's clock ticks on the shelf!   220
Might not the dial scorn itself
That has such hours to register?
Yet as to me, even so to her
Are golden sun and silver moon,
In daily largesse of earth's boon,
Counted for life-coins to one tune.
And if, as blindfold fates are toss'd,
Through some one man this life be lost,
Shall soul not somehow pay for soul?

   Fair shines the gilded aureole   230
In which our highest painters place
Some living woman's simple face.
And the stilled features thus descried
As Jenny's long throat droops aside, —
The shadows where the cheeks are thin,
And pure wide curve from ear to chin, —
With Raffael's, Leonardo's hand
To show them to men's souls, might stand,
Whole ages long, the whole world through,
For preachings of what God can do.   240
What has man done here How atone,
Great God, for this which man has done?
And for the body and soul which by
Man's pitiless doom must now comply
With lifelong hell, what lullaby
Of sweet forgetful second birth
Remains? All dark. No sign on earth
What measure of God's rest endows
The many mansions of his house.

   If but a woman's heart might see   250
Such erring heart unerringly
For once! But that can never be.

   Like a rose shut in a book
In which pure women may not look,
For its base pages claim control
To crush the flower within the soul;
Where through each dead rose-leaf that clings,
Pale as transparent Psyche-wings,
To the vile text, are traced such things
As might make lady's cheek indeed   260
More than a living rose to read;
So nought save foolish foulness may
Watch with hard eyes the sure decay;
And so the life-blood of this rose,
Puddled with shameful knowledge, flows
Through leaves no chaste hand may unclose;
Yet still it keeps such faded show
Of when 'twas gathered long ago,
That the crushed petals' lovely grain,
The sweetness of the sanguine stain,   270
Seen of a woman's eyes, must make

Her pitiful heart, so prone to ache,
Love roses better for its sake: —
Only that this can never be: —
Even so unto her sex is she.

    Yet, Jenny, looking long at you,
The woman almost fades from view.
A cipher of man's changeless sum
Of lust, past, present, and to come,
Is left. A riddle that one shrinks   280
To challenge from the scornful sphinx.

    Like a toad within a stone
Seated while Time crumbles on;
Which sits there since the earth was curs'd
For Man's transgression at the first;
Which, living through all centuries,
Not once has seen the sun arise;
Whose life, to its cold circle charmed,
The earth's whole summers have not warmed;
Which always — whitherso the stone   290
Be flung — sits there, deaf, blind, alone
Aye, and shall not be driven out
Till that which shuts him round about
Break at the very Master's stroke,
And the dust thereof vanish as smoke,
And the seed of Man vanish as dust: —
Even so within this world is Lust.

    Come, come, what use in thoughts like this?
Poor little Jenny, good to kiss, —
You'd not believe by what strange roads   300
Thought travels, when your beauty goads
A man to-night to think of toads!
Jenny, wake up. . . . Why, there's the dawn!

    And there's an early waggon drawn
To market, and some sheep that jog
Bleating before a barking dog;
And the old streets come peering through
Another night that London knew;
And all as ghostlike as the lamps.

    So on the wings of day decamps   310
My last night's frolic. Glooms begin
To shiver off as lights creep in
Past the gauze curtains half drawn-to,
And the lamp's doubled shade grows blue, —
Your lamp, my Jenny, kept alight,
Like a wise virgin's, all one night!
And in the alcove coolly spread
Glimmers with dawn your empty bed;
And yonder your fair face I see
Reflected lying on my knee,   320
Where teems with first foreshadowings
Your pier-glass scrawled with diamond rings:
And on your bosom all night worn
Yesterday's rose now droops forlorn
But dies not yet this summer morn.

    And now without, as if some word
Had called upon them that they heard,
The London sparrows far and nigh
Clamour together suddenly;

And Jenny's cage-bird grown awake   330
Here in their song his part must take,
Because here too the day doth break.

   And somehow in myself the dawn
Among stirred clouds and veils withdrawn
Strikes greyly on her. Let her sleep.
But will it wake her if I heap
These cushions thus beneath her head
Where my knee was? No, — there's your bed,
My Jenny, while you dream. And there
I lay among your golden hair   340
Perhaps the subject of your dreams,
These golden coins.
               For still one deems
That Jenny's flattering sleep confers
New magic on the magic purse, —
Grim web, how clogged with shrivelled flies!
Between the threads fine fumes arise
And shape their pictures in the brain.
There roll no streets in glare and rain,
Nor flagrant man-swine whets his tusk;
But delicately sighs in musk   350
The homage of the dim boudoir;
Or like a palpitating star
Thrilled into song, the opera-night
Breathes faint in the quick pulse of light;
Or at the carriage-window shine
Rich wares for choice; or, free to dine,
Whirls through its hour of health (divine
For her) the concourse of the Park.
And though in the discounted dark
Her functions there and here are one,   360
Beneath the lamps and in the sun
There reigns at least the acknowledged belle
Apparelled beyond parallel.
Ah, Jenny, yes, we know your dreams.

   For even the Paphian Venus seems
A goddess o'er the realms of love,
When silver-shrined in shadowy grove:
Aye, or let offerings nicely plac'd
But hide Priapus to the waist,
And whoso looks on him shall see   370
An eligible deity.
   Why, Jenny, waking here alone
May help you to remember one,
Though all the memory's long outworn
Of many a double-pillowed morn.
I think I see you when you wake,
And rub your eyes for me, and shake
My gold, in rising, from your hair.
A Danaë for a moment there.

   Jenny, my love rang true! for still   380
Love at first sight is vague, until
That tinkling makes him audible.

   And must I mock you to the last,
Ashamed of my own shame, — aghast
Because some thoughts not born amiss
Rose at a poor fair face like this?
Well, of such thoughts so much I know:

In my life, as in hers, they show,
By a far gleam which I may near,
A dark path I can strive to clear.

Only one kiss. Good-bye, my dear.

— Dante Gabriel Rossetti

Generating Writing

1. In a sense Alice Walker's essay is a revision of several previous texts about women. Assign an essay in which students analyze the way she rewrites the descriptions of women provided by Jean Toomer (a black man) and Virginia Woolf (a white woman). Why does Walker feel the need to correct or amend these previous texts? What are the main issues upon which she disagrees with these writers? How would students characterize the view of women that emerges from her revisions of these earlier views?

2. The metaphors in this essay are many and varied. Have students write an essay exploring the significance of the metaphors Walker borrows and creates to describe her female forebears' creativity. Make sure they distinguish between the metaphors she implicitly or explicitly critiques and the metaphors she endorses.

Barbara Lazear Ascher

Mothers and Sons

Teaching Strategies

Your approach to this essay will have to depend, perhaps even more than usual, on students' response to it. Although Barbara Lazear Ascher is certainly voicing one feminist position, not all feminists — in fact, not even all feminists who speak out in this chapter — would agree with her. This will provide a good opportunity for your students to realize that there is not *one* undisputed viewpoint shared by all feminists.

You might begin with the question "How did you like this essay?" in order to gauge their response. Suppose that most of the male students say they liked it and that most of the females say they didn't. Although this might sound like an unexpected response to a feminist essay, it is not an unlikely response to this essay. How many men could resist the urge to blame their own ignorance and insensitivity on a woman and, what's more, to be able to quote a woman as their authority for doing so? If there are male students in the class who succumb to this urge, you will have two resources ready, not including your own response: the epigraph by Marilyn French — who writes, "Women, not men, are considered responsible for the children of Western society and are blamed for our children's fates. Therefore, we have smothering mothers, schizophrenic mothers, mothers who cause anorexia, bulimia, autism, neuroses, and psychoses" — and the arguments forwarded by the female students in the class who object to the fact that Ascher makes women responsible for men's shortcomings.

What do you do with the women who dislike the essay? You can't just let them leave class with only the insights and opinions they brought to class. Ask them if there are any values that they, as feminists, share with Ascher. Are they in favor of solidarity among women? Ascher's entire essay is written as an attack on gender treachery. Ask them if they have ever experienced, and deplored, instances of gender treachery in their own lives. How do they feel, for instance, if a friend starts to neglect her women friends when she acquires a male lover? (If any students notice that Ascher's attack on mothers could also be classed as a gender treachery, you might have to concede the point. If no one else notices, you might have to make the point yourself.)

Of course, some women will probably agree with Ascher. They may cite Ascher's popularized version of Freud to question the relevance of the epigraph by Marilyn French: after all, even if men start taking an equal share in the responsibility for raising children, women — not men — have psychological reasons for the "blind love" they feel for their sons. You might point out that if women really did receive the respect they deserve for their own merits, a mother would have no motive to mold her son into "a man who thought she was important." If there are feminists in the class who agree with Ascher — as there may well be — you might direct their attention to the epigraph by Audre Lorde in Chapter 18, "The Feminist Movement Today." Lorde writes that "women of today are still being called upon to educate men as to our existence and our needs. . . . This is a diversion of our energies and a tragic repetition of . . . patriarchal thought." Ask them if the fact that Ascher is not calling on all women, but rather on mothers in particular, to "educate men as to . . . our needs" makes a difference, and if so, why?

Finally, there may well be some men in the class who did not like the essay. Most of the direct swipes at mothers are simultaneously thinly disguised swipes at sons. Besides, sexism on the part of males is certainly not incompatible with a fierce protectiveness when it comes to what are perceived as threats to the sexist's own mother or sisters. If some male students exhibit signs of protectiveness, you may want to refer them to Nancy Mairs's "A Letter to Matthew" (see Chapter 18), in which she reveals the assumptions behind male protectiveness toward females and explores the political consequences of that kind of thinking.

Additional Activities

Nancy Mairs's "A Letter to Matthew" would also interconnect with Ascher's essay in that both deal with sexism in its seemingly benign forms: Mairs draws out the implications of the pedestal upon which many American women perch, and Ascher mentions, among others, the "boss who addresses one as 'sweetie.'" You might want to initiate a discussion of the insidious effect of such socially acceptable forms of sexism.

Generating Writing

1. Barbara Lazear Ascher gives several examples of how *not* to raise children, particularly sons, but only one example of a child-rearing technique she approves of. Assign an essay in which students invent a scheme for raising children so that they will help to break the cycle of sexism. They may wish to write this essay in the form and style of a guide to child-rearing, à la Dr. Spock, or to choose a more contemporary model, Judith Martin. Judith Martin's *Miss Manners' Guide to Rearing Perfect Children*, by the way, offers next to no advice regarding gender, so you may tell the students that the field is wide open! As an alternative to this assignment, you might suggest that students read a classic child-rearing guide and write an essay critiquing it from an enlightened standpoint regarding gender roles.

2. Students can learn a valuable lesson in composition from Ascher's essay. Many of her paragraphs follow a pattern that is well worth imitating: a statement is followed by anecdotal evidence. You might assign an essay, on a topic of the student's choice, that utilizes the several brief anecdotes as evidence. Point out that Ascher's anecdotes do not all illustrate precisely the same point, but that the points they do illustrate are all logically related.

WRITING ABOUT THE CHAPTER

1. For each author in this chapter, the personal *is* the political. Assign an essay in which students discuss the ways this principle is developed in each essay. Ask them to discuss the

gender implications of this question: Why is, or why isn't, a question about the personal approach to political issues somehow more suited to a chapter on motherhood than, say, to a chapter on fatherhood? They should argue for or against the idea that Steinem, Walker, and Ascher unwittingly endorse the sexist notion that a woman's natural sphere of influence is the domestic, the private rather than the public.

2. Gloria Steinem writes that it "was a strange experience to look into those brown eyes I had seen so often and realize suddenly how much they were like my own." In trying to understand her mother, she inadvertently learned something about herself. Have students look again at the exploratory drafts they wrote before reading the selections in this chapter. Are there any revelations about them tucked in between the lines about their mothers? Have them revise that earlier draft, this time focusing on the anecdotes that reveal as much about the person who chose them and wrote them down as they do about that person's mother. How have students' efforts to understand their mothers led them to understand their mothers' legacies in them?

20

Fathers

Sherwood Anderson, Discovery of a Father

Max Apple, Bridging

Bharati Mukherjee, Fathering

WORKING WITH THE CHAPTER

When Robert Frost wrote the words quoted in the epigraph to this chapter the contrast between a mother's role and a father's was clearer than it is today. "You don't have to deserve your mother's love. You have to deserve your father's. He's more particular." The difference he suggests, with such wry humor, is not a biological difference between the ways in which men and women respond to their offspring, but rather a function of the distance between a traditional father and his children, which enabled him to be "more particular." Alice Walker identifies the commonest source of this distance when she writes of her father that she "spent less time with him and knew him less well" than her mother. From the opening line of Sherwood Anderson's "Discovery of a Father," the idea of estrangement between a father and his child is emphasized: "One of the strangest relationships in the world is that between father and son." When he tells about the time he and his father went swimming in the rain, Anderson writes "Before that night my father had never seemed to pay any attention to me."

Fortunately, times are changing for fathers, and for their children. Mary-Lou Wiseman writes, with a touch of envy, of seeing today's "fathers changing diapers, playing catch, dressing their daughters for school, feeding them, waiting at bus stops, teaching them manners and how to fix a car." The father in Bharati Mukherjee's story and the father in Max Apple's story are both learning to cope with today's expanded definition of fatherhood. In the background of each story is a more traditional version of fatherhood. Jason, whose Vietnamese daughter pushes him to the outer limits of fatherhood, has twins who live with his ex-wife, children about whom he thinks "I never felt for them what I feel for her." And the narrator in "Bridging," a widower who is bringing up his nine-year-old daughter alone, realizes that he paid very little attention to his daughter before his wife died. In each story the father is given a second chance at fatherhood, a chance to redefine his role in relation to his daughter. Each of them meets this difficult and complex challenge with the kind of unconditional love that Robert Frost would have attributed to mothers, but never to their husbands. Of course, Frost never had an opportunity to meet one of today's fathers.

171

Teaching Strategies

You might generate a discussion of this entire chapter by calling your students' attention to the perspective from which each of the epigraphs and selections is written. The epigraph by Alice Walker and the essay by Sherwood Anderson are both written from the point of view of grown children looking back upon their childhood in an attempt to understand their fathers and themselves. (Here you might also bring in a discussion of "Ruth's Song" and "In Search of Our Mothers' Gardens," from Chapter 19.) Robert Frost and Mary-Lou Weisman both write about fathers in general, but their views seem informed by the feelings of adult children thinking back on their relationships with their own fathers, much as Walker and Anderson do. The two stories, "Bridging" and "Fathering," are written from the father's point of view. Ask students what difference point of view makes in each of these instances. Is there something about the nonfictional mode of the three epigraphs and the Anderson memoir that lends itself naturally to the child's perspective? Can they think of autobiographies written from the point of view of the parent? What is it about childhood, and our relationships with our parents, that makes such a fertile field for personal narrative?

A Writing-before-Reading Exercise

This exercise can be used in class or assigned as homework. Have your students brainstorm, individually and on paper, a list of memories associated with their fathers. Once they have constructed a substantial list, instruct them to choose a few items from the list, and to expand each into a narrative of one or more paragraphs. If you are using this as an in-class exercise, have the students break up into groups of three or four and read their paragraphs to one another. The listeners should help each writer by asking questions that might lead to development or clarification, and by giving the writer advice on which of the several incidents might form the best start for a longer paper about the writer's father. The writer should make note of his classmates' advice, but need not implement it until after reading the selections in the chapter. He may then choose to write a polished essay about his father, and his classmates' comments may come in handy.

WORKING WITH THE SELECTIONS

Sherwood Anderson

Discovery of a Father

Teaching Strategies

You might start by asking students to identify the point of view of "Discovery of a Father." By asking this question, and follow-up questions designed to refine their answer, you will show them that in essays, as well as in fiction, the author does have important decisions to make on such things as point of view. The mere fact that "Discovery of a Father" is an autobiographical essay did not force Anderson to write it in this way, and it does not mean that the distinction between author and narrator is irrelevant, or even uncomplicated. By using such words as *choose* and *decide* in your questions, you will make it clear that nearly every word we write involves some decision or choice. You might ask, for example, "Why did Anderson choose to write this essay from the point of view of his father's *grown* son? Why did he choose to mention that he has sons of his own? In what ways does he expand the point of view, explicitly and implicitly, beyond the son's perspective? Why would he choose to expand the limits in this way?"

Once you have discussed *how* the readers of Anderson's essay know what they know, you might shift the discussion to consider *what* the reader knows. Start, perhaps, by asking students what they can tell about Anderson's father from reading the essay. List their responses on the chalkboard, in a column marked "Father." As each student volunteers one of the father's characteristics, ask, "How do you know this characteristic?" This approach will encourage them to give textual evidence for their assertions, and to notice the difference between ideas that are expressed in the text and ideas that are implied by the text. It will also tie in to your opening discussion of point of view, for they will have gathered some of their knowledge about the father from the reactions of others in the essay besides his son.

Next, you might ask what the reader knows about the son, writing their responses in a column marked "Son," next to the column on the board. When appropriate, line up the son's attributes directly across from the corresponding attributes in the "Father" column. You might actually phrase the question about the son so as to focus on their similarities, asking, for example, "In what ways does the son resemble his father?" This part of the discussion might focus on their creativity and humor. You might want to emphasize the stories they tell and the allure of those stories: the narrator admits that his father's invented origins "seemed so real" that he almost believed them himself; later *he* makes up a story of his own origins — an adoption fantasy — about which he says, "I even made myself half believe these fancies."

To pursue the doubling motif in "Discovery of a Father," draw students' attention to the opening and closing paragraphs of the essay. In the first two paragraphs, the narrator seems to suggest that the positions of father and son are nearly interchangeable: because he has sons, and because he had expectations of his father that mirror a father's for his son, he makes the implicit claim that he knows how his father feels. But have your students carefully examine the equation he sets up: "You hear it said that fathers want their sons to be what they feel they cannot themselves be, but I tell you it also works the other way. I know that as a small boy I wanted my father to be a certain thing he was not." They should discover that he has erased the son's inadequacy from the second half of the equation, leaving it lopsided. The same impulse that made the boy run "down an alley back of some stores" to escape the scene of his father's supposed humiliation deforms the narrator's logic in this sentence; he is eager to distance himself from what he sees as his father's failings.

Invite students to discuss what happens to the doubling motif in the final episode of the essay. Where do the identities of the father and son seem to merge? They might notice that this episode is in part a rite of passage that leaves the son briefly on the same adult male level that his father, for the moment at least, inhabits: "It was as though I had been jerked suddenly out of myself, out of the world of the schoolboy." Then their inequality — the natural inequality of an adult father and a young son — asserts itself: the former is the "strong swimmer" and the latter is "the boy clinging to him in the darkness." Finally, the mother reduces them to doubles again, but this time as children: "I remember that she called us 'boys.'" Ask students to identify the end result of all this shifting of position. Is the initial imbalance created by an irresponsible father corrected by this final episode? Where does the final equilibrium, if there is one, rest?

Additional Activities

If you'd like to use Anderson's essay as an example of a technique that your students might like to use in some of their own narratives, draw their attention to his use of aspect. More than half of his narrative (the first half) is written in the habitual aspect. Verbs such as *would* and *might* and tag phrases such as *let's say* and *or something* are the linguistic signs of the habitual. Many writers use the habitual to weave a background against which to set an instance in the simple past tense. Anderson's use of this device, however, is especially effective because the singular incident he recounts contrasts so sharply to the rest in *content* as well as form. The passages written in the habitual also add to the sense of distance that the narrator tries to maintain: the reader senses that only someone with the perspective afforded by time could have noticed this pattern and collapsed several similar incidents together to illustrate it. By calling your students' attention to the effects of such stylistic devices, you will make them more aware of the possible effects of such choices in their own writing.

If you'd like to connect this chapter with Chapter 19, "Mothers," one route would be to discuss the adoption fantasies in "Discovery of a Father" and "Ruth's Song," by Gloria Steinem. Ask how adoption fantasies differ according to the gender of the parent who is the cause of the child's shame, the target of the child's so-called hatred.

"Discovery of a Father" could also be taught in conjunction with autobiographical narratives about childhood in *The Winchester Reader,* including "Salvation," by Langston Hughes (see Chapter 3), "Two Kinds," by Amy Tan (see Chapter 2), and "No Name Woman" (Chapter 12) and "A Song for a Barbarian Reed Pipe" (in Chapter 30), by Maxine Hong Kingston, if you'd like to examine the topic of autobiography as fiction versus nonfiction; and, especially, "Gumption," by Russell Baker (see Chapter 2), because the little boy in his story ends with the same revelation about his vocation — indeed, even the same vocation — as the little boy in "Discovery of a Father."

Generating Writing

1. Assign an essay in which students explore the repercussions of the word *strange* (and *stranger*) in "Discovery of a Father." Anderson uses this word repeatedly throughout the essay. Why? To what effect(s)? Encourage them to think of several possible connotations and associations for the word, and the appropriateness of these meanings and reverberations in the context of this essay. Ask them if the word seems to undergo a transformation during the essay.

2. You might also suggest that students explore the significance of talking and silence in this essay. What is the meaning and effect of the father's habitual volubility? What is the meaning and effect of his silence during the swimming episode? If students choose this essay topic, they should address the ending of the story: Why does the son recognize a connection between himself and his father as two storytellers at the conclusion of a *silent* experience with him?

Max Apple

Bridging

Teaching Strategies

The father in "Bridging," like the one in "Discovery of a Father," has a lot in common with his child. In the Sherwood Anderson selection, however, the child must come to realize that he and his father are alike, whereas in "Bridging," the fact that the father and daughter are on parallel journeys is almost a given: when, in Part I, the therapist describes Jessica's fears, her father says, "That's pretty much how I feel too." Both of them have to "learn to trust the world again" after the death of Jessica's mother. You might begin by asking what happens in this story. If the narrator already knows that he and his daughter need to learn to trust the world, that the Girl Scouts are capable of "sticking and sewing their lives together in ways" that are unavailable to him and his daughter, then what, if anything, does he learn in the remainder of the story?

If your students see an evolution in the father's character, have them give evidence for their opinion. What, for example, does the opening description of a scene in the

Astrodome, a place where he emphatically is *not*, say about him? How does the phrase "Vicki died" strike the reader? What does its placement in the third of the story's three sections say about the evolution in his character? Ask students if they can identify a climax in this story. Their answer will of course depend on what they think the narrator has to learn, and whether they think he learned it. Some will cite the moment when the father, who holds season tickets to a spectator sport, finds himself in the midst of the Girl Scouts, "not watching and keeping score and admiring from a distance but a participant, a player."

Others might point out that because the father seems to have all the necessary knowledge from the beginning of the story, it is Jessica who needs to come to a realization. After all, the narrator focuses most of his energy on trying to help *her* character evolve. Does this story have a climax if one reads it as a story about Jessica? If so, when does it occur? If not, why not? What is the effect of the final scene?

Other students may decide that it is irrelevant to talk of climaxes in such a story. They may argue that the story focuses on the "slow steady process" of grieving and healing, rather than a product such as health, trust or normalcy, and that to look at the story for a climax is to trivialize the process, as if it could magically be resolved in an instant. You might look at Vivian Gornick's extended metaphor from psychoanalysis, in "Who Says We Haven't Made a Revolution" (see Chapter 18). Her description of therapy as a process of coming to the same insights over and over again should be useful in this context.

Once the idea of narrative climax has been called into question, it might be interesting to look at the organization of the story as a whole. How does Max Apple frustrate the normal expectations of readers of fiction when it comes to organization? Look at the transitions — or lack of transitions — between many of his paragraphs. Can students identify a principle or pattern at work in his juxtapositions? Look too at the abrupt time shifts. What is the effect of the short paragraphs and quick shifts? Why might Apple have chosen to write his story in this way? Do the stylistic features reflect the mental state of the narrator? If so, how? Do they reinforce the themes of the story?

Additional Activities

Because his wife has died, the narrator of "Bridging" has taken on the responsibilities traditionally allocated to mothers, about which he apparently knew little before her death. He has even volunteered to be an assistant leader in a Girl Scout troop, for which he performs the kinds of mindless tasks usually reserved, Kay Randall points out, for women. Ask students how this story comments on gender stereotypes. They will want to consider the character of Kay Randall as part of the evidence for their answer. You may want to juxtapose this story about a man who "swoop[ed] past thousands of years of stereotypes" to become a Girl Scout Leader with "Mr. President," by Bob Greene (see Chapter 22), an article about the first boy to be named president of the Future Homemakers of America.

Generating Writing

1. When the narrator is out cavorting with a bunch of nine-year-old girls, and his daughter is home listening to a ball game, he comments that the situation seems "upside down." Assign a paper in which students explore the theme of role reversal in "Bridging." In what ways and to what extent is it possible to declare that the adult and the child in this story have exchanged places? What causes this kind of role reversal? How, if at all, is it resolved? Your students may want to expand their essays to instances of parent-child role reversal in "Discovery of a Father," by Sherwood Anderson, or "Ruth's Song," by Gloria Steinem, or both.

2. Images and metaphors drawn from baseball permeate this story, as do images and references to hands and fingers. Have students focus on one set of imagery in the story, and write an essay exploring its larger implications.

Bharati Mukherjee

Fathering

Teaching Strategies

Because "Fathering" is a first-person narrative, the key to understanding the story is understanding the narrator. Ask students to describe Jason. Because he seems caught in a tug of war between Sharon and Eng, an obvious response is to characterize him as a peacemaker in an impossible situation. If this is your students' first response, spend time listening to evidence from those who sympathize with Jason. He does seem to be genuinely trying to make up for a lot: the blank space that was Vietnam and the "screw-ups" in his personal life. He seems to take all the responsibility for everyone's pain and trouble: when he sees that Sharon looks "old, harrowed, depressed," he thinks "What have I done to her?" He's Mr. Fix-it on every level: even when Sharon seems to be deserting him, he feels the urge to run down and help her with the latch. Finally, he provides the kind of fairy-tale, heroic ending that the reader of this tale of relentless conflict may very well crave.

Still, it's important for the reader to question Jason's reliability as a narrator as well. There are many avenues of approach to such a critique, and doubtless some students will start the ball rolling by questioning the version of Jason's character that is being forwarded by those who sympathize with him. They may question his motives: anyone who blames himself for *everything* inevitably draws suspicion: What might motivate such martyrdom? Also, the flip side of his feeling of responsibility is a feeling of ownership: he refers to Eng and Sharon, for example, as "my women." An observation about his proprietary instinct might lead to other observations about his sex and gender biases: he refers to his ex-wife as a "lesbo," and focuses on the tiny feet of Eng's mother, proving that he has swallowed a cultural stereotype of female beauty.

Of course, the stereotype he has swallowed is more prevalent in Asian culture than in American culture. Ask students to characterize Jason's attitude toward Vietnamese culture, and to the Vietnamese people. You might want to draw their attention in particular to paragraph 11, where he describes the "mumbo jumbo" of the Vietnamese women, and to paragraph 43, where he seems to be struggling with internalized racism: "I can't help wondering if maybe Asian skin bruises differently from ours, even though I want to say skin is skin; especially hers is skin like mine." He says that "Vietnam didn't happen" because he was on drugs. What does he mean? Does he mean merely that he doesn't remember much about his wartime experiences, or that he wasn't responsible for his wartime experiences? How might his acute sense of responsibility in the present relate to his denial of responsibility in the past? Do students believe that Jason doesn't feel responsible for the war in Vietnam? What details about the war can they read between the lines of Jason's narrative? What is he not saying?

To elicit further evidence for Jason's unreliability as a narrator, you might ask students to identify places in the text where they see implications that Jason does not (or refuses to) see. Why, for instance, does he read a story about invading aliens to Eng, even though she plugs her ears when he does? Doesn't he realize the implications of the story? What do the contents of his parka pockets say about him that he does not realize he's revealing? How does the fact that Eng tries to heal herself with coins just as the enemy Viet Cong women did complicate the issue of enemies and allies beyond the black-and-white conflict set up in movies such as *Rambo*, which Jason mentions? Emphasize that although the narrator is not always aware of what he's revealing, the author can generally be assumed to know what *she* was doing.

Of course, that Jason is an unreliable narrator does not mean he is a villain. Just as Eng is a product of her environment, so too can many of Jason's blind spots be attributed, at least in part, to his cultural environment. The tug of war between Eng and Sharon is urgent enough to grab most of the reader's attention, but the tug of war inside Jason, who has a daughter who is both an alien and a part of him, may be more important. By choosing to rescue Eng in that dramatic way, Jason certainly puts a physical end to the external tug-of-war. Ask students if the fairy-tale ending shows that Jason has also resolved his internal conflict.

Additional Activities

Ask students to analyze the character of Eng. Do they agree with Sharon that Eng is manipulating Jason? How was Eng's personality formed? Why does she ask Jason to show her his scars, and offer to show him hers? Why does Mukherjee decide to give her the flu? Help your students to see Eng as a portable, personal embodiment of the effects of war.

The authors of this manual had an opportunity to interview Bharati Mukherjee about her story, "Fathering," and about her way of writing in general. Mukherjee began by saying that "Fathering" is about "the Vietnamization of America and the reconstitution of the American family." Americans can't just leave Vietnam behind them: we have to "acknowledge the moral consequences." Asian (and other) immigrants are here to stay; they have even, many of them, entered our homes and our families. By focusing on the changing complexion of American life, Mukherjee "turns the *New Yorker* story, the white-relationship story, on its head."

Mukherjee said that the narrator, Jason, is the center of this story. She agreed that he is an unreliable narrator, in that author and reader can see things he is unaware of; nonetheless, she sees the ending as a real revelation on Jason's part. To the question of the real-life efficacy of what could be seen as a fairy-tale heroic solution on Jason's part, she answered, "Jason knows it can't be worked out in real life"; he knows that his life with Eng won't be problem-free. Mukherjee said that Jason "chooses to become a magical hero"; whether or not he is conscious of it, his decision to rescue Eng proves that for him "the world of uneasy subjectivity is no longer enough."

In response to our comment that despite our mixed feelings, we were still cheering for Jason when he chose Eng in the tug-of-war between Eng and Sharon, Mukherjee emphasized that Sharon is not an evil person. She said that the world is full of "good-enough people" like Sharon, whose goodness is not sufficient when it comes to difficulties this great. Even Dr. Kearns is not evil; he just doesn't understand Eng. He wants to "scrub down her exogenousness so she can be controlled." In a statement that combined realism and optimism, Mukherjee commented, "There are no bad guys in the story. It's just that they can't come together — yet."

Eng, of course, is "the ghost of Vietnam." For Jason, Eng is "a call from the unconscious"; and, Mukherjee says, "these calls work themselves out in unexpected and sometimes violent ways." Warn your students not to be too quick in trying to fit Eng into the pattern of the American child: according to the author, "Eng is not Americanized." Her delirium, for instance, is "*not* a war flashback." If an American soldier in a story experienced such a state of delirium, that would signal a mental breakdown. But Eng comes from a different culture, and, Mukherjee asks, who's to say she isn't really seeing her grandmother? The dead are present to many Asian peoples in a way that is hard for Westerners to understand. According to Mukherjee, for American writers from other cultures, as for Eng, "death doesn't exercise the same fascination, hold, and fear" that it does in Western culture.

The story of the Engs of this world, and the American family's adjustment to Eng and others like her, has long fascinated Mukherjee as a theme. This theme comes to fruition in her novel, *Jasmine*, in the character Du (pronounced "Yo"). If your students liked "Fathering," you might suggest *Jasmine* as further reading.

When asked about her writing process, Mukherjee answered that "Fathering" came to her "fully formed — very much a voice story." In fact, most of her stories come to her in the form of voices, this time Jason's voice. Mukherjee claims that selecting point of view is a writer's most crucial decision. If the stories present themselves as an idea or an image first, then she finds she has to work until she hears a voice: "until then, it's not ready." Once the character starts going, she or he often creates situations Mukherjee hadn't anticipated. The ending of *Jasmine* is one such surprise.

In response to further questions about her writing process, Mukherjee explained that a combination of "poverty and ambition" led her to develop a method whereby stories "write themselves" at the back of her head, no matter what she is doing at the time (including being interviewed!). At one time, she was working three jobs at a time. The stories jelled in the back of her mind as she worked at her other jobs, then she would write them down during a few precious hours beginning at 3:00 A.M., or during twenty-two-hour weekend writing marathons.

Stories require many hours of solid work. The most recent story she wrote (her first "California story") took three months of hard work. She made several false beginnings. She wrote it from one point of view, realized that wasn't exactly what she wanted, and then revised it from another point of view. She never shows anyone her rough drafts, but when she feels she is finished with a story, she always shows it to her husband, who is also a writer. (They met in 1963 at a writers' workshop, and married in 1964.) She said she always takes his feedback very seriously.

We've found that students, when given a chance to interview published authors, always ask about their writing process. Their questions reveal a genuine interest in the process of writing. If possible, you might invite a local writer to visit your class. If direct contact with professionals is not possible, written accounts of interviews, such as those in this manual and other sources such as *The Paris Review Interviews,* can help to sate your students' healthy curiosity while teaching them a valuable lesson: each writer must discover a working style that works best for him or her.

Generating Writing

1. In the opening paragraph, Mukherjee gives vivid character sketches of both Eng and Sharon, and establishes the sense of conflict between them, in a few deft strokes — strokes on a doorknob, in fact. Doorknobs, latches, buttons, and snaps reappear throughout the story. Assign an essay in which students explore the significance of this constellation of related images.

2. Drawing on the idea of Jason as a fallible narrator, assign a creative essay in which the student writes the same series of events, or a series implied in "Fathering," from the point of view of Sharon, or Eng, or Jason's ex-wife. Those among your students whose parents are divorced will perhaps recognize, and distrust, statements such as "I brought the twins up without much help ten years ago." They will assume that his ex-wife would have a different tale to tell, if she were given a voice. In fact, anyone involved in a dispute has probably experienced the phenomenon of conflicting versions of the same events. This essay assignment will give them the chance to create a different version, and perhaps to give a voiceless character a voice.

WRITING ABOUT THE CHAPTER

1. The authors of all three selections in this chapter write about the father and child being alone together, "just the two of us," apart from the rest of the world. Ask students to write an essay exploring the psychological implications of the father–child relationships in these selections. What are the forms and functions of fusion and separation between father and child? What difference does the child's gender make?

2. Offer students the option of writing an essay about their own father, drawing on the material in the Writing-before-Reading exercise they did at the beginning of this chapter. To help them avoid the clichés that are often written about fathers, you might encourage them to take an example from Sherwood Anderson, choosing incidents that seem to capture their dominant childhood view of their father, and then setting off one incident

against this backdrop, an incident that seems anomalous in some way. Ideally, students will focus their essays on a turning point in their relationship with their father, but sometimes an instruction to do so will backfire, because only hackneyed turning points will leap into their minds. For this reason, it's good to sneak up on the concept of epiphany. We like Nancy Sommers's (Associate Director of the Expository Writing Program at Harvard University) method for doing so: she advises her students to focus on an incident they don't yet understand. The chances are very good that this method will produce more complex, sophisticated essays, and the students will learn something as they write, so that the feeling of sudden revelation will be fresh. It is certainly true that Anderson did not understand the significance of his late-night swim with his father when it happened, and possibly true that he came to understand it only by writing about it. As instructors, we like to provide our students with as many opportunities for discovery as we can.

21

Gender Roles and Stereotypes

Alexis de Tocqueville, How the Americans Understand
the Equality of the Sexes

Thomas Edison, The Woman of the Future

Jamaica Kincaid, Girl

Bruce Curtis, The Wimp Factor

WORKING WITH THE CHAPTER

This chapter addresses one of the major sources of irritation and complaint among many Americans about their identity in the contemporary world. The brief quotations from Germaine Greer, Janet Chafetz, David Potter, and Dorothy Sayers that appear at the beginning of this chapter provocatively introduce the myriad issues in thoughtful discussions of gender stereotypes. David Potter and Dorothy Sayers recapitulate many of the stereotypes that have circumscribed identity over the years. Ask your students to discuss how the observations and claims of each are organized. What do they make of the repeated word *if* in the Sayers excerpt? What assumptions lie behind and what consequences would David Potter's discussion of gender stereotypes apparently produce?

Follow these questions by examining carefully the general identities established in the Greer and Chafetz epigraphs. What assumptions lie behind their attitudes toward stereotypes? The pace and intensity of this discussion can be accelerated markedly if you ask students to talk about whether men and women are equally affected by stereotypes. Have them discuss specific examples in detail, pushing beyond the surface features of these stereotypes to analyze the assumptions and cultural traditions that form them.

You might then ask for specific examples of how various stereotypes influence economic status, leading into discussion of Thomas Edison's "The Woman of the Future."

Help students distinguish between gender and sexual stereotypes and ask them if men and women are equally affected. Here the de Tocqueville essay will work especially well. He alludes to a sexual double standard for European men and women. Discuss double standards in the United States today and their advantages and disadvantages. Bruce Curtis writes that it is culturally unacceptable for men to express their emotions. How does this restraint affect interpersonal relations? How do all stereotypes affect the balance of power between men and women? Finally, you might close the chapter with Jamaica Kincaid's "Girl," a powerful statement about stereotypes and cultural conditioning — without saying a word about it.

Whichever order you choose for the materials in this chapter, your students will have a great deal to think, talk, and write about.

Teaching Strategies

The following exercise, if used early in the semester, is both an effective introduction to the chapter and a hands-on beginning lesson in composition. This activity, occupying two full class periods, will amply repay the expenditure of class time.

Photocopy an advertisement trading in gender stereotypes and distribute copies. At the same time, hand out scraps of paper — the backs of discarded rough drafts, cut in eighths, will do nicely. Ask students to mark up the ad freely, writing down anything they notice about the text or the picture. If they look confused at your request to "mark up the ad," you may have to do some modeling: choose an engaging ad and briefly explore its implications. Now give students ten minutes to write their observations.

Next, ask what they've written, copying the responses all over the board in random order. Do not organize the various points for them; later, each will be responsible for creating order from this miscellany of ideas. As you write on the board, students should write each response on a scrap of paper. After fifteen or twenty minutes, they can sort their scraps into piles, according to topics or similarities that occur to them. Of course they can feel free to re-sort the scraps to their own satisfaction, discarding any that don't seem to fit in any pile. They may be reluctant at first, because the activity is unfamiliar, but soon they will actively think and sort and discard. The paper may begin to fly as unwanted scraps make their way to the floor.

When they are satisfied with their piles, students should sort them into logical order. They should now set aside any piles that are no longer relevant, or even reshuffle the contents of each pile. During this sorting and organizing, a provisional thesis is likely to strike: have them write it down. This stage should take fifteen minutes.

Next, have students pair up and read their theses to each other. Have a few read their boiled-down theses aloud to the class. Both you and they will be amazed at the varied theses that arise from applying individual minds to a common task, not only to the same one-page ad, but also to the identical data base (the words on the scraps). In one class period students offered theses about dehumanizing women, stereotyping men, sexism masquerading as enlightenment, effectiveness of ads built on gender stereotyping, and the copywriter's values. Your students too may come up with unexpected and original theses.

At the end of the period, have students write a two- to three-page draft for homework, and bring four copies to the next meeting, at which time they can form groups for peer editing. Their polished drafts will be due in the following class period.

The exercise works best very early in the semester, because it takes students through each phase of composing, from brainstorming through revision, in one week. Physically manipulating the scraps of paper helps make the sequence tangible. And they learn a graphic lesson: a thesis will form out of a body of evidence, instead of the other way around. The principles and skills they learn in this week can carry through in all their writing, whether they apply the brainstorming method on scraps of paper, or apply the principles more abstractly. The advertisement also provides ample evidence of the gender stereotyping perpetuated by the media, and that students themselves discover all the sexism in the ad will help to prevent skepticism when the class discussion of the roots of sexism begins in earnest.

A Writing-before-Reading Exercise

What kinds of behavior do you find appropriate and inappropriate for a person of your gender? Consider dating protocol, physical contact with members of the same sex, choice of clothing, interaction with children, and so on: Where did your opinions on gender-appropriate behavior originate? Write a rough draft of an essay exploring these sources. Focus on the source that most directly influences your idea of yourself as male or female. How has this source, or cluster of sources, affected your own habitual behavior? How do you expect it will affect your future choices? If you can't see how your gender has made or will make any difference in your behavior, it might help to imagine the specific ways in which your life would differ if you had been born in the other gender.

WORKING WITH THE SELECTIONS

Alexis de Tocqueville

How the Americans Understand the Equality of the Sexes

Teaching Strategies

This passage forms an important part of Alexis de Tocqueville's celebrated view of nineteenth-century American sociocultural values and behavior, *Democracy in America* (1835–1840). Your students will readily discover that between the lines of de Tocqueville's enthusiastic account of American life lies a clear portrait of the gender stereotypes and limitations of individual identity bound into the separation of the sexes that dominated American society well into the second half of the twentieth century. The de Tocqueville précis of the specific differences between male and female identity will strike many students as quaint, even deeply sexist, especially with his seemingly secure impression of his enlightened opinions. These students have the advantage, after all, of being able to draw on a century and a half of experience, commentary, and insight on "equality of the sexes." Still, some of de Tocqueville's opinions, such as his assumption that equality in gender is "eternally based in human nature," are not completely obsolete. You might find that students, at first amused by his sexism, will find it enlightening to examine how their own late twentieth century assumptions about gender still bear traces of de Tocqueville's assumptions and attitudes.

A useful way to encourage students to grapple with the stereotypes built into de Tocqueville's discussion of "the equality of the sexes" is to ask each student to choose a profession or occupation — the one perhaps each of them is considering as a career. Ask them to reread paragraph 2 of the de Tocqueville selection, in which he outlines characteristics that would "make men and women into beings not only equal but alike." Then invite them to assess how well women in the profession they have chosen have achieved equality with men. When they discover that some inequalities remain, have them identify the socioeconomic and cultural factors that might account for the origins of these inequalities. The conversation will provide ready access to the issue and to the sociocultural and economic consequences of gender stereotypes.

Two principal features of de Tocqueville's observations about relations between the sexes in America — as well as of most writing that establishes or reinforces stereotypes — are his frequent use of generalization and his unsupported assertions. Consider the end of paragraph 2 in this selection, where de Tocqueville claims that efforts to make "one sex equal to the other" will "degrade both," resulting in nothing more than "weak men and disorderly women." Invite students to work with the assertions and generalizations in this and similar paragraphs — and press them to seek evidence validating his contentions. Most students will quickly understand the problems generated by unsupported assertions and sweeping generalizations about such complex subjects as gender identity and "equality of the sexes." (Also direct them to paragraph 6, where de Tocqueville claims that the "most virtuous" women "attach a sort of pride to the voluntary surrender of their own will" to male conjugal authority. So too, explore with students what de Tocqueville means when he writes of a woman's "holiest duties.")

Another distinctive feature in writing that encourages or underwrites stereotypes is a tone of certainty and the use of seemingly logical connectives between sentences, as in paragraph 4. Ask a student to read the paragraph aloud. How would the reader and listeners describe de Tocqueville's voice in this paragraph? Which words and phrases provide the clearest sense of tone? Once students can describe the speaker's voice, ask them to explore de Tocqueville's choices in diction and syntax that anticipate the tone displayed in paragraph 4. To follow through, invite them to consider whether or not that tone remains consistent throughout the chapter.

In the opening sentence of the selection, de Tocqueville observes that "up to the present day," the inequality of the sexes "has seemed . . . to be eternally based in human nature." Ask for specific ways in which de Tocqueville does or could ascribe inequality to "human nature." Which other passages support or subvert this assumption.

De Tocqueville mentions that American women "never manage the outward concerns of the family" (para. 4). What do students understand him to mean? If it is reasonable to infer that, how would de Tocqueville define "inward"? He also ascribes to American women "a masculine strength of understanding." How might he define this phrase? To what might it stand in opposition?

De Tocqueville spends much time and energy in the middle of the selection on elaborate distinctions between gender stereotypes in European and American society. With what moral vision does he credit Americans that Europeans lack? How would students characterize the diction describing women in America? Compare and contrast that diction with the descriptions of women in Europe. Discuss inferences they might draw from the choices de Tocqueville has made.

Additional Activities

Spend time helping students develop a detailed comparison and contrast of the selection from de Tocqueville's *Democracy in America* and de Crèvecoeur's *Letters from an American Farmer* (Chapter 7). What assumptions about American society and behavior do these two writers share? How do their visions of America and American experience differ?

De Tocqueville's essay would also work well with Chapter 26, "Freedom of Expression," and, more specifically, with Walter Lippmann's "The Indispensable Opposition." With de Tocqueville's paragraph 6, help prepare a detailed critique of his version of an ideal society in which women who do not agree with the status quo are expected to remain silent. They can gather what women silenced by de Tocqueville's essay might say if given an opportunity to speak from Elizabeth Cady Stanton's "Declaration of Sentiments" (Chapter 24), published a few years after de Tocqueville's book.

This de Tocqueville selection is good for first-hand research that might lead to an extended essay or a research paper. The goal is to see if de Tocqueville's assumptions about men's and women's work were shared by less celebrated, writers in mid–nineteenth-century America. Students could search the library's holdings under such subjects as diaries of pioneer women and women's autobiographies, select a title or two that interest them, and then read through a representative sampling of these materials to ascertain whether his assumptions and assertions were endorsed by the women's lives and prose. They would present their findings in class or in a formal paper.

Generating Writing

1. In an essay entitled "Some Individual Costs of Gender Role Conformity" (1971), Janet Saltzman Chafetz, who teaches sociology at the University of Houston, surveyed male and female undergraduates to assess advantages and liabilities of the traditional roles associated with their gender. She opens the essay with this observation:

It is probably true that very few individuals conform totally to their sex-relevant stereotypes. Roles of all kinds . . . are sociocultural givens, but this is not to say that people play them in the same way. Indeed, individuals, like stage actors and actresses, interpret their roles and create innovations for their "parts." The fact remains that there is a "part" to be played, and it does strongly influence the actual "performance."

It is also important to recall that the precise definitions of gender-role stereotypes vary within the broader culture by social class, region, race and ethnicity, and other subcultural categories. Thus, for instance, more than most other Americans, the various Spanish-speaking groups in this country (Mexican-American, Puerto Rican, Cuban) stress domesticity, passivity, and other stereotypical feminine traits, and dominance, aggressiveness, physical prowess, and other stereotypical masculine traits. Indeed, the masculine gender role for this group is generally described by reference to the highly stereotyped notion of *machismo*. In fact, a strong emphasis on masculine aggressiveness and dominance may be characteristic of most groups in the lower ranges of the socioeconomic ladder. . . .

From your experience, how accurate are Chafetz's assertions? Choose one of the factors she mentions that form gender stereotypes — social class, region, race and ethnicity, and the like — and assess how evident it is in the stereotypes in the communities in which you participate. Write the first draft of an essay exploring how that factor affects the development of gender stereotypes.

2. Ask students to write an essay in which they assess the accuracy of Chafetz's final assertion: that a "strong emphasis on masculine aggressiveness and dominance may be characteristic of most groups in the lower ranges of the socioeconomic ladder."

Thomas Edison

The Woman of the Future

Teaching Strategies

Thomas Edison's "The Woman of the Future" proudly announces an industrial revolution in the design and management of the American home, in which technology will be the principal cause of women's liberation. Yet, the very case Edison makes for women's freedom and intellectual development quickly turns into an even more hardened version of the original gender stereotypes from which he sought to free women. Edison's efforts eventually impersonalize, if not dehumanize, women's lives.

Edison's article appeared in the October 1912 issue of *Good Housekeeping*, one of the most popular magazines in the early twentieth century. As its title suggests, the magazine published articles on household affairs, fashions, and furnishings in a style that its intended audience, middle and lower-class women, would find both informative and "homey." In 1900, the magazine established a special institute to test and evaluate products, awarding those which satisfied its standards "the *Good Housekeeping* seal of approval," a phrase that quickly became synonymous with high quality.

When *Good Housekeeping* first appeared in 1885, it carried the subtitle *A Family Journal Conducted in the Interests of the Higher Life of the Household*. Open a discussion of Edison's "The Woman of the Future" by asking students to comment on the appropriateness of publishing Edison's essay in a magazine dedicated to "the Interests of the Higher Life of the Household," whose editors took great pride in helping the public define and maintain standards of excellence.

Edison's "The Woman of the Future" can help students learn a great deal about writing for a specific audience. One of the most remarkable aspects of Edison's "prophecy," first presented in interview form and then transcribed and edited into the printed version, is that his primary audience was women. Considering his subject and his attitude toward women and machines, does Edison's language reflect any special efforts to speak to women, and especially to demonstrate his sensitivity to their problems? Mention Edison's diction in the article. More specifically, how technical does he allow his language to become as he presents his vision of the woman of the future and the new life he has created for her through "the greatest of all handmaidens, electricity"? If you focus on the audience imagined for Edison's article, ask students to create a socioeconomic portrait of the readers he seems to expect. Using the language of the essay, identify the financial circumstances Edison assumes for his audience and examine the class distinctions that he seems to build into his remarks.

Edison seems aware of, and often endorses, the gender stereotypes that constricted American women at the turn of the century, and well beyond. Identify the stereotypical notions in the duties he imagines that a mother has toward her daughter. But the gender stereotypes extend far beyond that parental responsibility; they dominate Edison's conception of the functions of the "housewife" of the future. Students can quickly identify these stereotypes; he reveals them, for example, in envisioning the relationship between a housewife and the machines in her home.

Edison makes it clear that his view of women depends on established stereotypes: she is a "domestic laborer" (para. 1) to be reborn into a "domestic engineer." She is an "undeveloped creature," and is "vastly man's inferior," yet a creature whose brain is "finer and more capable of ultimate aesthetic development than man's . . . " (para. 2). Edison imagines a world in which, in response to his belief that "Direct thought is not at present an attribute of femininity" (para. 17).

The world of efficiency Edison foresees is governed by absolutes, in diction and syntax as much as in design and production. This is a world in which uniformity and standardization will simplify life and language by correcting imperfections or by eliminating them. In such a world standardization reinforces rather than eliminates stereotypes.

To get discussion going, ask what strategies Edison uses to align himself with women? With their domestic problems? Does Edison identify with the women he addresses? Where and how is this interest presented? With what effects? What aspects of his experience does Edison draw on in presenting and developing the ideas in this article, and with what results?

Edison applies the word *revolutionize* to the effects of technology on American housewives. Does he take into account the political effects of his inventions? Consider the political implications of such statements as those about "the children of the future," and "stop the cry for more births and raise instead a cry for better births." What are the implications of such assertions as "The less of that space [the world's] which is occupied by the unfit and the imperfect, certainly the better for the race." In what sense might it be said that his remarks are aimed at "perfecting" the human race? Identify, and assess the implications, of other instances of such talk. Is the tone of the essay self-promotional at the expense of larger political and social issues? Explain. List the inventions mentioned or alluded to in this essay. Are Edison's remarks about these inventions aimed at persuading American women to purchase these machines? What other goal or goals seem implicit in his remarks?

Edison builds his argument on "revolutionizing" women's identities on the notion of freeing them from the daily drudgery of housework. And yet the alternatives he sketches for them seem nearly as uniform, standardized, and tradition-bound as the stereotypes from which he apparently seeks to free women. Choose one of these alternative identities, and decide how much the inventions Edison discusses have freed women from the traditional constraints.

Edison sees his work as an effort to organize and standardize experience, particularly that of women. Do these efforts extend to Edison's own writing? Characterize the structure and logic in his remarks. Is there variety in his sentence structure? In his tone of voice? How do you account for his penchant for aphorisms?

Additional Activities

Balance Edison's viewpoint on women's identity with a few views from the other side: Elizabeth Cady Stanton (Chapter 24), who adds considerably to Edison's idea of what's needed if women are to be treated as equal with men; Vivian Gornick (Chapter 18), who looks back on a revolution, as opposed to Edison, who looks forward to one; and Gloria Steinem and Alice Walker (Chapter 19), who, in describing their own mothers' lives, show how two very different women coped with the realities of "women's work."

For an entirely different pairing, try Edison's "Woman of the Future" with Swift's "Modest Proposal" (Chapter 27). Both writers have plans for bringing about a utopian future; both sound rational, even "scientific," in their plans. Students could benefit by pinning down the difference between reading Swift and Edison. Does something in the language prove Swift to be ironic and Edison in deadly earnest? Or is the difference between the lines?

To extend discussion of the gender stereotypes in the Edison selection or to measure Edison's "prophecy" against the domestic lives and stereotyped identities of women later in the twentieth century, read Ruth Schwartz Cowan's "Less Work for Mother?" in *Invention and Technology* (Spring 1987). She concludes that modern technology reinforces the stereotype of the housewife by allowing her "to do much more in the house than ever before" while exacting a severe personal cost for this "progress."

Similarly, Edison's essay might be reread with Frederick Taylor's *Principles of Scientific Management* (1911), an influential movement that was aimed to increase America's efficiency in early twentieth-century American business and a good deal of the nation's social and domestic life as well. More specifically, reexamine Edison's essay by comparing and contrasting the gender stereotypes it promotes with those in the spate of domestic engineering books popular in the second decade of this century. The most prominent of these household management books were *The Business of Home Management: The Principles of Domestic Engineering* (1915), by Mary Pattison, and *Household Engineering: Scientific Management in the Home* (1919), by Christine Frederick. These volumes and numerous others were grounded in the same stereotypes that pervade Edison's vision of a future when a woman "will be rather a domestic engineer than a domestic laborer."

Generating Writing

1. Most of us, at one time or another, have sought to organize the clutter and crowded schedules of our daily lives and to make ourselves more efficient managers of our own experience. Reread Edison's essay, focusing on the efficiency he seeks as well as on the principles that underpin that vision. Try to adapt those principles and procedures to your own experience. Write the first draft of an essay in which you imagine how you might make your daily life more efficient than it currently is. As an undergraduate, how might you make each day's business of going to classes, reading course material, and writing papers far more efficient? What tone of voice will you need to adopt in presenting these ideas to your readers (other students as well as your instructor)?

2. Edison talks about "microscopical examination and exact measurement" of experience in an effort if not to "perfect" it then certainly to improve it, to eliminate as many of its flaws as possible. Consider the developments in the recording industry over the past twenty years or so. How have the dramatic advances in stereophonic sound recordings changed responses to and interest in attending concerts? Are concertgoers less willing to tolerate or perhaps more understanding about "flaws" in live performances by musicians? Write an essay in which you explore this issue from the vantage point of your own experience, of those you know, and of research you conduct on the subject.

Jamaica Kincaid

Girl

Teaching Strategies

Jamaica Kincaid makes a powerful statement about cultural conditioning in "Girl" without saying a word about it. The mother whose voice dominates this nearly uninterrupted dramatic monologue speaks in imperatives and declarative sentences that admit no backtalk. Your students will probably enjoy this story in the way one enjoys a dramatic monologue by, say, Robert Browning: they can eavesdrop on a person from an exotic land, and, more important, they catch this person in the act of inadvertently revealing more than he or she realizes. In Kincaid's story, the mother exposes at least one source of gender stereotyping. The Jamaican setting of this story should create enough distance for most students to feel comfortable discussing how gender stereotypes are perpetuated in the home, starting with the example in the story, then moving closer to home. Students may get carried away finding evidence of the mother's sexism once they realize that this is the subtext of her instructions. This is a productive first response: encourage them to find subtler evidence for this assertion. Of course the mother's beliefs are not idiosyncratic, and responsibility for the sexism clearly is not hers alone. The evidence that she genuinely cares for her daughter's welfare should lead students to realize that her warnings about sexual promiscuity spring from the same source as her instructions about etiquette: she is transmitting her culture's gender expectations to her daughter with the probably benign intention of making it possible for her daughter to live in that culture without friction.

If possible, have a student read this story aloud to the class; it's obviously meant to be heard. For this reason, you might want to use this story to teach tone. Help them to identify the features, including diction and syntax, that make the mother's voice vivid and forceful.

The story could also spark a discussion of point of view. Have students identify the point of view, and then brainstorm situations in which such a perspective might be effective. Discuss the reader's position toward speaker and listener in such a text. Your students probably are already familiar with persuasive methods designed to win a reader to their point of view. Discuss indirectly persuasive methods in "Girl" that nudge the reader into a position not directly represented in the text. Ask about their experience with other ironic texts. Have they ever felt confused about the position the author wished them to take? How would they construct an ironic text so as to make the reader side with them — without, of course, directly stating their own position?

Why does the mother give her daughter all this advice? Ask students to categorize the kinds of advice she offers. Why is it sometimes difficult to sort the mother's statements neatly into boxes labeled, perhaps, *survival, etiquette,* and *morality,* or *social* and *personal?* Look at this quotation from the story: "this is how to hem a dress when you see the hem coming down and so to prevent yourself from looking like the slut I know you are so bent on becoming." Can they find other sentences in which one kind of statement slips unexpectedly into an entirely different kind of statement? What is the effect of these juxtapositions? How are seemingly discrete categories such as survival, etiquette, and morality intertwined?

Not one man speaks in this story. Nonetheless, a pervasive yet subtle male influence stands behind the mother's words. Find the references to men and boys. What can you tell about the men behind the scenes? What can you infer about the mother's relationship to the father? What can you infer about the balance of power between the genders in the community in which the daughter is being raised?

Additional Activities

Kincaid's story could be taught in conjunction with Jonathan Swift's "Modest Proposal" (Chapter 27) and Judy Brady's "I Want a Wife" (Chapter 22) in studying irony. Students will discover differing degrees of difficulty in their attempt to pin down each author's unstated position.

"Girl" also fits nicely with the selections in "Family Stories" (Chapter 12), especially with "No Name Woman," by Kingston. The mothers in both pieces speak cautionary words aimed at saving their daughters from the consequences of promiscuity. Students may want to explore the differences between a text in which the mother is reticent, forcing the daughter to fill in the blanks, and a text in which the mother hardly closes her mouth long enough for her daughter to get a word in.

Generating Writing

1. The daughter in "Girl" speaks only two lines, both of which are italicized. Still, it is possible to infer something about her character even though her mother does most of the talking. Ask students to analyze the daughter's character, both from what she says and from what she hears (if they believe that she filtered these words of wisdom from an endless stream provided by her mother).

2. In conjunction with "Girl," ask students to read Robert Browning's poem, "My Last Duchess" (reprinted here). Using features of dramatic monologue drawn from both pieces, they should construct a dramatic monologue of their own. They may write in verse or prose. Remind them to use Kincaid and Browning as models for the *form*, but not the *content*, of their own work.

My Last Duchess
FERRARA

THAT'S my last Duchess painted on the wall,
Looking as if she were alive. I call
That piece a wonder, now: Frà Pandolf's hands
Worked busily a day, and there she stands.
Will't please you sit and look at her? I said
"Frà Pandolf" by design, for never read
Strangers like you that pictured countenance,
The depth and passion of its earnest glance,
But to myself they turned (since none puts by
The curtain I have drawn for you, but I)
And seemed as they would ask me, if they durst,
How such a glance came there; so, not the first
Are you to turn and ask thus Sir, 'twas not
Her husband's presence only, called that spot
Of joy into the Duchess' cheek: perhaps
Frà Pandolf chanced to say "Her mantle laps
Over my lady's wrist too much," or "Paint
Must never hope to reproduce the faint
Half-flush that dies along her throat:" such stuff
Was courtesy, she thought, and cause enough
For calling up that spot of joy. She had
A heart — how shall I say? — too soon made glad,
Too easily impressed; she liked whate'er
She looked on, and her looks went everywhere.
Sir, 'twas all one! My favor at her breast,
The dropping of the daylight in the West,
The bough of cherries some officious fool
Broke in the orchard for her, the white mule
She rode with round the terrace — all and each

Would draw from her alike the approving speech,
Or blush, at least. She thanked men, — good! but thanked
Somehow — I know not how — as if she ranked
My gift of a nine-hundred-years-old name
With anybody's gift. Who'd stoop to blame
This sort of trifling? Even had you skill
In speech — (which I have not) — to make your will
Quite clear to such an one, and say, "Just this
Or that in you disgusts me; here you miss,
Or there exceed the mark" — and if she let
Herself be lessoned so, nor plainly set
Her wits to yours, forsooth, and made excuse,
— E'en then would be some stooping; and I choose
Never to stoop. Oh sir, she smiled, no doubt,
Whene'er I passed her; but who passed without
Much the same smile? This grew; I gave commands;
Then all smiles stopped together. There she stands
As if alive. Will't please you rise? We'll meet
The company below, then. I repeat,
The Count your master's known munificence
Is ample warrant that no just pretence
Of mine for dowry will be disallowed;
Though his fair daughter's self, as I avowed
At starting, is my object. Nay, we'll go
Together down, sir. Notice Neptune, though,
Taming a sea-horse, thought a rarity,
Which Claus of Innsbrück cast in bronze for me!

— Robert Browning

Bruce Curtis

The Wimp Factor

Teaching Strategies

Bruce Curtis's article, first published in *American Heritage* (November 1989), adds to the chapter on gender stereotypes by focusing on sexist stereotypes directed at men. As this article illustrates, neither women nor men are immune to the pressures and limitations gender places on them, and no individual power can deflect gender-based expectations and criticisms: even the president of the United States is subject to a continual critique of his "manliness." Assigning "The Wimp Factor" will help keep your classroom from becoming unproductively polarized: if male students feel accused and female students feel self-righteous, no one will learn anything. And, as any instructor who has brought gender issues to bear in the classroom knows, the most entrenched sexist viewpoints do not inevitably come from male students. Gender stereotyping is so prevalent that even Curtis, who should after all be on the lookout for such pitfalls, falls prey to the sexist assumption that journalists of the future will all be "men" (para. 38). Some stereotypes are worn so thin by overuse that they are nearly transparent. For this reason, essayists analyzing the fabric of our culture provide an essential service for any reader, male or female.

"The Wimp Factor" is a good model for students who will need to write fairly substantial research papers for college courses, but can't fully imagine how to move past the traditional five-paragraph essay structure. Have them analyze the structure of Curtis's essay, not only describing the organization of his main points but also speculating on the reasons for that organization. What, for example, is the effect of starting with contemporary examples before backtracking into history? Have them identify Curtis's thesis, and then explore the ways in which he complicates his argument without diverging from that thesis. One good way for students to improve their organization when revising a long paper is to write a one-sentence summary of each paragraph, stringing these sentences together to form a new paragraph (or series of paragraphs, depending on the length of the original paper) that forms a condensed version of their original paper. Any difficulty in making the sentences cohere into paragraphs may warn of an organizational problem in the original paper, or perhaps an idea that hasn't been thought out and articulated clearly enough. The whole class might try this technique on Curtis's essay as a practice run before applying it to their own drafts.

"The Wimp Factor" is a nice model for their research papers for at least two reasons other than development and organization. First, Curtis integrates supporting quotations with grace and economy. And second, his style is very personable. Students sometimes need to be shown that a stiff and stuffy tone is not the only one appropriate for essays that incorporate research on such weighty topics as politics and history.

Curtis analyzes the language of political campaigns and other relevant political statements to illustrate his point about mandatory machismo. He gives examples of metaphors drawn by past United States presidents from such stereotypically masculine domains as wrestling, poker, football, and boxing. He also demonstrates "wimp-baiting" language, such as images of emasculation, with which the press sets out to discredit candidates. Ask students why this linguistic evidence matters? How does Curtis show that language used by press and politicians can have serious repercussions? What might be some real-life results of their choices of diction and imagery?

Curtis ends his essay with restrained optimism because recent challenges to "traditional images of racial superiority and inferiority" have had "considerable success." Do you agree with Curtis that such challenges have succeeded? Support your answer with incidents from the news or your experience. Why do you think Curtis foresees new and more flexible gender definitions because of new images on race? What connections do you see between these two spheres? Can you decipher a historical connection between the two waves of feminism Curtis mentions and the struggles for racial equality?

Additional Activities

This essay has many similarities to those making up Chapter 32, "Language and Politics." And because Curtis's so often examines the repercussions of language by analyzing metaphors, his essay could also be successfully taught with Chapter 33, "The Power of Metaphor."

You might also teach it in conjunction with Chapter 11, "A National Obsession" and Chapter 16, "Consumer Culture," to focus on the effects of popular culture. Students often enjoy writing analyses of pop culture. They get a chance to feel like experts for they are generally more familiar with the latest popular genres. An added advantage is that in writing their assignments, they may undergo transformation from passive receptacles to informed critics of culture.

Try putting your students into groups (made up of both males and females), and have each group brainstorm ideas for four lists: (1) words (nouns, adjectives, similes) conventionally used to describe women, (2) words often used to describe men, (3) words often used to describe men who behave in ways considered "female," and (4) words often used for women who behave in ways considered "male." When they have fairly substantial lists, ask each group to compose a short skit, in which a male and a female character face the same situation (such as asking the boss for a raise, or asking someone to dance). After the skits have been performed, reconvene the class to discuss not only how the lists and the skits were composed (did they decide to have their characters act according to conventional gender expectations or not?), but also the audience's reaction to the skits. (Did students laugh when a male character acted in ways traditionally perceived as feminine? How did they react to a female character behaving in ways usually seen as masculine?) Encourage them to analyze their reactions to this classroom exercise.

You may find that several students have never voted. To help them understand the power of the press to influence decisions, discuss originality — many students may not realize how difficult it is to have even one original opinion in this age of mass media. You could start discussion by asking questions like these: Have you ever found yourself in the position of voting for someone who didn't turn out to represent your values, or buying something that didn't turn out to fit your sense of personal style, or expressing an opinion that surprised you the instant you heard it coming out of your own mouth, because you had no idea where that opinion originated? How did you feel when that happened? Can you track the origins of your "choice"? How many influences are tangled up inside you? Do you believe that a sense of personal style, or an independently formed opinion, even exists? How would you know if you had hit upon the real, unadulterated you?

Ideally, of course, you will have to pose only the first of these questions. After students come up with examples, the follow-up questions should arise spontaneously from the discussion.

Generating Writing

1. Bruce Curtis gathers his examples of wimp baiting from, among other sources, *The New Republic, Time,* and the *New York Review of Books.* Choose a current event that is receiving a great deal of media attention, and examine several newspaper and magazine accounts of that event. Do these accounts seem perfectly objective? Or do their authors use loaded language, such as that Curtis discovers in the press coverage of every American president since Thomas Jefferson? Write a paper in which you analyze the language of the articles you've found. Upon examination, do the sources all reveal the same subtext, or are differing attitudes subtly promoted by different journals?

2. Curtis describes the condemnation risked by men who support the women's movement — "the Alan Aldas of their day." He also describes the double bind in which women politicians are caught: "if gentle, they are womanish; if tough, they are not womanly." Both men and women are restricted to gender roles that are sanctioned by public opinion, and public opinion often is not flexible enough to allow people to follow their own conscience, or show their true feelings. Have you ever found yourself in a position that would have been easier to handle if you'd had the full range of attributes and behaviors open to you? Write a paper in which you narrate that experience, and meditate on its full implications.

WRITING ABOUT THE CHAPTER

1. Using Jamaica Kincaid's story as a model, have students revise the draft they wrote before reading the selections. This time, instead of writing from their own point of view, encourage them to borrow a voice from one of the people who helped shape their gender identity. They may choose, as Kincaid did, to write from the point of view of one person — a parent, perhaps, or a teacher — or they may create a medley of voices as from family members or the media. Encourage them to go back into memory and listen for the voices that told them how to act, who they were. Tell them to write down those words without commenting on them; let their message, like Kincaid's, be implied rather than stated.

2. Among the epigraphs is a quotation from Dorothy Sayers, who imagines a world in which men are treated as women are every day in the real world. Say to the students: Write an essay in which you create a mirror universe in which gender stereotypes are the reverse of those in your own world. You may choose to limit your description to one gender, describing either your own experience in dealing with the gender expectations traditionally imposed on people of the other gender, or, as Sayers does, turning the tables on people

of the other gender. Another option to consider is to describe the experiences of both men and women in that mirror universe. (If you choose the latter, you will need to remember to work with a manageable number of examples.)

3. Bruce Curtis analyzes the language of campaign speeches, editorials, and political cartoons to illustrate his thesis about the underlying sexism in these public statements. Using Curtis's method as a model, choose either Thomas Edison's or Alexis de Tocqueville's article, and then analyze the author's language. Is the woman who interviewed Edison accurate when she says that his message "will wipe offense away"? What are the implications of de Tocqueville's preference for an equal but different status for women? You may need specific evidence from the text to support your assertions about the subtext of the essay.

22

Resistance to Stereotypes

Virginia Woolf, Thoughts on Peace in an Air Raid

Judy Brady, I Want a Wife

Bob Greene, Mr. President

WORKING WITH THE CHAPTER

Some of the most exciting moments in teaching come when students begin to scrutinize the assumptions and preconceptions they have always taken for granted. Our role in helping this growth along is challenging and rewarding; sometimes clichés and prejudices can be firmly rooted, requiring a bit of judicious excavation by the instructor. The best revelations are the ones students discover on their own (or, perhaps, with a little indirect direction). This chapter's selections should help inspire reflection and reassessment on the issue of stereotypes.

Virginia Woolf examines how stereotypes left unquestioned help shape a vicious circle of war and destruction. Judy Brady's and Bob Greene's selections are lighter treatments of the issue, focusing on housework as an epitome of the burdens placed upon us by sex roles. Chapter epigraphs come from various eras and sources, giving perspectives as diverse as Sojourner Truth's and Paul Theroux's on the restrictions stereotypes impose.

As a whole, the chapter elucidates the conflict between individual freedom and the limitations of stereotypes. Students' responses will be quick and passionate; they should find here powerful resonances with their own experience.

Teaching Strategies

The epigraphs for this chapter neatly summarize the complexity of the issues. You might want to start with Sojourner Truth's view, as reported by Frances Dana Barker Gage. This passage is a quotation from an account of a speech by Truth; students may be familiar with her career on the Underground Railroad and as an activist for the rights of African-Americans and women after the Civil War. How do students feel about hearing her views through a third party? What do they think about the use of dialect here?

Ask students to imagine a dialogue between Truth and Brady. How might she respond to Brady's request for a wife? What does the conjunction of these two selections reveal about how time, place, class, and race influence gender expectations?

Rita Mae Brown, like Brady, uses irony to make a serious point. How do students react to this epigraph? Do they find it funny? They may want to challenge the validity of Brown's description of courting behavior and how women treat men. Discuss this issue; do students feel compromised by the behavior expected of them in dating? Are these roles exclusive to heterosexual relationships, or does gay and lesbian culture have its own versions? How do dating roles differ from the sex roles required in business, school, or other aspects of life?

Paul Theroux's epigraph might be interestingly paired with Greene's article on Thomas Lucas. Ask students how that piece might have been different if Theroux (himself a journalist) had written it instead of Greene. Does Greene seem to feel that the masculine role is "a hideous and crippling lie"? Does Thomas Lucas?

Theroux's epigraph also seems to echo Woolf's view of the male role as leading to dangerous and destructive behavior. *Soldierly* clearly has a negative meaning for Theroux, as it has for Woolf. How might this role be emotionally damaging? How might its damage to individuals harm society as a whole?

A Writing-before-Reading Exercise

Ask students to write a brief description of some ways in which they have challenged stereotypes in their own life. How do they feel about those challenges? Were they successful? Next, have them discuss an occasion when they felt limited by a stereotype but failed to challenge it. How did that make them feel? If they had a time machine set to return to that moment, what would they do differently?

WORKING WITH THE SELECTIONS

Virginia Woolf

Thoughts on Peace in an Air Raid

Teaching Strategies

This essay is subtle, thoughtful, and perhaps a little difficult to grasp on first reading. Encourage students to reread the piece; ask them to take down questions they may have and discuss them in class. Some students may require background to understand the essay thoroughly; you might want to remind them that, in 1940, America was not yet involved in the war. How does that information change their view of Woolf's tone and intent? What might the purpose of this essay be?

One place to start might be to address the question of Woolf's audience. The essay was written for an American symposium on women, and it is explicitly addressed to women — those at the symposium and, by extension, women everywhere. These are the women Woolf seems to mean by "we," throughout. Discuss this audience with the class. Do male students feel excluded? Point out that this is a response to war rhetoric, which included statements like "we will fight them on the beaches," where "we" excluded that half of the population not permitted to enlist. Does the rhetoric of peace need to exclude men? Does the rhetoric of war need to exclude women?

Discuss Woolf's career with the class. How might her identity as novelist and feminist help define her position on war and its origins? What agenda might she be expected to have? The style of the essay could be challenging for students; they may find it unusual for political writing. How does Woolf's avoidance of a traditionally "political" approach support her claim that complete social reconstruction is vital? Does her refusal to adopt the "role" of pundit or philosopher reinforce her call for rejecting roles?

Paragraph 1 sets the tone for the piece, and needs careful attention from students. They may not be familiar with the details of World War II; you might bring in photographs of London during the Blitz to illustrate the urgency of Woolf's fear for her own, and her nation's, life. What do they think of her phrase, "unless we can think peace into existence"? What might that mean? How does it challenge a "war mentality"?

Talk about Woolf's metaphor of ideas as weapons. You might discuss the "war effort," in which civilians had so vital a part; World War II was the last war in which American and European civilian populations participated significantly. How does this arrangement differ from our current experience of war and armed conflict? Show students how Woolf uses a wartime government's own rhetoric against it; she answers the incessant propaganda calls to make clothing, weapons, food for the war effort with her own cry to make peace for the peace effort. This was a daring move in the England of 1940; how might the courage of her stand forestall claims about the cowardice of pacifism?

Woolf quotes from Blake's "And Did Those Feet" (also known as "Jerusalem"). You may want to read the poem aloud to the class; does her allusion to it reinforce her theme of rebuilding and rebirth? Why are the Christian elements of Blake's vision missing from Woolf's?

One main point Woolf makes in this essay appears in her statement, "If we could free ourselves from slavery we should free men from tyranny. Hitlers are bred by slaves." You might first point out that *should* here means *would* in American usage — Woolf does not mean that if women freed themselves from slavery then they ought to free men from tyranny, but rather that one would follow the other naturally. Ask students what Woolf means here by *slavery*. What is meant by her evocation of dressed-up, made-up women as the mothers of Hitlers? Part of the allusion may be biographical, for Allied propaganda maintained that Hitler was the illegitimate child of an amateur prostitute, but what else could Woolf imply? Do students agree with her view of power and sexuality?

Invite students to analyze Woolf's characterizing a soldier's motivation. Do nations go to war because of romantic ideals about the nobility of battle? How might that possibility be avoided? Is Woolf's parallel with the mythologies of motherhood accurate? Discuss the statement, "We must compensate the man for the loss of his gun." What is meant here? What honors could societies award for peace?

Ask the class how Woolf ties the limitations of sex roles to militaristic ideology. Is a society that forces roles on its citizens more apt to try to force its will on others? Why, or why not?

Additional Activities

Examine this essay in conjunction with Elizabeth Cady Stanton's "Declaration of Sentiments and Resolutions" (Chapter 24). What principles do Woolf and Stanton seem to share? How might their visions of a just and equal society differ? You might also want to look at the selection from Lakoff and Johnson's *Metaphors We Live By* (Chapter 33) while keeping in mind Woolf's admonition to "think peace into existence." How might we *talk* peace into existence?

Ask students what they know about women in protest movements. (The Frances Dana Barker Gage epigraph on Sojourner Truth might also be brought in for discussion.) Students may want to research this topic; some places to start might be women's part in the pacifist movement today (Dr. Helen Caldecott is only one example), in the Black Nationalist movement of the 1960s (Angela Davis, among others), or in other nations, such as South Africa (Winnie Mandela, Nadine Gordimer, and the women's group Black Sash are three who spring to mind). How do gender roles help or hurt positions of protest?

Generating Writing

1. Ask students to write an essay outlining their view of a future without war. One way into this subject may be for them to discuss how war changes history; how else might political

changes come about? What ways of resolving conflict might replace war? If we do "think peace into existence," how might we enact that thought?

2. Assign a personal essay on students' experience of war. If they have had no direct or second-hand experience of war, they may want to discuss images of war in the media and their psychological effect. How do they feel their gender influences their perception of war? How do they feel their exposure to images of war has helped shape their views of sex roles?

Judy Brady

I Want a Wife

Teaching Strategies

This essay has a lighter tone, although Brady's irony cuts deep. First published in 1971, it is (one hopes) a bit dated, and yet the problems Brady addresses are still here in one form or another. Its agenda is fairly straightforward, and students should not have much difficulty grasping it.

One approach to teaching the piece might be to have students read it aloud, alternating between genders. How do the words sound different to the class when read by a man or a woman? What kinds of feelings does the essay and its tone raise in students?

The question of audience might be addressed here as well. The essay was published in *Ms.* magazine's first issue, and therefore may safely be assumed to be primarily directed toward women interested in equal rights. Does Brady seem to be describing her own experience here, as a whole or in part? Is it an experience likely to be shared by her audience? Ask students to recall similar experiences of their mothers, aunts, or older friends. If you have older students who can be coaxed into autobiography, their comments may be tremendously valuable.

What kind of background does Brady seem, from her essay, to have? Are the things she demands from her "wife" (help in attending college or graduate school, for instance) things that the majority of men in society demand from their wives? What does that say about Brady's relative position of privilege? How might a poor or uneducated woman have framed her protest against the pressures of wifehood?

Ask students how much of Brady's complaint is accurate today. What do they, men and women, expect from women? What do they expect from men? How does each gender perceive the other's roles and duties? How do they perceive their own?

You might want to do a role-playing exercise, inviting students to discuss this essay from the opposite gender's point of view. Have the men in the class take Brady's side as the women argue against her. After discussion has gone on for a while, ask students to switch back to their usual roles. How did they feel about adopting the other gender's perspective? Discuss how people rationalize their stereotypes. What kinds of social pressures help maintain gender roles? What does society invest in them?

How does Brady's tone affect the force of her argument? How can humor be an effective form of protest? Why is Brady's statement, "I want a wife," funny? What taboos does it seem to challenge or break? How?

Additional Activities

Return to Thomas Edison's "The Woman of the Future" (Chapter 2). What do the woman he is describing and Judy Brady's ideal wife have in common? How do they differ? Why is Brady's essay satire and Edison's not? How can we tell from the authors' language? How much context do we need to know that Edison is serious and Brady sarcastic?

How might Vivian Gornick respond to the charge that very little has changed for women and wives since the time of Brady's article? Refer students to her essay on the women's movement (Chapter 18). Which of Brady's points might she echo today?

You may want to bring in some of the myriad books, comic strips, movies, and television shows that deal with the supposedly hilarious situation of a man having to perform housework and child-care duties. (The syndicated comic strip "Adam," television shows like "My Two Dads" or "My Three Sons," and movies like *Mr. Mom* or *Three Men and a Baby* are just a few examples of the genre Jay Leno calls, "Mom's dead, let's have a party!") Why is the depiction of a man trying unsuccessfully to change a diaper funny? What does that say about the relative values of sex roles? How might Brady comment on these?

Generating Writing

1. Ask students to prepare a rebuttal to Brady's essay, entitled "I Want a Husband." They should adopt the point of view of an aggrieved husband feeling the pressures of his role. How might a "husband" help husbands in our society?

2. Have students rewrite Brady's essay as a straightforward, nonhumorous discussion about the unfair demands of a wife's role. How do they feel about the argument? How did her presentation help or hurt her in getting her point across?

Bob Greene

Mr. President

Teaching Strategies

Students may already be familiar with Bob Greene's work, because his column is widely syndicated in newspapers. His reports on offbeat Americana are funny and good-natured, generous rather than satirical. Remind students about the genre of the "human-interest story," beloved of family newspapers and television shows. Is this a classic human-interest story?

Ask students what they know about Future Homemakers of America. What might the purpose of such an organization be? Who do they think might be its members? Were they surprised to find that 11 percent of its membership is male?

Greene mentions early that Thomas Lucas was a defensive tackle for his high school's football team. Why might Greene have included this fact? What stereotypes do we have of football players and other athletes that might conflict with our stereotype of homemakers? Are the roles necessarily at odds?

Discuss Greene's portrayal of Lucas's parents and their reactions to his choice of extracurricular activities. What does his stepfather say about Lucas's interest in homemaking? Does Greene's description of his encounter with the family cast doubt on the sincerity of Mr. Brown's enthusiasm for homemaking? The first time Thomas's mother appears, she is described as entering "from the kitchen, where she had been preparing dinner." Later, she calls from the kitchen that "dinner is served." In her discussion of Thomas's help around the house, no mention is made of Mr. Brown's help; this seems a significant omission. How might this absence support Thomas's contention that "the bad stereotype comes from adults"? Do students feel Greene is exposing Brown's lack of interest in domestic chores on purpose, as irony, or do they feel Greene, a member of Brown's generation, just doesn't notice?

What does Greene's attitude toward Thomas Lucas seem to be? What linguistic and stylistic clues do students find to support their answer to that question? Does Greene respect Lucas's achievement? Does he invite his readers to do so? This essay was first published in

Esquire magazine, which is aimed at a primarily male readership. What influence does that background have on their reading of the essay and of Greene's intentions in it?

What are students' attitudes toward Lucas as he is depicted in the piece? Do they agree or disagree with his statements about the importance of homemaking for both sexes? What do they think about his friend's assessment of Lucas's accomplishment? Would they agree with his statement that "it's about time for boys to learn stuff that has always been thought of as women's stuff"? Ask them to list some duties or tasks that they feel have always been thought of as part of a feminine social role. Have them list other responsibilities tradition-ally assigned to men. How valid are these traditions today? Discuss this issue, then ask students to list some responsibilities that they feel are still rightfully women's. Why? Have them list tasks that they think are necessarily masculine. Why do they find them so?

Additional Activities

Scott Russell Sanders's "The Men We Carry in Our Minds" (Chapter 23) is an interesting complement to this piece. How might Sanders assess Thomas Lucas and his ambition? What might Lucas think of Sanders's essay? How might he respond?

How is the story of Thomas Lucas a response to the questions raised in Bruce Curtis's "The Wimp Factor" (Chapter 21)? Does Greene go out of his way to show that Thomas Lucas is not a wimp? Does Lucas seem uneasy about possible accusations of wimpiness? Do his parents?

Students interested in this topic may want to look at some recent work on the philosophy of masculinity and the problem of the male role in society. One good place to start is with John Stoltenberg's book *Refusing to Be a Man: Essays on Sex and Justice* (London: Collins, 1990), which provides an absorbing and comprehensive account of one man's experience and a view of the growing movement to restructure masculine roles. Perhaps colleagues involved in this issue will speak to the class on the problems wound up in our society's definition of *man*.

Generating Writing

1. Have students "enter" two imaginary essay contests — one to determine the presi-dency of the Future Homemakers of America and one to determine who will be head of the Junior Business Achievers' club. Ask each student to write the best essay he or she can, regardless of how little they care about homemaking or business (for incentive they may need an imaginary cash prize). When they have finished, ask them to evaluate their own work. How did their gender color their view of themselves as president of the organizations? Have students discuss their work in groups, perhaps passing essays around with names covered, trying to guess which essays were written by men and which by women.

2. Ask students to write a personal essay on housework and gender, and what the connection between the two means to them. They may want to focus on their mothers' experiences, or inequities among siblings in assignment of household chores, or perhaps their plans for division of labor in a future household. Can housework be a symbol of more than inconvenience and difficulty?

WRITING ABOUT THE CHAPTER

1. The Brady and Greene selections are complementary enough to inspire a number of compare-and-contrast assignments. Students might want to compare tone, say, or contrast the ways in which housework is depicted in the two essays. The selections could also form the basis for a longer assignment on how sex roles have changed over the last twenty years; this could be a project for group or individual research, class discussion, or student presentations.

2. The Woolf essay is perhaps the least accessible in the chapter. In some ways, though, it is the most important, for it leads the discussion of stereotyping's harmful effects out of the private sphere and into the public. Ask students to examine how strongly gender stereotypes influence the political world. You could assign them to collate coverage of male and female politicians and compare the adjectives describing them and the approaches taken toward them by members of the press. How great a part do gender stereotypes occupy in our ideology of war? Students might give presentations on sex roles in novels, plays, movies, or television programs depicting war. What does a running joke like M*A*S*H*'s transvestite Corporal Klinger say about our views of manhood and war?

23

Conflicting Loyalties

June Jordan, Waiting for a Taxi

Paula Gunn Allen, Where I Come from Is Like This

Scott Russell Sanders, The Men We Carry in Our Minds

WORKING WITH THE CHAPTER

Teaching Strategies

Because of relatively recent shifts in gender paradigms, many men and women find themselves falling into the gap between traditional gender roles. Olga Silverstein identifies a "younger generation of women" who "are often denying the feminine voice, and yet they can't take on the masculine voice either." Terry Allen Kupers, in his epigraph to this chapter, writes of the dilemmas facing today's "feminist men." The women and men described by these two authors are trying to invent new ways of constructing relationships in a world in which the dividing line between male and female roles is continually being eroded.

The essays in this chapter explore some of the factors that can complicate one's perspective on gender. As Scott Russell Sanders points out in "The Men We Carry in Our Minds," one's class status can make an enormous difference in one's perspective. Sanders grew up in rural Tennessee and Ohio, the son of poor, hardworking parents, and his experience with oppression made him first envy and then identify with the plight of women. Racial factors also come to play in one's response to gender, as we see in Paula Gunn Allen's essay "Where I Come from Is Like This." Allen, a Native American woman, finds herself in a "bicultural bind": she and women like her have to "identify with two hopelessly opposed cultural definitions of women." It is clear from the essays by Sanders and Gunn Allen that no two cultures define gender roles in precisely the same ways, and often, when two cultures come into contact, as they do when a lower-class boy gets a scholarship to an expensive college, or when one race vanquishes another, people can find themselves torn between conflicting value systems.

June Jordan's essay combines the concerns of each of the other two essays — gender, class, and race — and then attempts to rise above them. For this reason, Jordan's piece can be seen as a capstone to this chapter. She experiences the conflicting loyalties that come from being both black and female, but she also seeks a principle that will transcend identity politics. The epigraph by Vivian Gornick is relevant in this context. She describes her Jewishness as an asset because it has allowed her to "think analogously about 'them' and 'us'": she can "think more inventively" about gender oppression for having experienced racial oppression. Her emphasis on the structure of oppression is reminiscent of bell hooks's thesis in "Feminism: A Transformational Politic" (see Chapter 18). Although their solutions differ, Jordan and hooks would make a productive interconnection, because their goals are so similar.

A Writing-before-Reading Exercise

Ask students to think back to a specific time when they experienced a sense of conflicting loyalties. Ask them to choose an incident that brought previously existing, incompatible loyalties to the surface. This could be the moment when they first became aware of their own internal tug-of-war, or a moment that would encapsulate that tug-of-war for a reading audience. Next have them represent that moment of conflict, not in narrative form, not even in sentences, but rather on a map. Instruct them to represent their internal conflict pictorially or symbolically, and to write or draw in the details — snatches of dialogue, images, feelings, childhood memories, and so on — in appropriate places on the map, to represent the alliances and discordances that fed into the incident.

Some students may be a little uncomfortable with this kind of assignment at first: they might not expect to produce nonlinear work for an English class. Their expectations are one good reason for trying such exercises as mapping: the more often you can surprise students, the better your chances of jolting them into a new insight. Assure these students that their maps will not be graded or judged in any way; this is just an opportunity to try something different. If, in the course of a semester, you show them many different ways of starting the writing process, you will be providing an opportunity for the students, many of whom are still discovering their intellectual styles, to learn which methods work best for them.

WORKING WITH THE SELECTIONS

June Jordan

Waiting for a Taxi

Teaching Strategies

This essay may be difficult for students: as in her essay, "Nobody Mean More to Me than You and the Future Life of Willie Jordan" (see Chapter 32), the author combines personal experience with political rhetoric in a way that can be confusing to people reading her work for the first time. You may want to teach the two pieces by Jordan in tandem, to give students a stronger sense of her style and its underlying purposes. Let them ask the first questions, so you can get a sense of their problems and insights regarding the essays. Many will wonder what the murder of the black man in "Nobody Mean More to Me" has to do with the issue of black English, which is discussed in the same essay. Others will wonder what the opening incident in "Waiting for a Taxi" has to do with Jordan's argument against identity politics. They will wonder how Jordan's revelation in Paris connects with her revelation in Liverpool.

You may need to walk through this essay with students step by step. Look first at the incident in Paris. Ask them why it is significant that this incident takes place on the anniversary of the French Revolution. How do the words *Liberté, Egalité, Fraternité* reverberate in later parts of the essay? Ask them to paraphrase the meaning of the cab drivers' refusal to stop and pick up Jordan and her companions. What does she mean when she says that "the problems of our identity" surfaced? At this point in the essay, whose narrow-mindedness is being exposed?

After a line break, Jordan translates the literal taxi into a metaphor for a solution to identity politics, which she defines as "politics based on gender, class, or race." Thus far in the essay, it seems as if the people who are guilty of identity politics are people such as the racist cab drivers — enemies who can affect one, but only from the outside. If this is the case, why does Jordan write the following paragraphs in the first person plural, beginning with the statement "Many of us function on the basis of habits of thought that automatically concede paramount importance to race or class"? (Make sure students understand the explanation of the fallacies and evils of identity politics as they are explained in these paragraphs. Shelby Steele's essay "Black and Middle Class" (see Chapter 6) might facilitate their comprehension of these ideas.) Beginning in paragraph 14, Jordan explains how oppressed people themselves have come to identify themselves by their race, class, or gender. Gloria Naylor's essay "A Question of Language" (see Chapter 34) might be a helpful interconnection here, because Naylor gives an expansive illustration of what Jordan means when she writes that "we have created these positive implications as a source of self-defense." At this point students should be realizing that Jordan's main purpose is not to rail at external perpetrators of racial injustice, but rather to revolutionize the ways in which "those of us who began our lives in difficult conditions," including herself, see themselves. She wants to move past identity politics, and she rejoices in evidence that a new kind of thinking that "underlies or supersedes" identity politics is possible. In the remainder of the essay, Jordan recounts personal experiences — which you will want to examine with the class — that have shown her the dangers and irrelevance of identity politics. She also proposes a solution to the kind of narrow-minded thinking she deplores: she finds this solution in concepts such as justice, equality, and tenderness. How do these concepts come to Jordan's rescue in the course of the essay? Does her solution appeal to students?

At the end of the essay, Jordan returns to the rainy night in Paris with which she opened her essay. Ask students to analyze the shift in her attitude from the first time she told this story and this final mention. Why has her exhilaration returned? How have the taxi drivers been transformed from enemies into brothers? Can your students relate the taxi drivers to any other characters in the essay, without falling too deeply into the traps of identity politics? What is the overall effect on the reader of this spiral structure, in which the author circles back to her original topic?

Additional Activities

Chapter 6, "Divided Identities," would also make a natural pairing with this chapter. The authors in both chapters find themselves torn between and among the various facets of their identities, and all of them try to find a way to resolve their inner conflicts. You might consider teaching the two chapters in succession, and assigning one paper in which students could draw on any of the essays in either chapter — perhaps a paper comparing and contrasting the various resolutions discovered by the authors.

You might also want to analyze Jordan's examination of language. In paragraph 16 she writes that "race and class . . . are not the same kinds of words as grass and stars." What difference is she positing? How do words contain the histories, the contexts in which they have been used? What other differences can students spot between "race and class" on the one hand and "grass and stars" on the other? Do they notice that the first pair is more abstract than the second? Two paragraphs later she proposes three abstract concepts as an alternative to identity politics. Ask students to speculate about why she would choose to set these abstractions, rather than something more concrete, in opposition to the abstractions of race and class.

You might also have them look at Jordan's writing style. What words and phrases does she repeat, within a paragraph or series of consecutive paragraphs? What is the effect of this repetition? How does her language help her to effect the transitions between the different sections of her essay? How would students describe her style and tone throughout the essay? Do they sense any shifts in style or tone? Point out the last sentence in the essay. What is the effect and significance of such shifts?

Generating Writing

Assign an essay in which students explore the role of habit in "Waiting for a Taxi." How have the habits Jordan describes come into being? What could be seen as their positive function? What, on the other hand, are the dangers of remaining within existing "habits of thought"? What kinds of experiences encourage the breaking of such habits? What are the benefits of breaking free of the force of habit?

June Jordan embedded a poem, "Solidarity," within her essay. This poem stems from the same incident that opens "Waiting for a Taxi." Have students write a comparison/contrast paper about the poem and the essay. What do the two have in common? How do their emphases differ? Ask them to consider the different demands and possibilities of the poetic and essayistic genres. What can Jordan accomplish in the poem that she could not accomplish in the essay, and vice versa?

Paula Gunn Allen

Where I Come from Is Like This

Teaching Strategies

This essay explores the conflicting messages that a "half-breed American Indian woman" such as Paula Gunn Allen might receive from her cultural environment. Because the essay is written in a straightforward style, students shouldn't have any trouble comparing and contrasting the tribal definitions of women and the industrial and postindustrial non-Indian definitions. Instead of asking students to identify each culture's expectations of women, then, you might open by asking if there was anything in Gunn Allen's description of the tribal view of Indian women that surprised them. Before reading her essay, did they think of Indian women as practical, strong, reasonable, intelligent, witty, and competent? If not, how *did* they picture Indian women? Where did they pick up their ideas about Indians in general, and Indian women in particular? Where and to what extent have they encountered the images of Indians as bloodthirsty, quaint, or exotic? Ask them to put themselves in the place of an American Indian, and imagine what it must feel like to be surrounded by images that clash with those they have picked up about their own people through daily contact with them.

If your non-Indian students make that imaginative leap, they will have no trouble believing Gunn Allen when she describes the "cultural bind" that makes her and her Indian sisters "vacillate between being dependent and strong, self-reliant and powerless, strongly motivated and hopelessly insecure." These pairs of adjectives illustrate, in a minor key, some of the basic principles underlying her essay. Most obviously, the opposing pairs encapsulate the opposition between two cultures' views of women. To read these pairs — and other similar constructions, large and small, throughout the essay — in this way is to reveal our own "western adversarial and dualistic perceptions of reality." We mustn't forget, however, that Paula Gunn Allen is half white, and that it is she who wrote these phrases.

A less obvious perspective, but one that students should be able to come to after having read this essay, would suggest that we describe these pairs as balanced, rather than opposing. Early in the essay the author identifies two Western images of women: the madonna image is "countered (rather than balanced) by the witch-goddess/whore." Thus, in the third paragraph of her essay, Gunn Allen sets up a contrast between the whites, who see the world as a series of adversarial dualisms, and the Indians, who prize balance above all. Have students look through the essay to find other places where the idea of balance figures in her discussion. How does balance differ from dualism? Do they find this to be a useful distinction? Do they think that Gunn Allen adheres mostly to a balanced structure for her essay? Why or why not? Does Gunn Allen, as a half-breed, find herself suspended in the precise center between the Indian and the non-Indian versions of her identity as a woman? If they find that her essay is more heavily weighted toward the Indian point of view, ask them if there is another, implied point of view against which she might be balancing her words.

Additional Activities

Paula Gunn Allen's essay has a lot in common with the selections in Chapter 12, "Family Stories." Direct students' attention to the information she gives about the stories her mother told her, and ask them what they can infer about the function of stories in a tribal culture such as the one she describes. Why does she repeatedly connect the oral tradition with the image of the "web"? Why is it essential that the Indians keep telling their own stories about themselves? Why, in the context of her essay, is it important that the women be the ones who tell the stories? What does she mean when she writes that "all life is a circle"? You might want to bring "No Name Woman" from Chapter 12, "Family Stories," into the discussion.

Generating Writing

1. Have students choose an image of Indian women from popular culture — from a movie, a television show, or an advertisement, for example. Have them analyze the implications of that image: What are its assumptions about Indian women? How, if at all, is their power represented? Whence does the image derive its allure, if indeed it is alluring? What white values are perhaps inadvertently revealed in the conception of the image?

2. Gunn Allen mentions several Indian religious stories in which women figure prominently, legendary women such as White Buffalo Woman, Tinotzin, Yellow Woman, Coyote Woman, and Grandmother Spider. As an exercise in library research, have students find a written account of one such story, starring an Indian goddess. Have them analyze the story, including in their paper an examination of its implications regarding gender. A variation on this essay assignment would be to have students look up various versions of the "same" Indian myth, and to identify and account for the differences in the versions. Or, if there are any Indian tribes in your area, suggest that students, working individually or perhaps in pairs, try to set up appointments to speak with some of them. If they can secure interviews with several Indians, they might be able to compare various versions of one tribal tale. Or, depending on your own contacts, you may be able to invite a Native American to visit your class. Ask students to prepare questions for her or him ahead of time. Have them show their questions to their peer editing group during the class period preceding the visit, so that they can help each other choose the most productive and interesting questions (and weed out any that are unintentionally offensive). They can then use the material and insights they gain from the guest speaker's visit as the basis for their essays.

Scott Russell Sanders

The Men We Carry in Our Minds

Teaching Strategies

Early in the essay, when his friend Anneke remarks that men have to search their souls, Scott Russell Sanders searches his, only to discover that he feels "confused" toward women. You might use this admission as a starting point, suggesting to students that they take Sanders at his word. How would they characterize Sanders's attitude toward women? Some might point out his initial resemblance to the "feminist man" model set out in the epigraph by Terry Allen Kupers. His first line is sympathetic to women: "This must be a hard time for women." Ask students to explain, using evidence from the text, how he acquired this sympathy. The first time he met women who said that "men were guilty of having kept all the joys and privileges of the world for themselves," he was "baffled." How did he move from not understanding women's complaints to a position where he felt comfortable voicing their complaints for them?

Some students may suggest, and rightly so, that Sanders can sympathize with the woman's position because he has been in an analogous position himself: as a working-class man, he experienced oppression firsthand, from the perspective of the oppressed. He lists "dirt-poor farm country . . . mining country . . . Hispanic barrios . . . the shadows of factories [and] Third World nations" as places "where the fate of men is as grim and bleak as the fate of women." You might want to tie in the essay "Feminism: A Transformational Politic" (see Chapter 18), in which bell hooks argues that the overall structure of oppression, rather than any one particular oppressive structure such as patriarchy, should be the focus for change. Ask students if Sanders seems to be focusing on the entire structure of oppression, as hooks advocates, or if he seems to be privileging class over gender in a form of identity politics such as June Jordan warns against in this chapter's first essay.

Other students might point out, again with reason, that Sanders finds a kinship with women in their shared desires: he writes, "The daughters of such men wanted to share in this power, this glory. So did I. They yearned for a say over their future, for jobs worthy of their abilities, for the right to live at peace, unmolested, whole." It is doubtful that any of your students would deny to men or women a share in these basic human rights. He ends that paragraph, and the essay as a whole, with a kind of plea to women to believe in his sympathy: "If I had known, then, how to tell them so, would they have believed me? Would they now?" Ask the women in the class to respond to his question. If the class has been finding evidence of the foundations of his sympathy with women, many of them will doubtlessly proffer the assurance he craves.

What if some women in the class are finding it hard to take Sanders's feminism at face value? What if they think he's just as "confused" at the end of the essay as he was at the beginning? What other explanations might such a reader offer, for example, for Sanders's sympathetic opening remark? What reason does *he* give for the extension of his sympathy? He says that women "have so many paths to choose from, and so many voices calling them." And later he says that "women feel pressure to be everything, do everything. . . . Career, kids, art, politics. Have their babies and get back to the office a week later. It's as if they're trying to overcome a million years' worth of evolution in one lifetime." Who were the women whom he envied for their lives of comparative "ease"? How do they differ from the women for whom he feels sorry? How would students characterize the description of the women's lives in the town where he grew up? Do they think he was seeing those lives clearly? What does the nostalgia that permeates his description of the "expansiveness" of women's days suggest about his attitudes toward women's liberation?

Some of your students may draw a distinction between the author and the narrator. After all, the author decided to give most of the good lines to a woman, Anneke, to whom he also awarded the mug that signifies wisdom. It is certainly worth arguing that the author was aware of some of the implications of the narrator's words — implications of which the narrator seems ignorant. But it is equally worth arguing that a first-person essay is unlikely to feature a large gap between author and narrator.

Additional Activities

Many descriptive passages in this essay are crammed with a kind of physical detail that makes them almost palpable. Look with the class, for example, at paragraphs 11, 12, and 13. Ask students why the vivid description appears in the passages describing men engaged in brutal physical toil. It is as if the men's bodies are inscribed by the work they do. Why is there no comparable physical description of the women he saw as a boy? Why don't their bodies "remember" their work? It is possible, of course, to point to the essay's title as justification for his focus on the men, but it is not as if he doesn't describe the women's lives — he just doesn't concentrate on the physical part of their lives. What kinds of work *are* the women doing, in all likelihood? What kinds of work are women traditionally in charge of? Who, for example, is traditionally in charge of the family's emotional house-work? Consider bringing in Thomas Edison's essay "The Woman of the Future" (see Chapter 21) in this context. Sanders mentions the shame of men who have lost their jobs; why doesn't he put himself in the woman's place as well, to imagine the emotions she might have to deal with?

Generating Writing

1. Sanders's title, "The Men We Carry in Our Minds," suggests the process whereby images and their attendant ideas are formed. In view of the importance of images in this essay, you might consider assigning a paper in which students examine the assorted images Sanders employs in his metaphors. What do these images, taken together, suggest?

2. Early in the essay, Sanders wonders about the depth of the past, in the context of a discussion of male guilt. He asks himself, "Do I have to scour memory back through father and grandfather? Through St. Paul? Beyond Stonehenge and into the twilit caves?" For the purposes of his essay, he apparently decides that his own personal memories go back far enough. Here a useful contrast might be provided by Adrienne Rich, who finds it necessary, when writing "Split at the Root" (Chapter 6, "Divided Identities"), to go back to her father's childhood. However, his questions might hit a nerve for any students who have been thinking a lot lately, as they read about race and gender issues in *The Winchester Reader* and elsewhere, about the origins and limits of guilt, or perhaps responsibility. If they are struggling with guilt feelings about what the white man did to the Indian (after having read Paula Gunn Allen) or about what the white man did to the black slaves, this might be a good time to assign an essay in which they explore this issue. It will be a difficult exploration, one that will entail both self-scrutiny and abstract thought, but for many students the mere attempt to write about such a topic will be salutary.

WRITING ABOUT THE CHAPTER

1. Have students take out the maps they constructed before reading the essays in this chapter. Assign an essay, to be based on the map and any new insights they have gained while reading and discussing the selections, recounting a time when their conflicting loyalties came to a head. What was the outcome of the incident? Did they find themselves choosing one loyalty and rejecting the other, or, like June Jordan, did they discover a concept that would help them rise above the conflict?

2. Scott Russell Sanders describes the men he carries in his mind; similarly, Paula Gunn Allen describes many of the women who provided her with role models as she was growing up. Ask students to write an essay in which they describe the role models, negative or

positive, that they carry in their minds. They can focus on memories of adults of their own gender or race, or any other people whom, in the words of Sanders, it was their "fate to become." If possible, have them include a description of the first such people that they remember seeing — just as Sanders begins with the convicts and guards. Ask them to comment on the significance of their memories: Why did their minds retain these particular pictures among all those they had to choose from?

Enduring Issues

24

Declarations of Independence

Thomas Jefferson, The Declaration of Independence

Ho Chi Minh, Declaration of Independence of the
Democratic Republic of Viet-Nam

Elizabeth Cady Stanton, Declaration of
Sentiments and Resolutions

Martin Luther King, Jr., I Have a Dream

WORKING WITH THE CHAPTER

It is easy sometimes to forget that a nation is primarily its own creation. Like people, nations grow by self-examination and must attempt to define themselves and their aims before taking their place among peers; and, like people, one of their best means for achieving self-definition is autobiography.

Declarations of independence are, above all, national autobiographies, the epitome of a people's thought and feeling at a particular moment. The statements and manifestos of groups within a nation offer refinements to the original declaration, new editions of that people's autobiography. Students may not see these links at first; one aim in this chapter is to emphasize the self-definition shared by groups with aims as various as Thomas Jefferson's and Ho Chi Minh's.

The chapter's epigraphs, by John Locke, Barbara Jordan, and Mary Wollstonecraft, give some perspective on the kind of thinking that projects and reacts to declarations of independence; Locke and Wollstonecraft comment from a time just beginning to feel a drive toward national and personal individualism, and Jordan gives a view from today's America, heir to generations of struggle to make the Revolution's ideals accessible to all our nation's people.

Teaching Strategies

The Wollstonecraft and Locke epigraphs might best be used to give students some perspective on the historical background of the ideal of freedom. Many students might be unfamiliar with traditions of monarchy and systems of government focused more on citizens' responsibilities to the state than on states' responsibilities to their citizens. How do students imagine life under other systems of government? What rights and privileges do they take for granted that are of relatively recent invention?

Who is Wollstonecraft's audience? Is she attempting to strike a sympathetic chord with women or persuade men of a problem in their approach to issues of gender? The class might be interested in a brief summary of Wollstonecraft's life and work; a student could be assigned to research her for a short presentation. Does Stanton's "Declaration of Sentiments" respond to the issues Wollstonecraft raises?

Barbara C. Jordan's view is a personal perspective on our nation's movement toward freedom. How is her career as a member of Congress and a respected political writer and thinker an emblem of the slow realization gained by Jefferson's, Stanton's, and King's visions? How are all three of these documents vital in constructing and maintaining a just society? How do they fill in one another's gaps?

A Writing-before-Reading Exercise

Before students have had an opportunity to look at the chapter, ask them to summarize, briefly, what they think the Declaration of Independence says, and what its importance was in the development of our nation. What do they believe its significance is today?

WORKING WITH THE SELECTIONS

Thomas Jefferson

The Declaration of Independence

Teaching Strategies

The Declaration is, like much of the rest of our heritage, so widely advertised and so poorly taught that the average student has a real distaste for it that stems from forced pseudo-knowledge of it. Urge students to read it carefully. You may want to read it out loud in class, clarifying the meaning of difficult and archaic words or phrases as you go. See if students can hear its fiery tone; one way to bring out its air of jeremiad is to read it aloud yourself in the style of a fire-and-brimstone evangelist.

Discuss the document's role in Revolutionary hostilities. At whom is it aimed? Who was its intended audience? What was to be gained by it?

Ask the class to examine the declaration's first sentence. Who is the speaker? What effect does the omniscient tone of the opening have? Why does the first paragraph have no active indicative verbs, personal pronouns, or references to specific events? What does Jefferson have to gain by generalizing the American situation?

The second sentence introduces the Declaration's speaker. Who is "we"? (The Barbara Jordan epigraph might well be introduced here.) To whom is "we" speaking? How emotional is this paragraph's tone? What are the worries? Discuss the rhetorical power of the phrase, "we hold these truths to be self-evident." What might "self-evident" mean here? Are all truths self-evident? Is everything self-evident true?

What effect does the declaration's invocation of a "Creator" have? What claims does that invocation make for equality? Ask students what they think "life, liberty, and the pursuit of happiness" could mean. What relation do we feel governments have to happiness today?

Paragraph 4 sets the stage for the list of George III's abuses; how is it reminiscent of paragraph 1? How do these paragraphs of detached, abstract commentary on rights and responsibilities enhance the weight of the grievances that follow? Why the passive construction in the last sentence of paragraph 5?

One way to start discussing the grievances might be to list them, as objectively as possible, on the board as they are read aloud. When the section is finished, read the list on the board aloud. Why doesn't the class list have the power of Jefferson's? What does that tell us about literary style in this document?

What effect do the repetitions have? Do they remind students of anything? Two of the greatest influences here seem to be classical epics and the Bible; remind students of the incantatory force of lists in ancient literatures. How does the list limit and contain the colonies' enemy, the King? How might it be a national rehearsal of antagonism, a way of working ourselves up for the battle ahead?

What does the concluding paragraph's pomp and circumstance achieve? How does the passage's authoritative tone help reinforce the document's authority? What is the effect of the final sentence? Those who signed the Declaration of Independence were putting themselves in very real danger; how does their courage validate the aims of the struggle the Declaration inaugurates?

Additional Activities

How could the Declaration of Independence be understood in the relation to Desmond Morris's view of "territorial behavior" (Chapter 14)? Might it represent the staking of a verbal claim analogous to the physical claim-staking that occurs in crowded areas?

How is the Declaration of Independence a "family story"? Who is the antagonist? the protagonist? With which selection in Chapter 12, "Family Stories," does it have most in common?

Students interested in further reading on this topic might well start with Garry Will's classic *Inventing America: Jefferson's Declaration of Independence* (Garden City, N.Y.: Doubleday, 1978), a lively and detailed analysis of the Declaration of Independence and its genesis. A more specialized work that may also interest them is Bernard Bailyn's *The Ideological Origins of the American Revolution* (Cambridge, Mass.: Harvard UP, 1967).

The movie *1776* might be viewed by the class or individually. This charming musical comedy traces events leading up to the composition and signing of the Declaration. Some leeway is taken with dates, facts, and figures, but the show stays remarkably close to history throughout and may help spark students' interest in the period.

Generating Writing

1. Ask students to write a brief essay answering these questions: How does Jefferson seem to define "independence"? Whom does the definition include? Whom does it exclude? How does Jefferson's definition of independence differ from your own?

2. You might also assign a personal essay here; have students write their own declaration of independence. They may assert independence from family, friends, or society; ask them to structure their declaration like Jefferson's, with an assertion of authority, a list of grievances, and a vow of action. Ask students to append a one or two sentence description on the emotions involved in writing such a document.

Ho Chi Minh

Declaration of Independence of the Democratic Republic of Viet-Nam

Teaching Strategies

Before beginning to discuss the document at hand, you will certainly need to refresh students on the history of the Vietnam conflict. They will probably need to be reminded who Ho Chi Minh was, and what the French had to do with Vietnam. Even the most astute students will probably be confused by Ho's usurping our political traditions; you might briefly explain that the Vietnamese declaration was written at a time when Ho and the American government were, if not friends, at least not open enemies. A helpful source here is Barbara Tuchman's *The March of Folly: From Troy to Vietnam* (New York: Knopf, 1984).

What is the purpose of Ho's paraphrase of the Declaration of Independence? What is gained in his restatement of it in the next paragraph? Are the same aims served by his quotation from the Declaration of the Rights of Man?

How does Ho's list of grievances against the French echo Jefferson's list of grievances against the English? How do they differ? Why are Ho's grievances more specific than Jefferson's? In paragraphs 14 through 18, Ho gives names, dates, and events. What might be his purpose?

What is Ho's voice throughout the declaration? Who is speaking? To whom? Who is "we" meant to signify? What ideological buzzwords are used in the document, and why?

It may be a little difficult to integrate discussion of Ho with the class's views on national goals of autonomy and independence. Discuss the similarities between Ho's and Jefferson's situations. How are they, as educated representatives of what might be considered violent guerrilla movements, under pressure to produce an articulate defense of their nation's rights and demands? To what common ground do they appeal?

Additional Activities

Students could be assigned to gather information on aspects of the Vietnamese conflict and give brief presentations to the class. Ask some students to compile a brief biography of Ho Chi Minh and outline his thought. What kind of figure was he? How did he differ from other revolutionary leaders of his time?

An interesting group project might be to research contemporary Vietnamese society, comparing current conditions with the ideals set out in Ho's declaration. How does Vietnam live up to its stated aims and founding principles?

Generating Writing

1. Ask students to briefly summarize the Vietnamese struggle as Ho Chi Minh depicts it in his Declaration of Independence. Then ask them to consult an American source on the subject (you might photocopy and distribute a short encyclopedia article, perhaps from the *Colliers Encyclopedia* or the *Academic American Encyclopedia*). How do their presentations of Vietnamese history differ? How are they the same? Which events does Ho include, and why? Which does he leave out of his narrative, and why?

2. Have students write a brief comparison and contrast of the American and Vietnamese declarations of independence, emphasizing their style. How do Jefferson's and Ho's different stylistic choices reflect their different aims? Is Ho's evocation of Jefferson misleading?

Elizabeth Cady Stanton
Declaration of Sentiments and Resolutions

Teaching Strategies

This selection, too, requires background if students are to comprehend its meaning and significance. A brief history of the Seneca Falls convention could help the class by defining the document's intended audience. Margaret Forster, in *Significant Sisters: The*

Grassroots of Active Feminism, 1839–1939 (New York: Knopf, 1984), surveys the convention and its organizers, with some useful material on the women's movement of the time.

Ask students what kind of statement Stanton intended to make by adapting Jefferson's language to express women's interests. How might that step have been daring for her time? What is the effect (para. 2) of the change from "all men are created equal" to "all men and women are created equal"? Read it aloud. Did Jefferson mean to include women in his statement? Does their inclusion seem shocking, rhetorically? What does Stanton mean by *government*? She seems to include not only men's public attitudes and decisions toward women, but also the private and even domestic relations of power between the sexes. Is this a valid metaphor? How were (or are) women like a nation? How are they unlike? What interests do women, as a group, share with new or developing nations?

Stanton's list of grievances clearly echoes Jefferson's stylistically, but has some important differences in content. For instance, Stanton protests (para. 6) that women are denied rights "which are given to the most ignorant and degraded men — both natives and foreigners." What prejudices does this statement seem to betray? Is it inconsistent with Stanton's earlier assertion that all men and women are created equal? Her statement (para. 8), "He has made her, if married, in the eye of the law, civilly dead," was, of course, literally true. You might quote the old legal saying, "Man and wife are one, and that one is the husband." Students may not be aware that nineteenth-century American women were not permitted to own property or to participate in any legal or civic undertaking (contracts, business partnerships, or other formal agreements), nor could wives legally charge their husbands with assault, rape, fraud, or other crimes, because they were considered, under the law, mere extensions of the husband.

What is the meaning of Stanton's charge that male society has made woman "morally, an irresponsible being"? Why might that condition have seemed more important in Stanton's day than today? Christian values seem significant here. Explain *chastisement* in this context. How does the word *master* used of a husband play on the values of an audience of northern political activists in 1848? Stanton says that man has "usurped the prerogative of Jehovah himself" in directing women's lives. This was a serious and even shocking accusation in an era of widespread and fervent Christian revival. What influence do students feel this statement might have had? Advocates of women's subordination then, as now, used religion and especially Biblical tradition to support their position (you might remind students of the Wife of Bath's fifth husband). How is Stanton's charge a daring reversal of her opponents' claims to authority?

In the last paragraph, Stanton sums up the odds against the declaration as "no small amount of misconception, misrepresentation, and ridicule." Why ridicule? How might the aims of the declaration have been seen as ridiculous? Why? In whose interest was it to suppress and detract from the growing activity on behalf of women's rights? Point out that this declaration's signatories can pledge each other nothing but promises of action, for they have no property and their lives, liberties, and even their honor are not, strictly speaking, their own.

Additional Activities

Look at this essay in conjunction with Vivian Gornick's "Who Says We Haven't Made a Revolution? A Feminist Takes Stock" (Chapter 18) and bell hooks's "Feminism: A Transformational Politic." What goals does the Seneca Falls Convention share with contemporary feminism? How do their aims diverge?

You might want to bring in and distribute or read to the class antifeminist editorials contemporary with Stanton's declaration (they are, unfortunately, very easy to find). What rhetorical weapons are used against the women's cause? Students interested in the history of the women's movement may wish to give brief oral reports on different participants in the Seneca Falls convention. You might also wish to distribute or read the sections of

Stanton's autobiography, *Eighty Years and More* (1898) on the convention and her composition of the Declaration of Sentiments.

Generating Writing

1. Have students analyze Stanton's list of grievances carefully, and ask them to prepare a progress report on each. Are all now completely redressed? Are women still less than equal in any of the ways outlined by Stanton? Discuss students' findings in class; encourage the class to challenge and defend one another's assertions.

2. What influence might this document have had? Ask students to imagine themselves as Stanton's contemporaries who have just seen the Declaration of Sentiments reprinted in a newspaper. Have them compose two brief letters to the editor in response to the declaration and its publication, one supporting Stanton and one opposing her. (You might ask them to assume a different gender role for one of the letters.)

Martin Luther King, Jr.

I Have a Dream

Teaching Strategies

It seems essential in teaching this work to give students the opportunity to hear the audio recording of this speech (20th-Century Fox Records); King himself gives the most powerful interpretation imaginable of his words. Ask students how familiar they are with King's life and work; you may want to view the episodes of the series *Eyes on the Prize* (PBS Video, 1989), discussing the leader and his influence on the civil-rights movement.

What are King's ruling metaphors here? How might they be related to the context in which this speech was made? Ask students what they feel about equating social and financial responsibility. Is King's metaphor of the "bad check" of emancipation making a point about the economic aspects of oppression? Discuss what these might be.

Remind students that the "great American in whose shadow we now stand" is Lincoln (the speech was delivered from the steps of the Lincoln Memorial), and that the phrase "five score years" is a reference to Lincoln's Gettysburg Address. How is King's speech a response to Lincoln's? Bring the Gettysburg Address in for the class; you might want to read it aloud. How does King echo Lincoln's rhetoric? What effect does his evocation of Lincoln have? How do the two works differ?

How does King use Christian imagery for greater effect? How might phrases like "the dark and desolate valley of segregation" and "the solid rock of brotherhood" effect his immediate audience? (Remind students of the Baptist hymn that begins, "On Christ the solid rock I stand / All other ground is shifting sand.") How might they be received by the larger audience the speech was certain to gain?

Discuss with students the paragraph beginning, "We cannot walk alone." How does King's list of demands without which the civil-rights movement cannot be "satisfied" mirror Jefferson's list of England's offenses against America? How do they differ? What purpose does the list serve? What is the effect of juxtaposing general ideas of justice and their specific violations? How might this portion of the speech be received by African-Americans in King's audience? By others?

What part do King's references to children have in the construction of his argument? How do they serve as a metaphor? What meanings are attached to children here? Is it significant that King does not mention women explicitly in the speech, but that he does mention girls?

How does King's quoting "America" lend his speech greater power? What significance does this patriotic song have for us? How does its use in King's speech force us to reexamine its meaning? Discuss the rhetorical force of King's associating this national hymn with the spiritual "Free at Last." What point is King making about our common cultural heritage?

Additional Activities

Discuss this selection along with Shelby Steele's "On Being Black and Middle Class" (Chapter 6). Might King have anticipated some of Steele's difficulties? How might Steele find some of the grievances King lists irrelevant to his own situation? Is King's speech a challenge to today's "middle-class" values, black and white? Has his point of view been at least officially incorporated into our society's perception of justice and social responsibility?

You might also want to look at Ishmael Reed's "America: The Multinational Society" (Chapter 7). Ask students how deeply the cultures of different ethnic and racial groups touch their own perception of an American national identity. Is King a hero to Americans of all origins and backgrounds? What other African-Americans are our heroes and heroines?

Interested students might be assigned to do further research on King or on the civil-rights movement. What problems does that movement have today? You might ask colleagues in African-American studies to address the class on King's legacy and the problems still to be conquered. Students might write or call the NAACP or other organizations for information on their activities.

Generating Writing

1. How might King have updated his speech if he had lived to deliver it again today? Ask students to imagine they are his aides and to submit suggestions for revision and amplification reflecting past and current events.

2. Invite students to write about their own dreams for our country's future, and our world's. Ask them to refer in their own work to King's, as he referred to Lincoln's. They might want to focus on his vision of children in unity, for instance, or on his images of struggle and separation. Have students briefly describe the ideal location and occasion for their speeches. Who might their audience be?

WRITING ABOUT THE CHAPTER

1. Ask students to consider Stanton's and King's work together. You might ask them to write a comparison and contrast of the two pieces, focusing perhaps on style or metaphor. What do Stanton and King have in common? Does their lack of official backing, armies, or governments to enforce their prescriptions, make their work different from Jefferson's and Ho's? How is their work complementary?

2. Accepting that Jefferson's Declaration is the acknowledged model for Stanton's and Ho's, ask students to write an essay analyzing how the later writers use Jefferson in their work. What effect do references to Jefferson have in each? Which aspects of this work do Stanton and Ho include? Which do they choose to leave out? Why might they do so?

3. Ask students to write an essay addressing the conventions of public speech. What kinds of things can be said in documents like the Declaration of Independence? What kinds of things must be left out? How does public speech misrepresent specific situations? How does its reliance on general truths make it more or less useful?

25

The Debate on Abortion

Judith Jarvis Thomson, A Defense of Abortion

Richard Selzer, What I Saw at the Abortion

Ellen Willis, Putting Women Back into
the Abortion Debate

WORKING WITH THE CHAPTER

The selections in this chapter attempt to illustrate various perspectives on a debate increasingly central to American society. Both Ellen Willis and Richard Selzer address the question of abortion in personal, subjective essays; Judith Jarvis Thomson, on the other hand, constructs her argument as a formal moral enquiry. As a whole, the chapter provides a balance of contemporary opinion.

Teaching Strategies

This issue is both difficult and important to discuss with students. Many of the dangers in debating topics like abortion stem from a lack of mutual understanding about definition or terms and basic assumptions. It is helpful to encourage students to examine the assumptions contained in the chapter selections as a prelude to an inquiry into their own, and their classmates', assumptions.

See what students' understanding of the terms *left* and *right,* as used in selections and epigraphs, are. You may be surprised at their interpretations. A brief discussion of these traditions might be helpful in fostering comprehension of the debate and its aims. Stress the flexibility of these labels. Remind students to consider the source when evaluating their accuracy.

It might be informative to bring your state's abortion statutes to class and distribute photocopies. Some students may not be aware of the law in this matter; you might compare legislation of several states as an introduction to the variety of possible civic responses to the question. The abortion laws of other countries and eras may also provide grounds for discussion. You may want to write to organizations on both sides of the abortion rights issue for their most recent brochures and publications; if students are reminded to read them critically, they could serve as a valuable additional resource.

The epigraph from Sagan and Druyan might serve as a relatively neutral starting point for class discussion. What do students think about the rhetorical power of the terms *pro-choice* and *pro-life*? What would they think if the orientation of the terms was shifted to, say, *anti-choice* and *anti-life*? (You may want to look at the selection from Hayakawa [see Chapter 34] in relation to this question.)

Florynce Kennedy's famous comment is inflammatory enough to need careful handling. The reaction of male students will most likely be defensive; there is probably more to be gained here by encouraging a rational discussion than by allowing gender antagonism to run wild. It could be interesting to plan discussion of this epigraph as a more-or-less formal parliamentary debate ("Resolved: If men could get pregnant, abortion would be a sacrament"). This degree of structure might give students enough distance from their personal feelings to allow for an exchange of ideas.

The Kennedy quote might also be considered in the light of Anna Quindlen's view. This epigraph (from a remarkable op-ed piece you may want to assign as further reading) offers a perspective few students will have on the issue. (If you are lucky enough to have older or nontraditional students who are themselves mothers or fathers, this selection will certainly encourage them to express their own views, as parents, on the topic.)

As a fictional treatment of abortion, "Hills Like White Elephants" may be a "safer" place to begin discussion. Gender issues will, no doubt, arise; students may feel more comfortable expressing attitudes about fictional characters than about actual persons. Hemingway's, and his characters', tone here is a helpful place to start: you may want to assign the entire story to the class as a whole, or to interested individuals.

Thomson's essay may require more nuts-and-bolts work than the others in the chapter. You may want to walk through the major points in her argument with the class, perhaps outlining its structure on the board. One way to integrate it into a discussion of the selections by Selzer and Willis might be to challenge students to turn one of their arguments into a Thomson-like formal inquiry. This would work well as a class discussion, because students may want to debate each others' attempts to pin Selzer or Willis down to a particular position. (Rewriting a personal essay as a formal argument might also give students an object lesson in the mutability of form and content.)

One interesting approach to the remaining essays might be through the question of authority. Because both Selzer and Willis draw heavily on their personal experience, your asking students about their views on the validity of personal experience in this matter could lead to an absorbing class discussion. Who is qualified to make statements about abortion? Is every member of society equally affected by the question, or are some groups more directly concerned than others? The Quindlen and Kennedy epigraphs might be reintroduced into the discussion at this point.

Discuss Selzer's essay in the light of the Anna Quindlen epigraph. Like Selzer's, her experience with a developing fetus has caused a revision of her ideas about pregnancy and life, but it has not changed her view of abortion rights. Is Selzer's position, then, the necessary outcome of his personal experience? What assumptions does he leave unstated?

Similarly, Ellen Willis's view of the morality of abortion was not altered by her own pregnancy. Willis, however, is very explicit about her own underlying political assumptions. Where might Selzer's assumptions differ? How might that have shaped their differing views? One place to start might be in Selzer's first paragraph. Why was he entitled to witness a stranger's abortion? What is his attitude toward the patient? Why does he mention that she is Jamaican? She is referred to consistently as "the woman," but one assumes that the attending nurses, if not one of the physicians, were also female. What rhetorical purpose, if any, might this serve?

A Writing-before-Reading Exercise

Before beginning serious work on the selections, ask students to draw up their own definitions of concepts such as "life," "rights," "humanity," and "responsibility." Discuss their conclusions, encouraging them to challenge and defend each other's assumptions. After some work with the chapter, the exercise may again be called into play.

WORKING WITH THE SELECTIONS

Judith Jarvis Thomson

A Defense of Abortion

Teaching Strategies

One of the problems presented by "A Defense of Abortion" is that its primary audience is the philosophical community. Thomson uses words such as *rights, direct,* and *responsibility* in a discipline-specific way. It is important to underscore that these words have a technical meaning in philosophy that differs from their meaning in everyday speech. One place students may have some trouble grasping the fine points of her argument is in her discussion of the concept of moral decency (paras. 33–37). Thomson is very careful to make a clear distinction between those things one ought to do (which, if not done, would violate moral decency) and those things one must do (which, if not done, violate others' rights). The distinction is, as she points out, rarely observed in everyday life. Students may, understandably, miss this distinction and become confused and angry with Thomson's conclusions, finding them inconsistent. Try to get them to challenge the assumptions of the argument itself — is the distinction between what one ought to do and what others have a right to a valid one?

Thomson uses the Kitty Genovese murder case as an example of the failure of minimal decency. It is doubtful that today's students will be familiar with this case; you may need to give them some background on it, or illustrate it further with some analogous, more recent example.

How valid do students find the example of the diseased violinist? You may want to discuss the tradition of hypothetical examples in law and philosophy as a way of getting your classes to accept Thomson's arguments on their own terms. Encourage students to invent their own hypothetical examples and to challenge each other on their applicability.

One approach that may be fruitful is to assign small groups to each of Thomson's sections and urge them to come up with one defense of, and one challenge to, each part of Thomson's argument. Breaking the argument down into its constituent parts may help students perceive it as a formal, rhetorical entity. Close examination of structure and syntax could provide particular examples of how the author's style serves to reinforce her argument. How do students feel about her tone? What connection do they make with the piece — do they find it too abstract, or do they think it is a compelling examination of the issue? Ask whether they think Thomson's academic approach and use of hypotheticals distance the issue from the real-life choices involved in the politics of abortion.

The last sentence of the article seems deeply problematic. Students may feel cheated by it; you might use these feelings in a discussion of what kind of arguments are satisfactory or unsatisfactory. What kind of intellectual maneuver is Thomson making here? Does her tactic tend to undermine the integrity of the argument up to that point?

Additional Activities

An analysis of Thomson's language might be done in light of the selections found in Chapter 32, "Language and Politics," particularly Orwell. Thomson's argument might also be compared with Tocqueville's (see Chapter 21); despite their profoundly different aims, they employ similar rhetorical devices to achieve their desired effect. The authoritative and dispassionate tone of both arguments could serve as the center of a discussion about the powers of language and their uses.

The ideas of right and responsibility raised in this selection (and in the chapter as a whole) might be a focal point for an examination of the varying concepts of freedom stated in Chapter 24, "Declarations of Independence." Expect this discussion to be passionate; it might best take place in one of the later classes on the chapter, where students may have ammunition more substantive than their own strong feelings.

The abortion issue, needless to say, occupies an ever-increasing share of public attention. You might assign students to bring in related clippings from newspapers or magazines, or citations from television and radio news, each day the chapter is discussed. They may be surprised at the extent of the coverage of the abortion controversy; ask them to scrutinize these treatments of the issue with the same care they have given to the chapter selections. You may want to focus especially on assumptions, and on the things a reporter or an editorial writer takes for granted. This exercise could refresh the interest of students who found Thomson dry and too academic; you might even use this as an opening to discuss the different things we, as readers, require from different genres of writing.

Students may be interested in further research on the concept of Good Samaritanism and its enforceability by law. The work recommended by Thomson, *The Good Samaritan and the Law* (James M. Ratcliffe, ed.), is a good place to start. Your state's laws may provide specific cases and limits to citizens' responsibilities to others; some students might wish to give an oral presentation on this topic. A mock trial could even be arranged if enough students want to become involved.

Generating Writing

1. You might ask students to treat Thomson's central hypothesis as if it were an actual case in law. Assign some students to be the defense attorneys for the Society of Music Lovers and others to be the prosecutors for the state on behalf of the violinist's unwilling Good Samaritan. Have students prepare a brief, singly or in groups, that uses the principles of responsibility raised by Thomson as their guide. Encourage them to make the strongest case possible for their claim; the hypothetical distance may allow them to argue passionately without fear of offending other classmates' beliefs.

2. Ask students to analyze Thomson's argument for its underlying assumptions. They may draw up a list, or brainstorm in class. Words and phrases such as *plain, clear,* and *it is obvious* may offer a way into these assumptions. Are the issues Thomson finds "plain" and "clear" problematic for students? An essay could then be assigned on the use of assumption in argument, or on the nature of the student's own assumptions and how they affect his or her perceptions of an issue. The Writing-before-Reading exercise could provide the basis for students' assessments of their individual preconceptions of this complex controversy.

Richard Selzer

What I Saw at the Abortion

Teaching Strategies

The tone of Selzer's essay differs greatly from Thomson's; his is a more subjective approach, containing strong appeals to emotion. You may want to discuss the issue of his intended audience; this piece was originally published in *Esquire* magazine. Ask students what bearing, if any, they feel that has on Selzer's argument or approach. (If they are not familiar with *Esquire,* you may want to discuss its history and philosophy with them — its subtitle, for example, is "Man At His Best.")

How do students react to Selzer's opening paragraph? What kind of voice do they see him as trying to establish? The statement "I am a surgeon" might be seen either as straightforward descriptive journalism or as a claim to rhetorical authority. Ask the class to evaluate Selzer's statement about aspects of human physiology ("I do not make symbols of them") in the light of his argument's conclusion.

What uses does Selzer make of emphasis? How does his choice of words and phrases to italicize advance his point of view? What do students make of his tone here? It may be a little difficult to draw them out on this; you might want to ask class members to read aloud to illustrate the high emotional pitch of Selzer's narrative — it seems impossible to read this piece aloud calmly.

How do students respond to Selzer's description of fetal development? Do they find this to be a convincing argument against abortion? Point out that the abortion Selzer is describing was, at the time of writing, allowed by law. Abortion at a later stage of pregnancy was, of course, impermissible, as he points out in his antepenultimate paragraph. Does the class find this to be a sensitive topic? Discuss Selzer's assertion "Does this sound like argument? I hope not. I am not trying to argue" (para. 57). How seriously can readers take this claim? What kind of argumentative strategy is Selzer using here?

One of the most fascinating passages in the essay is Selzer's imaginative reconstruction of the aborted fetus's experience. This is certainly an affecting piece of writing, but do students find it to be a valid argument? Would it be correct to compare this with Thomson's hypothetical situations?

Selzer's last paragraph, like Thomson's, is frustrating. Discuss his final assertion, "You cannot reason with me now" (para. 58). Do students find this representative of Selzer's approach? What part does (or should) reason play in moral judgment? Does Selzer's essay in fact describe the process of developing a moral stance?

Additional Activities

Selzer seems to present his experience at the abortion as a moment of epiphany. Discuss this in light of Chapter 3, "Moments of Recognition." How is Selzer's repulsion and horror in the operating room similar to, and different from, Orwell's terror and disgust at shooting the elephant? How valid are these kinds of experiences in forming and arguing moral judgments?

After reading this highly dramatic re-creation of an abortion, students may be interested in poems, plays, fiction, and films that depict or discuss abortion. "Hills Like White Elephants" is perhaps the best-known short story "about" this question, but students should be encouraged to range farther afield. If the film *Story of Women* (France, 1990, directed by Claude Chabrol) is available on video, interested individuals or groups might be assigned to view it and give a short presentation. Each new season brings various miniseries, television movies, and after-school specials about abortion; these, too, might be assigned for individual or group viewing.

Generating Writing

1. Much of Selzer's argument depends on the authority of his perspective. Have students analyze the rhetorical creation of this authority. Why does it matter what "I" saw at "the" abortion? Ask students to rewrite the narrative from the point of view of one of the other participants — the doctors, the nurses, even the patient herself. How might "What I Saw at My Abortion" be a different story?

2. How does Selzer both invoke and dismiss opposing arguments? What might this have to do with the overall strategy of his essay? Try to draw out some of the "ghost" arguments that appear in the piece. How might the doctor, for example, justify his position? How might Selzer respond? To whom is he speaking, at the essay's end, when he says, "I know, I know . . ."? How does he discount their claims?

Ellen Willis

Putting Women Back into the Abortion Debate

Teaching Strategies

This selection is, paradoxically, both easy to teach (as a journalistic essay, its form may be familiar to students) and difficult (its tone is highly polemical, and students may have difficulty evaluating it as an argument). Some discussion of Willis's intended audience might be helpful here; the essay originally appeared in *The Village Voice*. The class may be unfamiliar with the *Voice* and its traditions of counterculture journalism; you might remind students that the author here is drawing on assumptions she presumes are shared by her readers. This might be the place for class discussion of what is meant, and by whom, when labels such as *right-wing, left-wing,* and *feminism* are used. No two of the chapter's authors, and probably no two students, have exactly the same definitions of these highly charged terms.

Point out that the phrase "seamless garment" has very specific Christian resonances. Why does Willis use the metaphors of the very group she is opposing? Does it add to the effect of her argument?

How do students feel about the introduction of Willis's personal experience of pregnancy into the essay? Does it enhance her authority? You might ask them if they find that the personal tone of Willis's argument makes it more or less forceful than Thomson's abstract approach. Are women who have been pregnant more qualified than others to discuss abortion? In whose interest would a "yes" or "no" answer to that question be?

Willis confronts the issue of sexuality far more directly than either Thomson or Selzer. What bearing do attitudes about sexuality have on attitudes about abortion? How are authors' assumptions about sexuality embedded in their thinking on abortion?

Willis's conclusion reveals an essential assumption underlying her argument — that modern American society is, as she puts it, "male-supremacist." This is a delicate question to introduce in class, although the result is guaranteed to be lively. You might ask students a two-part question: Do they think that contemporary American society *is* male-suprema-cist? And if it is not, how does that detract from Willis's argument?

Additional Activities

Willis's essay is, in many ways, a sermon to the converted. The question of context is central here; her language is charged with particular political meanings, not all of which may be immediately clear to students. It might be helpful to review class discussion and work on Chapter 18, "The Feminist Movement Today." How are Willis's views part of a particular political agenda?

Her most disturbing assumption, that contemporary America is a male-supremacist society, should also be examined in light of Chapter 18, as well as Chapter 21, "Gender Roles and Stereotypes." How do students feel about this assumption? What impact, if any, does it have on their assessment of Willis's argument?

Generating Writing

1. The selection's context as a journalistic essay provides a ready-made option for generating writing — the letter to the editor. Ask students to draft such a letter in response to Willis's piece. They may cite arguments from the chapter's other selections to support their own claims. The brief length of the letter form (perhaps 250 to 500 words) might

force students to formulate their opinions concisely. This assignment could also work well as a prelude to a longer essay or research project.

2. Willis's conclusion raises the interesting question of other issues that might also be interpreted as "pro-life," such as opposition to the death penalty or the struggle for economic justice. Do students see these concerns as aligned with particular positions on abortion? You might have them do a close analysis of the relevant portions of Willis's argument as a way into their own views on these complex issues. The Writing-before-Reading exercise on the definition of life could also help them begin their self-examination.

WRITING ABOUT THE CHAPTER

1. Have students return to the definitions of key terms they wrote before reading the chapter. Ask whether the assigned readings have led them to question these definitions. Have students rewrite these definitions in light of the issues the chapter selections raise. Then have them select one of the key terms and write an essay addressing the complexities of the term.

2. Willis's and Selzer's essays are similar enough in form and approach to lend themselves to a traditional compare-and-contrast assignment. Ask students to analyze the authors' arguments and approaches closely. How do they use similar techniques of persuasion to make their opposing points?

3. Some students may be interested in mapping the progress of the abortion controversy in a particular journal or periodical. *The Village Voice* has been a forum for debate on this issue for decades, both in its editorial pages and in its frequently fiery Letters to the Editor pages with writers like Willis and Vivian Gornick speaking out for abortion rights and others, led by columnist Nat Hentoff — see, for example, his column in the October 16, 1990, issue of *The Village Voice* — taking a contrary position. Students might collate various discussions of abortion in their chosen journal over a given space of time. How has the debate changed? What, if any, conclusions have the journal and its readers come to agree upon? The project could be oriented differently, with students surveying different periodicals over a brief interval. How do different publications present the debate? What relationship, if any, does this position have to the periodicals' overall political orientations?

26

Freedom of Expression

Walter Lippmann, The Indispensable Opposition

Henry Louis Gates, Jr., 2 Live Crew, Decoded

Susan Brownmiller, Let's Put Pornography
Back in the Closet

WORKING WITH THE CHAPTER

After some years out of the spotlight, the idea of freedom of expression is once again fiercely contested. Educators, of course, have a personal interest in the right to free expression, but the issue should be a central concern for students, too. The chapter selections supply a rich context for discussion of this question, as well as widely varying perspectives on the controversy that surrounds it.

Teaching Strategies

The epigraph from Montaigne supplies some historical background on the debate, as does the passage from Mill and Taylor. More modern views are given in the Becker and Russell epigraphs and in the selection by Walter Lippmann. Brownmiller and Gates provide contemporary case histories of the principle in action, using traditions of inquiry into the issue to adjudicate the merits, or demerits, of individual instances of free and unpopular speech.

Lippmann's interpretation of the doctrine applies it strictly to political discussion and debate. Gates, on the other hand, maintains that obscenity standards must be applied with an eye to cultural difference, thus combining the political aspect of free expression with its impact on guidelines regarding the sexually explicit. Finally, Brownmiller argues that the aesthetic and moral choices involved in pornography are also political choices that cannot be forced upon members of a free society. None of the writers sees freedom of expression as an entirely unrestrained right. How are their limits the same? How do they differ?

The chapter's epigraphs provide a historical context for the principle of free expression and its discussion. Montaigne's view is a good starting place for an explanation of the development of our concepts of civic rights and responsibilities. Is his view more personal than our own? Might it depend on his situation as an aristocrat and intellectual? This might be contrasted with Chapter 24's epigraph by Locke. The quotation from Mill and Taylor is an interesting illustration of a nineteenth-century liberal view of liberty. How is this echoed in Lippmann? How might Gates find this inadequate? What might Brownmiller's view be?

Bertrand Russell provides the chapter with a viewpoint from academic philosophy, fittingly enough a philosophical examination of academia. Do students agree with Russell's position? How do they find it to apply in their own experience? Ask students how they respond when classmates or instructors challenge their beliefs. Can the results be positive?

The quote from Carl Becker offers another view from Lippmann's generation. You may need to give a little background on Mussolini and the Italian Fascists; what did people mean when they said, "At least he makes the trains run on time"? Can that ever be a valid defense of political repression? If comfort and freedom were mutually exclusive, which might we choose? How might Becker's statement that we must "be prepared to take the consequences" of free speech be countered by Brownmiller?

Brownmiller's and Gates's arguments seem to be fundamentally at odds. One way to examine their difference might be to discuss whose rights are at stake in each author's view: Gates focuses on the right of the artist to express those ideas which he or she wishes to express; Brownmiller focuses on the right of the bystander not to become involved with material he or she might find offensive. How might these arguments work if their focus was shifted? For example, how might Brownmiller defend 2 Live Crew's unwilling listeners (shoppers in stores that played their music, neighbors of 2 Live Crew groupies)? How might Gates defend the publishers of the pornography to which Brownmiller objects?

A Writing-before-Reading Exercise

Bring a copy of the Constitution to class and write the First Amendment on the board. Ask students first to translate it briefly into everyday language, and then to list some situations in which they think it might apply. Have them list some situations in which they think it might not apply. You may also want them to write a paragraph or two on what impact free speech and expression has on their lives; are they enthusiastic about openly depicted sexuality in movies, books, television, and art? Or are they offended by what they see as obscenity? Similarly, do they find uncensored political debate and discussion socially useful or destructive to public consensus? Remind students that the issue of free expression deals with our right to criticize political figures and decisions as well as our right to disseminate violent or sexually explicit material.

WORKING WITH THE SELECTIONS

Walter Lippmann

The Indispensable Opposition

Teaching Strategies

It may be helpful to provide students with some context on Walter Lippmann's life and career. Briefly, he was, from 1914 until his death in 1974, one of America's most influential journalists. A founder of *The New Republic*, he was also the author of a widely syndicated newspaper column and several important books. Lippmann's orientation was toward progress and reform; he was a champion of the underdog and the seemingly lost cause. He was also highly respected for his dedication, thoroughness, and fairness.

In some ways, then, Lippmann's position is self-interested; as a working journalist, he has more than most at stake in the question of freedom of expression. Or has he? Ask students whether they feel the press finds the First Amendment more significant than the average citizen might. How might Lippmann counter this charge?

You may need to remind students who Voltaire was and the historical context of his famous remark; perhaps they have heard the quotation before. What does it mean to them? Do they agree with Lippmann's view of it?

Unpack Lippmann's metaphor of the doctor's diagnosis. Do students find this to be a valid comparison with the ideal of free discussion, specifically of freedom of the press? How is the health of society like the health of an individual? Discuss Lippmann's use of the pronoun *we* here, and elsewhere in his argument. To whom is he referring? Do students feel included in this "we"? Why, or why not?

The center of Lippmann's argument is his assertion that the "creative principle of freedom of speech" is not to grant permission to err, but rather to find the truth. This needs to be discussed in detail. How likely do students find it that two opposed parties would agree on the truth? How do they think consensus comes about? You may want to use specific social issues as examples.

The same point is made in his discussion of "the necessity of listening." Surely students will agree, at first, with Lippmann that "the fool is compelled to listen to the wise man and learn" and that "the wise man can increase his wisdom by hearing the judgment of his peers" (para. 16). Ask them to unpack this statement, though. Who will decide, then, who is wise enough to instruct others and who is foolish enough to need to listen and learn? Isn't there an underlying assumption here about social consensus? Lippmann's view may be almost Utopian; one key to his assumptions about learning and debate may be in his constant repetition of the term *civilized countries*. What do students think Lippmann means by that? What might his criteria for civilization be?

What do students think of Lippmann's assessments of the different media as purveyors of opinion? (The essay was, of course, written before the development of television.) How accurate now is his statement that producers of movies avoid political controversy? Does the rise of talk radio have any impact on our views of radio censorship? Do they agree with his assertion that the public does not support regulation of newspapers except in unusual cases of personal injury (libel, for example)? Ask them what views on television censorship they think Lippmann might have expressed had he revised his essay in the 1960s or 1970s. How might his opinions have changed today?

You may want to discuss Lippmann's statement that, in a democracy, "the party in power should never outrage the minority." What might be meant here by *outrage*? How valid do students find this view? What does a society gain by allowing the expression of dissenting views? What, if anything, might it lose?

Additional Activities

This selection would be interestingly paired with Virginia Woolf's "Thoughts on Peace in an Air Raid" (see Chapter 22). How do the two essays differ on the role of opposition in public decision (declarations of war being perhaps the most serious of all public decisions)? To what principles do both writers appeal? How do their concepts of civilization vary?

Vivian Gornick's essay "Who Says We Haven't Made a Revolution?: A Feminist Takes Stock" (see Chapter 18) offers a view from inside the opposition. How does Gornick's history of the feminist movement illustrate the principles Lippmann lays out? How does the experience she recounts differ from his theory?

Interested students may want to read Lippmann's book *Public Opinion* (Free Press, 1965) for a fuller statement of his views on civic debate and freedom of the press. Students may also wish to research his career, perhaps to give a presentation to the class on his changing view of the First Amendment throughout his lengthy and distinguished professional life.

Lippmann mentions Italy, Russia, and Germany as countries where freedom of speech is denied or compromised.

Some students might be interested in researching the specifics of censorship and restriction for these places and times. Others might want to find out which countries restrict individual and public discussion even today. Is freedom of expression a universal value, or is it tied to particular social goals?

An interesting class exercise might be to stage a political discussion with mock censorship. Divide the class into two teams; one will be the public and the other will be the censors. Have the "censors" agree in advance on topics, names, and opinions to be considered forbidden; you might want to discuss a campus issue and permit no mention or criticism of college administrators, for example, or urge people to talk about their childhoods and not allow them to discuss their parents. Encourage "censors" to intervene freely; the frustration of restricted speech will become sharply apparent.

Generating Writing

1. Using Lippmann's discussion of the regulation of media as a jumping-off place, have students write a brief essay on the limits of freedom of expression. They may select one medium and discuss ways in which it can, or cannot, acceptably be regulated. Some questions to consider might be: Can one legally yell "Fire!" in a crowded theater? Are threats or other aggressive verbal behavior protected by freedom of speech? How might television news manipulate images to give false impressions of events? Should advertising for potentially harmful products, such as alcohol or cigarettes, be regulated or eliminated?

2. One of the central assumptions of this essay is the vital importance of debate and discussion as a way to knowledge. Assign students a personal essay; on what occasions in their lives has a discussion with someone else, or in the media, changed their minds? How did their new perspectives influence their behavior? When have they persuaded others in an argument? What difference did they feel they made?

Henry Louis Gates, Jr.

2 Live Crew, Decoded

Teaching Strategies

This selection may be easier to teach than the previous one; its form might be more familiar, and the issue is very contemporary. The obvious first step in a class discussion of the piece might be to play a selection from the album *Nasty As They Wanna Be*. This may not be possible or desirable in your specific classroom situation. The lyrics to one or more of their songs might also be photocopied and passed out, although this, too, might be less than ideal. Even if class reaction tends toward offense and outrage, it would seem only fair to give the group under discussion a hearing if circumstances permit.

You may want to discuss Gates's position as an African-American and a professor of English. How do these personal characteristics qualify him to discuss the 2 Live Crew controversy? Does his professional concentration on African-American studies make him a more informed observer than others might be? What impact, if any, does his gender have on his assessment of the group's lyrics and attitude?

This essay was originally published in the *New York Times* opinion section. Does that context lead to a different assessment of the piece? For what audience is Gates writing? How does that overlap with the audience 2 Live Crew is presumed to address? How do they differ?

You may need to remind students of the meaning of hyperbole and its significance in satire. Discuss the ideas of satire and parody; how do students understand these terms? Try to get the class to come up with a group definition. What kinds of attitudes do they think satire and parody express toward their subjects?

How valid is Gates's defense of 2 Live Crew's lyrics and behavior as exaggeration for parody's sake? Ask students to discuss other examples from popular culture. The performer Andrew "Dice" Clay is often accused of racism and sexism, yet he defends his act on the grounds that it is a parody of racism and sexism. How much of a role does context play in these interpretations? There are many instances throughout history of parodies being understood as serious arguments in favor of the cause they intend to deride. (One example you may want to discuss is Swift's "A Modest Proposal" (see Chapter 27), which caused an uproar as recently as the 1980s, when it was read aloud at a Dublin theater festival and several people responded with shocked letters to local newspapers.)

You might want to explain briefly the concept of "carnival" to students; they will certainly be able to produce many examples of licensed irresponsibility from their own experience. Is the idea of carnival a valid defense of outrageous speech? In what contexts do we find outrageousness to be socially acceptable? To what ends? What do students think of Gates's near-dismissal of 2 Live Crew's sexism? Do students familiar with the group's work find his response to be valid? Do different standards for tolerance apply in minority communities? Should they? How might we evaluate the opposing claims of groups such as the Nation of Islam and the Aryan Nation? Should they be judged by the same standards? What about divisions within minority groups? Can certain subgroups be excluded? (For example, the term *African-American,* although accurate for many Americans of color, seems to exclude some persons [blacks in the Caribbean and West Indies, among others] who were formerly described as "black.")

Discuss Gates's concluding paragraph. What qualifications does it seem to require from those who would regulate free speech? The specter of intentionality seems to be haunting this essay; can judges and regulating bodies evaluate artists' and authors' intentions? What other criteria could they use in separating parodies of an offensive view from expressions of it?

Additional Activities

Ishmael Reed's "America: The Multinational Society" (see Chapter 7) offers another respected African-American scholar's perspective on the interaction of majority and minority cultures. How do Reed and Gates agree? How do they differ?

Shelby Steele's, "On Being Black and Middle Class" (see Chapter 6) discusses the problems that arise when cultural values conflict. How might Steele respond to Gates's argument? Where might 2 Live Crew, as described by Gates, fit into the world depicted by Steele?

Ask students to be on the lookout for challenges to performers, journalists, artists, and others involved professionally in self-expression. Almost any week should, alas, provide one or two newsworthy items about this issue. Invite students to follow particular controversies and bring clippings to class. Debates and presentations are just two of the forms class discussions could take.

You might bring in the documents relating to James Joyce's *Ulysses* and its obscenity trial (published in the foreword to the Random House edition) as an example of how the "obscene" can become the "classic" in one generation. The Hays Code (for motion pictures) of 1933 might profitably be compared to the current guidelines of the Motion Picture Ratings Association. George Carlin's classic routine about the seven words forbidden by radio could also be an enlightening experience for students of today.

Generating Writing

1. Ask students to examine Gates's use of academic language — "allegories," "the carnivalesque," or "decoding," for example. How might they rewrite the essay in colloquial language? What do they make of the linguistic split between Gates and the performers he is defending?

2. Have a group discussion on the persistence of racial and sexual stereotypes. Which are the most frequently encountered? How are they used? In what situations are they seen as acceptable? Is their acceptability dangerous, even in specific situations? Assign a personal essay on students' experience with stereotypes. They may want to react to incidents from their own lives or to uses of stereotypes in literature, politics, or popular culture; or they may want to engage particular abstractions on their own terms. What have these stereotypes meant to them? How have they hurt them, either as victims or aggressors?

Susan Brownmiller

Let's Put Pornography Back in the Closet

Teaching Strategies

It may be difficult to discuss this essay without first discussing what is, and is not, pornography. You may want to read local or state ordinances aloud; students might offer testimony from their own experiences about what is available to them at the local newsstand, movie theater, or video store. The dividing line between what is "pornographic" and what is "sexually explicit" differs, of course, radically from individual to individual; it might be instructive, though, to at least attempt to arrive at a group consensus.

Brownmiller's definition of pornography explicitly includes any visual depiction, staged or not, of any person being restrained, tortured, raped, or humiliated sexually. (She seems to include some other things by implication as well, but the use of force would seem to be her main criterion of pornography.) Do these things violate the "community standards" of your classroom? What else do students feel is pornographic? How are these things dealt with by law?

How do students react to Brownmiller's assertion that pornography is everywhere, that a visit to a newsstand is "a forcible immersion in pornography"? Do their own experiences bear this out? Sexually explicit materials of all kinds are regulated; only adults are allowed access to them, and only adults are legally permitted to participate in their creation or distribution. How does this compare with the legal status of potentially harmful substances, such as cigarettes, alcohol, or other drugs? Does the availability of pornographic materials make them unavoidable, or can adults make an informed choice as to whether to obtain them?

How dangerous might the vagueness of the Supreme Court's ruling in *Miller v. California* be? Who is to decide what is "patently offensive"? Discuss the assumptions about cultural homogeneity that underlie the language of the ruling. How can it be decided whether an image or series of images appeals to "prurient interest"? One traditional method that publishers used to avoid being branded as pornographers was to claim that a magazine of nude photographs was a study of nudism (hence "scientific" and therefore acceptable). How might similar strategies be used to evade the regulation or banning of pornography today?

The question of "hard-core" and "soft-core" pornography is also a difficult one. What are students' interpretations of the difference between these categories? How about the dividing line between sexually explicit material and soft-core pornography? The differences between "R" and "X" ratings might be a good way into this question.

Is Brownmiller's concluding argument — that although pornography is permissible under the First Amendment, other social considerations should prohibit its public display — a convincing one? How does your experience in your community argue against this or bear it out? Might Brownmiller be satisfied with local conditions in this regard? Why, or why not?

How do students respond to Brownmiller's tone? They may be perplexed by her sense of urgency and outrage; ask the class to examine their own attitudes toward pornography. Are they able to "screen it out"? Do their communities or circumstances insulate them from it? In some countries (Japan and Sweden, for example) there is very little regulation of pornography distribution, sale, or display, and many people find it acceptable to read pornographic literature openly on buses and subways or in restaurants. How would students react to this situation? How might they expect Brownmiller to react?

Additional Activities

Brownmiller's essay frequently invokes the feminist community in support of her claims. Is feminism today a monolithic entity? Can there really be one "feminist perspective" on any given issue? Compare Vivian Gornick and bell hooks (see Chapter 18) on this. How might students' definitions of feminism differ from any, or all, of these writers'?

The issue of pornography is one where many people experience a conflict of loyalties. Many of those who the strongest supporters of free speech also find pornography most injurious and offensive. How does this conflict of loyalties compare with those described in Chapter 23?

What contribution might pornography and the images associated with it make to women's conceptions of their own bodies? Compare Nora Ephron (see Chapter 13). How does the depersonalization of pornography's subjects change the ways in which we view ourselves and our world?

Generating Writing

1. It might be interesting to ask students to reconsider their earlier definitions of pornography in light of the issues Brownmiller raises. Have them prepare a brief essay comparing and contrasting their definitions of pornography with Brownmiller's. Encourage them to challenge and defend her claims.

2. Brownmiller feels that the line between pornography and more conventional forms of expression has been blurred. Do students agree? You might ask them to survey current advertising campaigns for images that might meet Brownmiller's definition of pornography. (Guess? jeans and Calvin Klein are two companies whose advertising often includes depictions of bondage and humiliation.) Have students write a brief narrative of the story each of these pictures tells. How do these images sell the product? Why?

WRITING ABOUT THE CHAPTER

Students who are involved with campus newspapers, radio or television shows, or student government may wish to discuss their own encounters with censorship on campus. Perhaps a dean or other administrator might give a brief talk on the community's limits on freedom of expression. What guidelines must campus art galleries, theater groups, and film societies obey? How does the administration meet challenges to these guidelines?

27

Denigrating the Species

Jonathan Swift, A Modest Proposal

Fyodor Dostoyevsky, Confession of Faith

Mark Twain, The Damned Human Race

WORKING WITH THE CHAPTER

This is a chapter that introduces big questions about humanity that students should find morally and intellectually challenging. Are people inherently evil? Is humanity, which likes to congratulate itself on being the highest, actually the lowest of the species? Is there any hope that the human race can be improved? The selections raise doubts about our religious and political ideals, and they do so with a biting sarcasm. These are selections many of your students will remember for a long time.

Teaching Strategies

The three epigraphs will prepare your class for the nastiness to come. They present an unflattering view of humanity, portraying people as naturally incapable of competent political choice, of altruistic behavior, and of peaceful cooperation. The American essayist and satirist, H. L. Mencken, points out what he believes is a brutal fact of democracy. Ask your students if they instinctively agree with Mencken's comment. His remark, they should see, assumes that democracy is not bad but that people are collectively stupid and will always fall for fraudulency rather than honesty. Still, your students should notice that Mencken acknowledges the possibility of honest individuals; his objection is really to the behavior and intelligence of people acting collectively; he calls them "the mob."

The novelist [Janet] Taylor Caldwell — whose subjects have included munitions manufacturers, Genghis Khan, and Nazi Germany — forms an even more negative objection to humankind, which she sees as "the most selfish species this world has ever spewed up from hell" (images of hell and the damned, by the way, appear throughout the Mark Twain and Dostoyevsky selections). You might invite discussion about Caldwell's examples in this comment; why does she bring in "misers," "whores," and "robbers"? Ask students why Caldwell believes such people uphold ethical and moral values. Do your students agree with her opinion. Are they also baffled by their "fellow man"?

You might want to introduce the passage from the seventeenth-century British philosopher Thomas Hobbes by informing your students that this is one of the most famous quotations in the history of political thought. They probably will find the language tough going, and so it might be a good idea to go through the epigraph slowly. You could get discussion moving by asking students what Hobbes assumes about human beings: why does he think that warfare is "the natural condition of mankind"? What does he mean by a "common power"? Invite your class to consider what Hobbes says: many may think that he advocates war. They should see that Hobbes lacks a taste for war. He clearly sees it as destroying civilized values; but he believes that the human species is such that unless there is authority and power there can be no peace. This view of humankind could provide some interesting pro and con discussion, as members of your class begin to fall into opposing camps: those who believe the species is ultimately good and that the human spirit is thwarted by authority, and those who believe the species is ultimately evil and the human spirit is preserved by authority.

The selections show three world-famous writers taking a pessimistic view of humankind. But more than hostility toward the species unites these three classic selections. You may want to alert your students ahead of time to the irony and invective that form such a large part of these writers' styles. Each selection presents — in the form of either a persona or a character — a rationalistic, scientific-minded speaker confronting the cruelty and irrationality of man. Interestingly, the word *man* in these selections is not used in its philosophical sense but for the most part refers to the male of the species, because *male* cruelty is specifically a theme. Each writer graphically describes the terrible abuses men are willing to inflict on other people — and the Swift and Dostoyevsky selections focus on abuse to women and children. You might concentrate, too, on the animal imagery that pervades these selections. In Swift, the imagery clusters around butchering and eating; in Twain around a reversal of Darwinian theory; and in Dostoyevsky around torture and beatings. The general sense is not that men are like other animals — but that men are worse than other animals.

A Writing-before-Reading Exercise

This chapter gives your students a chance to engage in some large ideas. Ask them to decide what they think is the worst quality of humankind. They should then draft an essay in which they describe that quality as accurately as they can and discuss how broadly this quality affects their overall view of human life.

WORKING WITH THE SELECTIONS

Jonathan Swift

A Modest Proposal

Teaching Strategies

If freshman composition can be said to have a canon, this is one of its texts. You might even begin discussion about this classic essay by inviting speculation about *why* it occupies so prominent a place in so many anthologies. Is it because its topic is horrible: cannibalism? Or is it because of the author's masterful use of irony? Or is it the savage political satire? Do your students share the critical opinion that for decades has included this essay as a main document in composition studies?

Satirists like to kill two birds with one stone; they take a satirical attitude not only toward a topic but also toward the literary vehicle typically used to present that topic. Swift's main subject in the essay is economic oppression, and he makes his point about it by inventing a reasonable-sounding person who offers a solution he believes is reasonable to correct a terrible problem. But he also satirizes the literary form in which such solutions are couched — in this case, the proposal. With its parliamentary style of address, its use of "official" sources, and its statistical "evidence," "A Modest Proposal" is a remarkable parody of the governmental or "think-tank" document that purports to provide a rational solution to a grievous social problem. You might want to point out to students that Swift lives at a time when demographic and statistical data are just being recognized as important sources of social information. The essay is prescient: Swift keenly seizes on such data to show how easily they can be used for social and political control. The speaker of Swift's "proposal" offers perhaps one of the earliest examples of the technique we now call "blaming the victim." How can we relieve eighteenth-century Dublin's poor and homeless? By encouraging them to sell their children to the rich so that they can be murdered for food. It sounds preposterous, of course, but by making the preposterous sound reasonable Swift achieves his ironic purpose.

One reason that this essay has played so well for so long in composition courses is, of course, that it offers instructors a chance to teach irony. Ford Maddox Ford commented that the commonest error the general public makes in reading is that it doesn't distinguish between the author's opinions and those of the characters. Ford was talking about fiction, but the same problem often occurs in the essay, especially when the author has created a character or a "voice" that seems identical to the writer's but isn't. Swift sustains this voice so thoroughly — that is, he presents his plan with such a "straight face" — throughout the essay that many readers in his time took his "modest proposal" seriously and were outraged.

You might get into the issue of irony here by inviting students to characterize the unnamed person who is ostensibly writing this proposal. They should try to identify some of his characteristics: how he presents himself as caring deeply about Dublin's poor and wants to do something about them; how he has thought long and hard about what to do; how in the final paragraph he identifies himself as entirely lacking in self-interest and cares only about the public welfare (your students might want to consider alternative explanations of the essay's final sentence). Ask them to consider the speaker's explicit self-presentation: Why do they think he wants his readers to think of him in this way? They should also examine his language and style, noticing his repetition and his continual efforts to appear deferential, humble, and sincere (all words he uses). His proposal is "modest" in two senses: it is presented as a reasonable, *moderate* plan, and it is presented by a reasonable and *modest* person.

Obviously, there is a clash here between the moderate tone of voice and the violence of the plan. A large part of Swift's irony comes from this clash of moral attitudes — the speaker is appalled by the poverty and deplorable condition of women and children (and appalled that impoverished women would abort their pregnancies) but he is not at all appalled by the idea of murdering one-year old infants and selling their flesh for food. Swift expects, of course, that this moral inconsistency will tip his readers off that *his* views are not the same as his speaker's. To demonstrate this point more clearly, invite your class to look closely at paragraph 17, where the speaker discusses the inadvisability of a plan to cannibalize young adolescents. The strategy (common to the rhetoric of proposals) is a good one: make your own position appear reasonable and moderate by showing that others hold views more extreme than your own. It even gives the speaker the opportunity to show himself as a very feeling person: "it is not improbable that some scrupulous people might be apt to censure such a practice (although indeed very unjustly), as a little bordering on cruelty; which, I confess, has always been with me the strongest objection against any project, how well soever intended." One of the best ways to justify one's own repugnant ideas is morally to draw the line to say, for example: "I may propose *x*, but I would never propose *y*." Your students should notice here Swift's fine ironic touch — the speaker doesn't believe the proposal to use adolescent flesh is really cruel; he merely (and notice all the negative couching) believes that "scrupulous people" might "unjustly" think it "a little bordering on cruelty."

Other instances of inconsistency show that Swift has created a special type of "voice" here; the speaker frequently acknowledges his repetitiveness and digressions, yet tells us that he is "studious of brevity." This is a joke on the speaker that Swift expects readers will notice, just as they will pick up the irony in the speaker's abhorrence for cruelty. He injects jokes on others, too: Americans come off as barbaric cannibals, though the speaker never directly says so; and we find Protestants who wouldn't mind seeing the number of Catholics reduced.

But is the prime target of Swift's irony only this individual speaker? Is he the one Swift is making fun of for his moral callousness, his officialese? You might want to discuss this issue at some length in class. You first may need to invite your students to see what this speaker represents — that behind the speaker's attitude is a dangerous rationalism willing to sacrifice human life in the name of a benevolent social program. Any plan, Swift says, regardless of how much misery it may cause or how it may harm innocent people, can be made to sound utterly reasonable, equipped with the requisite calculations and its supposed advantages. You might read aloud in class this synopsis of an article ("The Economics of Legalizing Drugs," by Richard J. Dennis) that appeared in the November, 1990, *Atlantic Monthly* and ask your students how closely they think it resembles the style of argument in Swift's essay: "From a strictly economic point of view, the author argues, legalizing illegal drugs makes a great deal of sense: It would save taxpayers billions of dollars and put drug lords out of business. And, he contends, it would not cause an unmanageable increase in the number of addicts."

The target of Swift's irony is, students will see, the English landlords who have devastated the Irish economy. You might demonstrate this aim by examining paragraph 12: "I grant this food will be somewhat dear, and therefore very proper for landlords, who, as they have already devoured most of the parents, seem to have the best title to the children." This short paragraph opens up a problem of tone, for the speaker's attitude here seems to break out of the ironic frame and directly state the situation not as he sees it but as *Swift* apparently sees it.

You might point out the puns in this passage. The food is *dear* not only because it will be expensive and thus affordable only to landlords; but it may also be *dear* to the parents whose child it once was. Here we may assume that the speaker, whose terms are strictly monetary, may intend only one level of meaning for *dear;* the other, human level will be supplied by the reader (we thus have a lesson in irony contained in one word). But *devour* presents us with a different level of consciousness on the part of the speaker, because he intends the word both literally and figuratively, to eat and eat up. It would be interesting to assess the range of student response to this passage: Do they think that it is out of character for the speaker to admit this accusation, or is it still in character? In other words, do they think Swift allows his own opinion to break directly through the ironic pose?

This is clearly a difficult discussion question — analyzing levels of irony always are — but in asking students to reflect on Swift's method you will be raising essential questions about the distance between authors and speakers that is vital to understanding literary works in their fullest complexity.

Additional Activities

To show how relevant "A Modest Proposal" is to today's world, invite your class to read Jonathan Kozol's "Distancing the Homeless" (Chapter 8) and compare the "official" explanations of homelessness criticized by Kozol with Swift's speaker's similar explanations. Students should be able to identify several comparable strategies. You also might use the example of drug legalization above as a model for similar recent articles. Divide the class into a few groups and encourage them to find a recent proposal that promises to remedy some current social problem. They should make a copy of the proposal and bring it to class, ready to discuss its reasonableness and the self-image the proposer attempts to create. Discussion should focus on the writer's strategies to make his or her proposal acceptable to the reader.

Generating Writing

One good way to learn about irony is to try using it in writing. You might ask students to take one of the positions from Jonathan Kozol's or Sallie Tisdale's essays (see Chapter 8) — or another similar article not in this collection — and use the opinions or attitudes as a basis for an ironic essay in the manner of Swift. Students will need to invent the reasonable voice of a proposer who wants society to implement his or her "benevolent" plan.

Fyodor Dostoyevsky

Confession of Faith

Teaching Strategies

This well-known excerpt from *The Brothers Karamazov* includes one of the famous lines of modern religious rebellion: "It's not God that I don't accept," says Ivan Karamazov, "only I most respectfully return the ticket to Him."

Why Ivan returns the "ticket" is the subject of this extended conversation between the cynical Ivan and his innocent younger brother Alyosha, who wants to know why Ivan can't accept the world. Ivan proceeds to recount stories of human atrocity — especially to children — to show that humankind cannot be loved, that it is too cruel and undeserving. "I think if the devil doesn't exist," he says, "then mankind has created him."

Your students will surely find Ivan's stories of cruelty to children moving and graphic. You might point out their philosophical resemblance to the Twain selection: "People talk sometimes of bestial cruelty, but that's a great injustice and insult to the beasts; a beast can never be so cruel as a man, so artistically cruel" (para. 7). Point out, too, another similarity between Ivan and Twain — they both take examples of cruelty and horror from newspapers. And in paragraphs 11 and 12, Ivan offers as evidence of cruelty administered under the name of religion an anecdote Twain would have relished: "And they chopped off his head in brotherly fashion, because he had found grace."

Ivan's stories of child abuse will strike a more modern chord with students. You might want to examine carefully Ivan's anecdote of the child set upon by his master's hounds and killed in front of his mother (paras. 18–21). This is a key passage because Ivan gets Alyosha to think his way and then turns the tables. You might ask your class to discuss why Alyosha responds "To be shot." Does he mean it? Or is he simply carried away by Ivan's tale? Ask students, too, why Ivan concentrates on atrocity to children and what he wants done. Does Ivan seem more bothered by the type of suffering? Does he care as much about children going to bed hungry or being denied proper shelter or medical attention?

Ivan's reasons are explained in the final paragraphs of the selection. Ivan can finally accept the suffering of adults — they are sinners and culpable — but he can't accept the suffering of innocent children. Nor can he accept any "higher harmony" that allows their suffering to exist for ultimate ends; you might want to ask what that "harmony" might be. But this is a good place at which to invite students to say what they think Ivan truly wants. Is it revenge? Is it justice? The answer is not simple, and so there's plenty of opportunity for open class discussion.

Students will see that Ivan's and Alyosha's conversation is essentially religious. You might want to open up discussion to see how different students will respond to Ivan's dilemma. Can anything be done about the suffering of children? Can it be explained in any way? How do different religions explain the suffering of innocent people? Invite students to suggest religious or philosophic answers to this question. Are those answers dealt with by Ivan? For example, do the answers offer a "higher harmony" or a "hell for oppressors"? If so, do your students still find them satisfactory? Do they think Ivan has missed the point about suffering?

You will need, of course, to remind your students that this is an excerpt from a long novel that treats these themes in far more detail. The intellectual discussion between Ivan and Alyosha, for example, is far more extensive than this excerpt conveys. But it's also important to realize that Dostoyevsky works out these intellectual and spiritual problems not by reasoning but by action.

Additional Activities

Though there would be too little time to read the entire novel, you might want to introduce students to the film version of *The Brothers Karamazov*. Of the several versions, at least one is readily available on videocassette (MGM/UA, 1957). Students should view the film from the point of view of Ivan and Alyosha's discussion about suffering. How do they think the movie version resolves the issue?

Generating Writing

Invite students to write an essay in which they answer Ivan's question in paragraph 31: "How are you going to atone for them?" The essay could answer this question according to religious, legal, or philosophical belief. If they want, students might pretend that they are part of the conversation and jump in there with their response to Ivan. But Ivan is clever, and so the response should be well thought out.

Mark Twain

The Damned Human Race

Teaching Strategies

When Mark Twain was a young printer in Cincinnati he roomed with a self-educated worker who advanced a pre-Darwinian evolutionary theory. But — as Twain writes in his autobiography — according to this theory, "Development was progressive upon an ascending scale toward ultimate perfection until *man* was reached; and that then the progressive scheme broke pitifully down and went to wreck and ruin!" Twain never forget this theory, and "de-evolution" long exerted a fascination for his thought. It began to dominate his thinking toward the end of his life, when he began writing some of his darkest works, such as the sketches in "The Damned Human Race."

The excerpt reprinted from that posthumously published work clearly demonstrates Twain's reversal of the Darwinian theory that humankind ascended from lower forms of life. According to Twain in this selection, the correct theory should be one of man's *descent* from higher animals. In a parody of "scientific method," Twain has his speaker recount man's many atrocities as inductive proof that he could not under any circumstances be considered a superior creature. In the great chain of being, man is at the bottom. Cruelty, greed, revenge, sexism, racism, indecency, obscenity, vulgarity — these are all characteristics of men, the speaker argues, not of any other animal.

Make sure your class understands that Twain was writing this sketch around newspaper clippings that he planned to append. Twain was a great reader of the daily paper and liked to cut out stories that showed human folly and atrocity. The clippings are mentioned in the text — they are not necessary for comprehension — but their mention may lead students to think that something is currently missing from the work.

Invite your class to discuss the speaker's scientific method in the selection. What sort of experiments does he perform? You might look closely at the first one (para. 7) — in what sense is it an experiment? Does your class feel that it conforms to the standards of scientific experiment? Can we take it seriously? Look also at the experiment in paragraphs 20 and 21. Invite your class to speculate about Twain's point in these "experiments." Do they find them effective, or do they think Twain could have made his point in better ways? You could ask, too, if your students think that Twain's theory is proving his experiments rather than the other way around.

You might want to point out that Twain proceeds by a tried-and-true method of satire — reversal. Most of the reversals go from high to low. By reversing Darwin's evolutionary scheme, Twain stands the conventional hierarchy of creatures on its head. He also reverses the usual claims about humankind's moral sense: instead of seeing it as the source of humankind's superiority, Twain regards it as the source of his degradation. The moral sense is, he maintains, in a reversal of definition, "the quality which enables him to do wrong."

In paragraph 28, Twain turns to man's physical inferiority, again using as proof specific instances. A good example of the rhetorical effectiveness of a list occurs in paragraph 28, where we are given an exhaustive account of diseases and infirmities. But though lower than animals morally and physically, humankind — the speaker acknowledges in the final paragraph — does possess one superiority: the intellect. But then Twain invites us to reflect on why, with our superior intelligence, we have provided no heaven for our finest quality to enjoy itself. This is a good question to ask your class to reflect on. Do they think Twain really believes that in intelligence humankind is superior, or is this more satire? And what does he mean that we have been offered no heaven for our intelligence? Why does it lead to his conclusion about our sense of importance?

Additional Activities

Invite your class to try Twain's method of researching human folly and atrocity. Ask them to run through a few days' issues of recent newspapers and clip any items that show humankind at its ugliest. Each person should bring in one or two clippings and be prepared to display the findings. Class discussion could focus on specific themes the items have in common and how they reinforce Twain's point.

Generating Writing

You might ask your students to consider this question in an essay: Does Twain's attack on humankind amount to a denial of what is today called "speciesism" — the belief that human beings have an inherent right to kill other species? Students might research some articles on speciesism as preparation for the essay. They should discuss whether or not they think Twain's work provides evidence that speciesism is wrong.

WRITING ABOUT THE CHAPTER

1. If you asked your students to try the Writing-before-Reading exercise, you might return to it after reading the selections. Your students should have noticed several ways in which to revise their papers: they might want to use a satirical or ironic point of view; they might want to use specific anecdotes, especially from newspapers; they might want to set up a fictional discussion that deals with their topic. Invite them to rethink their essay with some of these strategies in mind.

2. Much of the language and imagery that appear in this chapter go back to the view of man articulated in Psalm 8, one of the most famous Psalms in the Old Testament. Invite your students to pay close attention to the language of the Psalm and how it relates to the

various selections. The Psalm, of course, is infused with a far more positive view of humankind than are the selections. Your students should choose one selection and write an essay comparing it with the Psalm. They should demonstrate how the selection specifically echoes the Psalm's language and imagery, and how the writer has chosen a different view. They might want to argue which view of humankind they prefer.

Psalm 8

O Lord our Lord,
how excellent is thy name in all the earth!
who hast set thy glory above the heavens.
Out of the mouth of babes and sucklings hast thou ordained strength
because of thine enemies,
that thou mightest still the enemy and the avenger.
When I consider thy heavens, the work of thy fingers,
the moon and the stars, which thou hast ordained;
What is man, that thou art mindful of him?
and the son of man, that thou visitest him?
For thou hast made him a little lower than the angels,
and hast crowned him with glory and honor.
Thou madest him to have dominion over the works of thy hands;
thou hast put all things under his feet:
All sheep and oxen,
Yea, and the beasts of the field;
The fowl of the air, and the fish of the sea,
and whatsoever passeth through the paths of the seas.
O Lord our Lord,
how excellent is thy name in all the earth!

— The Holy Bible, King James Version, 1611

28

Visions of the Land

Henry David Thoreau, *From* The Maine Woods

Wendell Berry, The Journey's End

N. Scott Momaday, A First American Views His Land

WORKING WITH THE CHAPTER

Americans have always enjoyed a passionate relationship with the territory they inhabit. All cultures have their own ways of expressing the beauty and complexity of the connection between nature and humanity; our multicultural heritage combines these perspectives into a uniquely American vision of the land.

Teaching Strategies

Ask students what land means to them; what do they think of as "their" land? One way into this subject might be to discuss the lyrics of Woody Guthrie's "This Land Is Your Land" or Robert Frost's poem "The Gift Outright." How close do these words come to expressing students' views of the land? Where might they take issue with Guthrie and Frost?

The chapter selections approach the idea of the land from various angles. The epigraphs might be the easiest place to begin; ask students what kind of views these passages represent. The quotation from Heinmot Tooyalaket (Chief Joseph) offers a window on the traditional Native-American view of the land. Ask students what they know about Chief Joseph and his part in Native Americans' struggle for autonomy; this might be a good topic to assign for research and oral reports. How much of an influence do students feel the Native-American outlook has on mainstream American culture? Have them brainstorm about the possible results of the cultural clash between Chief Joseph and the United States government. How is our political philosophy diametrically opposed to the world view outlined in Chief Joseph's words?

Noel Perrin's summary of the origins of the wilderness movement throws some light on Thoreau s project in *The Maine Woods.* How do students assess Thoreau's proposal for municipal conservation projects? How might things have been different if Thoreau's plans had been carried out and wilderness was preserved on the local level, rather than in state and national parks? You may live in an area where municipalities do maintain conservation land; how does this protection seem to affect overall city or town environments? Does it improve citizens' quality of life? Ask students if they feel Perrin's assessment of nineteenth-century reactions is accurate. Do we still feel that we have unlimited wilderness nationwide? Worldwide?

The epigraph from Brigid Brophy may be most fun for class discussion. Invite students to discuss Brophy's tone; is she "serious"? Do they ever have feelings like this about nature? Fran Lebowitz once wrote in *Metropolitan Life* (New American Library, 1988), "Nature is what you go through on the way to a taxi." Might Brophy be parodying some contemporary attitudes about the countryside? Ask the class if they have ever had the experience of wanting to rebel against expectations of nature worship (students who are veterans of Boy and Girl Scouts almost certainly will have). How does our society go overboard in mythologizing the wilderness? From what acute problems might knee-jerk naturalism distract attention?

Ask students how Chief Joseph might react to the selection from Thoreau. How might he take issue with Thoreau's portrayal of his Penobscot guide, Joe? What kinds of agreement do you see between Chief Joseph's philosophy and N. Scott Momaday's? What differences might they have?

How does Brigid Brophy's attitude differ from those of the oblivious consumer of nature Wendell Berry inveighs against? How does Noel Perrin's characterization of nineteenth-century Americans still, in Berry's opinion, hold true? Have the class compare and contrast N. Scott Momaday's and Berry's visions of the land. How might the things Berry sees as an integral part of a territory's history be viewed by Momaday as an intrusion, and perhaps a desecration? What attitude does the class take toward the cabin Berry views as vital to our perception of the Red River? Is the human element vital to a territory's character? How might this realization bring out the contrast between European and Native-American ways of thought?

A *Writing-before-Reading Exercise*

Have students write a brief essay answering the question, "Where do you live?" Ask them to consider issues such as where they are in the state, in the country, in the world. Invite them to imagine what their surroundings looked like one hundred years ago, or two hundred, or a thousand. How does the place where they live affect their lives? What other places are important to them, and why?

WORKING WITH THE SELECTIONS

Henry David Thoreau

From The Maine Woods

Teaching Strategies

This essay is rather challenging. You may want to urge students to read it carefully and make notes for class discussion. Remind them to read the footnotes, and to look up words they find confusing or unfamiliar. It might be helpful to bring in a large map of Maine (or perhaps an overhead projection) and trace Thoreau's journey for the class. Pictures, film, or videos of the Maine wilderness would also provide context for this selection: the Maine Department of Tourism has several publications that could be used as an additional teaching resource. Make sure students are clear about the sequence of events in Thoreau's narrative, and about its setting and cast of characters.

Thoreau is most likely to be best known to students as the author of *Walden* and *Civil Disobedience*. Most of us today are apt to overlook the travel writing that formed the largest part of his work; in his own lifetime, Thoreau earned more renown as a naturalist than as a philosopher. What relationship do students see between Thoreau's nonconformist attitudes and his fascination with the wilderness? Does Thoreau's writing in *The Maine Woods* seem to reflect social and political interests?

You may need to offer students help with the selection's vocabulary; for example, they may not be familiar with *birch* for canoe, or with a canoe's *painter* (the rope attached to the bow and used for towing).

What is Thoreau's stated purpose in this expedition? How does he seem to question it during his account? The most obvious contrast seems to be between paragraph 5, in which Thoreau writes, "Though I had not come a-hunting, and felt some compunctions about accompanying the hunters, I wished to see a moose near at hand, and was not sorry to learn how the Indian managed to kill one," and the later statement, "It is no better, at least, than to assist at a slaughter-house." Similarly, Thoreau says of the logging-company "explorers," "I have often wished since that I was with them" (para. 8); later, though, his assessment is not so favorable: "explorers and lumberers generally are all hirelings, paid so much a day for their labor, and as such they have no more love for wild nature than wood-sawyers have for forests" (para. 34). What might be the roots of this deep ambivalence? Discuss with the class Thoreau's statement, "What a coarse and imperfect use Indians and hunters make of Nature!" (para. 34). What kind of assumptions might this thought betray? How does Thoreau discount motivations like survival in favor of more refined and aesthetic ideals?

Although the narrative is about a voyage into the wilderness, images of civilization remain close at hand. Why does Thoreau set out to document his expedition in precise detail? Read closely the episode in which he measures the moose (para. 28). What purpose might be served by this attention to statistics? Elsewhere Thoreau is careful to name the plants and animals he observes, and to define Indian words. What is the rhetorical effect of his thoroughness? How is this technique at odds with his evocation of the rapture of the wild?

Thoreau also uses images drawn from the inhabited world to describe the natural one: "a perpendicular forest-edge of great height, like the spires of a Venice in the forest" (para. 11). Does the vocabulary of wilderness or civilization seem more essential to Thoreau? How does his use of these metaphors shape the experience for the reader? For himself?

The characterization of Joe is a fascinating example of Thoreau's conflicting attitudes toward humanity's place in the wilderness. How does Thoreau seem to find Joe unsatisfactory? You might want to focus on the passages in which he describes Joe, or on the varying assessments he gives of Joe's hunting and tracking ability. What does Thoreau seem to expect from Native Americans? Why is he disappointed by some of Joe's traits (such as his use of popular slang) and fascinated by others (his ability to walk quietly in the woods)? What kinds of impulses does Joe seem to represent for Thoreau? Later, Thoreau says of Indians, "No wonder that race is so soon exterminated" (para. 34). What do students make of this statement?

Reread with the class Thoreau's summing-up of his experiences on the Penobscot and the readjustment of his thinking that they inspired. (You may want to read this passage aloud, to help students focus on its tone.) What kind of relationship to nature does Thoreau seem to be projecting here? Do students agree or disagree with such statements as, "There is a higher law affecting our relation to pines as well as men" (para. 36)? What might that higher law be, for Thoreau? For us today? What kind of issues does his maxim, "Every creature is better alive than dead, men and moose and pine-trees" (para. 36) force us to confront? How might Thoreau be inconsistent here?

Thoreau's conclusion is that "the poet" (by which he seems to mean all creative and artistic thinkers) is the truest lover of nature. Do students agree or disagree with this claim? Who, in their opinion, is closest to nature in today's society? Which of us seem to be furthest away?

Additional Activities

This selection might best be understood in company with Thoreau's other travel writings; you may want to assign a brief selection from each of Thoreau's nature works for individual reading and oral presentation. Some students may be interested in presenting selections from *Walden* in conjunction with this work. You may also want to ask them to research the current state of the wilderness Thoreau describes; how has it changed over the last century? How has it remained the same?

It could be interesting to look at this selection with George Orwell's "Shooting an Elephant" (see Chapter 3, "Moments of Recognition"). How are the situations of Thoreau's and Orwell's observers the same? How do they differ? How is each writer affected by the necessary and yet tragic death of an impressive animal? To what shared conclusions do they come?

Generating Writing

1. Ask students to write an essay on Thoreau's attitudes toward the uses of nature. How is he ambivalent about the logging industry, for example? About Native Americans? Have the class tease out the oppositions underlying Thoreau's conception. How can his ideals coexist with the necessities of life? How are they at odds with the necessities of his own journey? What might the results for society be if Thoreau's conclusions about our place in nature were adopted by all?

2. Have students try to write a brief account of this journey from the points of view of the other participants in it. What might Joe's view of this trip, and of Thoreau, be? How might Thoreau's companion, Ed Hoar, have described it? What perspective could the lumbermen have offered?

Wendell Berry

The Journey's End

Teaching Strategies

The first task might be to fill students in on Daniel Boone's life and role in our nation's exploration. In *Regeneration through Violence: The Mythology of the American Frontier, 1600–1860* (UP of New England, 1973), Richard Slotkin discusses the myth of Daniel Boone and its influence on American self-definition. How much does the figure of Boone matter in Berry's argument? Is Berry interested in Boone as an individual or as part of a movement he sees as vital to our history? How does his evocation of Boone shape his narrative? Does Boone's name "sell" the hut in the same way as it sold fried chicken, or a television show?

Berry characterizes the hut as "a vital clue to our history and our inheritance, turned into a curio" (para. 4). How are our national landmarks compromised by preservation? What concessions are necessary if we are to maintain and exhibit significant items from our country's past? Ask students to discuss Berry's contempt for those who cite "convenience" in their attempts to control nature. How are the opposing claims of wilderness and society to be balanced? Discuss Berry's statement that when people "must be divided by a fence from what is vital to them, whether it is their history or their world, they are imprisoned" (para. 5). How might the builders of the fence (the Parks Service, presumably, or a local authority) have differed from Berry? How have students reacted to the presentation of landmarks and the control of their spectators? Ask them to share their own experiences of similar situations. How did their physical separation from the object or site they were visiting change their perceptions of it?

Discuss Berry's describing the grove of timber as a "virgin place." What does the virginity metaphor mean in this context? What is its effect? What kinds of attitudes might the use of this metaphor indicate? Is Berry's tribute to the untouched places slightly at odds with his defense of the hut? Which kinds of human creation are considered as part of nature? Which are not? What underlying conceptions might that reflect?

Ask students what they make of Berry's experience in the timber grove. How does he shape his encounter with nature? What traditional ways of expression does he use or adapt? How might the class agree or disagree with his attitudes about his walk in the woods? To what possible characterizations of the author does this passage lead?

How do students react to Berry's powerful evocation of a forest three centuries gone? How might his description of the early frontier differ from their own? What is the effect of this section of the essay? How does it reinforce Berry's conclusions? Are these the reflections that he would, ideally, wish the hut to inspire? Discuss the significance of Berry's mediation of this experience. Is his writing analogous, in some way, to the fence that encloses the hut? How is an essay about the importance of direct experience of nature and history a self-defeating proposition? What response might Berry make to that idea?

Discuss Berry's final metaphor of the lost map. He views it as the symbol for his discovery of the wilderness and his relinquishing the idea of control over it. Do maps interpose an illusion of control between ourselves and our surroundings? How is the concept of mapping representative of our attempts to dominate nature? Is Berry's abandoned map a token of his move closer to the actual experience of the land?

Additional Activities

You may want to look at this selection in connection with students' work on Chapter 4, "Public Space." How are our nation's landmarks an example of public space? What territorial claims are made there, and by whom? What kinds of power are exercised?

If practical, a field trip to a local historic or natural site could provide the class with an analogue to Berry's experience. How do they perceive the space as being presented? What mediates their experience of the site?

Students may want to compare and contrast this essay with Gretel Ehrlich's "The Solace of Open Spaces" (Chapter 4). How similar are Berry's and Ehrlich's views of our emotional and psychological relationship to the wild? How do the authors differ?

Generating Writing

1. Ask students to briefly dissect and summarize Berry's view of nature. What does he see as its powers? What does he perceive as threats to it? Invite students to formulate their own philosophy of our land and its history; how do they agree with Berry's? How do they differ?

2. Berry writes that the virgin timber is the best place in which to think about Daniel Boone's hut, just as the hut itself gives us a way into imagining the great forest that surrounded it when it was built. How do our perceptions of the wilderness shape our ideas of history? How does history help to define our experience of nature?

N. Scott Momaday

A First American Views His Land

Teaching Strategies

Discuss the essay's title with the class. What rhetorical point does Momaday make by using the phrase "a first American"? How might the title's effect have differed if the wording were "a Native American" or "an aboriginal American," for example? What is the signifi-cance of the description, *"his* land," given Momaday's statements about Native-American attitudes about land and ownership? Does Momaday mean to say that the first American's land might be his in the way a car might be his, or rather that it is his in the way of a family, nation, or language? Discuss Momaday's charge that our society perceives land as "a lifeless medium of exchange." Ask students their own views on this issue: is America something of which they feel they own (or could own) a tangible piece, or is our possession of the land less material than that?

How do students react to Momaday's integrating a poem into his essay? What kind of statement does this inclusion make? Does Momaday's willingness to cross the boundaries of genre mirror Native-American unwillingness to acknowledge territorial boundaries? Ask the class to evaluate Momaday's tone. How might it represent an attempt to incorporate some features of oral history into the traditional essay form? How might this rhetorical choice reinforce Momaday's argument for the claims of America's Indian heritage?

What do students make of Momaday's description of how Native American civilization developed? Read closely the passage in which Momaday describes the fifteenth-century Indian hunter. How is this portrait idealized? Why has Momaday chosen to leave out contributions by Native American women? Many of the skills he mentions here were traditionally female ones such as the cultivation of corn, the gathering of fruit and nuts, and in many tribal cultures, the practice of herbal medicine. How do students react to Momaday's presentation of the Native American as a lone male hero rather than part of a community? What European-American traditions does this depiction mirror?

Discuss Momaday's view of Native-American aesthetic perceptions. How is the Native-American view of the earth part of mainstream culture? How could it be integrated further into popular perceptions? What role do Native-American traditions have in our public lives? In New Zealand, traditional Maori dances are performed at many national ceremonies, even though the dominant culture and the majority of the population is descended from the same Europeans who conquered the Maori and appropriated their lands. Ask students to imagine a similar situation in America today. What might be the effect if we included Indian rituals in our civic observations? Might this combination, ultimately, be hypocritical, or would it reflect understanding of, and confrontation with, our culture's inherent oppositions and contradictions?

How would our appreciation and adoption of Native-American ideas of the land change our interactions with nature? With each other? How might these ideas deepen our commitment to the environment and its preservation?

Additional Activities

Students may want to look at this selection in conjunction with Chapter 7, "What Is an American?" What part do Native American traditions have in our national self-defini-tion? How is our view of the land a blend of the immigrant's and the original inhabitant's?

Some class members may be interested in researching and presenting different Native-American views of the land and human relations to it. *Black Elk Speaks* is a fascinating documentation of one Native American's philosophy on this and other issues. Indian women's views of the earth are represented in a number of oral histories, folklore collections, and autobiography; one of the most accessible is *Papago Woman* by Ruth M. Underhill (Waveland Press, 1985).

Generating Writing

1. Ask students to write a brief essay detailing how the Native-American view of the earth, as presented by Momaday, differs from their own. How do their views coincide? How has their knowledge and perception of Native-American traditions affected the creation of their own philosophy of nature?

2. Have students draw up notes for a challenge to, or defense of, Momaday's claim that the "ancient ethic of the Native American . . . must shape our efforts to preserve the earth and the life upon and within it" (para. 29). What other traditions must (or must not) be taken into account? How is the Native American tradition incomplete or inadequate in our contemporary struggle on behalf of the environment?

WRITING ABOUT THE CHAPTER

1. Ask students to write an essay comparing and contrasting the selections by Berry and Momaday. How do the authors' presentations of nature differ? From what traditions do they draw their philosophies of the land? How would Momaday react to Berry's view of the hut and of its importance in our history? Might he not see it as a desecration of a site properly wild, rather than as an important historical landmark? (Daniel Boone was not noted for his tolerance of Native Americans.) What view do students take?

2. How are all three writers' perceptions of the land and our attitude toward it influenced by gender? What alternative perspectives might women authors have offered? Discuss how sex-segregated occupations like hunting and logging influence our connection to the wilderness. Do women's relationships with the land differ from men's? How?

3. Which of the authors seems, in students' opinion, to have the clearest understanding of the compromises forced on nature by social necessities? Which of the authors seems most idealistic? How does each writer present civilization and its requirements? From which of the essays could readers develop the most constructive outlook and plan of action?

29

Environmental Action

Lewis Thomas, Natural Man

Charlene Spretnak, Ecofeminism: Our Roots and Flowering

Cynthia Hamilton, Women, Home, and Community:
The Struggle in an Urban Environment

WORKING WITH THE CHAPTER

National and global environmental problems are rapidly becoming issues that unite people of all political outlooks and affiliations in the vital struggle to preserve the natural world we live in. Many students will already be interested and involved in the environmental movement; others may have received some education about the topic in school, from their communities, or through the media.

Teaching Strategies

Ask students what their exposure to environmental issues has been. Poll the class on their greatest worries about the ecological future of their community, country, and planet. Write their responses on the board, and encourage the class to discuss and debate these problems and their possible solutions. What kinds of priorities must we set? How shall we balance opposing claims when something so essential as the global habitat is at stake?

The selections in this chapter survey some primary perspectives in the environmental movement today. You might want to ask the class their perceptions about the differences among environmentalists. What are some commonly shared interests? How, in their opinion, do different groups define and order ecological issues?

It might be best to start with the chapter epigraphs as a way of introducing students to some of the main questions. Joy Williams's epigraph may be the most challenging; you might want to read longer selections from her essay (published in *Esquire* in February, 1989) as a way of giving a context for her thought. Whom does the class think she is addressing when she writes, "You must change?" What is their reaction to her tone? Do they agree with her recommendations for change?

The passages from J. E. Lovelock and Aldo Leopold supply the point of view of the most traditional camp in the environmental movement. Some students may be familiar with Leopold's *Sand County Almanac* (New York: Oxford UP, 1949). Sections of it could be assigned for reading and brief presentations; it is one of the great classics of nature writing. Other students may be interested in researching work by other pioneers of ecology, such as John Muir and Rachel Carson. Lovelock's work is more recent, but he is heir to the classic tradition of inquiry into our place in the world around us. Ask students how they feel about the issues Lovelock raises. Do our wishes for economic and social progress sometimes conflict with the well-being of the natural world? How might these conflicts be resolved? Does Leopold's idea of a "land ethic" help in understanding and solving these problems?

The land ethic is a major theme for today's environmental movement. Discuss with the class how this idea has changed in time. You might want to fill them in on some points of view that are not represented in the chapter selections, such as the Green Party platform, and the ideas of deep ecologists and allied groups such as Earth First! This might be an ideal basis for a class research project, with students each contributing sections of a group report. Have students follow the environmental debate in journals and periodicals, and ask them to briefly summarize its disparate trends. Collate results and ask the class to edit their report as a committee; they will gain insight into how fact-finding commissions and other research bodies compile their data for publication.

Lewis Thomas's essay seems closest in spirit to Leopold's philosophy. Ask the class how they feel Spretnak differs from the environmentalist mainstream. Where does Hamilton fall on the spectrum? Is she closer to Thomas, Lovelock, and Leopold than Spretnak is? Which of the authors might be most inclined to agree with Williams? Discuss how the aims of the essays are alike, and how they differ. How does each author define the issues at stake?

A Writing-before-Reading Exercise

Ask students to describe a natural spot that is important to them. This may be a place they have visited, such as fields or woods near their homes, or some distant location they know only through film or photographs, such as the rain forest or Mount Kilimanjaro. Now ask them to describe some possible threats to that site. How could these be avoided? What would the students do to help maintain this environment's integrity?

WORKING WITH THE SELECTIONS

Lewis Thomas

Natural Man

Teaching Strategies

Thomas's essay gives less-informed students a way into the environmental debate, and his thought is complex enough to sustain the interest of class members more involved in the issue. You may wish to remind students about Thomas's position as a medical and scientific essayist, originally trained as a physician. He usually focuses on humanistic interpretations of science and technology; "Natural Man" is from Lives of a Cell one of his best-known collections of essays. How might Thomas's medical and scientific training influence his approach to ecological issues?

Ask students to evaluate the claims in Thomas's first paragraph. Are they aware of any examples (past or present) in which an environmental hazard was judged by economic standards? You might want to suggest some situations in which such standards are continually applied. The nuclear power industry is constantly subjected to scrutiny by environmentalists, as are the fishing industry and heavy manufacturing. What negative effects would society feel if these industries' powers were sharply limited? What positive effects might result? What criteria do we use to balance these opposing claims?

Discuss Thomas's précis on the history of environmental thought. How accurate do students find it? What underlying assumptions might it reveal? Ask students which position they feel best matches their own. Do they agree with Thomas's opinion that humanity's great power over other species carries greater responsibility? Or do they feel that we are no more custodians of the earth than any other form of life? Few students are likely to admit to the view that human beings have, or should have, untrammeled sovereignty over the planet. How are remnants of this view still visible in our society?

Define *morphogenesis* for students and discuss it with them. What kind of world view might this idea fit into, and how acceptable is that to students? How is Thomas's proposal for our contract with the earth a restatement of traditional European and Judeo-Christian ideas of humanity's place in the great scheme of life? Could Thomas's philosophy be used to justify the same excesses and violations of nature as did previous characterizations of man as steward of nature?

What do students think and feel about Thomas's proposal for a human-centered ecology? Some have argued that the major problem with deep ecologists and other radical environmentalists is that they do not accord the same rights to human beings as they do to other species. Discuss this claim; what rights do people have? What rights do other species have? We do not, cannot, and should not stop animals from ravaging, torturing, and plundering other species (we can bell our pet cats to protect the birds in our yard, but we can hardly bell lions to protect gazelles); why should we not, as part of the cycle of prey and predator, be free to do whatever we can to maximize our species' success? It seems obvious that we must impose limits on ourselves, but what must those limits be? What claims should we take into account? Where should our first loyalties lie?

How enthusiastic are students about a role as "handyman of the earth?" How do they think that self-perception might affect human interaction? Our attitudes toward the environment? How accurate do they find the description?

Additional Activities

You may want to have a representative of a local or national environmental organization speak to the class about that group and their work. The Sierra Club has an information outreach program, as do Greenpeace and many other groups. Your city or town may employ a municipal environmentalist, or appoint a conservation commission; these individuals might want to address the class, or students could observe their meetings or work and give brief presentations on current problems and issues these officials face, and the means they have to solve them.

This essay could profitably be taught in conjunction with Virginia Woolf's "Thoughts on Peace in an Air Raid" (see Chapter 22). How is Thomas's call to action like Woolf's belief that we must "think peace into existence?" What does Thomas want us to "think into existence?" What interests do he and Woolf seem to share? How do the essays differ?

Generating Writing

1. Ask students to find coverage of an environmental controversy in a newspaper or magazine. The issue could be local, national, or global; it might relate to a proposed power plant, an oil spill, or a report on the rain forests. Have them read a few articles about the issue and take a position on it. Ask them to draft a letter to the editor outlining their opinion and the reasoning behind it. The letter can be brief (250–500 words), but students should be as specific as possible, and support their position with thorough knowledge of the problem.

2. Invite students to come up with their own definition of humanity's position in relation to other species. How are we different from them? How are we similar? What interests do we share with other living things, and how do ours run counter to theirs? Ask students to compare and contrast their view with Thomas's.

Charlene Spretnak

Ecofeminism: Our Roots and Flowering

Teaching Strategies

Spretnak's essay is a helpful introduction to one of the most important currents in today's environmental movement. Ecofeminism may not be familiar to many students, but its influence is widely felt and publicized. Ask the class what they know about the women's antinuclear movement, both in this country and in Europe. Students who listen to women's music may already be aware of ecofeminism. Some popular artists, such as Ferron and Holly Near, are actively involved in this movement.

Some members of the class might wish to challenge Spretnak's thesis that women have a particular interest in ecological action. Ask students to read carefully the paragraph that begins, "Ecofeminism grew out of radical, or cultural, feminism . . ." (para. 6). What assumptions underlie Spretnak's argument? Do students find these assumptions to be valid? What do students make of a phrase like, "patriarchal culture with its hierarchical, militaristic, mechanistic, industrialist forms?" Encourage the class to debate the accuracy and usefulness of this characterization. What point could Spretnak be trying to make here?

Spretnak's assertions about religion, spirituality, and their relation to our attitudes about nature might be fairly challenging to the class. What is their understanding of feminist critiques of Western spirituality? Find out how familiar they are with the various alternative goddess-centered religions and their historical and anthropological justifications. What do they think about Spretnak's claims for these spiritualities as a means to understanding the earth and our relationship to it?

The part of Spretnak's essay that may be most accessible to the majority of students is her discussion of our alienation from nature. Read closely the paragraph that begins, "Extremely important is a willingness to deepen our experience of communion with nature" (para. 12). Does the class agree that we can be cut off from nature even while we are thinking most intently about it? How might that problem best be addressed? Of what might it be a symptom? Spretnak writes that she was shocked into awareness of nature when a colleague drew her attention to birds' songs. Ask students if they have ever had to confront their own distance from the natural world. What event or events brought it to their attention? How did realization make them feel? What did they resolve to do to strengthen their relationship to nature?

Spretnak's discussion of the relationship between ecofeminism and deep ecology may be difficult for students not familiar with the terms of the debate among environmentalist factions. Ask students to make notes on questions they may have, and discuss them in class. How do students evaluate Spretnak's analysis of how political problems contribute to environmental crises? What things might she be overlooking? What assumptions underlie her argument?

Discuss Spretnak's proposals for action under a new regime of ecofeminist awareness. What does she mean when she says "we must lead by example?" Whom is she addressing? How might her general recommendations be transformed into specific behaviors? How different, ultimately, is her vision from more traditional ecologies?

Additional Activities

Be sure to compare this essay with students' work on Chapter 18, "The Feminist Movement Today." How does Spretnak's work mirror some of the concerns expressed by Nancy Mairs and bell hooks? Where might ecofeminism fit into the range of feminisms described by Vivian Gornick?

Some students may be interested in researching alternative spiritualities and presenting short reports on them to the class. How accurate does the class find Spretnak's indictment of Western religion's attitudes toward nature? How is nature accommodated in other traditions? How are its claims denied?

Generating Writing

1. Ask students to analyze Spretnak's conclusion and to extrapolate from it a plan for specific interactions between human beings and the rest of nature. How could Spretnak's philosophy best be expressed in action? Are there any dangers to which it might lead?
2. Have students return to Leopold's epigraph. If he were alive today to read Spretnak's essay, how might he respond to it? Where would the authors agree? Where might they disagree?

Cynthia Hamilton

Women, Home, and Community: The Struggle in an Urban Environment

Teaching Strategies

Hamilton's essay, like Spretnak's, might be classified as ecofeminism, but the two works have a number of significant differences. Hamilton shares certain interests with Spretnak, specifically those related to women's, minority, and Third-World issues, but her approach to solving these problems seems informed by an ideology that varies greatly from Spretnak's. Discuss with students how these two essays can be seen as part of the same movement. What range of opinion might ecofeminism include?

How do students react to Hamilton's revelations about the unfair burden placed on minority communities by pollution? Do their own experiences bear this imposition out? Discuss the relation between socioeconomic class and political activism. What kind of issues are the underprivileged generally seen as interested in? The privileged? Are these generalizations fair? Ask students to think carefully about their own preconceptions. One way to get into the issue is to talk about the never-ending stream of celebrity events for charity; are people more likely to give money to a cause in which Sting or Elizabeth Taylor are involved than to an individual soliciting funds on the street? Why, or why not?

Does Hamilton suggest that the movement against the Los Angeles incinerator was founded with an explicitly feminist agenda? Talk about the times when individual interests coincide with group ideologies. How might feminism, as a movement, represent the feelings of the incinerator's opponents? How might it not reflect their interests?

Ask students to return to Lovelock's epigraph. How does the incinerator conflict provide a real-life example of Lovelock's projected environmental dilemmas? What might Lovelock's opinion be of the neighborhood activists and their project? Robin Cannon, one of the women involved in the protest, expressed skepticism about the city's promise of economic gains in return for environmental losses, saying, "They're not bringing real development to our community" (para. 13). What might environmental hazards be worth to a disadvantaged community? Can students imagine any conditions in which an ecologically compromising installation, such as an incinerator or waste dump, would be welcomed by those directly affected for the financial advantages it would bring? (One response to the idea that high-pollutant sites can make good economic sense might be that the directors of such sites take great care not to live anywhere near them, even though they are the ones enjoying the most direct financial benefits.)

How are the experiences of the incinerator protestors specific to women? How might male opponents have acted, or been treated, in a similar confrontation? Using their own experience as a guide, do students find Hamilton's explanation of masculine and feminine approaches to conflict a fair one? How does Hamilton describe the supporters of the incinerator? How does she describe its opponents? Does she attempt to present proincinerator arguments in a reasonably objective way?

Do students agree with Hamilton's conclusion that the reason for the success of the incinerator protests was that the protestors rejected "normal" (which seems, by implication, to mean "male" here) ways of organizing around issues and confronting their opposition (para. 20)? What other explanations might there be? Would Hamilton's model be applicable anywhere a community's interests are threatened?

Additional Activities

Interested students might be encouraged to use this essay as the basis for an oral-history project. Ask them to interview community activists about their experiences, and then compare and contrast the subjects' views of organizing and protest with Hamilton's. How do factors like race, class, or gender influence an individual's manner of protest? How do these variables shape people's views of a community crisis and the optimal response to it?

This chapter could be approached in conjunction with Chapter 23, "Conflicting Loyalties." How are the women's gender, race, and class interests at odds? How are they complementary? Shelby Steele's essay, "On Being Black and Middle Class" (see Chapter 6) might also provide an interesting perspective on the issue; how might he characterize the different impulses of the incinerator protestors? How might he respond to Hamilton's charges that persons of color bear an unfair share of technology's risks?

Generating Writing

1. Ask students to imagine that their homes and families were being threatened by a proposed industrial site, such as the Los Angeles incinerator. Have them draft a letter to the protestors asking for their advice on how to start a similar action in their community. Encourage them to come up with specific requests; they may want to respond directly to the statements made by spokespersons such as Robin Cannon and Charlotte Bullock. What aspects of the protest would they like to know more about?

2. Have students write a brief essay responding to Hamilton's claims about the differences between male and female political behavior. Does their own experience suggest these claims to be true? Ask them to include a short discussion of their own attitudes and beliefs about social and political action. What part do they feel their gender plays in these beliefs?

WRITING ABOUT THE CHAPTER

The essays by Spretnak and Hamilton would make an interesting comparison-and-contrast assignment. How might the women Hamilton quotes respond if asked to read Spretnak's essay? How do Hamilton's real-life examples bear out Spretnak's theory? How do they challenge it?

Students might work with the Thomas selection and Leopold and Lovelock epigraphs to try to develop their own definitions of the land ethic and their relation to nature. How do they act on their feelings of responsibility to the environment? What actions would they like to have the opportunity (or the courage) to take?

The class might also want to consider Spretnak's and Thomas's essays as examples of widely divergent lines of thought within the same movement. How do the writers' views differ? What assumptions do they make, explicitly and implicitly? What critiques might they offer of each other's view? Ask students to align themselves with one point of view or the other. How does their own experience bear out their choice of opinion? What challenges might they raise to the other side?

Another approach might be to return to the Writing-before-Reading exercise and ask students to draw up a personal environmental manifesto. (Their work on Chapter 24, "Declarations of Independence," might be helpful here.) How have they changed their own lives to accommodate the claims of ecology? How might they urge others to change? Through what means should change come?

The Power of Language

30

The Languages of Home

John Edgar Wideman, The Language of Home

Paule Marshall, From the Poets in the Kitchen

Maxine Hong Kingston, *From* A Song for a Barbarian Reed Pipe

Grace Paley, The Loudest Voice

WORKING WITH THE CHAPTER

Teaching Strategies

In reading this chapter, students will be exposed to many different languages and dialects, some of them directly and others indirectly. In a sense this chapter celebrates the richness of linguistic diversity in the United States today. By all means take this opportunity to have students read aloud in class: let them actually *hear* the power in the black dialect spoken by Barbara Mellix to her daughter; let them feel the rhythm of the Barbadian dialect spoken by Paule Marshall's mother. Help them to imagine what it would be like to hear language as pure, smooth sound, the way that An-Thu Quang Nguyen experienced his mother's voice on warm summer nights. If possible, go to a music library and check out tapes or albums in foreign tongues so students can experience language that seems as if it doesn't "actually have *meaning.*"

Of course, students who are not from Vietnam will not experience the sounds of Vietnamese the same way that An-Thu Quang Nguyen does, even though he claims not to understand the language. The poignancy built into many of the selections and epigraphs in this chapter comes from a linguistic chasm between generations. For these writers, progress, too, often entails loss. The epigraph by Richard Rodriguez reveals its author in a state of limbo: he can no longer use the tender Spanish words of his childhood when addressing his parents, but the all-American alternatives are equally impossible. Maxine Hong Kingston's parents don't speak English, and John Edgar Wideman and Paule Marshall write here in a standard English that has been polished smooth of the rhythms of the English spoken in their homes. The topic "the languages of home" just might have a sense of loss built into it: the languages of home exist in memory, but the authors of the essays write in a more homogenous style, and their children may never be exposed to the linguistic diversity that was *their* parents' heritage.

Encourage students to look for the signs that the authors in this chapter, like Edmund Wilson, have found in their parents' language "a valuable heritage," "a model for [their] literary style." In some of the selections, the traces of the languages of home will be hard to find; in others, such as "The Loudest Voice," by Grace Paley, they will be impossible to miss. This chapter can be a valuable testing ground for the theory that form should reflect and reinforce content. Of course, the content of these essays is more complex than a mere celebration of the languages of home. Have students also be on the lookout for evidence of the conflicts that inevitably arise when two languages, the products and vehicles of two cultures, collide.

A Writing-before-Reading Exercise

You might try taking your students through a guided reverie, a mental voyage that will allow them to listen for their own languages of home. Ask your students to close their eyes, empty their minds, and concentrate on a scene in their childhood homes. Start, perhaps, by saying "You are a small child again. You are at home with your family. It is evening, and the whole family is eating dinner together. Imagine the room where you used to eat dinner. Look around the table and see each face. Take your time. Now listen. What are they saying? . . ." You might also want to take them to bedtime, to listen to their bedtime stories, or just their parents' last "good-nights" before they drifted off to sleep. And have them listen to the sounds of their family on a busy school-day morning. What do they hear? Whose voice is the loudest? What is he or she saying? What other tones do they hear? What feelings do these voices evoke?

Bring students back to the here and now by telling them to open their eyes but also to remember the voices they heard on their journey home. Have them write down any snatches of dialogue they brought back with them. Ask them to try to capture the nuances of the languages of their homes. This is not an essay assignment, nor even a prompt for a rough draft; rather it is a way of brainstorming in preparation for reading about others' languages of home, and eventually writing about their own, if they choose to do so.

WORKING WITH THE SELECTIONS

John Edgar Wideman

The Language of Home

Teaching Strategies

Your students might find this essay difficult, because its structure is not transparent. You might want to focus your questions in class discussion around the transitions, asking how Wideman gets from point to point, and how the various ideas are connected. You could start with the first paragraph. He ends that paragraph by saying that as a writer he always returns to his home, a black neighborhood in Pittsburgh. But the second paragraph, instead of picking up where the first paragraph left off, shoots us out to the "green woods of Maine," about as far from Homewood as one could get, and then he mentions, in the same sentence, that his present home is in Wyoming. Ask students why he jumps around the map in this way. Does his tactic throw them off the trail, at least momentarily? Help to bring them back onto the trail by asking questions such as the following: Why does he tell us about his writing rituals? What is the "return home" that these rituals facilitate? You might want to remind them at this point of the guided journey they took back to their own childhood homes at the start of this chapter's work.

You might next ask them where the *content* of his journey home lies. Where in the essay do they actually see Wideman at home, or hear the language of that home? He writes, for example, about his treks up Negley Avenue, into the rich white neighborhood, or about the time when he stole a piece of "stuck-up, siddity white folks'" language. He also talks about the importance of Ralph Ellison's work to the Afro-American writer and lists the art forms that preserve black culture: "Double-entendre, signifying, mimicry, call-and-response patterns of storytelling, oratory and song . . ." But nowhere in the essay does he bring us, as readers, back to his childhood home, to hear the language spoken there. This might seem odd in an essay titled "The Language of Home," and it might very well explain your students' confusion upon reading the piece: it seems like an essay with a hole at the center.

If students agree that there's a hole at the center of this essay, ask them why Wideman might have constructed it that way. They might point to the fact that this is a piece of writing about *writing* about home, not about home itself — that he is therefore writing at one remove from the subject of home. They may point to the fact that he gains his inspiration from the geography and climate of Maine: "Whatever kind of weather they happen to be producing, the elements are always perfectly harmonized, synchronized." It's not the content of the weather, but rather the form that matters. "Whatever mood or scene I'm attempting to capture, the first condition is inner calm," Wideman says, revealing a privileging of the writer and the writing over the scene he writes. Students might also point to his use of the image of the mirror, either because it implies a certain amount of distance from one's subject matter or because it suggests a focus on the self.

But if he's focusing on himself, why does he avoid a focus on himself at home, in his community? You might ask if he has indirect ways of airing the language of his home. Have students look at his discussion of the songs that used to play in his head as he worked his paper route. How could his comments about the songs also apply to the language of his home? The songs, for instance, let him "imagine a shape for [his] feelings." In order to make the implications for literature written in black English explicit, you might bring in Paule Marshall's description of discovering the poetry of Paul Laurence Dunbar, in "From the Poets in the Kitchen." Wideman also writes that "the songs were protection, a talisman, but they also could betray me." In what sense could it be said that the language of his home, black English, could similarly both protect and betray him? How might he be betrayed if he were to sing out in his native dialect?

It is clear that language is the site of political "skirmishes," that the oppressors would rather see a black kid with "a watermelon in his mouth" than to give him access to an education that might simultaneously give him access to some of the power (you might bring in the ideas expressed in Chapter 32, "Language and Politics"). What is not as clear is Wideman's relation to black culture, to the language of Homewood. Why, for instance, does he find "each book a voyage home, each a struggle up a steep incline whose familiarity makes it more rather than less difficult" — why, that is, does he borrow an image for his writing from the climb to the rich white neighborhood? Why does he find himself, at the completion of each book, "in an alien place, whistling, singing to keep away the strangers who own the hilltop and everything else," if his books are journeys home? It's certainly possible that he's referring to the hegemony of whites, the people who "own" everything. His account of the struggle to write and the results of that writing sounds like a nightmare, in which he makes his way home only to discover that his parents' faces are actually the faces of the kidnappers who had been pursuing him. You might discuss the particular difficulties of having an uncomplicated relation to one's culture if one is not born a member of the dominant culture.

Some students in the class might suggest that Wideman's structural choices in writing this essay constitute an instance of race betrayal, similar to his inability to assert his own way of talking and walking when he was hanging out with the white guys outside Liberty School gym. You will want to ask for evidence for and against this position, perhaps ending with a sense that not all of the elements fall into an easy "harmony," despite Wideman's desire to emulate "the elements." Or, perhaps, students will come up with lots of built-in contradictions in the essay, and they will decide that these contradictions add up to an honest portrayal of what "makes [Wideman] what he is."

Additional Activities

As a writing instructor, you might want to focus on Wideman's insights regarding the writing process. What lessons about writing — regarding methods, motives, and so on — can students carry away from this piece? Have them look in particular at the beginning and ending of the essay, where Wideman explicitly treats matters of composition. You might ask them if they can think of ways to develop "the habit of looking long and hard," which Wideman finds crucial to the vocation of the writer.

You might teach this essay in conjunction with Chapter 4, "Places in the Heart," in particular with "Ringgold Street" by David Bradley, whom Wideman mentions in his essay. Look specifically at the distancing techniques of both writers. How do they create distance between themselves and their subjects? What might motivate this distance?

Generating Writing

1. In paragraph 4, Wideman tells about the centrality of race in his writing: he fought for years to "believe again in my primal perceptions, my primal language, the words, gestures, and feelings of my earliest memories. . . . The blackness of my writing inheres in its history, its bilingual, Creole, maroon, bastardized, miscegenated, cross-cultural acceptance of itself in a mirror only it can manufacture." Ask students to write an essay answering the question of how Wideman *shows* (as opposed to merely tells) that this is true of his writing. What evidence of the influence of "double-entendre, signifying, mimicry, call-and-response patterns of storytelling, oratory and song, style as cutting edge, as a weapon against enforced anonymity" do they find in his essay?

2. Assign an essay in which students analyze the structure of Wideman's essay. Why does he put the ideas in the order in which they appear? Have them concentrate particularly on any pieces that seem out of place — they will find intriguing answers if they ask themselves hard questions. Does Wideman explicitly state his structural principle anywhere in the essay? If they think he does, they might try using that statement, in his words, as the thesis for their essay.

Paule Marshall

From the Poets in the Kitchen

Teaching Strategies

The first thing students will probably notice about Paule Marshall's essay is that it celebrates "common speech," or rather the *un*commonly powerful, evocative "common speech" of a group of women from Barbados. Give them the opportunity to discuss this language: What are its characteristics? Where does its power come from? Marshall discusses the language of her mother and her mother's friends in terms of its style, but she also discusses it in terms of its functions. Discuss these functions as well. Some of the functions she mentions coincide with the observations made by other black women writers in *The Winchester Reader,* for instance Gloria Naylor (see Chapter 34), who would agree with Marshall about language's power to reaffirm self-worth, and Alice Walker (see Chapter 19), who also celebrates women who created art "in the only vehicle readily available to them."

Students will probably notice that Marshall, Walker, and to some extent Naylor all focus on women's speech, women's art. In fact, Marshall foregrounds the issue of gender by opening her essay with the remark about women writers, spoken by the male novelist, but quickly taken up by Marshall herself. Discuss the portrait of women that Marshall paints in this essay. How do the women of her mother's generation challenge the stereotypes about women? Look at the subject matter of their talk: they indulge in "the usual gossip," a stereotypical genre for women, who are expected to take great interest in matters considered trivial by men. (Judith Ortiz Cofer's essay, *"Casa:* A Partial Remembrance of a Puerto Rican Childhood" [see Chapter 12], provides a contrasting example of women whose talk is mostly confined to traditionally defined women's genres.) But they also talk about politics and economics, in ways that show that these topics are vital and immediate concerns in their lives.

Your discussion of gender should lead naturally into a discussion of some of the underlying antitheses in this essay. (Remind students of the "fundamental dualism in life" expressed by the Barbadian women for whom "contradictions make up the whole.") How would students characterize the interaction between male and female voices in this essay? Paule Marshall quotes women's voices throughout the essay: the voices of her mother and her mother's friends, the voices of published writers such as Grace Paley (who has a story in this chapter) and Flannery O'Connor. But she also quotes men: male authorities on women's language (the male novelist) and on the experience of exile (Czeslaw Milosz). Considering the distance between her own prose style and the style of her mother's phrases, which are enclosed within quotation marks and often translated into standard English, the issue of writing in a foreign tongue so that one's words sound natural must have been a live one for her. It's no wonder, then, that she also quotes Joseph Conrad, whose vehicle, written English, was not his native tongue. Ask your students to speculate about why Marshall quotes both male and female authorities. Do they feel she is quoting the best source, regardless of gender? If so, what would be the implications? Are the "poets" who didn't "spend their days in an attic room writing verses" just as valid as the men from the ivory tower? Have them support their answers with evidence from the text.

Another antithesis in this essay comes from Marshall's focus on both oral and written language. In paragraph 36 she writes that when she was eight or nine she "graduated . . . from the spoken to the written word." Here you might want to bring in Gloria Naylor's "A Question of Language" once more, because Naylor, unlike Marshall, privileges spoken over written language. Ask students why Marshall considers her move to the spoken word a "graduation." What does this hierarchy do to her argument about the primacy of her mother's "wordshop," if one considers that the women there "never put pen to paper except to write occasionally to their relatives in Barbados"? On a similar note, you might ask why Marshall announces her academic credentials ("I was teaching a graduate seminar in fiction at Columbia University") in the very first line of her essay. After all, Paule Marshall *is* one of "these New York children." Even though this essay is ostensibly and titularly about the "poets in the kitchen," Marshall's heritage as a writer does not flow solely from that stream.

Additional Activities

You might teach this essay in conjunction with any number of selections in *The Winchester Reader* whose authors are also from mixed backgrounds, including the pieces in Chapter 6, "Divided Identities," and Chapter 23, "Conflicting Loyalties." Selections by Maxine Hong Kingston (in this chapter and Chapter 12) would have a special relevance, because Kingston and Marshall are first-generation Americans, and both inherit something from their mothers while simultaneously creating a place for themselves in today's United States. All of these suggested essays focus more explicitly on the conflicts or tensions between competing worldviews, whereas Marshall only implies a paradigm conflict, but the insights from the other essays might help you to help students bring the underlying antitheses to the surface in her work as well.

Generating Writing

Despite the fact that Marshall's essay style has a lot more in common with Joseph Conrad's style than with her mother's speech patterns, there are signs that she inherited some stylistic features from the poets she overheard in the kitchen as a young girl. Assign an essay in which your students identify and discuss the evidence of her mother's style embedded in her own style. They will probably also want to discuss similarities in the uses to which both mother and daughter put language.

Maxine Hong Kingston

From A Song for a Barbarian Reed Pipe

Teaching Strategies

Like the other authors in this chapter, Maxine Hong Kingston is caught between two cultures. In this excerpt from "A Song for a Barbarian Reed Pipe," the last chapter in her autobiography, *The Woman Warrior*, we see what can occur when the language of a child's home is not the language spoken at school or in the neighborhood stores. Maxine is almost like two children, running and shouting with the others during her breaks from Chinese school and chanting with the others during Chinese school itself, but unable to speak in her American classroom, where she is expected to speak as an individual. It's no wonder, then, that she repeats the contradictory explanations given by her mother for why she cut her frenum: because "a ready tongue is an evil," and so that Maxine "would not be tongue-tied." Of course, nothing in *The Woman Warrior* is simple or schematic: Maxine's mother says that "things are different in this ghost country" (the United States), but Maxine doesn't end up with the "ready tongue" that Americans apparently prize except when she is speaking Chinese.

Maxine Hong Kingston attributes her silence as a child, and her difficulty in speaking as an adult, to an attempt to make herself "American feminine"; apparently the attempt backfired, because she and the other Chinese girls she describes ended up whispering "even more softly than the Americans." Much of this selection is taken up in the story of the quiet girl whom Maxine tortures. Ask your students why, in a selection that seems to be about Maxine Hong Kingston's difficulty in speaking, the emphasis is shifted to this nameless little girl who is even more silent than Maxine.

They will probably notice similarities between Maxine and the quiet girl — both girls are chosen last for team sports, and both follow the silent girl's sister around. As the incident in the basement lavatory progresses, their similarities increase, until their cries are both echoing off the same walls. Given the fact that Maxine and the quiet girl have so much in common, you might ask why Maxine tortures her so cruelly. Have them look at the catalog of physical traits that Maxine notices, and despises, in the quiet girl. What is Maxine's response to each of these hated traits? Why is she so anxious to distinguish herself from the quiet girl? Some students may also call attention to paragraph 75, where Maxine projects a bleak future for the quiet girl. How can we tell that her words spring from her anxiety about her own future?

As the incident progresses, Maxine's tactics change. Have students identify the different methods Maxine employs in her attempt to get the quiet girl to speak. Why does she lower the ante in paragraph 73, where she says she will settle for a scream instead of a word, and then, in paragraph 76, why does she switch from threats to bribes? Why does she want so desperately for the quiet girl to succeed?

Additional Activities

You will probably also want to take this opportunity to discuss cultural differences between the Americans and the Chinese who are represented in this selection. What can students tell about those differences just from reading this piece? What, for example, are the differences between American school and Chinese school? What happens when the customs and beliefs of one culture are not understood by the people of the other culture — for instance, when the boy says that his mother calls her husband "father of me" (para. 68)? Have students find and discuss other examples of the two cultures coming into contact, and producing results that suggest a lack of perfect understanding. Also ask them to list the cultures other than Chinese and American that come into play in this selection, and to describe their function in the piece as a whole.

At least one student will inevitably ask if Maxine's mother really cut her frenum when she was born. Of course, there is no way to know for sure the answer to this question, but you might point to the following evidence that would lead one to question the mother's veracity: Maxine herself admits the possibility that her mother might have been lying; and her frenum looks just as precise and unscarred as those of the other kids whose frena she inspects. Students may also have noticed that a child's perspective often infuses Kingston's style ("which was a tic-tac-toe mark, liked barbed wire, on the map"), and that this child's perspective, like that of many children, is both cruel and vivid: witness the graphic descriptions of torture in the lavatory. It is certainly plausible that Maxine Hong Kingston, the "outlaw knot-maker," might have invented the story of her cut frenum herself, or, at the very least, that her mother really said it, and that Maxine's own proclivities made her remember and repeat it with such relish.

The authors of this manual had the opportunity to ask Maxine Hong Kingston a few questions about "A Song for a Barbarian Reed Pipe" and about her writing process. Our interview felt a little strange at first, because of the nature of *The Woman Warrior,* an autobiography that feels simultaneously like a work of fiction. We were a little hesitant to refer to the main character in "A Song for a Barbarian Reed Pipe" as "Maxine," because we were talking to Maxine Hong Kingston herself, but at the same time "you" didn't seem to be the right word either, because obviously there is some distance between the mature author and the little girl in the book. Kingston quickly smoothed away any awkwardness by referring to herself in the first person as the protagonist of *The Woman Warrior.*

Although her Western readers might often read fantasy and exaggeration into *The Woman Warrior,* to Maxine Hong Kingston this is pure autobiography. When asked to explain what she meant when she wrote that her mysterious disease, described at the end of the passage excerpted in *The Winchester Reader,* had "no symptoms" and "no pain," Kingston said that she had been diagnosed with rheumatic fever as a child, but that later, when she was an adult, doctors had tested her and found no evidence to suggest that she had actually had that disease. She added that she has met several others who tell similar stories about the rheumatic fever they ostensibly had during their childhoods. She spoke about this disease, or absence of disease, as if she was just as baffled (and amused) by it as her readers might be. When asked whether, in the context of the torture of the quiet girl, this disease could be seen as retribution, however, she readily agreed.

We also asked her about the episode in which her mother either did or did not cut her frenum, suggesting that there are several textual clues that imply that she did not. Kingston agreed that the straight line of her frenum might seem to suggest that it wasn't cut, but she also offered an opposing explanation: her mother, who was a surgeon, might have cut it so skillfully that she didn't leave a scar. On the topic of the truth or fictionality of her autobiography as a whole, Kingston told us about a graduate student who was researching a thesis about *The Woman Warrior.* This student visited the nursing home where Kingston's parents lived and asked the residents about several of the events that happen in the book. She was told that the book was full of lies. Kingston seemed outraged that the student would believe their version rather than her version of her own life.

Maxine Hong Kingston told us that she writes for at least five hours every day, except on the days when she teaches, when she manages to devote two to two and a half hours to her writing. She prefers to write in the morning. *The Woman Warrior* took three years to write, because she had to write ten or twelve drafts of it before she was satisfied. She told us that she never shows her rough drafts to anyone. (The Bancroft Library, on the University of California at Berkeley campus, however, owns her typescripts, which are interesting in spite of the fact that they so closely resemble the published version. For details drawn from that typescript, see the Kingston essay "No Name Woman" [Chapter 12]). She told us that when she first drafts a piece it is "incoherent," mostly just "sounds and images." Only as she reworks it does it gradually take shape. The openness of Maxine Hong Kingston and other professional writers about their writing processes can help to dispel the romantic myth that works of literature spring fully formed from the minds of their creators. If you have any students who are discouraged because their initial attempts at writing don't resemble the ideal versions they treasure in their imaginations, you might want to use Kingston as an encouraging example for them.

Generating Writing

1. The language of Maxine Hong Kingston's home is at once very literal and highly symbolic. Assign an essay in which students analyze the passages in which Kingston talks about Chinese ideographs, Chinese sayings, or the Chinese language in general. It is always productive to examine a language's assumptions, but a language whose alphabet is not phonetic but rather symbolic is especially fertile ground.

2. Assign an essay about the doubling motif in "A Song for a Barbarian Reed Pipe" and at least one other selection, of the student's choice, from *The Winchester Reader*. They may elect to analyze the *first* chapter of *The Woman Warrior*, "No Name Woman," included in Chapter 12, "Family Stories." Other possibilities would include "Once More to the Lake," by E.B. White (see Chapter 4), "Shopping," by Joyce Carol Oates (see Chapter 10), or "Discovery of a Father," by Sherwood Anderson (see Chapter 20). Have them analyze the function of the double in each story. Does the author or narrator use the double to express a feared part of him- or herself, for example, or perhaps to play out a fantasy version of his or her own life?

Grace Paley

The Loudest Voice

Teaching Strategies

The Loudest Voice" is a joyous, exuberant story about a Jewish girl who interacts with the dominant culture, as do the other speakers in this chapter, but, unlike them, she comes out victorious without compromising herself a jot. Students may point out that this is the only fictional piece in this chapter, and if they see the conjunction of these two facts as more than coincidental, so be it.

First you might ask students to identify the "certain place" that Paley describes in the first line of the story. If they say "Shirley's home," they are only half right. This story is set in the childhood home that now exists only in the narrator's memory. There is evidence (which students may or may not have caught), for instance, that her mother has died since the events recounted in this story occurred. Ask students what difference it makes to set this story in the irrecoverable past. Do they ever get the impression, as they read this story, that it isn't perfectly realistic? How, for instance, do they read such lines as "They are not insulted" (para. 8) or "They weren't ashamed and we weren't embarrassed" (para. 24)? Is this an innocent, child's-eye view, translated through the consciousness of someone who, unlike the child, would be able to think of the possibility of shame and insult? Is this a dream world, or a case of protesting too much, or both? How could it be both? What clues do they get to the racial prejudice that exists just outside Shirley's sphere of perception? You might draw their attention to the arrogance implied in Miss Glace's assumption that English is *"the* language."

The main action of this story is a Christmas play, which most students should recognize despite its unfamiliar garb (including a Jewish prayer shawl). The parents in the story realize that the Christians are in power in the United States; Shirley's mother's final speech is priceless: "The English language they know from the beginning by heart. They're blond like angels. You think it's important they should get in the play? Christmas . . . the whole piece of goods . . . they own it." But the Jewish kids, who play all the key roles in the Christmas pageant, blithely make it their own. Ask students how the narrator's point of view affects the story of Christ's life. What is the effect of hearing "Eddie Braunstein" and "Marty Groff" in the place of the names in the original story? Ask students if the role played by Jews in the story of Christ's life as it is usually told (by Christians, of course) has an impact on the way they read "The Loudest Voice," or if the girl's innocence makes that reading irrelevant.

Additional Activities

Another difference between this piece and the others in the chapter is that the texture of the prose in "The Loudest Voice" is permeated with the rhythms of Yiddish syntax. Whereas the three nonfiction pieces showed subtle signs of the languages of home that were their subject matter, there is nothing subtle about the signs in this story. (The Kingston piece, which is a sort of fictional autobiography, might be seen to lie somewhere between this story and the two essays in this regard.) Ask students if they think that fiction is more susceptible to this kind of verbal contagion than are essays. Why or why not? Can they think of anything inherent in essays that might resist the stylistic features of nonstandard dialects? Interested students might go to the library and look up some of John Edgar Wideman's fiction, which he mentions in his essay, in order to find out if black English affects his writing when he is not working in the essay form. Similarly, they might compare the prose in Gloria Naylor's "A Question of Language" (see Chapter 34), in "Fighting Words," with the prose in one of her novels. This library assignment could easily turn into a topic for an essay.

Generating Writing

You might want to assign this creative essay promptly after discussing "The Loudest Voice." Have students retell a traditional or popular story from a point of view that is alien to the original version of the story, to see how a change in perspective changes the force of the story. They can either adopt a persona for the purpose of the assignment, or use their own perspective on a tale from a culture that is very different from their own. Suggest that they try to capture the wit that is everywhere evident in Paley's story.

WRITING ABOUT THE CHAPTER

1. Have students look over the notes they made directly following the exercise and write an essay about their own languages of home. They needn't be a member of an ethnic minority group, as is each of the authors in this chapter, in order to write an interesting account of the languages they heard and spoke as they were growing up, but they will have to be creative in order to make it interesting, no matter what their ethnic background. Tell

them to feel free to make use of personal narrative and dialogue, but also either to state or to imply some significance to the memories they choose to recount.

2. In "The Loudest Voice," Shirley's dad stands the perspective of the dominant culture on its head when he praises the Christmas pageant for "introducing us to a different culture": Christians in America are accustomed to viewing all other cultures as "different." Similarly, Lavinia in Wideman's "The Language of Home" effects a turnabout in the narrator's thinking when she shows him she values black culture over white; Wideman writes that suddenly "it dawned on me that there was a Negley Hill where my white buddies, those unconscious kings of the earth, would be scared to deliver papers." Assign a paper in which your students explore a change in their own perspective regarding the issue of dominance — either a change effected by their reading of the essays in this chapter or a change brought about by events in their own lives.

31

Bilingualism

Richard Rodriguez, Toward an American Language

James Fallows, Viva Bilingualism

WORKING WITH THE CHAPTER

One of the most critical issues in today's America is language and its role in our national identity. What will be the language of public and political dialogue? How are residents unfamiliar with a country's tongue to be a meaningful part of that country's voice? What can we learn from the experience of other multilingual, multicultural nations?

America's diversity is one of its greatest strengths; yet how are the claims of diversity and unity to be balanced? Bilingual education often serves as a focus for this debate. Advocates claim it can help students keep pace with English-speaking classmates; without it, they argue, the rest of foreign speakers' education would be put on hold while they acquired skill in English. Opponents believe that bilingualism segregates non-native speakers, putting them at a disadvantage they can rarely overcome. The issue is complex; both sides seem to have only the best motives at heart, and yet simply cannot agree.

Teaching Strategies

Ask students about their own experience with bilingual education. Did their elementary and high schools provide first-language instruction for non-native speakers? Was the emphasis in their school system on mainstreaming, or on parallel progress? What are their opinions on the topic?

Another question in the controversy is which linguistic and cultural groups are to be considered as candidates for bilingual education. The chapter selections are focused on the needs of Spanish-speaking Americans; they are certainly the largest demographic group of non-English speakers in this country today, but other groups, such as Cambodians, Vietnamese, and Haitians are growing quickly. The deaf, too, have recently been recognized as a significant group of Americans to whom English is a second language; what are our society's responsibilities to them? Discuss these issues with the class; you may want to structure part of the discussion as a formal debate, with students arguing for and against a specific position on bilingualism.

The class debate might be built around the epigraph from Tina Bakka, with some students supporting the position she calls "immersion," and others taking a stand for bilingualism. How do "immersion" supporters counter her implication that the method succeeds only with great psychological pain? When does students' discomfort or anxiety begin to outweigh an educational method's possible benefits? Ask the class to think of analogous educational experiences. How does the "sink or swim" model work in areas other than language?

The epigraph from S. I. Hayakawa is an interesting view from a non-native speaker's experience. Students may not remember Hayakawa; remind them that he was a distinguished United States senator and a well-known authority on semantics. How might his experience not be typical of the immigrant learner of English? Is society responsible for making achievement possible for all members of a group, or for only the most talented and motivated among them?

The Pulitzer prize–winning novelist Oscar Hijuelos movingly depicts in his epigraph one boy's fight to keep his linguistic identity. Hijuelos's work draws on our rich Hispanic culture, yet his prose is in the tradition of the great American writers. How might the bilingualism compromise produce powerful art? On the other hand, how might it marginalize writers from non–English-speaking cultures?

Hayakawa's view supports Rodriguez's strongly; you will certainly want to teach this epigraph and selection together. How might Bakka respond to the claims Rodriguez makes? How might Hijuelos challenge Rodriguez's view of the tensions between Spanish and English in America today?

Discuss the differences between Bakka's and Fallows's reasoning in support of bilingualism. How do their agendas differ? How are they the same? Which position do students find is closer to their own?

Fallows's and Rodriguez's essays need careful analysis: Exactly what is each writer arguing for and against? Which of the same issues do the essays address directly? Where do they seem to have structured the controversy differently? How do the motivations behind their positions seem different — are the two authors responding to the same circumstances and conditions? Which assumptions are shared or unshared?

A Writing-before-Reading Exercise

Ask students to write about the importance of language in their own education. When did linguistic deficiencies or difficulties hold them back? How might this limitation have been avoided? What do they remember about their own struggles in learning English, as a first or second language? If they are native speakers of English, how do their experiences in learning other languages influence their views of, and responses to, non-native speakers?

WORKING WITH THE SELECTIONS

Richard Rodriguez

Toward an American Language

Teaching Strategies

Richard Rodriguez is a well-known American essayist much of whose work is focused on large social and cultural issues. His is also an articulate voice from the Hispanic community; his autobiography, *Hunger of Memory: The Education of Richard Rodriguez*, is one of the best accounts of the conflicts and challenges that a bright and talented Spanish speaker faces in an English-speaking society.

Ask students where the voice in this essay situates itself. What kinds of choices does Rodriguez make in his diction and allusions? The piece begins with a reference to *Huckleberry Finn*, a classic of mainstream American culture. What rhetorical effect does this allusion have? Have the class talk about the force of the generalizations in Rodriguez's opening paragraphs. What do they make of aphorisms like, "Individualism is the source of America, the source of our greatness." Are they surprised at Rodriguez's seemingly unproblematic insertion of himself into the "us" of American rhetoric? Discuss this tricky issue with the class; who is entitled to claim entitlement? Do students feel that most of today's Hispanic writers would be comfortable making statements such as, "They taught us well, those old Puritans." Is Rodriguez's intrusion into the norm a courageous move?

Ask the class how far they agree with Rodriguez's interpretation of American culture. Are Puritan ethics and ideals the basis for our communal and civic values? Is Rodriguez overlooking the enormous influence of cultural diversity on America's social character? Discuss his statement, "the outsider is the archetypal citizen." Do students find this idea resonates with their own experience? Are the views Rodriguez espouses here those we traditionally associate with "the outsider"?

The center of Rodriguez's argument lies in his claim that "the classroom is the most subversive institution of America . . . chipping away at any tangible distance between us." Have the class evaluate this statement. Do their educational experiences bear it out? How does our country's public-school system work as a force for acceptance and assimilation? How does it emphasize and maintain differences between groups? Which of its effects is stronger? Ask students whether their own schooling gave them a sense of national identity. Do students feel included in America's past? In its present and future? Do they feel excluded?

What does the class make of Rodriguez's describing the probilingual forces as providers of intellectual training wheels? (And does this metaphor mean anything to urban students?) How does this attitude misrepresent the position in favor of bilingual education? Is Rodriguez's characterization valid?

Rodriguez stresses the need for classroom values to be public, not family, values. Do students agree or disagree with this idea? In what other educational situations might public and family values come into conflict? Is the class entirely comfortable with Rodriguez's use of "unsentimental" as praise? What word might an opponent of the author use here instead?

Discuss the link Rodriguez makes between the demand for bilingual education and the values of the turbulent 1960s. What kind of a rhetorical move is this? How does Rodriguez implicitly dismiss 1960s aims as antithetical to America's shared vision? Which generation's values does he seem to espouse?

The essay depicts the birth of a shared American culture in nineteenth-century schoolrooms. What issues and developments in our nation's history are overlooked here? The Civil War and the extermination of Native-American populations are just two of the divisive and destructive events that shook the country during the era when, Rodriguez says, "grammar school teachers forged a nation." Are positive steps toward unity, such as public education and a national culture, separable from efforts at forced homogenization? Rodriguez's references to *Huckleberry Finn* bring up another point students should consider — the civilizing and unifying nineteenth-century classrooms marginalized African-Americans or excluded them entirely; Huck's mentor Jim may have been the African-American many of these students knew best. What might be Rodriguez's intent in emphasizing women's roles in this educational effort? Are the values of America's Puritan and pragmatist traditions generally considered hospitable to women?

Rodriguez's conclusion includes this thought-provoking aphorism: "Diversity which is not shared is no virtue. Diversity which is not shared is a parody nation." Examine this assertion with the class; what might Rodriguez mean by it? Do they agree or disagree? How, in their opinion, is diversity best to be shared?

Additional Activities

Shelby Steele's essay, "On Being Black and Middle Class" (Chapter 6) seems an interesting complement to Rodriguez's. What view of mainstream America do these minority writers share? How do they encourage all Americans to demand a place of privilege, rather than focus on their own disadvantages? How do Steele and Rodriguez differ in resolving minority intellectuals' conflicts of loyalty?

Students may wish to read and report on other writers' stories about growing up bilingual. Maxine Hong Kingston's works might be a good place to start (see the selection by Kingston in Chapter 30, "The Languages of Home"); Rudolfo Anaya's novel *Bless Me, Ultima* movingly portrays a Latino boy's struggle to reconcile his Hispanic and American identities.

Your campus may have one or more action groups for Hispanic students; you might want to ask a group's leaders to speak briefly to the class on recent developments in bilingual education for Spanish speakers. Perhaps a dean or other college administrator might also participate in a forum discussing multilingualism and diversity; some students might organize this forum as a special project, or it could be taken on by the class as a whole.

Generating Writing

1. Rodriguez mentions a number of ways in which our encounters with fellow Americans might enhance our understanding and appreciation of diversity; our schools, our workplaces, and our consumer culture all, he feels, contribute to a shared national identity. Have students write a brief essay responding to this view; when are they made aware of cultural diversity? What makes them feel part of a unified nation? How do they interpret their own identity as Americans?

2. How, in students' opinion, are the ideals of individualism and consensus to coexist? What compromises must be made to preserve both? What compromises between the two have students made in their own education and life?

James Fallows

Viva Bilingualism

Teaching Strategies

The first part of this essay that requires close reading is its title. With whom is Fallows aligning himself? How might the rhetorical effect of "Long Live Bilingualism" be different?

How do students react to his portrayal of a xenophobic Japanese anthropologist as a metaphor for American antibilingualism? The class may not be aware of the controversy in Japan over the influence of cultures that some Japanese perceive as inferior, especially that of the United States. Is this situation analogous to our own?

Fallows cites Québec as an example of a culture impoverished rather than enriched by its bilingualism. Are students familiar with the state of affairs in Québec and its influence on Canada today? Some students may want to research recent developments in the conflict between Canada's French and English speakers. How does bilingualism work as a positive factor in Canadian life?

Discuss with the class Fallows's "two wives/two children" metaphor for language. How is this metaphor useful and descriptive? How is it inadequate? Are students put off by the metaphor's seeming sexism (after all, it would have been just as easy for Fallows to write "spouse" as "wife")? Ask the class whether their own experiences in acquiring language bear Fallows out. Do they find their understanding of their native language enriched by acquiring a second?

Fallows gives the experience of multilingualism in Singapore as a model. Students may need information on Singapore and its unusual history as an international port of call and trade center to judge if Singapore's experience applies to our own. How is Malaysia's solution to the same problem also determined by its idiosyncratic history and demograph-ics? Which aspects of American culture are analogous to those of these nations, and which are dissimilar?

One of the most problematic paragraphs in Fallows's essay brings out some significant issues in the bilingualism debate. In paragraph 11, Fallows writes of the multilingual Malaysians,

> I should emphasize that I'm talking about people who in no way fit modern America's idea of a rarefied intellectual elite. They are wizened Chinese shopkeepers, unschooled Indian night guards, grubby Malay food hawkers. . . . Yet somehow they all find room in their brains for more than one language at a time. Is it so implausible that Americans can do the same?

Are students at all uncomfortable with Fallows's assumptions here? This statement could be taken as offensive in many ways: that shopkeepers, night guards, and food hawkers have limited brain capacity, and therefore we should all be able to learn more than one language; that if Chinese, Indian, and Malay people can learn several languages, then Americans should certainly be able to; or even that those people in our society who are non-native speakers of English could not possibly be part of an "intellectual elite." Perhaps Fallows means none of this by his statement; what are the class's opinions? Is this kind of ambiguity unfortunate in an article about the politics of language and learning?

Fallows's attack on what he describes as the "second antibilingual assumption," that a multilingual culture threatens the integrity of English, raises interesting points. How do students feel our language is affected by our national diversity? Should language be a fixed entity, or should it grow with its speakers? How do students respond to Fallows's assertion that American society is constantly pressuring its members to participate in mainstream culture? Ask the class to offer its own examples pro and con. Do pressures for economic and social achievement provide significant incentives for non-native speakers to learn English? Do students agree with Fallows's contention that multilingualism makes American culture richer and better able "to deal with the rest of the world"?

Additional Activities

Colleagues in English as a second language might be asked to speak to your class on the challenges and rewards of educating our country's non-native speakers. In conjunction with this exchange, students could be assigned a selection from Leonard Ross's *The Education of H*Y*M*A*N* K*A*P*L*A*N** (Harcourt Brace Jovanovich, 1968), a comic fictional treatment of ESL education in the 1940s. How has the focus of ESL changed over the years? What problems do today's immigrants share with those of the past? How do their challenges and goals differ?

The growth of English as an international language is one of the major arguments against multilingualism's supposed dangers. You may want to view with the class the episode in *The Story of English* (R. MacNeil, director; PBS Video, 1988) in which the rise of English abroad is discussed. How is our language one of our nation's most precious commodities? Do opponents of multilingualism run the risk of isolating American English from the potential enrichment of cultural exchange?

Generating Writing

1. Ask students to imagine themselves suddenly transported to a city where a language that they don't speak is spoken. They may appropriate Fallows's description of living as an American in Japan, or draw on their own experiences traveling in other countries. Have them write a brief essay describing their typical day; what basic skills become challenges? What frustrations present themselves? How would they cope with this difficulty?

2. Fallows mentions how multilingual needs are integrated into our public lives, in "street signs and TV broadcasts and 'maintenance' courses." Assign a short personal essay

in which students discuss an encounter with multilingual address; they may want to talk about Spanish-language cable channels, or being addressed in languages other than their own by passersby or service personnel, or perhaps even the experience of wondering what nearby conversations could be about. How did they respond to this interaction with another language? Did they find the experience frightening, enriching, confusing, empowering? How do they feel their position as native or non-native speakers of English contributed to their understanding of the situation?

WRITING ABOUT THE CHAPTER

A comparison and contrast of Fallows's and Rodriguez's arguments seems an obvious and enlightening assignment for this chapter. You may want to encourage students to use ideas from class debate on the topic as a way of critiquing the authors' opposing views. Encourage students to identify and examine the assumptions the two writers share; are some of these assumptions antithetical to the ideal of diversity that each author espouses?

How might Hayakawa respond to Fallows's points about the invulnerability of English to multilingualism's pressures? How might Rodriguez react? Which authors in the chapter focus on individual experiences, and which on collective ones? How does that concentration help shape their arguments?

What kinds of authority do the chapter's authors implicitly claim? Who, in students' opinion, is most entitled to talk about the successes and shortcomings of bilingualism? Who is least entitled to discuss them? What weight should personal experience have in this debate?

32

Language and Politics

George Orwell, Politics and the English Language

Václav Havel, Words on Words

June Jordan, Nobody Mean More to Me than You
and the Future Life of Willie Jordan

WORKING WITH THE CHAPTER

Language radically shapes our world. Our understanding of experience is mediated by language and linguistic constructs, our interactions with others are utterly dependent on the success or failure of our communication, and even our self-image is defined by the words we and others use to describe ourselves. Is it any wonder, then, that language is vital in our political lives? The selections in this chapter offer some views on how language can be used politically, both as an instrument of repression and a tool for change. The chapter's epigraphs supply additional perspectives on the political side of language and its uses in our society.

Teaching Strategies

Students may already have some ideas about the links between language and politics. The power of political rhetoric is revealed to us over and over again, as every election brings technological advances in the war of words. How else does language serve as a means of civil control? You might want to discuss questions of law. How does the language of law — the proverbial "letter of the law" — help provide the foundation for our social structure? Talk about how law can be seen as a matter of definitions; discuss the idea of a contract whereby citizens sign a verbal agreement, binding themselves to perform specified actions. The penalties for defying that agreement, or "breaking their word," are spelled out in the law as well. Does this linguistic transaction have consequences that go beyond language? Law is not only a matter of words; if it were, no one would be kept in a prison cell or executed in the service of those words. It is not mere language that gives these powers; society uses its force to support and reinforce the connection between words and actions. Why? How might this system be abused? What does it reveal about the ways in which we understand language?

Ask students to think about how their own lives are structured by language. Their actions respond to commands, prohibitions, regulations, encouragement, and suggestions. How much influence does the language of others have on their thought? On their behavior? How much influence do social and political rhetoric have on their lives?

Walt Whitman's epigraph shows he understands the great power of language in American society. Whitman was well aware that we are a nation founded on a linguistic act — the Declaration of Independence — and that language is at the core of our way of perceiving and maintaining our national unity. Ask students what they make of Whitman's definition of language. Is this an important claim for a poet and writer to make about language? To what kinds of attitudes might it be a response? Does this view of language seem uniquely American? Encourage students to look at Whitman's view of the creation of language, about which he says "the final decisions are made by the masses." How could this democratic model of language differ from hypotheses proposed in other societies? Why might Whitman's statement have seemed even more daring in the nineteenth century, when he made it, than it does today?

The Randall Jarrell epigraph offers another poet's view of language in America. How might the decades separating him from Whitman have affected his perspective on the public uses of speech? What is Jarrell questioning here? Do his comments seem aimed primarily at advertising, journalism, fiction, or other uses of communication? Does Jarrell's metaphor about the forest of words that surrounds us seem positive or negative? What might he be protesting against? Do students sympathize with his claims?

James Baldwin's "If Black English Isn't a Language, Then Tell Me, What Is?" is a concise attack on those who would ignore the tremendous contributions African-Americans have made to American speech. Ask the class to read the epigraph carefully. Why might the author have chosen not to write his defense of Black English in Black English? What do students make of his almost coy parenthetical request, "if I may use Black English," to illustrate a point? Is it ambivalence? Discuss Baldwin's comments about the need to use socially acceptable language and speech, and the dangers of using prohibited languages. (Ask students to look back at the Oscar Hijuelos epigraph in Chapter 31.) Do Baldwin's assertions about speech in England, that the English are constantly revealing their background and education when they talk, hold true in America as well? What else might an individual's speech reveal?

Whitman, Jarrell, and Baldwin are all known primarily as literary rather than political figures. How might a professional speechwriter, a politician, or a newspaper columnist rebut their claims? What points of view might they not represent?

George Orwell's "Politics and the English Language" is one of the best-known treatments of language and its consequences in our public and private lives. Ask students to look at Orwell's writing, considering Baldwin's statements about Britain and the English propensity to judge others by their speech. How is Orwell's model of language unlike the democratic model proposed by Whitman? Might Orwell agree with Jarrell's assessment of how difficult it is to form opinions in a world of endlessly proliferating opinion and information?

Might Havel agree with Baldwin's statement that language is "a political instrument, means, and proof of power"? Would his personal experience bear this statement out? What do students imagine Havel's reaction to Orwell might be?

June Jordan's essay on Black English and the African-American struggle for justice seems a logical development of some ideas foreshadowed by Baldwin. How does the story of Jordan's class parallel the struggles by Havel and his colleagues? What differences might appear between their experiences? To which of the dangerous tendencies of linguistic "swindles and perversions" described by Orwell (para. 9) might the response to the class's protest be allied? What kind of language did the police officer use in his attempt to stonewall and defuse the class's grievance? How might Orwell have responded to it? What might Baldwin have made of Willie Jordan's decision not to write his essay on repression in Black English?

Ask the class to talk about the possible consequences, in our society today, of using the wrong word at the wrong time. How might speech be physically dangerous or even fatal? It is fashionable in some social groups to imply that one is affiliated with a gang or in some way involved in organized crime. What could the outcome of this suggestion be?

How might it be dangerous to reveal that one is a member of a minority group, such as homosexuals? How could individuals avoid some of these potential hazards? Should people need to watch what they say? How could society eliminate the possibilities of linguistic peril? What steps could be taken to ensure true equality and freedom of speech?

A Writing-before-Reading Exercise

Have students think about the judgments they make about others based on their speech. How do we assess the intelligence and education of people we meet for the first time? Does their speech tell us about the part of the country they are from? About their ethnic and racial background? About their social status? About their economic class? About their sexual orientation? Ask the class to remember, and briefly describe, some incidents in which they judged others by their speech. Were they ever mistaken? Ask them to recall an occasion on which they were judged, or misjudged, because of their own speech. How did this judgment make them feel?

WORKING WITH THE SELECTIONS

George Orwell

Politics and the English Language

Teaching Strategies

This essay is long and rather demanding; be sure students have read it carefully and understood Orwell's argument. You might want to break the argument down, in class discussion, into its two main branches: (1) his articulation of what was wrong with political writing in his day, and his identification of some potential abuses of political jargon and doctrine, and (2) his recommendations for avoiding these abuses in one's own writing and thought. To which aspect of his argument does Orwell give most attention? Which does the class find more interesting and relevant?

Paragraphs 1 and 2 of the essay hold the heart of Orwell's argument, that the decline of the English language is caused by social factors in the English-speaking world, but that by succumbing to the tendency toward confusion and obfuscation in political thought, writers and thinkers allow these detrimental trends to continue and gain momentum. He says, "an effect can become a cause, reinforcing the original cause and producing the same effect in an intensified form, and so on indefinitely" (para. 2). What do students make of this vicious-circle hypothesis? How can public acceptance of what should be unacceptable — confusing language used to express confused ideas — lead to dangerous precedents and bad habits that require a great deal of effort to break?

One example in our own time is the trend toward negative political campaigning. One side may not want to make direct personal attacks on the other side's candidate, but unless some action is taken, that side will wind up having to respond to the opponents' antagonistic rhetoric. In the next campaign, the second party may seize the offensive, hoping to avoid an attack, which might spur the first party on to even greater efforts to discredit the opposition. The cycle will eventually be so firmly established that drastic steps will be necessary to end it. Doesn't this sequence support Orwell's claim that it is vital to think our assertions through, carefully, word by word? How might a resolve to do this work affect the current state of our public rhetoric?

Ask the class to read Orwell's five examples of bad English carefully; they might read them aloud. Tell them that the first two passages quote leading British professors of

Orwell's day. Why might Orwell have chosen to single out academics for sloppy writing and thinking? The other three quotations are anonymous, but Laski and Hogben receive full discredit for their efforts. Do teachers and professors have greater responsibility toward language than other members of society? Why, or why not?

How do students respond to the passages of bad prose? Ask if any remind them of writing or speech they might encounter today. What do they think of Orwell's assertion, "The mixture of vagueness and sheer incompetence is the most marked characteristic of modern English prose, and especially of any kind of political writing" (para. 4)? How accurate is it as a description of these passages? How accurate is it as a description of writing in America late in the twentieth century?

Orwell identifies the major problem as reliance on clichés in discussing any potentially sensitive political issue. Do our politicians, writers, and thinkers act thus today? Ask the class for some examples of "dying metaphors" in our society. We have seen the merciful demise of the "Iron Curtain" as a political metaphor, but the "war on drugs" is still with us. Some of the metaphors in our political arena are incomprehensible but refuse to die, such as President Bush's famous "thousand points of light." The "verbal false limb" is inescapable in our public and private discourse, which sprouts as many of these appendages as a Hindu god. *At this point in time* for the simple *now* is one example that should be familiar to all students; *the fact that* has spread even further in the decades since Orwell wrote the essay. His "pretentious diction" category is still with us, as is the class of "meaningless words." What does the word *progressive* mean when it is used by a Republican? By a Democrat? By a Socialist or Communist? How could one word have meanings so various? Have the class think of other buzzwords with no fixed meaning, and discuss their political uses. What are some of the pitfalls in accepting a statement using some buzzword (or word with a private meaning) at its face value?

What do students make of Orwell's attack on political speech as a "defense of the indefensible" (para. 13)? How likely is it that obfuscatory speech is being used to cover up some outrage, offense, or outright crime? The Reagan administration's official response to findings about illegal dealings with Iran was that "mistakes were made." Is this kind of abuse of language an abuse of the public trust? Our nation's Department of Defense (which, until a few decades ago, was called the "War Department") is renowned for this kind of circumlocution. Ask students to bring in "official government statements" (as given to newspapers and magazines) and analyze them according to Orwell's guide. What is their response?

Additional Activities

Some students may want to read Orwell's *1984* and give the class a presentation on Newspeak. Is Orwell's literary invention of a repressive government's repressive language motivated by the same ideals as this essay? What parallels to Newspeak do we see in our society today?

Ask students to bring in short political articles from newspapers and magazines. (Editorials are an ideal length and style for this exercise.) Have them evaluate these articles using Orwell's criteria. How are the authors, or the language they use, confusing or misleading? What might their motivation be? How might their political opponents state the same issue differently?

Generating Writing

1. Have the class examine Orwell's "translation" of the passage from Ecclesiastes into bad English. Ask them to "translate" some well-known piece of straightforward writing into bad contemporary American. Choose a short poem (Robert Frost's "Fire and Ice" is an excellent example) or perhaps a few proverbs ("Look before you leap"; "Don't count your

chickens before they're hatched"). Have students read their "translations" aloud. (The results will be ridiculous, but emphasize that they illustrate a very serious problem.)

2. Ask students to write a brief essay on their response to Orwell's six rules of writing (para. 18). Do they agree with these rules? Might they use them in their own work? Do they consider valid his claim that adherence to these rules will help writers avoid stale thought and imagery?

Václav Havel

Words on Words

Teaching Strategies

Find out how familiar the class is with Havel and his personal and political history. Make sure they read the explanatory notes to this selection carefully; do they understand how this speech is itself a political act and a testament to a remarkable revolution?

Havel's career is an inspiring example of how words can make a difference. Remind students of his progress from harassed and imprisoned playwright to leader of antitotalitarian opposition to the Czechoslovakian head of state. Would this scenario be likely in America? Why or why not? How might the greater (though not absolute) freedom of speech that our government permits make intellectual critiques of national policy less vital and less serious than they might be in a more repressive society? What is our public attitude toward exposés, satires, and outright attacks on our government's rhetoric and deeds? How might that be our society's best insurance against revolution?

What might Havel mean when he states that speech is "the key to the history of mankind," and "the key to the history of society" (para. 3)? What do they make of his assertion that modern society uses "words to construct scientific theories and political ideologies with which to tackle or redirect the mysterious course of history" (para. 5)? How is history "mysterious"? How can our words redirect it, or channel its flow? Ask students to consider moments in their lives when they were conscious that history was being revised around them (most personal arguments, for example, are about whose version of history will be accepted). How does the role language plays in history making add to its power? Why might that be an important fact for a Czech president to mention at a German booksellers' convention?

Havel refers elsewhere in his speech to national history, stating, "I don't think I need to go to any lengths to explain to you of all people the diabolic power of certain words: you have fairly recent first-hand experience of . . . indescribable historical horrors . . ." (para. 22). Why does Havel shy away from naming Hitler and the Nazi regime directly? Discuss this reticence with the class. Does an oblique reference to Hitler have greater power than direct use of his name, which has become shorthand for all manner of evils? (A more difficult question would be why Havel refrains from naming Heidegger in the same paragraph.)

Have the class talk about Havel's vision of how the most powerful and transforming words can be drastically and dangerously misused. He sums up this idea best, perhaps, in his evocation of "ever mightier armies ostensibly to defend peace" (para. 40). How does this statement emphasize his main theme about the importance of words? What do students make of this vision? Is this misuse of the inspirational power of language confined to totalitarian governments, or do we see it in our own society?

Additional Activities

Students interested in Havel's life and work, and in the progress of the Czechoslovakian revolution and the social and political changes that have occurred there, might be encouraged to research specific topics and present brief reports to the class. Assign students to find out about suppression of free speech under the old regime; are the stories of persecution and imprisonment Havel relates exceptional or representative? You might also want someone from Amnesty International to speak to the class on censorship and violations of the right to free speech in the world today.

Look at this selection in conjunction with Chapter 24, "Declarations of Independence." How do those who openly defy repressive regimes risk, in Thomas Jefferson's words, their lives, their fortunes, and their sacred honor?

Generating Writing

1. Havel makes clear that words can have both constructive and destructive effects. Ask the class to analyze the examples he cites. How can the same concepts be used to help and to hurt? What makes the same words an instrument of attack in one context and a tool for building in another?

2. Have students extract Havel's recommendations for action from the speech. How does he feel we must think and behave if we are to avoid and combat the destructive possibilities of language? What are students' responses to these moral imperatives? Might they add other considerations?

June Jordan

Nobody Mean More to Me than You and the Future Life of Willie Jordan

Teaching Strategies

This may be a sensitive topic for your class; encourage students to keep an open mind and to respect one another's opinions. Jordan deals with a number of quite explosive issues here — the validity of Black English as a literary language, the conflict between African-American and mainstream culture, and the tension between the African-American community and the police. How would students describe Jordan's tone? How does it change through the essay? You might want to map this sequence with the class; Jordan's discussion of Black English, its history and grammar, is restrained and academic. How does her tone change when she begins to talk about her class (para. 5) and her experience with them? Notice the increased colloquialism in her diction: "At this, several students dumped on the book" (para. 13). What might be the reason for this change? What does your class make of Jordan's class experiments with Translated Black English? Students who are not African-American may not be quite sure of the humor here. How does the "translation" of Alice Walker seem ludicrous? How might a similar "translation" of such white dialect writers as Mark Twain (you may want to do a passage from *Huckleberry Finn* as a comparison) be equally foolish? Emphasize that what is funny here is not the idea of African-American characters speaking Standard English, but rather how grossly Standard English misrepresents a large and vital part of our culture.

How does Jordan's tone change further when she begins discussing Willie Jordan and her Contemporary Women's Poetry class? Look at her use of such phrases as "a young brother" and "all of us laughed a good while" (para. 23). Does Jordan's diction seem to grow closer to Black English as she and her class get closer to defining it?

Discuss the Rules and Guidelines of Black English with the class. Do students disagree with any of the formulations by Jordan's class? How might they render some of the examples differently? Talk about the ways in which class members used Black English in their writing. What do students make of the examples Jordan gives of her students' work? You might want to focus on Philip Garfield's rendition of the scene from *A Doll's House* (find a Standard English translation of the work to give your students a basis for comparison). Is Black English any better able to express the thoughts and speech of Ibsen's nineteenth-century Norwegians than Standard English gets Alice Walker's characters across?

To a casual reader, Jordan's story of the tragedy of Reggie Jordan may seem like a digression from the topic of Black English and its place in education. Thoughtful students will know better. How did the same social conditions that deprived Jordan's students of their voices as African-Americans deprive Reggie Jordan, because of his color, of his life? Did not the class's decision to write messages of condolence and protest in Black English reflect their feeling that linguistic and physical repression of minority groups are closely allied?

Discuss with your class why the issue of whether to write the group preface to their message of protest in Standard or Black English was such a sensitive one. What kinds of issues were at stake for Jordan's class? Why does Jordan say that "our decision in favor of Black English had doomed our writings" (para. 78)? Was the class decision to use Black English in their protest a courageous one?

Talk with students about Officer Charles's "explanation" of Reggie Jordan's death and the reactions of June Jordan and her class. How does Jordan convey her contempt for the police officer and his apologies for the system? Have the class look carefully at her tone. What kind of diction does Jordan use here? Why might her dismissal of Charles be written in Standard, rather than Black, English?

What conclusions does June Jordan seem to come to about her experiences with the class? How does she tie together their work with Black English and their response to Reggie Jordan's death? What connections does your class make between the two?

Additional Activities

Look at this essay together with Shelby Steele's "On Being Black and Middle Class" (Chapter 6). How might Jordan and her students, privileged enough to be college educated, have made the same kind of choices as Steele? Why might their choices have been different? How might Steele react to Jordan's essay?

You might also return to Virginia Woolf's "Thoughts on Peace in an Air Raid" (Chapter 22). How is the Black English project an example of what Woolf was talking about in her call to "think peace into existence"?

Some students may want to give presentations on Black English and its role in African-American culture. Invite students to bring in rap records they find significant, or to discuss the portrayal of Black English in literature, movies, and television. How is Black English essential to African-American identity?

Generating Writing

1. Why might Willie Jordan have chosen to write his final essay in Standard, rather than Black, English? Why does June Jordan choose not to write in Black English? Does this choice tell more about the limitations of society's attitudes than about a lack of courage or conviction on either Jordan's part?

2. Ask students to write a brief essay about a personal experience they have had in which language defined a community. They may have been an "insider" or an "outsider," but the incident discussed should be one in which some people were excluded, explicitly

or implicitly, because of language. How did this exclusion make them feel? What conclusions might they draw from their experience?

WRITING ABOUT THE CHAPTER

1. Have the class compare and contrast Havel's and Orwell's views of the political uses of language. You may want to ask them to focus on each writer's recommendations for action. What do Havel and Orwell feel we should do about the possible abuses of language? How, in each writer's view, can individuals challenge or perpetuate repressive and abusive systems by their own choices of language?

2. What linguistic violations do all three writers point out? How, in their opinion, do these violations of language lead to violations of rights? Which interests are unique to each writer? Why? Which two writers seem closest in their aims and approach? Which two of the chapter's authors are most dissimilar? What is at stake in each essay?

3. Ask students to write a brief essay about language and politics. They may draw on personal experience, as well as their work in this chapter. How does language control our lives? How can we be aware of this control and take steps to resist it effectively? How does language control their own life? What steps might they take to combat this control?

33

The Power of Metaphor

George Lakoff and Mark Johnson, *From* Metaphors We Live By

Susan Sontag, *From* AIDS and Its Metaphors

WORKING WITH THE CHAPTER

Teaching Strategies

The metaphor is one of the main tools with which we construct our experience. Metaphor gives shape to the world around us; it eases communication and makes of our talk and writing an aesthetic as well as a practical act. Students may not be aware of how deeply metaphor runs, an essential member in thought and language. The selections in this chapter are designed to get the class thinking about metaphor and its possible uses and abuses in our society; the epigraphs express views of metaphor from the classical age to the present.

Begin class discussion of metaphor by asking for a definition. What do they think *metaphor* means? What were they taught in school? The traditional formula that makes a metaphor a verbal comparison without the words *like* or *as* sadly misrepresents the figure's reach and significance. Metaphor is more than a grammatical mannerism, it is a way of thinking. Emphasize that the chapter's authors use the concept broadly, to denote both the figure of speech and the intellectual leap it expresses. This idea may be difficult to put across without examples. Discuss each example in detail; make sure the class clearly understands how each metaphor works.

The epigraph from Aristotle's *Poetics* illustrates how much weight metaphor carries in classical theories of language. Now may be a good time to discuss the word's etymology. It comes from the Greek, *metapherein*, to transfer or change, and its roots are in the words *pherein*, to carry, and *meta*, between. Is a metaphor a transfer of meaning? How does it carry meaning between words? Between people?

How accurate do students think Aristotle's assertion is? Is skill in metaphor essential in using language creatively? Try discussing this epigraph together with the Cynthia Ozick passage. Is metaphor integral to our imagination? Might our humanity be compromised without it? Ask how a doctor and patient might talk without using metaphor. (Remind them that *metaphor* here is used in its broad, not its narrow, sense.) What might the doctor ask? Something along the lines of "how do you feel?" The patient would almost certainly respond, "I feel like. . . ." Impress upon the class that this exchange is itself a use of metaphor. The patient might feel a stabbing pain, or perhaps a sensation of pins and needles. Perhaps one foot is asleep, or the feeling is "a lump in the throat." The patient depends upon the doctor to make the same or similar connections between two concepts so that the description's meaning will be understood. Without metaphor, what might the patient be able to communicate besides "it hurts here"?

The Bronowski passage also illustrates how much we need metaphor. Read the epigraph closely with the class: do they understand that the power to make metaphor is integral to scientific inquiry? How do they think theories of life, matter, and energy are arrived at in the scientific community? Where does the procedure Bronowski describes as "man's creative gift, to find or make a likeness" come in? Where would our traditions of science and knowledge be without it? We need metaphors to understand science. How were students taught basic scientific facts during their schooling? Most elementary- and high-school science teachers rely heavily on metaphorical demonstrations to get their ideas across. (Teachers often boil kettles under glass to illustrate condensation, or explain the solar system by likening the sun to a basketball surrounded by other objects, proportional in size and distance, representing the planets.) How did these metaphors shape their understanding of scientific models and the world they describe?

Judy Ruiz offers metaphor in action among students. What does the class make of Ruiz's plan to illustrate a talk about the world with a group peeling of oranges? Why were these disadvantaged students unable to make that metaphoric jump, but capable of other subtle responses to the oranges' possible significance? Why did Ruiz think this a healing experience? Discuss the Ruiz and Ozick epigraphs together. Do both writers see ability to use and comprehend metaphor as linked to our very humanity? Can metaphor establish contact between highly disparate groups or individuals?

The Ruiz and Ozick passages can also open up the Sontag selection. The Ozick epigraph is from, "The Moral Necessity of Metaphor." Sontag, too, treats metaphor as a moral entity. Might the moral metaphor Ozick describes counter the acts Sontag calls the immoral uses of metaphor surrounding AIDS? Might the simple metaphoric interaction Ruiz discusses also help us understand the power of AIDS and our own terror of it? How might metaphor serve as a link between the sick and the well? Could it reinforce connections between the isolated and the larger community? How might these things be accomplished?

Examine the Bronowski passage with the Lakoff and Johnson selection. Do Bronowski's examples illustrate what Lakoff and Johnson mean by "conceptual metaphor"? How might Bronowski characterize their lists of "metaphors we live by"? Where might that fit into the activity Bronowski calls "looking for intelligibility in the world"? What does *intelligibility* mean here?" How could metaphor help us to find it?

A Writing-before-Reading Exercise

Ask students to think carefully and come up with three metaphors they have encountered recently in everyday activities. These might be slang (his car is a piece of junk), lines from a popular song (she's a rainbow), or figures of speech in political oratory, journalism, or literature. How effective were these metaphors? Did they enrich their context? How different were they from a straightforward statement of the information they were meant to communicate? Have students "translate" these metaphors into plain language. Would the unadorned sentences have been awkward? Why do students think the metaphors were used?

WORKING WITH THE SELECTIONS

George Lakoff and Mark Johnson

From Metaphors We Live By

Teaching Strategies

This selection should help students understand metaphor in its broadest sense. Encourage them to read the piece carefully and list anything they don't understand. The selection is part of a larger work, which is itself based on extensive linguistic research. Does knowing the background of the work affect students' interpretation of it?

It is helpful to discuss the concept of "concepts" with the class before discussing Lakoff and Johnson's argument. Do students see clearly what concepts are? You may want to read some dictionary definitions aloud, and talk about which meanings Lakoff and Johnson might have had in mind. Some students may resist the idea that we perceive the world through a specific socially and culturally contingent conceptual system. Bring up some massive cultural differences in things we think of as universals or essential truths to illustrate the contextual working of thought. Many Australian aborigines, when shown a drawing or photograph of two persons, one in the foreground and one in the distant background, assume that they are seeing one large person and one small one, because their artistic tradition does not include perspective. Point out that medieval Europe also lacked this idea and that some of the most learned persons in our history would have made exactly the same mistake about a picture that in our society even a child has learned to "read." Many Amazon Indian tribes divide the color spectrum into two primary colors, the red half and the green half, rather than the red, yellow, blue of the European tradition. This is no more or less arbitrary than our own distinction; these peoples can perceive yellow, but as a secondary color (as purple might be in our system). Ask students to come up with their own examples of culturally defined perceptions. Might their own fundamental assumptions have been produced by education and experience?

Once the class is comfortable with the idea of conceptual systems, you may want to begin discussing Lakoff and Johnson's argument in depth. What do students make of their assertion that "on the basis of linguistic evidence, we have found that most of our ordinary conceptual system is metaphorical in nature" (para. 4)? Talk about the validity of "linguistic evidence." Can people's way of speaking about something be the best clue to their thoughts and feelings about it? What problems might there be with Lakoff and Johnson's method of inquiry?

A fundamental assertion Lakoff and Johnson make is that "metaphors as linguistic expressions are possible precisely because there are metaphors in a person's conceptual system" (para. 10). Analyze this idea with the class. How is language produced by our conceptual system? Is our conceptual system a product of language? Might the two work together to reinforce each other? Ask the class to come up with examples in which, for good or ill, ways of speaking have encouraged ways of thinking. Why might this influence make language a more dangerous instrument than it seems?

Go through Lakoff and Johnson's list of metaphors and their linguistic expressions with the class. Invite students to find more examples of each metaphor. Encourage them to challenge and defend one another's examples. How "live" are these metaphors? Are they aware that a statement like "The theory needs more support" is metaphoric when they make it? Do they feel that they are consciously making an equation of an idea and a building, or is the context making the equation for them?

Ask the class to talk about their response to this selection. Has it made them reexamine their own habits of speech and thought? Might it make them think more closely about the metaphors others use? How important do they feel Lakoff and Johnson's findings are?

Additional Activities

You will certainly want to look at this essay with Orwell's "Politics and the English Language" (Chapter 32). How does Orwell anticipate some of Lakoff and Johnson's ideas? Understanding Lakoff and Johnson helps students comprehend the urgency of Orwell's message that sloppy speech and writing are not only aesthetically unpleasant but politically dangerous.

One class project that could be fun and enlightening would be to bring in advertising from newspapers and magazines. What conceptual metaphors are implied in the ads' language? Do the ads use visual metaphor? How do these metaphors help advertisers sell goods? For example, cars may have the names of horses (Mustang, Maverick, Bronco) to suggest speed and power. Other product names connote qualities appropriate to their use: dishwashing liquids have names like Sunlight and Dawn, connecting the product with ideas of clarity and brightness. How effective are these metaphors? Do we perceive them as metaphors, or do we take them for granted?

Generating Writing

1. Ask students to list two or three other "metaphors we live by" and to come up with several examples of the linguistic expression of each. How "live" are these metaphors? Have they become accepted as part of our language, or do we think of them as metaphors in action? How might our use of them differ if we were constantly aware of their metaphoric quality?

2. Have the class take one of Lakoff and Johnson's examples of conceptual metaphor and write a brief essay discussing that metaphor's function in our society. Encourage students to pattern their discussion after Lakoff and Johnson's treatment of the metaphor "argument is war." Does our society act as if "love is madness," or "ideas are products"? Do social structures and conventions dealing with one side of the metaphoric equation model themselves after the structures appropriate to the other half?

Susan Sontag

From AIDS and Its Metaphors

Teaching Strategies

Students may find this essay very challenging, and well they might; Sontag draws on a wealth of cultural and literary references to compose a complicated moral and philosophical argument about the abuses of language in responses to AIDS. Remind the class to read the footnotes carefully and, as always, to take notes and ask questions about words and references they don't understand.

How do students understand the moral implications of such a word as *plague*? Sontag is careful to document the history of the word and show how it is used as a means of exclusion and for assigning blame. A "plague" does not come from within; it is brought to a society by carriers who can (and should, the metaphor implies) be isolated, quarantined, kept out at all costs. *Plague* is a word of fear, a curse, a powerful metaphor. Why must we be careful about how we use it? What does the class make of Sontag's discussion of "the usual script for plague" (para. 7) and "the classic script for plague" (para. 13)? Ask them to explain her metaphor. What might it mean to imply that a plague was in some way a performance, or a narrative, "scripted" by a society? What does Sontag suggest about the constructs we place on an experience? People certainly die of diseases every day, and yet some diseases are classed as plagues rather than others. Why is heart disease, for example, exempt from the "plague script"?

It seems important to discuss in class Sontag's citation of the two major mythological AIDS histories — the American and European belief that the disease originated in Africa and the African belief that it began in America. Might both be equally "true"? Why do societies need to believe that epidemics start somewhere else? What factors other than the data at hand might be involved in assigning blame for the origin of an epidemic disease? How can stereotypes come into play in these circumstances?

Talk about Sontag's assertion that "Plagues are invariably regarded as judgments on society" (para. 16). What are the potential dangers in this attitude? What could the results be if this interpretation of disease were followed to its logical conclusion? Again, consider heart disease, a leading cause of death in the United States. Why is heart disease, which claims thousands more victims than AIDS each year, not looked on as a plague or as a judgment on its victims, whose life-styles are often the direct cause of their disease and death? What might that attitude tell about our society's priorities?

What do students make of Sontag's discussion of the political uses of AIDS? Do they take issue with any of her claims about the ideological motivations of AIDS hysteria? (Discuss *ideology* with the class, to make sure that they are clear about the word, its definition, and its uses.) How might fascination with AIDS metaphors and fantasies distract society from the realities of the disease?

The selection concludes with a brief discussion of AIDS as metaphor. How does the use of AIDS as a metaphor reveal the ways in which we understand it? What do we think it is "like," or what is "like it"? Could our fascination with the idea of the virus reflect our obsession with, and terror of, AIDS? What might Sontag be suggesting about the way in which we have made AIDS part of our understanding of the world?

Additional Activities

Look at this essay with June Jordan's "Nobody Mean More to Me than You and the Future Life of Willie Jordan" (Chapter 32). Both writers believe language can be used as an instrument of repression. What might Sontag make of Jordan's urgent plea for self-expression? How might Jordan encourage persons with AIDS to reclaim language and assert themselves against the dominant AIDS metaphor?

Ask the class to do some research in newspapers, magazines, and periodicals. Are Sontag's claims about the uses of the AIDS metaphor borne out by examples? Which of the AIDS metaphors seem most powerful and most used? Do the media carry examples that might challenge any of Sontag's assertions?

Generating Writing

1. Ask students to review Sontag's argument carefully. What assumptions does she seem to have about language? What does she seem to assume about society and human interaction? How might these assumptions have shaped her argument? Ask them to select one of Sontag's assumptions and challenge or defend its validity and usefulness in her argument.

2. Have the class write a brief personal essay on how the metaphors surrounding AIDS have shaped their understanding of the disease. How have the metaphors affected their attitudes and actions? How do these metaphors hold up under examination? Has their work with this selection changed their views about AIDS and the rhetoric of the disease?

WRITING ABOUT THE CHAPTER

1. Ask students to compare and contrast the Sontag selection with the Lakoff and Johnson selection. They may want to focus on the authors' assumptions and on the different projects. What assumptions do Lakoff and Johnson share with Sontag? How do their assumptions differ? How is their work unlike hers? How are the projects similar? How might the selections' authors respond to each other's work?

2. Using Sontag's essay as a model, have the class select one of the "metaphors we live by" and discuss its influence on society. How might the metaphor be used for political and social control? To what ideological uses could it be put? Is this metaphor currently significant in our political or social system? What events might occur that would make it a more important part of our world view?

3. You might want to assign a personal essay on metaphor. Ask students to discuss a metaphor they have found restrictive or enabling. They may want to talk about a stereotype that limited their horizons or others' understanding of them; or they might want to celebrate a religious or aesthetic idea that changed their perceptions of themselves and the world around them. How aware were they of the idea as a metaphor? How might awareness that it was metaphoric help them to understand it better?

34

Fighting Words

S. I. Hayakawa, Words with Built-in Judgments

Gloria Naylor, A Question of Language

Anne Roiphe, The WASP Sting

WORKING WITH THE CHAPTER

In an epigraph to this chapter, Charles R. Lawrence quotes from the "fighting words" exception to the First Amendment: "The Supreme Court has held that words which 'by their very utterance inflict injury or tend to incite an immediate breach of the peace' are not protected by the First Amendment." Several writers in this chapter insist upon the potentially harmful effects of language. Barbara Lawrence, in an epigraph excerpted from "Four Letter Words Can Hurt You," writes that sexual, racial, and ethnic obscenities "deform identity [and] deny individuality and humanness." And Anne Roiphe points out that racial epithets injure Caucasians as well as ethnic minorities: the acronym "WASP" reduces the people to whom it refers to "an insect, a thing lower than a human being"; it undermines their pride in their own background.

Of course, groupings of symbols on a page, or combinations of sounds issuing from voice boxes, are not in themselves injurious. Gloria Naylor writes in "A Question of Language" that "Words themselves are innocuous; it is the consensus that gives them true power." Naylor writes about a group of people who have taken the fighting word *nigger* and stood it on its head, pitting their own consensus — about their own identity — against the consensus of the dominant culture. Still, the consensus in the dominant culture is not easily toppled, and a linguistic revolution depends upon a social revolution. S. I. Hayakawa observes, "When racial discrimination against blacks is done away with, the word [*nigger*] will either disappear or else lose its present connotations."

Teaching Strategies

Barbara Lawrence writes that people today are reluctant "to admit that they are angered or shocked by obscenity." How do your students react to that statement? Do they see value in the anger Lawrence advocates? Or do they admire the distance — or perhaps sophistication — implied by the other alternative, the reaction by people who show they are "bored, maybe unimpressed, aesthetically displeased"? How does Lawrence tie the issue of obscenity to that of offensive racial epithets? Do your students see the parallel she is drawing? Ask them if they react differently to sexual obscenity and racial obscenity, and if so, why?

This chapter, especially if taught in tandem with Chapter 26, "Freedom of Expression," is a fine opportunity for a discussion on free speech. Most of your students probably approve of free speech in principle. Do any of them revise their positions when asked to consider instances of racial or sexual slurs? How would they define the limits of free speech, so that each person's right to express himself or herself would not violate another person's right to freedom from molestation?

A Writing-before-Reading Exercise

Ask your students to think back to a time when they were offended by words spoken by another. These words might have been sexual or racial epithets, insults directed toward an individual, insensitive remarks, or any other offensive language. Have them draft a personal narrative in which they recount the incident, including their thoughts and feelings upon hearing the offensive language. Ask them to try to analyze the source of the offense. Has something in their own background sensitized them to this form of offensive language? Did the person who spoke the words intend to offend? Does intentionality enter into their decision to consider the remark offensive? Ask them also to recount their reaction upon hearing the offensive remark. If they remained silent, did they later think of a response they wished they had made? Instruct them not to worry about mechanical considerations, but rather to get their thoughts and feelings down on paper; they will have the chance to revise this draft after reading the selections.

WORKING WITH THE SELECTIONS

S. I. Hayakawa

Words with Built-in Judgments

Teaching Strategies

If your class has already discussed Chapter 32, "Language and Politics," they are probably aware that any discussion of language is at least implicitly also a discussion of politics. And an essay such as this one is acutely political in its implications. Hayakawa is a semanticist; because he analyzes language as a biologist studies life forms, students may mistake him for an objective writer with no political agenda. By the end of your class discussion of his essay, however, they should realize that the effect of racial epithets is not as cut and dried as the molecular structure of sea creatures. You might begin by discussing his position on the question of language, and then move to his implied political position.

In the second selection, Gloria Naylor writes that she will not "enter the debate . . . about whether it is language that shapes reality or vice versa." Ask students whether or not Hayakawa seems willing to enter that debate. What can they infer from a sentence such as this (para. 4): "Because the old names are 'loaded,' they dictate traditional patterns of behavior toward whom they are applied." Here he seems to ascribe great power to language, the power to "dictate . . . behavior." Ask if they find any other evidence that this is actually his position. How do they read his argument in favor of euphemisms (para. 3)?

If words have the power to "hinder clear thinking," if they can help us discover new ways of dealing with old problems such as crime, then it seems Hayakawa is assigning primacy to language. But encourage students to look more closely at the very sentences in which he seems to be ascribing such power to language. Look particularly at the passive constructions: *who* "loaded" those words? By whom has the word *Mexican* "been used with contemptuous connotations"? It is apparent that words acquire their connotative force from usage. But *whose* usage confers these connotations? Students might point to the communities in the southwestern United States, where "there is a strong prejudice against Mexicans." You might want to refer them to the essay by Gloria Naylor, also in this chapter, for a fuller explication of how community consensus determines connotation.

If it is true that Hayakawa would agree with Naylor about the role of consensus in the making of meaning, then what is the status of this remark: "The words 'Japs' and 'niggers,' for instance, although often used both as a designation and an insult, are sometimes used with no intent to offend." If consensus determines both meaning and connotation, then can an individual user of a language decide for himself or herself what the connotations of his or her words will be? Discuss how intention affects connotation. Do your students consider ignorance a sufficient excuse for the use of offensive language?

Move next to Hayakawa's discussion of *sensitive* and *easily offended* people (paras. 9, 10). What do students make of his ridiculing the delegations who are attempting to exclude the word *nigger* from the dictionary? Do students accept his analogy about the county register of births? Can they find any fault in his logic here? Do they think his position in this paragraph consistent with that earlier in the essay? How does this opinion jibe with his earlier remarks on the power and primacy of language?

Ask students to try to infer Hayakawa's political position from his remarks on language. What groups does he ridicule in the essay? What kinds of solutions to the problem of racial prejudice does he seem to favor? Do students believe that such solutions are workable? The first writing exercise will help them come to an understanding of Hayakawa's implicit political position in this essay.

Additional Activities

Hayakawa states that "the strength of [the prejudice against Mexicans] is indirectly revealed by the fact that newspapers and polite people have stopped using the word 'Mexican' altogether, using the word 'Spanish-speaking person' instead." Here, despite his defense of euphemism in the following paragraph, he seems to realize that polite avoidance of a term often signals a more deeply seated prejudice than free use of the same expression would suggest. You might couple this insight with a similar one from Adrienne Rich's essay "Split at the Root" (see Chapter 6): "so charged with negative meaning was even the word 'Negro' that as children we were taught never to use it in front of Black people. We were taught that any mention of skin color in the presence of colored people was treacherous, forbidden ground. In a parallel way, the word 'Jew' was not used by polite gentiles." You might use these two passages to prompt discussion or an in-class writing assignment on the racism inherent in *not* speaking some words. How does prohibiting speech such as the expressions described here measure up against utterance of fighting words?

Generating Writing

1. Assign an essay in which your students analyze Hayakawa's own use of language. He must have been very aware of how "loaded" language can be every time he chose a word in writing and revising this essay — what linguistic choices did he make because of that awareness? Have them pay special attention to evidence of his own prejudices. Do they find that he has "found more interesting grounds on which to base [his] insults"?

2. Hayakawa writes a brief defense of euphemisms (para. 3). Suggest to interested students that they write an essay arguing against use of euphemistic language. Hayakawa addresses a few of the common defenses of plain speaking in his essay; be sure your students move beyond these points already stated to construct a defense of their own.

Gloria Naylor

A Question of Language

Teaching Strategies

You may want to approach this essay by asking students to compare and contrast it with the essay by Hayakawa. Naylor, unlike Hayakawa, is a novelist by profession. In this selection, however, she takes on the role of a semanticist, like Hayakawa. She similarly sees that words are defined by their usage, and that connotations can change according to context. She analyzes the various meanings of the word *nigger*, meanings that vary according to the speaker, the listener, and the context in which the word is spoken. Ask students how they reacted to her analysis. Were they surprised that *nigger* could have such a range of meanings? Naylor is very specific about such criteria as gender and number — did her precision convince them her claims were valid? Do they find her essay more or less convincing than Hayakawa's? Which do they consider more scholarly?

Naylor, unlike Hayakawa, makes her own position within her argument quite clear. Your students may have inferred from Hayakawa's name that he is Japanese, but he doesn't reveal his own reactions to the word *Jap*, for instance. Instead, he reports the reaction of an elderly Japanese woman of his acquaintance. How did your students react to the personal narratives embedded in Naylor's essay? Do they feel that Naylor's openly stated personal stake in the issues make her seem more or less biased than Hayakawa? Why does she take a two-paragraph excursion from the main line of the argument to describe the home life of her extended family? What does this excursion add to her argument?

Look at the different definitions of *nigger* and *girl* provided by Naylor. What can students tell about the community that uses these words with these meanings? What do they value, and what warrants their censure? Call students' attention to the part community has in the definitions. Besides language, morality — or "decency" — is also defined by the community. Give students the opportunity to discuss the extent to which community defines standards of morality in general.

Additional Activities

Gloria Naylor anticipates an opposing viewpoint when she writes, "I don't agree with the argument that the use of the word nigger at this social stratum of the black community was an internalization of racism." If you teach Naylor's essay in conjunction with Shelby Steele's "On Being Black and Middle Class" (Chapter 6), students will see that Steele at least considers the possibility of internalized racism in his family's use of the imaginary character Sam, who embodies all the negative stereotypes about blacks. You could use these two essays, perhaps, along with Kesaya Noda's "Growing Up Asian in America" (Chapter 6), to open discussion of internalized racism.

Naylor's semantic analysis of the word *nigger* would complement June Jordan's linguistic description of Black English in "Nobody Mean More to Me Than You and the Future Life of Willie Jordan" (Chapter 32). It is entirely probable that many of your students are unaware that Black English, like any other legitimate language, has a structure. They may think of Black English and other dialects that diverge from so-called standard English as more or less random assortments of words and phrases. To facilitate their sensitivity to linguistic patterns outside of the classroom, you might assign the first essay topic, below.

Generating Writing

1. Instruct students to choose a word that has several meanings or connotations — not in the dictionary, but rather among a group of people with whom they associate. This group

could be members of an extended family such as Naylor's, or of their high-school class. Have them write a semantic breakdown of the many uses for the word, specifying the context in which each meaning is understood, and the limitations on its use.

2. Gloria Naylor ends her essay on an open note: "And since she knew that I had to grow up in America, she took me in her lap and explained." Invite students to write a paper in which they explain to a child like Gloria Naylor whatever she needs to know in order to grow up in America. What would a parent in this situation want to explain? How could one put a concept such as racism into words that a child could understand, while avoiding an escalation of the problem?

Anne Roiphe
The WASP Sting

Teaching Strategies

You might start class discussion of this essay by asking why, if her subject is the epithet WASP, Anne Roiphe opens her essay with two anecdotes about Jewish stereotypes. Who is the intended audience for this piece? What might be the intended effect of this opening on the audience she has in mind? What main point is she trying to get across to them?

The way in which Roiphe chooses to write this essay can provide valuable insights into the message she is trying to convey. How would your students describe her style in paragraph 7? What might be her purpose in employing those clichés? She writes too that Jewish culture has made gentiles "feel no good, not up to par, not up to us with our warm, huggy capacity to eat foods of all kinds and express everything the moment we feel it" (para. 6). Ask why, if she objects to stereotypes, Roiphe has slipped into reciting the most common Jewish stereotypes. Whose perspective on Jews is she reciting here? How can they tell? Discuss the idea that stereotyping one group automatically leads into stereotyping the group that provides the contrast.

Roiphe describes a situation in which Jews take linguistic power into their own hands, reducing white Anglo-Saxon Protestants, "in one verbal swipe," to a pale, stiff stereotype. Ask how, if at all, this figurative power translates into literal meaning. Is Jewish stereotyping of Protestants precisely parallel to Protestant stereotyping of Jews? If not, what makes the two situations different? (You may want to bring in the material in Chapter 21, "Gender Roles and Stereotypes," and juxtapose the effects of stereotypes on males and females with the effects of stereotypes on Jews and Gentiles.)

Additional Activities

This essay might be included in discussing internalized racism, as suggested in the Additional Activities section of this manual's treatment of Gloria Naylor's essay, because Roiphe writes about both Jews and WASPs who have internalized and help to perpetuate stereotypes about themselves. She also discusses the "walls behind which we stand as we throw stones at one another," suggesting a connection with Chapter 8, "Bridging Distances."

Roiphe entertains the idea that "the nasty implications of the word WASP are, after all, true, and therefore we should feel free to express them" (para. 12). She ends up rejecting that definition of freedom of speech. You may want to teach this selection along with the Chapter 26, "Freedom of Expression."

Generating Writing

Roiphe writes, "Jews have been the butt of so many stereotypes . . . yet sadly this has not stopped us from developing and enjoying our own brutal stereotypes of others" (para. 2). She implies that the victims of prejudice should become so sensitive that they will be unable to inflict prejudice on others — but she finds that they are not. Assign an essay in which students explore this idea, either on a large scale — researching the behavior of an oppressed ethnic group at a chosen historical moment — or on a small scale — writing from their own experience as victims of prejudice.

WRITING ABOUT THE CHAPTER

1. Anne Roiphe was the target of an unthinking remark against Jews in her childhood. At the time, she remained silent, as some of your students may have when confronted with the incidents recounted in the first draft written in response to this chapter's Writing-before-Reading exercise. Later, however, she wrote an essay on the deleterious effects of bigoted remarks such as the one spoken by her friend's mother. Invite students to think of the second draft of their essay as an opportunity to redress the wrong they recounted in the first draft. They may either incorporate the offensive remark that spawned their essay into an anecdote in the essay, as both Naylor and Roiphe do, or keep their remarks impersonal, as Hayakawa does. This is a chance to have their say about offensive language.

2. Charles Lawrence writes that "University officials who have formulated policies to respond to incidents of racial harassment have been characterized in the press as 'thought police.'" Several other writers in this chapter emphasize the distinction between controlling offensive language and eradicating racism. People who do not voice their prejudices are not necessarily free of prejudice. Assign an essay in which your students explore solutions besides censorship to the problem of prejudice. What would it take to bring about the seemingly Utopian world described by Hayakawa, in which racial discrimination is "done away with"?

The Pleasures of the Mind

35

Sight into Insight

Annie Dillard, Seeing

Barry Lopez, The Stone Horse

Walker Percy, The Loss of the Creature

WORKING WITH THE CHAPTER

Yogi Berra put the theme of this chapter nicely: "You can observe a lot just by lookin'." Students might think that sounds simple enough, almost redundant, but Yogi really meant that people usually don't observe much because they don't bother to look. This chapter introduces your students to the art of seeing and reminds them that seeing is more than an automatic instinct. We must learn to see. As the selections show, seeing things properly demands that we rid ourselves of preconceptions and preformulations and try to observe the world from a fresh perspective.

The selections in this chapter are literary, philosophical, and intellectually challenging. For Annie Dillard, Barry Lopez, and Walker Percy, seeing is a struggle against our habitual blindness and our expectations. To see things truly, Dillard says, is a "discipline requiring a lifetime of dedicated struggle" (para. 36). Much of the struggle, according to Walker Percy, is undertaken to recover our individual sight from experts and theorists who have "packaged" knowledge for us. For Percy, seeing is a struggle for self-empowerment. The personal sovereignty Percy recommends in our confrontation with the world can be seen in Barry Lopez's "The Stone Horse." Lopez's description of his early-morning encounter with a centuries-old Native-American rock engraving can almost serve as a model of careful observation.

Teaching Strategies

"How to Use Your Eyes" is the compulsory course Helen Keller wanted to establish in colleges. Blind and deaf from birth, Keller overcame these handicaps, and others, to become a prominent and influential author. Students may not know of her, and so you may want to include this information about her if you use the passage from "Three Days to See" to open discussion. As someone who doesn't take sight for granted, she wants to stimulate those who do to reawaken their "dormant and sluggish" vision. You might invite students to try her thought-experiment; if they had only three days left of sight, what things would they most want to see? This discussion reappears when you get to the account of the "newly sighted" in Annie Dillard's "Seeing," where she covers the opposite movement — people blind since birth who, because of an operation, are suddenly able to see.

Though brief, the quotation from the Nobel Prize–winning physicist Werner Heisenberg (who founded quantum mechanics and is best known for his Uncertainty Principle) offers students an important insight into observation: "What we observe is not nature itself but nature exposed to our method of questioning." You might invite students to reflect on this comment so that they fully understand its implications, which extend, of course, far beyond scientific investigation. You may discover that many of your students haven't considered the complexities of observation but simply assume that they are seeing the world exactly as it is. It will be interesting to discuss the ways in which what they see is shaped by their culture, their expectations, and their method of observation (the dominant method today is rational-empirical). Heisenberg's remark is essential in discussing Walker Percy's "Loss of the Creature," where mediated experience is the key topic.

The final epigraph reminds us that observation deeply influences our emotional lives. Wanting to describe his mother's face, the British writer and social critic Richard Hoggart searches his memory for the right detail. All the terms he comes up with seem "vague and distant" (a feeling all writers have had). But his memory finally leads him to the one observation, the one detail, which tells the whole story. You might use this passage to demonstrate how writers search for specificity and detail to particularize their experience. Hoggart wanted to describe *his* mother, not mothers in general. Notice, too, how his memory is triggered by words, all of which he discards until he hits exactly the descriptive language he is looking for.

Wittgenstein says somewhere that philosophy is a struggle against the fascination that forms of expression exert upon us. This remark describes observation as well. Annie Dillard says seeing is "very much a matter of verbalization." Yet at the same time, she also realizes, we must try to see things without the labels and conceptual baggage our consciousness carries. Barry Lopez works hard at seeing on the desert floor a stone horse that unobservant travelers might casually step right over; Walker Percy makes us aware of how difficult it is to see anything outside of the prepackaged context provided for us by educators, social planners, and other experts. The struggle to see truly informs all the selections in this chapter.

A *Writing-before-Reading* Exercise

You might use the Helen Keller passage as a way to get writing started. Invite your class to try her experiment. Students should imagine that they had only three days left to see; they should then draft an essay describing what they would most want to see in that time. It will be interesting to compare papers later to see how many select the same type of thing: major landmarks, loved ones, natural objects. (If any blind students are in the class, you might invite them to do what Keller says she will do; she will imagine what she would want to see if she were given the use of her eyes for three days.) You could also vary the assignment by using other senses: hearing, taste, and so on.

WORKING WITH THE SELECTIONS

Annie Dillard

Seeing

Teaching Strategies

Annie Dillard's "Seeing" is not only a remarkable piece of personal writing but its subject will also open the way to productive discussion about topics that bear directly on observation, reflection, and writing. The essay is challenging and may be tough going for some students; but jump in, for the issues it raises are basic and applicable to everyone's experiences.

"Seeing" is, of course, an essay on perception, on the ways in which we observe or fail to observe the world around us. Packed tight with detail, the essay doesn't simply tell us about the importance of attentive observation, it *shows* us those observations through the writer's astonishing power of description. The writer is someone who, as she modestly expresses it, keeps her eyes open. To see what can happen if one keeps one's eyes open, you might direct students to the impressive descriptive passage in paragraphs 11 to 13, where the writer waits patiently in the growing darkness "watching for muskrats."

This is a critical passage for understanding the main work of Dillard's essay. The moment doesn't culminate in a detailed description of a muskrat but rather in a sudden blur: "Head and tail, if there was a head and tail, were both submerged in cloud. I saw only one ebony fling, a headlong dive to darkness; then the waters closed, and the lights went out." The critical point to make about Dillard's essay is that it is as much about not-seeing as seeing. She doesn't actually see the muskrat but she does describe beautifully and convincingly the process of "missing" it. In that sense — and this explanation accounts for a great deal of the essay's literary craft and complexity — she describes the act of seeing what she doesn't see.

It's this oscillation between seeing and not-seeing, of now catching and now missing objects and events in the natural world, that keeps Dillard's essay moving. Nature is quick and elusive, a "now-you-see-it, now-you-don't affair" (para. 4). Much of Dillard's success as a writer grows out of her tough-minded, honest approach to the ebb and flow of her immediate perceptions. Her own admission of her observational limitations (she is never the "expert" or the "specialist") has the effect of making those observations all the more valuable. There's a big difference between finally seeing a well-camouflaged frog (para. 7) and finally seeing a tree transfigured in a mystical flood of flame (para. 38), but the hard time she has in spotting the frog actually helps convince us that she does indeed see that "tree with the lights in it."

You might want to begin discussion by looking closely at Dillard's way of opening the essay. She begins with a one-paragraph section. Invite students to examine how this paragraph relates to the essay as a whole. The opening paragraph of "Seeing" may confuse students who may not at first understand its relation to the rest of the essay. You might want to read the paragraph aloud in class, asking students how images introduced here are picked up later in the essay. First-year writing students usually have not yet learned to see how writing can be organized by patterns of interlocking images, and this is a perfect opportunity to demonstrate this fundamental reading ability.

Start with the hidden pennies. In what way do Dillard's pennies represent something of value? In what sense is one of her pennies a "gift from the universe"? Her large words alone should alert students that something more is at stake here than pennies. Notice in the next paragraph that Dillard confronts this matter of value and reintroduces the penny; but this time pennies are natural gifts. An arrow, too, reappears — this time, pointing the way to the sight, not of a penny, but of a different "reward," "a muskrat kit paddling from its den" (another image that will be picked up later in the essay [paras. 11–13]). These natural sights are like pennies, valuable only to those who "cultivate a healthy poverty and simplicity." Most people nowadays don't stoop to pick up a penny (ask students how many of them routinely do so); do they also routinely ignore the natural "pennies" of the world, those small and apparently valueless moments of seeing?

If economic metaphors are reintroduced throughout the essay (notice the "coppers" at the end of paragraph 4, the pearls in paragraph 37, and the use of "spending" in paragraph 38), so too is the image of *hiding*. To show how the hidden pennies of paragraph 1 acquire a new meaning, you might examine the image of the Osage orange with its hidden birds (para. 4). Then notice (para. 5) the metaphor of nature as a children's puzzle (a tree in keeping with the preceding image and pointing toward the essay's final one) with hidden objects; this image then gives way to the hidden things specialists can find in nature. Once they catch on to this metaphor, students should be able to perceive related images throughout the essay — image clusters that surround drawing and art; light and shadow; earth, air, water, and fire. They should then be in a good position to appreciate that the essay is organized around patterns of imagery.

Another avenue to pursue, of course, is the essay's explicit topic: seeing. Invite your class to consider what Dillard means when she says that "Seeing is of course very much a matter of verbalization." Dillard mentions two kinds of seeing (paras. 31–33); one is a matter of verbalization, the other "involves a letting go." Students should be aware that much of what we see depends upon our putting something into words. For example, houses have many types of roofs — pitched, mansard, gabled, hip and valley, and so on. If we can identify by name the types of roofs (as could an architect), we are far more likely to really see the roof of a house than we would if we only knew the one word *roof*. The same holds true when looking at objects in nature; the person who knows the specific names of various flowers, herbs, trees, and so on, is far more likely to notice these natural objects than someone who has no knowledge of such distinctions. Dillard realizes that a large part of seeing depends upon this "running description" in our heads. This kind of "verbalized" seeing, she adds, helps us in analysis and study.

But there is another type of seeing, according to Dillard, which dispenses with our interior commentary and which approaches the mystical. It requires discipline and "a lifetime of dedicated struggle." This deeper seeing, unlike the verbalized kind, cannot be willed. It comes unbidden — it is a gift — and also comes as "a total surprise." Dillard then offers two moments in which she experienced this deeper seeing, one in paragraph 34 and the other in her concluding paragraph.

To get into the subject of Dillard's writing style, you might ask students about her frequent use of wordplay. Why does she, for example, deliberately use a hackneyed expression such as "What you see is what you get"?

Dillard's writing is full of idiomatic wordplay and puns — though the use of these in her style is (like Thoreau's) quite subtle and students may not catch them. The ordinary tough-talk expression — "What you see is what you get" — is given a new meaning here because "what you see" refers not only to an object one is purchasing (as it does in the ordinary use of the expression) but to the act of seeing, to perception itself. We get what we can see. The common expression also plays into her economic metaphor, because it brings together both seeing and getting. Notice, too, in a preceding sentence, a similar literalization of the expression "make your day." A good example of subtle punning comes toward the end of her essay: "But I couldn't sustain the illusion of flatness. I've been around too long" (para. 29). That turn very nicely takes an ordinary expression and gives it a new spark of life. Students should be encouraged to go through the essay and find other examples of puns and idiomatic play.

Additional Activities

As a literary exploration into the nature of perception, Dillard's essay invites comparison with many American poems. Two frequently anthologized (and thus easily accessible) poems you might introduce in class for comparison with "Seeing" are Robert Frost's "The Most of It" and Richard Wilbur's "The Beautiful Changes." Each poet takes up issues found in Dillard; the Frost would work very well in conjunction with paragraphs 11 to 13, where the essayist waits in the dark for the muskrats.

Generating Writing

Invite your students to imagine that they are the newly sighted patients Dillard writes about. They could then try writing a description of something of which they are especially fond as though they had never before seen it. What, for example, would a car seem like if they had never seen one — or a cat or dog or hamburger? What mental "images" might they have formed of these things? Then, they should imagine that they suddenly see the thing for the first time. What do they think their reaction would be?

Barry Lopez

The Stone Horse

Teaching Strategies

Barry Lopez's essay combines two types of writing — he gives historical information about the archeological treasures of the southern California deserts and offers a first-person account of the aesthetic pleasure experienced at one of the sites. You might begin by drawing your students' attention to the divisions of the essay. It is in three parts: (1) historical background on the development of the California desert and the destruction of archeological sites (this part deliberately has no first-person pronouns); (2) the personal narrative in which Lopez visits the site of the stone horse; and (3) a reflective conclusion in which Lopez leaves the solemnity of the site and returns to the world. The conclusion pulls the parts together and makes the reader aware that the essay has been about history all along.

After referring to the historical sweep of the opening section (where Lopez moves from prehistoric times to the present desert), you may want to focus on the heart of the piece — his encounter with the stone horse. But first, you may want to establish clearly in your students' minds what it is he is looking at. Lopez, who always tries to use the precise word, calls it an intaglio, which is an incised carving. The carvings were usually made — as was Lopez's stone horse — by scraping away surface pebbles so that the lighter undersoil would be exposed in outline. Many such enormous figures or symbols appear throughout the desert landscapes of the American Southwest. (Some of your students may have read sensationalist explanations that these carvings were designed as signals to extraterrestrials).

In any popular magazine this essay would have been accompanied by photographs of the horse. But the essay appeared in *Antaeus* — a prominent literary magazine — with no illustrations. You might want to ask your students why no picture appeared and why Lopez devoted his efforts to painstaking verbal description. (Attentive students will cite the aerial photograph of the horse that Lopez finds unsatisfactory [para. 31].) Lopez's rejection of photographic support here might be a good occasion to introduce discussion of description in general. Many students find description boring and overly detailed and have no patience for it. They accept the journalistic adage that "a picture is worth a thousand words."

A photograph can, of course, give us a fairly objective representation of a scene or an object, but it can rarely communicate what we *think* about it. Unless it is being used by a highly talented photographer, a camera (you might remind your class) can go only so far. The photograph of the horse that Lopez looks at is clearly not the horse he saw — alive and moving with the light — and he doesn't want to give his readers that substitute. Students should realize that he doesn't accept the aerial view, because having observed how light plays across the intaglio, he believes that the carving was originally intended to be seen from the ground; this is also his reason for rejecting the idea that the artist wanted it to be seen from the heavens. It's important to the descriptive power of the essay that Lopez explicitly rejects the photographic version of the horse; otherwise, readers would be left wondering why the article carried no picture. Make sure your students know why Lopez rejects the photograph. It would be useful for your students as readers to understand that for many writers the real wonders of nature and art lie hidden between the frames of photographs, almost beyond range of vision. In that sense, a few incisive words, the exact metaphor, may be worth a thousand pictures.

But if your students want something graphic, you might invite them to draw the horse from Lopez's detailed description. This might be an enjoyable in-class assignment. It would encourage students to see the accuracy of descriptive language, and you might want to pass around various depictions to see the varied ways in which the class has interpreted Lopez's description.

Descriptive language depends on knowing the right names for things. Annie Dillard says in her essay that seeing was "very much a matter of verbalization." Lopez states how important it is to make careful distinctions: "You have to do it to be able to talk clearly about the world (para. 25)." To demonstrate Lopez's feeling for precise terminology and fine distinctions, you might invite the class to examine his diction. A good place to look is paragraph 20, where Lopez describes how the intaglio was made. Ask students to go through this paragraph and mark the words they find unfamiliar or unexpected. You might want to point out that the paragraph takes its strength from three sets of terms; one drawn from geology ("desert pavement," "matrix," "oxides," "desert varnish," "bermed"); another from art ("patina," "glyph," "intaglio," "negative image"); and the third from the horse ("brow," "rump," "withers"). Students should see that Lopez's language does more than convey his desire for accurate observation. His familiarity with the proper words makes us aware that he knows terrain, art, and horses; in other words, he knows what he's talking about. These three sets of words will surface and resurface throughout the essay.

Thoreau said "only by observing for the sake of observing and not for the sake of acting, will the Absolute reveal itself." In this essay, Lopez does just that — observes for the sake of observing — and he encounters a kind of Absolute: our presence in history.

Additional Activities

Books and magazine articles have been written on intaglios, prehistoric rock art, and geoglyphs. You might want to use Lopez's essay as the basis for more extensive research on the topic. Students could form groups and each group could do research and report on a different aspect of this art: its aesthetic value; whether it was designed for gods or extraterrestrials; the vandalism; and so on. If slides are available from the art department, such aids might be especially useful for discussion.

Generating Writing

Though Barry Lopez treats an object that is physically inaccessible to most people, he does offer a model of observation that is applicable to anything we want to look at attentively. Invite students to train their own power of observation on an art form more accessible to them — a statue on campus, an architecturally interesting building, a mural, an intriguingly placed poster, even some striking graffiti. Part of the challenge of the assignment should be to discover something that most people fail to notice.

Walker Percy

The Loss of the Creature

Teaching Strategies

This is not be an easy essay for most readers. Percy's argument is complex; the intellectual attitudes he objects to will not be obvious to most students; and his comic use of examples may be confusing. The essay is about something important, however, and is worth the challenge.

The best way into discussing the essay might be to ask your students to respond to this conversation overheard in a diner between a state trooper and a waitress: Trooper: "Hey, Linda, did you ever get out to the Grand Canyon for vacation?" Linda: "We sure did. It was beautiful! It looked just like the postcards." This is a familiar comment; your students may have heard similar ones from other people about sights they've seen. Invite your class to consider Linda's remark. Do they find anything odd about it? Do they consider it strange that the postcard takes priority over the scene, that it — and not the place itself — validates Linda's experience? From this "real-life" dialogue you may be able to turn more easily to Percy's similar observation (para. 5).

This incident, in a nutshell, is what Percy's essay is about — the way in which our experiences are prepackaged and preformulated by art, education, cultural expectations, the media, and so on. Though he uses sightseeing — and the Grand Canyon — as examples of how some experiences become inauthentic, his essay is really about experience itself (and for ambitious instructors could be profitably paired with Emerson's classic essay, "Experience"). As Percy says, it is almost impossible to see the Grand Canyon today because "the thing as it is, has been appropriated by the symbolic complex which has already been formed in the sightseer's mind (para. 5). By seeing such sites "under approved circumstances," we lose them. Percy's objection to most education is directly connected to this phenomenon of loss — most of what we learn in school is also learned "under approved circumstances" and is thus inauthentic.

Percy's terminology is frequently that of existentialist philosophy, and your students will probably find that his language puts them off. The way around this problem is to encourage them to grasp the idea first in words from their own experiences — surely, they've confronted things for the first time in a context of educational and cultural expectations. Once they've realized how common this event is, they can begin to understand the meaning of *appropriation, authenticity, expropriate,* or *concreteness.* Percy wants to restore the individual's "sovereignty" in knowledge (the educationally fashionable label now is *empowerment*).

To stimulate debate about Percy's point, you might ask the class to examine his opening paragraphs. Notice that exploration and discovery are his key images throughout. He begins by citing Cardenas's discovery of the Grand Canyon, and he uses that moment as the criterion by which to judge other experiences of the site, suggesting that the experience becomes — like a copied-over cassette — somehow degraded with every subsequent sightseer (he even whimsically offers a mathematical formula for this phenomenon). But your students may want to discuss a few matters that Percy doesn't touch on: (1) Cardenas was only the first *European* to see the Grand Canyon — not the first human being; does that then, according to Percy's logic, make Cardenas's experience less authentic? And (2) why should Cardenas's experience be regarded as primary, for didn't he, too, gaze on the place with preconceived attitudes about landscape, beauty, and empire (he was on a military expedition at the time) derived from his sixteenth-century culture and education? Cardenas, of course, had no pictures or travel brochures about the Grand Canyon to feed his expectations or predetermine his response, and that is Percy's main point.

Your students should also notice that the main impetus of Percy's essay, for all his talk of loss — is optimistic: Percy believes that even if we can't be the one to *discover* a phenomenon like the Grand Canyon, we can still *recover* it if we struggle against the officially approved view of it endorsed by experts, educators, theorists, artists, or other "privileged knowers" (para. 33). You might point out to students how the theme of discovery and recovery explicitly appears in the essay's first two paragraphs. Make sure, however, that your students are aware of the complexity of "recovery." You might want to see if the class can summarize Percy's four methods of recovery (paras. 9–14).

Once your students understand Percy's point about how we surrender our "sovereignty" to others, you can introduce the second part of the essay. You might point out how this part, too, begins with references to discovery. The second half of the essay is about our educational process. Invite your students to discuss Percy's point about the dogfish and the sonnet. Why does he use these two examples? (Your students might be interested to know that Percy is both a novelist and a physician. You might point out, too, how he has used examples throughout the essay. His examples sometimes start out as illustrations of a point but then suddenly, and at times humorously, take on a life of their own). Do they agree with his educational assessment? (He is very tough on classrooms throughout.) In paragraph 52 he makes a surprising proposition that is worth debating: "I propose that English poetry and biology should be taught as usual, but that at irregular intervals, poetry students should find dogfishes on their desks and biology students should find Shakespeare sonnets on their dissection boards." Percy is serious about this idea. What do your students think? Does it make sense to them? Do they understand why Percy makes this proposal? You might wrap up discussion by focusing on this educational plan. How does changing the instructional context of the dogfish and sonnet grow out of Percy's earlier attitudes toward discovery and recovery? And what have his examples to do with our attitudes toward the humanities and the sciences?

Additional Activities

To pursue further Percy's observations about tourism and sightseeing, invite your class to find travel advertisements or brochures for vacation spots. These are easily found in magazines, newspapers, and at local travel bureaus. The material should be discussed in the context of Percy's attitudes toward seeing: how many ads, for example, invite the tourist to "discover" X or Y? What would Percy say about that notion of "discovery"? What other kinds of "prepackaged" attitudes can students find in the advertisements?

Generating Writing

To test Percy's ideas, students might try their own thought-experiment. Invite them to write an essay in which they consider if it is possible, as Percy suggests, "to come face to face with an authentic sight." Does that necessarily mean seeing something for the first time? Or do they think it is possible, say, to visit a notorious tourist location such as the Eiffel Tower in Paris and truly see it? How would Percy define that kind of authentic seeing? In their essays students should consider a significant site that they have visited.

WRITING ABOUT THE CHAPTER

1. If your students worked on the Writing-before-Reading draft, they should now revise accordingly. With the range of detail and information in this chapter, they should reconsider Helen Keller's experiment from several new perspectives. If, for example, they chose sites to see for a last time, did Walker Percy's essay change their attitude about how they would see them? Did the essays in this chapter suggest ways of observing that students would now want to incorporate into their papers? And what about diction and specificity — did the essays make them aware of how important the precise word was to both authenticity and authority?

2. Annie Dillard in her essay "Seeing" cites another writer's advice on how to see deer: "As soon as you can forget the naturally obvious and construct an artificial obvious, then you too will see deer." This is an intriguing, if difficult, concept. Invite your students to speculate on this remark. What do they think it means? Once they've come up with a sense of the distinction between the "naturally obvious" and the "artificially obvious," they should suggest why understanding this distinction could make us better observers. Would the distinction apply to looking at a baseball or football game, a painting, a dancer?

36

The Unexpected Universe

Stephen Jay Gould, Sex, Drugs, Disasters, and the Extinction of Dinosaurs

Loren Eiseley, The Star Thrower

K. C. Cole, Much Ado about Nothing

WORKING WITH THE CHAPTER

Teaching Strategies

At the core of all the writings in this chapter is a feeling that might be called humility, the humbleness of the Indian who drew an immense ring in the sand, saying "This is where the white man and the red man know nothing." This image from the epigraph by Carl Sandburg is, fittingly, a primitive form, like those described by Albert Einstein in his epigraph: "To know that what is impenetrable to us really exists, manifesting itself as the highest wisdom and the most radiant beauty, which our dull faculties can comprehend only in the most primitive forms — this knowledge, this feeling, is at the center of true religiousness." For the Indian as well as for Einstein, the reader knows that the humility is caused by awe, brought on by a knowledge of the universe so large that it can begin to glimpse that which is beyond human knowledge.

The scientists in this chapter tackle the expressing the unknowable in different ways. K. C. Cole uses analogies, each as primitive as the circle in the sand, expressly knowing the inadequacy of each to describe the universe. "A fish," she writes, "can't imagine (if a fish could imagine) that the surface of the water marks the end of his water universe any more than we can contemplate an edge to our universe, a beginning or an end to time." Loren Eiseley brings out the spiritual implications of a point of view vaster than any we can imagine when he writes, "Out of the depths of a seemingly empty universe had grown an eye, like the eye in my room, but an eye on a vastly larger scale. It looked out upon what I can only call itself." Both Cole and Eiseley use paradox to try to break the mind free from the grasp of the purely rational, so that it can perceive the unexpected universe.

Stephen Jay Gould doesn't express awe or humility directly, but he does argue against the anthropocentrism that makes humanity the end goal of evolution. And he drastically reduces the stature of homo sapiens by expanding his argument to a scale measured in 26-million-year cycles. Similarly, Eiseley reduces human identity to "an illusion": "We gaze backward into a contracting cone of life until words leave us and all we know is dissolved into the simple circuits of a reptilian brain." Even Charles Darwin, whom Eiseley criticizes for his tendency to fall into anthropocentric fallacies, sees "grandeur" in the fact that "from so simple a beginning endless forms most beautiful and most wonderful have been, and are being evolved." It is this beauty and this wonder that make up the unexpected universe.

A Writing-before-Reading Exercise

Ask your students to think about the division between the so-called hard sciences and the humanities. It's a familiar distinction, replicated in the structures of most universities. Have them write a rough draft in which they examine that dualism critically. Do they see any overlaps between the two, perhaps in their subjects or in their methods? In their own studies in the sciences and the humanities, have they noticed any connections? Were they ever encouraged to notice such connections, perhaps by the teachers of core courses whose syllabi were designed to be compatible? If not, can they imagine any points of commonality between courses in these two categories? Why do they suppose this division arose? Whom does it serve, and how? What are the potential dangers in keeping the two realms separate?

WORKING WITH THE SELECTIONS

Stephen Jay Gould

Sex, Drugs, Disasters, and the Extinction of Dinosaurs

Teaching Strategies

Although his title mentions the "extinction of dinosaurs," and although Stephen Jay Gould spends much of the essay testing three theories about the cause of their extinction — "sex, drugs, and disasters" — Gould's thesis is not about dinosaurs but rather about science. His very first sentence lays it out: "Science, in its most fundamental definition, is a fruitful mode of inquiry, not a list of exciting conclusions." It's a fairly controversial thesis, at least to the lay reader, for whom this essay is obviously intended. You might illustrate its measure of controversy — one gauge of a good thesis — in class by asking your students if they know what scientists have been doing in the twentieth century. Write their answers on the board. How many mention "exciting conclusions," such as $E = mc^2$, or that light is both a particle and a wave, or superconductors, and how many can identify the "mode of inquiry" that led to the discovery they name?

Someone is likely to protest here that this is an English class, and they shouldn't be expected to know about the experiments that showed light to be both particle and wave. If no one does voice this protest, you can be sure that some are thinking it, but are too polite or politic to mention it. If they don't voice it, maybe you should — and let *them* argue against *you*. Gould, they may say, would blame the writers of "popular presentations of science" for our ignorance. K. C. Cole might find his charge leveled at her, for example. Even if your class has yet to read her essay, some may want to argue with Gould on this point. Isn't it possible that science has really so progressed that lay people couldn't understand the implications of scientific experiments even if they were explained, and that without the work of such popularizers the public would have no access to scientific knowledge at all?

Gould, of course, has structured his essay so as to refute such a position. He proves, by briefly emulating their technique, that the popularizers put their readers in a position where it is impossible for them to make up their own minds: it's not that lay readers cannot think about these questions, but rather that they have been trained not to. Have your class turn to his summaries of the three proposals on the extinction of dinosaurs. Ask them to characterize these summaries. Do they notice the bald, declarative sentences giving the kinds of conclusions that Gould deplores? Do the summaries themselves show any evidence by which we as readers can judge which of the statements are predicated on mere speculation and which on falsifiable evidence?

Some of your students will probably have the scientific knowledge necessary to know, for example, that livers and testes do not fossilize. But nothing in the summaries suggests this limitation. These summaries resemble the mysteries solved by Perry Mason: the vital case clue is always withheld from the audience, so that the viewer cannot figure out for himself or herself who committed the murder. Of course, people have figured out how to solve those "Perry Mason" mysteries by structural means: they have found that it's always the least conspicuous character, or the character whom the camera picks up at a precise moment in the courtroom scene. Similarly, most people familiar with stories such as "Cinderella," "The Three Billy Goats Gruff," and any fairy tale involving three brothers, three sisters, or three tests is likely to know by "intuition" that Gould's third option is the correct one. But any mystery fan will tell you that a story that does not provide all the clues necessary for its solution is not a good mystery. And Gould himself as much as admits that his withholding the vital clue was unfair: "much of the popular commentary has missed this essential distinction by focusing on the impact and its attendant results, and forgetting what really matters to a scientist — the iridium."

Additional Activities

Gould's essay, by explaining how the three hypotheses evolved, lets us see which are mere speculation, and which is properly falsifiable and expansive, thus meeting his criteria for good science. Because he describes the "mode of inquiry" and not just the "enticing conclusions," his essay meets his own expectations. After your class has examined his thesis and argument, you might want to direct their attention to his language. What, for example, is the status of such words as *titillating, enticing,* and *primally fascinating?* Is Gould using these words to imply a criticism of the press for playing upon the reader's baser emotions in order to seduce their interest in scientific theory? If he is, then where would Gould's essay stand in relation to the articles he judges in this way? After all, his essay has a titillating title. Or look at his use of the word *intriguing* (para. 5 and throughout). He obviously finds science intriguing, but at the same time he considers "intriguing ideas" not "good science." Similarly, you might ask if Gould would consider *fertile imaginations* and *speculation* (para. 15) good or bad. If they protest, with some reason, that "good and bad" are value judgments, with no place in a discussion of science, then point to any of Gould's many uses of that dichotomy (for example, "Good science is self-corrective" [para. 16]). Does "good and bad" imply a moral judgment in this context? Why does Gould refer to his own argument as "preaching" (para. 5)?

Generating Writing

1. Have students go to the library and find back issues of *Discover, Omni,* or other journals that provide popular accounts of scientific advances. Instruct them to use Gould's criteria to judge the essays they have chosen from these journals. They may choose two essays covering the same breakthrough to analyze their relative merits. Or they may choose to compare and contrast an essay from a popular science journal (or from the science section of the *New York Times,* for example) with one of Stephen Jay Gould's other essays, from any of his books on science written for a lay audience. Does Gould's own writing live up to his criteria? How, if at all, does it differ from the other essay your student has chosen?

2. Assign an essay in which students examine Gould's tone in this essay. When does he use the diction and syntax of the serious scientist, and where does he become more colloquial? How, if at all, does Gould's silliness differ from the silliness he criticizes in

Siegel's statement that "elephants drink, perhaps, to forget . . ."? What is the effect of his shifts in tone? What might be the intention behind the stylistic choices that create those shifts?

Loren Eiseley

The Star Thrower

Teaching Strategies

"The Star Thrower" is a very difficult essay, but will amply repay a close and careful rereading. Treatment of this essay will probably take up two full class periods. When your students come to class having read the essay the night before, the chance is very good that most will be baffled. If so, you might take this as a perfect opportunity to teach them to mark up the text in such a way that their reading will be slowed in a productive way. Read Seccho's epigraph and the first paragraph together as a class. Start by asking if anyone has already made marginal notations next to the epigraph. If so, they should read their comments, and everyone should write those comments alongside the epigraph. Then ask the class to name the species of comment: is it a question? an observation? an interpretation? speculation? identification? and so on. Emphasize that any kind of comment is useful, because writing marginal comments signals interaction with the text. As different kinds of interaction arise during your discussion, write them on the board so that the students will have a full repertoire of choices when they go to mark up sections of the text themselves.

Here are a handful of comments that the opening of this essay has elicited: *the Way* is underlined, with the comment "Zen"; *Seccho* is identified, drawing on information later in the essay (remember, this is a rereading) as "a Buddhist sage"; someone speculates from the epigraph that "it's a spiritual quest by a scientist, apparently"; another asks about the first line in the first paragraph, "does this get contradicted by the Star Thrower?"; beside the line *my perceptions have frequently been inadequate or betrayed,* someone writes "sounds like it's *him* that's at fault — inadequate — but also like someone or something else is betraying his perceptions — not his fault"; another circles *what man may be,* identifying this as "what he's seeking knowledge of"; another comments that the *terrible question* is "unstated — is it man's potential ? (so far that's all I can infer)." Your students will probably suggest other comments, either some they wrote as they were reading the essay, or comments they think of during the class exercise. They should be able to come up with enough kinds of marginal notations on just paragraph 1 to provide a good sampling for group work.

To set up group work, divide the class into eight teams. Divide each of the essay's four parts in half, and assign one half-section to each group. They are to collaborate on the task of marking up that section of the text, very thoroughly and interactively. They will of course be interacting with each other as well as with the essay as they perform their task. This exercise is likely to take up the remainder of the class period, meaning that you'll have to postpone whole-group discussion of the essay until the next meeting. As homework, assign a careful rereading of the text, suggesting that they use the marginal-notation techniques they have just practiced on the entire essay as they reread. During the discussion at the next class meeting, the members of each group will be considered "experts" on their own section of the text, but everyone will be expected to be able to discuss the essay as a whole.

In this rich and complex essay, almost any question you ask will lead, eventually, to every question you could ask. This being a chapter on science, you might begin arbitrarily with a question about that: What is Eiseley's view of science? Your students might notice that Eiseley, unlike Gould, does not claim to know what science is: "With such an eye, some have said, science looks upon the world. I do not know." What is the consequence or relevance of his doubting posture? What is the significance of his metaphor for science —

"the dead skull and the revolving eye"? What does it mean that the same symbol stands, in the epigraph to this selection from Seccho, for a "man walking in the way"? What does science have to do with spirituality? Ask your students to trace the movement of "the dead skull and the revolving eye" in the essay. When does Eiseley throw off that symbolic identity? When does he resume it? What is the significance of his shifts in attitude toward the skull and the eye?

When you ask about science, some of your students may focus on his geographic analogy instead, pointing to the two views of science implied in his contrast between the "level plains" and the "glacial crevasses" (para. 27). If these are the two alternative views of science, which does Eiseley seem to support? Why? Ask students to find other places in the essay where Eiseley endorses the model of the rift, beginning with paragraph 1. How is this simple dichotomy complicated? How does the question mutate into a meditation on the mind of man? What are the various accounts and definitions of man that Eiseley gives in this essay? What motivates each account? You will want to encourage your students to discuss the connections between science and religion, science and philosophy, science and superstition, and science and poetry. Notice that nowhere does Eiseley, the scientist, persist in valuing science more highly than the humanities, even though, like Gould, he criticizes other scientists (here Darwin) for being anthropocentric.

The struggle between Loren Eiseley the scientist and Loren Eiseley the humanist is pivotal in this essay. Ask your students about the function of the material about Eiseley's mother in this essay. Why does it take him so long after he first recognizes the eye that is haunting him as his mother's to get around to recounting the story of his discovery of the photograph? What does he gain by allowing himself to think about her, and to feel his feelings toward her? How does this episode tie in to the essay as a whole? How does his eventual openness to the memory about his mother enable him to go out searching for the star thrower? No matter what avenues your discussion takes, you will definitely want to discuss the significance of the star thrower. Ask your students to explain Eiseley's initial response to the star thrower, his quick defense against that response, and his final response to the star thrower, upon their second meeting. What does it mean that he was finally able to join the star thrower? What does it mean that from "Darwin's tangled bank of unceasing struggle, selfishness, and death, had arisen, incomprehensibly, the thrower who loved not man but life"? How does Eiseley resolve the conflict that has sent him wandering so restlessly along the shores at Costabel?

Additional Activities

Loren Eiseley sees a connection between modern science and Eastern philosophy. Interested students might consider reading and reporting on other books that make a similar connection, the most famous of which is probably *The Tao of Physics,* by Fritjof Capra. You might also assign "Emptiness," by Shuryu Suzuki (Chapter 39) together with "The Star Thrower," or refer your students to other sages of Eastern philosophy.

Eiseley repeatedly states and suggests that the poets understand much that the scientists miss. The "natural supernaturalism" (a phrase from M. H. Abrams) of the English Romantic poets seems to permeate the background of his essay. In particular, Coleridge's "Rime of the Ancient Mariner" and Wordsworth's "Resolution and Independence," both reprinted here, provide interesting points of comparison. The narrator of the former sheds the albatross when he blesses the water-snakes "unaware," in a gesture of cross-species compassion comparable to that of the star thrower. And the narrator of the latter, like Eiseley, gains a valuable insight from a brief conversation with an eccentric man he meets during a solitary walk.

The Rime of the Ancyent Marinere

In Seven Parts

ARGUMENT

How a Ship having passed the Line was driven by Storms to the cold Country towards the South Pole; and how from thence she made her course to the tropical Latitude of the Great Pacific Ocean; and of the strange things that befell; and in what manner the Ancyent Marinere came back to his own Country.

I

It is an ancyent Marinere,
   And he stoppeth one of three:
"By thy long grey beard and thy glittering eye
   "Now wherefore stoppest me?

"The Bridegroom's doors are open'd wide
   "And I am next of kin;
"The Guests are met, the Feast is set, —
   "May'st hear the merry din.

But still he holds the wedding-guest —
   There was a Ship, quoth he —
"Nay, if thou'st got a laughsome tale,
   "Marinere! come with me."   10

He holds him with his skinny hand,
   Quoth he, there was a Ship —
"Now get thee hence, thou grey-beard Loon!
   "Or my Staff shall make thee skip.

He holds him with his glittering eye —
   The wedding guest stood still
And listens like a three year's child;
   The Marinere hath his will.   20

The wedding-guest sate on a stone,
   He cannot chuse but hear:
And thus spake on that ancyent man,
   The bright-eyed Marinere.

The Ship was cheer'd, the Harbour clear'd —
   Merrily did we drop
Below the Kirk, below the Hill,
   Below the Light-house top.

The Sun came up upon the left,
   Out of the Sea came he:
And he shone bright, and on the right   30
   Went down into the Sea.

Higher and higher every day,
   Till over the mast at noon —
The wedding-guest here beat his breast,
   For he heard the loud bassoon.

The Bride hath pac'd into the Hall,
   Red as a rose is she;
Nodding their heads before her goes
   The merry Minstralsy.   40

The wedding-guest he beat his breast,
   Yet he cannot chuse but hear:
And thus spake on that ancyent Man,
   The bright-eyed Marinere.

Listen, Stranger! Storm and Wind,
  A Wind and Tempest strong!
For days and weeks it play'd us freaks —
  Like Chaff we drove along.

Listen, Stranger! Mist and Snow,
  And it grew wond'rous cauld: 50
And Ice mast-high came floating by
  As green as Emerauld.

And thro' the drifts the snowy clifts
  Did send a dismal sheen;
Ne shapes of men ne beasts we ken —
  The Ice was all between.

The Ice was here, the Ice was there,
  The Ice was all around:
It crack'd and growl'd, and roar'd and howl'd —   60
  Like noises of a swound.

At length did cross an Albatross,
  Thorough the Fog it came;
And an it were a Christian Soul,
  We hail'd it in God's name.

The Marineres gave it biscuit-worms,
  And round and round it flew:
The Ice did split with a Thunder-fit;
  The Helmsman steer'd us thro'.

And a good south wind sprung up behind,
  The Albatross did follow;   70
And every day for food or play
  Came to the Marinere's hollo!

In mist or cloud on mast or shroud
  It perch'd for vespers nine,
Whiles all the night thro' fog-smoke white
  Glimmer'd the white moon-shine.

"God save thee, ancyent Marinere!
  "From the fiends that plague thee thus —
"Why look'st thou so?" — with my cross bow
  I shot the Albatross.   80

II

The Sun came up upon the right,
  Out of the Sea came he;
And broad as a weft upon the left
  Went down into the Sea.

And the good south wind still blew behind,
  But no sweet Bird did follow
Ne any day for food or play
  Came to the Marinere's hollo!

And I had done an hellish thing
  And it would work 'em woe: 90
For all averr'd, I had kill'd the Bird
  That made the Breeze to blow.

Ne dim ne red, like God's own head,
  The glorious Sun uprist:

Then all averr'd, I had kill'd the Bird
  That brought the fog and mist.
'Twas right, said they, such birds to slay
  That bring the fog and mist.

The breezes blew, the white foam flew,
 The furrow follow'd free:
We were the first that ever burst
 Into that silent Sea.

Down dropt the breeze, the Sails dropt down,
 'Twas sad as sad could be
And we did speak only to break
 The silence of the Sea.

All in a hot and copper sky
 The bloody sun at noon;
Right up above the mast did stand,
 No bigger than the moon.

Day after day, day after day,
 We stuck, ne breath ne motion,
As idle as a painted Ship
 Upon a painted Ocean.

Water, water, every where
 And all the boards did shrink;
Water, water, every where
 Ne any drop to drink.

The very deeps did rot: O Christ!
 That ever this should be!
Yea, slimy things did crawl with legs
 Upon the slimy Sea.

About, about, in reel and rout
 The Death-fires danc'd at night;
The water, like a witch's oils,
 Burnt green and blue and white.

And some in dreams assured were
 Of the Spirit that plagued us so:
Nine fathom deep he had follow'd us
 From the Land of Mist and Snow.

And every tongue thro' utter drouth
 Was wither'd at the root;
We could not speak no more than if
 We had been choked with soot.

Ah wel-a-day ! what evil looks
 Had I from old and young;
Instead of the Cross the Albatross
 About my neck was hung.

III

I saw a something in the Sky
 No bigger than my fist;
At first it seem'd a little speck
 And then it seem'd a mist:
It mov'd and mov'd, and took at last
 A certain shape, I wist.

A speck, a mist, a shape, I wist!
 And still it ner'd and ner'd;
And, an it dodg'd a water-sprite,
 It plung'd and tack'd and veer'd.

With throat unslack'd, with black lips bak'd
 Ne could we laugh, ne wail:
Then while thro' drouth all dumb they stood
I bit my arm and suck'd the blood
 And cry'd, A sail! a sail!

With throat unslack'd, with black lips bak'd
    Agape they hear'd me call:
Gramercy! they for joy did grin
And all at once their breath drew in
    As they were drinking all.

She doth not tack from side to side —
    Hither to work us weal   160
Withouten wind, withouten tide
    She steddies with upright keel.

The western wave was all a flame,
    The day was well nigh done!
Almost upon the western wave
    Rested the broad bright Sun;
When that strange shape drove suddenly
    Betwixt us and the Sun.

And strait the Sun was fleck'd with bars
    (Heaven's mother send us grace)   170
As if thro' a dungeon grate he peer'd
    With broad and burning face.

Alas! (thought I, and my heart beat loud)
    How fast she neres and neres!
Are those *her* Sails that glance in the Sun
    Like restless gossameres?

Are these *her* naked ribs, which fleck'd
    The sun that did behind them peer?
And are these two all, all the crew,
    That woman and her fleshless Pheere?   180

His bones were black with many a crack,
    All black and bare, I ween;
Jet-black and bare, save where with rust
Of mouldy damps and charnel crust
    They're patch'd with purple and green.

Her lips are red, *her* looks are free
    Her locks are yellow as gold: —
Her skin is as white as leprosy,
And she is far liker Death than he;
    Her flesh makes the still air cold.   190

The naked Hulk alongside came
    And the Twain were playing dice;
"The Game is done! I've won, I've won!"
    Quoth she, and whistled thrice.

A gust of wind sterte up behind
    And whistled thro' his bones;
Thro' the holes of his eyes and the hole of his mouth
    Half-whistles and half-groans.

With never a whisper in the Sea
    Off darts the Spectre-ship;   200
While clombe above the Eastern bar
The horned Moon, with one bright Star
    Almost atween the tips.

One after one by the horned Moon
    (Listen, O Stranger! to me)
Each turn'd his face with a ghastly pang
    And curs'd me with his ee.

Four times fifty living men,
  With never a sigh or groan,
With heavy thump, a lifeless lump
  They dropp'd down one by one.   210

Their souls did from their bodies fly, —
  They fled to bliss or woe;
And every soul it pass'd me by,
  Like the whiz of my Cross-bow.

IV

"I fear thee, ancyent Marinere!
  "l fear thy skinny hand;
"And thou art long and lank and brow
  "As is the ribb'd Sea-sand.

"I fear thee and thy glittering eye   220
  "And thy skinny hand so brown —
Fear not, fear not, thou wedding guest!
  This body dropt not down.

Alone, alone, all all alone
  Alone on the wide wide Sea;
And Christ would take no pity on
  My soul in agony.

The many men so beautiful,
  And they all dead did lie!
And a million million slimy things   230
  Liv'd on — and so did I.

I look'd upon the rotting Sea,
  And drew my eyes away;
I look'd upon the eldritch deck,
  And there the dead men lay.

I look'd to Heaven, and try'd to pray;
  But or ever a prayer had gusht,
A wicked whisper came and made
  My heart as dry as dust.

I clos'd my lids and kept them close,   240
  Till the balls like pulses beat;
For the sky and the sea, and the sea and the sky
Lay like a load on my weary eye,
  And the dead were at my feet.

The cold sweat melted from their limbs,
  Ne rot, ne reek did they;
The look with which they look'd on me,
  Had never pass'd away.

An orphan's curse would drag to Hell
  A spirit from on high: 250
But O! more horrible than that
  Is the curse in a dead man's eye!
Seven days, seven nights I saw that curse,
  And yet I could not die.

The moving Moon went up the sky
  And no where did abide:
Softly she was going up
  And a star or two beside

Her beams bemock'd the sultry main
  Like morning frosts yspread;
But where the ship's huge shadow lay,
The charmed water burnt alway
  A still and awful red.

260

Beyond the shadow of the ship
  I watch'd the water-snakes:
They mov'd in tracks of shining white;
And when they rear'd, the elfish light
  Fell off in hoary flakes.

Within the shadow of the ship
  I watch'd their rich attire:
Blue, glossy green, and velvet black
They coil'd and swam; and every track
  Was a flash of golden fire.

270

O happy living things! no tongue
  Their beauty might declare:
A spring of love gusht from my heart,
  And I bless'd them unaware!
Sure my kind saint took pity on me,
  And I bless'd them unaware.

The self-same moment I could pray;
  And from my neck so free
The Albatross fell off, and sank
  Like lead into the sea.

280

V

O sleep, it is a gentle thing
  Belov'd from pole to pole!
To Mary-queen the praise be yeven
She sent the gentle sleep from heaven
  That slid into my soul.

The silly buckets on the deck
  That had so long remain'd,
I dreamt that they were fill'd with dew
  And when I awoke it rain'd.

290

My lips were wet, my throat was cold,
  My garments all were dank;
Sure I had drunken in my dreams
  And still my body drank.

I mov'd and could not feel my limbs,
  I was so light, almost
I thought that I had died in sleep,
  And was a blessed Ghost.

300

The roaring wind! it roar'd far off,
  It did not come anear;
But with its sound it shook the sails
  That were so thin and sere.

The upper air bursts into life,
  And a hundred fire-flags sheen
To and fro they are hurried about;
And to and fro, and in and out
  The stars dance on between.

The coming wind doth roar more loud;
  The sails do sigh, like sedge:
The rain pours down from one black cloud
  And the Moon is at its edge.

310

Hark! hark! the thick black cloud is cleft,
    And the Moon is at its side:
Like waters shot from some high crag,
The lightning falls with never a jag
    A river steep and wide.

The strong wind reach'd the ship: it roar'd
    And dropp'd down, like a stone!
Beneath the lightning and the moon
    The dead men gave a groan.

They groan'd, they stirr'd, they all uprose,
    Ne spake, ne mov'd their eyes:
It had been strange, even in a dream
    To have seen those dead men rise.

The helmsman steerd, the ship mov'd on;
    Yet never a breeze up-blew;
The Marineres all 'gan work the ropes,
    Where they were wont to do:
They rais'd their limbs like lifeless tools —
    We were a ghastly crew.

The body of my brother's son
    Stood by me knee to knee:
The body and I pull'd at one rope,
    But he said nought to me —
And I quak'd to think of my own voice
    How frightful it would be!

The day-light dawn'd — they dropp'd their arms,
    And cluster'd round the mast:
Sweet sounds rose slowly thro' their mouths
    And from their bodies pass'd.

Around, around, flew each sweet sound,
    Then darted to the sun:
Slowly the sounds came back again
    Now mix'd, now one by one.

Sometimes a dropping from the sky
    I heard the Lavrock sing;
Sometimes all little birds that are
How they seem'd to fill the sea and air
    With their sweet jargoning,

And now 'twas like all instruments,
    Now like a lonely flute;
And now it is an angel's song
    That makes the heavens be mute.

It ceas'd: yet still the sails made on
    A pleasant noise till noon,
A noise like of a hidden brook
    In the leafy month of June,
That to the sleeping woods all night
    Singeth a quiet tune.

Listen, O listen, thou Wedding-guest!
    "Marinere! thou hast thy will:
"For that, which comes out of thine eye, doth make
    "My body and soul to be still."

Never sadder tale was told
    To a man of woman born:
Sadder and wiser thou wedding-guest!
    Thou'lt rise to morrow morn.

320
330
340
350
360

Never sadder tale was heard
  By a man of woman born:
The Marineres all return'd to work
  As silent as beforne.

The Marineres all 'gan pull the ropes,
  But look at me they n'old:
Thought I, I am as thin as air —
  They cannot me behold.

Till noon we silently sail'd on
  Yet never a breeze did breathe:
Slowly and smoothly went the ship
  Mov'd onward from beneath.

Under the keel nine fathom deep
  From the land of mist and snow
The spirit slid: and it was He
  That made the Ship to go.
The sails at noon left off their tune
  And the Ship stood still also.

The sun right up above the mast
  Had fix'd her to the ocean:
But in a minute she 'gan stir
  With a short uneasy motion —
Backwards and forwards half her length
  With a short uneasy motion.

Then, like a pawing horse let go,
  She made a sudden bound:
It flung the blood into my head,
  And I fell into a swound.

How long in that same fit I lay,
  I have not to declare;
But ere my living life return'd,
I heard and in my soul discern'd
  Two voices in the air,

"Is it he?" quoth one, "Is this the man?
  "By him who died on cross,
"With his cruel bow he lay'd full low
  "The harmless Albatross.

"The spirit who 'bideth by himself
  "In the land of mist and snow,
"He lov'd the bird that lov'd the man
  "Who shot him with his bow.

The other was a softer voice,
  As soft as honey-dew:
Quoth he the man hath penance done,
  And penance more will do.

VI

FIRST VOICE

"But tell me, tell me! speak again,
  "Thy soft response renewing —
"What makes that ship drive on so fast?
  "What is the Ocean doing?

370

380

390

400

410

SECOND VOICE

"Still as a Slave before his Lord,
   "The Ocean hath no blast: 420
"His great bright eye most silently
   "Up to the moon is cast —

"If he may know which way to go,
   "For she guides him smooth or grim.
"See, brother, see! how graciously
   "She looketh down on him.

FIRST VOICE

"But why drives on that ship so fast
   "Withouten wave or wind?

SECOND VOICE

"The air is cut away before,
   "And closes from behind.   430

"Fly, brother, fly! more high, more high,
   "Or we shall be belated:
"For slow and slow that ship will go,
   "When the Marinere's trance is abated."

I woke, and we were sailing on
   As in a gentle weather:
'Twas night, calm night, the moon was high;
   The dead men stood together.

All stood together on the deck,
   For a charnel-dungeon fitter: 440
All fix'd on me their stony eyes
   That in the moon did glitter.

The pang, the curse, with which they died,
   Had never pass'd away:
I could not draw my een from theirs
   Ne turn them up to pray.

And in its time the spell was snapt,
   And I could move my een:
I look'd far-forth, but little saw
   Of what might else be seen.   450

Like one, that on a lonely road
   Doth walk in fear and dread,
And having once turn'd round, walks on
   And turns no more his head:
Because he knows, a frightful fiend
   Doth close behind him tread.

But soon there breath'd a wind on me,
   Ne sound ne motion made:
Its path was not upon the sea
   In ripple or in shade.   460

It rais'd my hair, it fann'd my cheek,
   Like a meadow-gale of spring —
It mingled strangely with my fears,
   Yet it felt like a welcoming.

Swiftly, swiftly flew the ship,
   Yet she sail'd softly too:
Sweetly, sweetly blew the breeze —
   On me alone it blew.

O dream of joy! is this indeed
  The light-house top I see?
Is this the Hill? Is this the Kirk?
  Is this mine own countrée?

We drifted o'er the Harbour-bar,
  And I with sobs did pray —
"O let me be awake, my God!
"Or let me sleep alway!"

The harbour-bay was clear as glass,
  So smoothly it was strewn!
And on the bay the moon light lay,
  And the shadow of the moon.

The moonlight bay was white all o'er,
  Till rising from the same,
Pull many shapes, that shadows were,
  Like as of torches came.

A little distance from the prow
  Those dark-red shadows were;
But soon I saw that my own flesh
  Was red as in a glare.

I turn'd my head in fear and dread,
  And by the holy rood,
The bodies had advanc'd, and now
  Before the mast they stood.

They lifted up their stiffright arms,
  They held them strait and tight;
And each right-arm burnt like a torch,
  A torch that's borne upright.
Their stony eye-balls glitter'd on
  In the red and smoky light.

I pray'd and turn'd my head away
  Forth looking as before.
There was no breeze upon the bay,
  No wave against the shore.

The rock shone bright, the kirk no less
  That stands above the rock:
The moonlight steep'd in silentness
  The steady weathercock.

And the bay was white with silent light,
  Till rising from the same
Full many shapes, that shadows were,
  In crimson colours came.

A little distance from the prow
  Those crimson shadows were:
I turn'd my eyes upon the deck —
  O Christ! what saw I there?

Each corse lay flat, lifeless and flat;
  And by the Holy rood
A man all light, a seraph-man,
  On every corse there stood.

This seraph-band, each wav'd his hand:
  It was a heavenly sight:
They stood as signals to the land,
  Each one a lovely light:

This seraph-band, each wav'd his hand,
　No voice did they impart —
No voice; but O! the silence sank,
　Like music on my heart.

Eftsones I heard the dash of oars,
　I heard the pilot's cheer:
My head was turn'd perforce away
　And I saw a boat appear.　　　　　　　　　　　530

Then vanish'd all the lovely lights;
　The bodies rose anew:
With silent pace, each to his place,
　Came back the ghastly crew.
The wind, that shade nor motion made,
　On me alone it blew.

The pilot, and the pilot's boy
　I heard them coming fast:
Dear Lord in Heaven! it was a joy,
　The dead men could not blast.　　　　　　　　540

I saw a third — I heard his voice:
　It is the Hermit good!
He singeth loud his godly hymns
　That he makes in the wood.
He'll shrieve my soul, he'll wash away
　The Albatross's blood.

VII

This Hermit good lives in that wood
　Which slopes down to the Sea.
How loudly his sweet voice he rears!
He loves to talk with Marineres
　That come from a far Contrée.　　　　　　　　550

He kneels at morn and noon and eve —
　He hath a cushion plump:
It is the moss, that wholly hides
　The rotted old Oak-stump.

The Skiff-boat ne'rd: I heard them talk,
　"Why, this is strange, I trow!
"Where are those lights so many and fair
　"That signal made but now?

"Strange, by my faith ! the Hermit said —
　"And they answer'd not our cheer.　　　　　　560
"The planks look warp'd, and see those sails
　"How thin they are and sere!
"I never saw aught like to them
　"Unless perchance it were

"The skeletons of leaves that lag
　"My forest brook along:
"When the Ivy-tod is heavy with snow,
"And the Owlet whoops to the wolf below
　"That eats the she-wolf's young.　　　　　　　570

"Dear Lord! it has a fiendish look —
　(The Pilot made reply)
"I am a-fear'd. — 'Push on, push on!
　"Said the Hermit cheerily.

The Boat came closer to the Ship,
  But I ne spake ne stirr'd!
The Boat came close beneath the Ship,
  And strait a sound was heard!

Under the water it rumbled on,   580
  Still louder and more dread:
It reach'd the Ship, it split the bay;
  The Ship went down like lead.

Stunn'd by that loud and dreadful sound,
  Which sky and ocean smote:
Like one that hath been seven days drown'd
  My body lay afloat:
But, swift as dreams, myself I found
  Within the Pilot's boat.

Upon the whirl, where sank the Ship,   590
  The boat spun round and round:
And all was still, save that the hill
  Was telling of the sound.

I mov'd my lips: the Pilot shrieked
  And fell down in a fit.
The Holy Hermit rais'd his eyes
  And pray'd where he did sit.

I took the oars: the Pilot's boy,
  Who now doth crazy go,
Laugh'd loud and long, and all the while   600
  His eyes went to and fro,
"Ha! ha!" quoth he — "full plain I see,
  "The devil knows how to row."

And now all in mine own Countrée
  I stood on the firm land!
The Hermit stepp'd forth from the boat,
  And scarcely he could stand.

"O shrieve me, shrieve me, holy Man!
  The Hermit cross'd his brow —
"Say quick," quoth he, 'I bid thee say   610
  "What manner man art thou?

Forthwith this frame of mine was wrench'd
  With a woeful agony,
Which forc'd me to begin my tale
  And then it left me free.

Since then at an uncertain hour,
  Now oftimes and now fewer,
That anguish comes and makes me tell
  My ghastly aventure.

I pass, like night, from land to land;   620
  I have strange power of speech;
The moment that his face I see
  I know the man that must hear me;
  To him my tale I teach.

What loud uproar bursts from that door!
  The Wedding-guests are there;
But in the Garden-bower the Bride
  And Bride-maids singing are:
And hark the little Vesper-bell
  Which biddeth me to prayer.

O Wedding-guest! this soul hath been
  Alone on a wide wide sea:
So lonely 'twas, that God himself
  Scarce seemed there to be.   630

O sweeter than the Marriage-feast,
  'Tis sweeter far to me
To walk together to the Kirk
  With a goodly company.

To walk together to the Kirk
  And all together pray,
While each to his great father bends,
Old men, and babes, and loving friends,   640
  And Youths, and Maidens gay.

Farewell, farewell! but this I tell
  To thee, thou wedding-guest!
He prayeth well who loveth well
  Both man and bird and beast.

He prayeth best who loveth best,
  All things both great and small:
For the dear God, who loveth us,
  He made and loveth all.   650

The Marinere, whose eye is bright,
  Whose beard with age is hoar,
Is gone; and now the wedding-guest
  Turn'd from the bridegroom's door.

He went, like one that hath been stunn'd
  And is of sense forlorn:
A sadder and a wiser man
  He rose the morrow morn.

— Samuel Taylor Coleridge

Resolution and Independence

1

There was a roaring in the wind all night;
The rain came heavily and fell in floods;
But now the sun is rising calm and bright;
The birds are singing in the distant woods;
Over his own sweet voice the Stock-dove broods;
The Jay makes answer as the Magpie chatters;   5
And all the air is filled with pleasant noise of waters.

2

All things that love the sun are out of doors;
The sky rejoices in the morning's birth;
The grass is bright with rain-drops; — on the moors
The hare is running races in her mirth;   10
And with her feet she from the plashy earth
Raises a mist, that, glittering in the sun,
Runs with her all the way, wherever she doth run.

3

I was a Traveller then upon the moor;   15
I saw the hare that raced about with joy;
I heard the woods and distant waters roar;
Or heard them not, as happy as a boy:
The pleasant season did my heart employ:
My old remembrances went from me wholly;   20
And all the ways of men, so vain and melancholy.

4

But, as it sometimes chanceth, from the might
Of joy in minds that can no further go,
As high as we have mounted in delight
In our dejection do we sink as low;   25
To me that morning did it happen so;
And fears and fancies thick upon me came;
Dim sadness — and blind thoughts, I knew not, nor could name.

5

I heard the sky-lark warbling in the sky;
And I bethought me of the playful hare: 30
Even such a happy Child of earth am I;
Even as these blissful creatures do I fare;
Far from the world I walk, and from all care;
But there may come another day to me —
Solitude, pain of heart, distress, and poverty.   35

6

My whole life I have lived in pleasant thought,
As if life's business were a summer mood;
As if all needful things would come unsought
To genial faith, still rich in genial good;
But how can He expect that others should   40
Build for him, sow for him, and at his call
Love him, who for himself will take no heed at all?

7

I thought of Chatterton, the marvellous Boy,
The sleepless Soul that perished in his pride;
Of Him who walked in glory and in joy   45
Following his plough, along the mountain-side:
By our own spirits are we deified
We Poets in our youth begin in gladness;
But thereof come in the end despondency and madness.

8

Now, whether it were by peculiar grace,   50
A leading from above, a something given,
Yet it befel, that, in this lonely place,
When I with these untoward thoughts had striven,
Beside a pool bare to the eye of heaven
I saw a Man before me unawares: 55
The oldest man he seemed that ever wore grey hairs.

9

As a huge stone is sometimes seen to lie
Couched on the bald top of an eminence;
Wonder to all who do the same espy,
By what means it could thither come, and whence;   60
So that it seems a thing endued with sense:
Like a sea-beast crawled forth, that on a shelf
Of rock or sand reposeth, there to sun itself;

10

Such seemed this Man, not all alive nor dead,
Nor all asleep — in his extreme old age:
His body was bent double, feet and head   65
Coming together in life's pilgrimage;
As if some dire constraint of pain, or rage
Of sickness felt by him in times long past,
A more than human weight upon his frame had cast.   70

11

Himself he propped, limbs, body, and pale face,
Upon a long grey staff of shaven wood:
And, still as I drew near with gentle pace,
Upon the margin of that moorish flood
Motionless as a cloud the old Man stood,   75
That heareth not the loud winds when they call;
And moveth all together, if it move at all.

12

At length, himself unsettling, he the pond
Stirred with his staff, and fixedly did look
Upon the muddy water, which he conned,   80
As if he had been reading in a book:
And now a stranger's privilege I took;
And, drawing to his side to him did say
"This morning gives us promise of a glorious day."

13

A gentle answer did the old Man make,   85
In courteous speech which forth he slowly drew:
And him with further words I thus bespake,
"What occupation do you there pursue?
This is a lonesome place for one like you."
Ere he replied, a flash of mild surprise   90
Broke from the sable orbs of his yet-vivid eyes.

14

His words came feebly, from a feeble chest,
But each in solemn order followed each,
With something of a lofty utterance drest —
Choice word and measured phrase, above the reach   95
Of ordinary men; a stately speech;
Such as grave Livers do in Scotland use,
Religious men, who give to God and man their dues.

15

He told, that to these waters he had come
To gather leeches, being old and poor: 100
Employment hazardous and wearisome!
And he had many hardships to endure:
From pond to pond he roamed, from moor to moor;
Housing, with God's good help, by choice or chance;
And in this way he gained an honest maintenance.   105

16

The old Man still stood talking by my side;
But now his voice to me was like a stream
Scarce heard; nor word from word could I divide;
And the whole body of the Man did seem
Like one whom I had met with in a dream;   110
Or like a man from some far region sent,
To give me human strength, by apt admonishment.

17

My former thoughts returned: the fear that kills;
And hope that is unwilling to be fed;
Cold, pain, and labour, and all fleshly ills;   115
And mighty Poets in their misery dead.
— Perplexed, and longing to be comforted,
My question eagerly did I renew,
"How is it that you live, and what is it you do?"

18
                                                                      120
He with a smile did then his words repeat:
And said, that, gathering leeches, far and wide
He travelled; stirring thus about his feet
The waters of the pools where they abide.
"Once I could meet with them on every side;   125
But they have dwindled long by slow decay;
Yet still I persevere, and find them where I may."

19

While he was talking thus, the lonely place,
The old Man's shape, and speech — all troubled me:
In my mind's eye I seemed to see him pace   130
About the weary moors continually,
Wandering about alone and silently.
While I these thoughts within myself pursued,
He, having made a pause, the same discourse renewed.

20

And soon with this he other matter blended,
Cheerfully uttered, with demeanour kind,   135
But stately in the main; and when he ended,
I could have laughed myself to scorn to find
In that decrepit Man so firm a mind.
"God," said I, "be my help and stay secure;
I'll think of the Leech-gatherer on the lonely moor!"   140

— William Wordsworth

Generating Writing

1. With a reading assignment of this complexity, it is probably wise to assign essays that encourage the writer to focus on one manageable element, such as an image, giving the student writer a way in to some of the larger ideas of the essay without confusing him or her. You might assign an essay in which they focus on the image of the eye, or the rainbow, or geographical images. Or, you might ask them to focus on one word that surfaces repeatedly, one with a slippery meaning. For this purpose, the word *natural* would do nicely. What does Eiseley mean by "natural" in each instance? How does its meaning evolve in relation to the words with which it is compared and contrasted?

2. A slightly more complicated assignment would be to analyze Eiseley's treatment of humanity's identity and place in the larger scheme of the universe. Instruct your students to pay special attention to the syntactic ways in which Eiseley brings humankind down to the level of other creatures, animate and inanimate. Have them also attend to the ways in which he personifies animate and inanimate entities other than homo sapiens. What is the larger purpose behind these techniques?

K. C. Cole

Much Ado about Nothing

Teaching Strategies

Three quarters of the way through her essay, K. C. Cole indirectly undermines her entire project of writing "Much Ado about Nothing" when she quotes Weisskopf as saying "you shouldn't be trying to explain things that you don't understand. It's not explainable, because it's not understood." You might start by asking your students if they agree with Weisskopf, from their understanding of Cole's essay. She has taken on an admittedly difficult task, "writing about the vacuum, because no subject is quite as hard to deal with as nothing" (para. 2). Ask your students to name the strategies Cole uses in an effort to counterbalance that difficulty. Ask them to identify the benefits and analogies in each strategy.

They might notice, for example, her casual use of metaphor: "a churning sea of invisible vibrating fields that continually erupt with particles" (para. 1). If the fields are invisible, the "sea" is obviously a metaphor employed to make the invisible visible, at least to the imagination, as is the word *erupts*, which readers will associate with volcanos and thus be able to imagine as well. Surely no one would challenge her intention to make such an abstract, even paradoxical, concept come alive in the reader's imagination, especially a reader with little or no scientific background.

They may also notice the analogies in the essay; some of them she borrows from other scientists and others she creates herself, for this essay. The first extended analogy is to a fish in water. In what ways does this analogy seem apt? What are its limitations; that is, where does the analogy break down? One difference between fish and human beings is that fish *can* get out of water — they just die if they do so — whereas for us there is no vantage point outside the vacuum. Look, too, at the jelly analogy: Cole herself admits the discrepancies between the vehicle and the tenor when she quotes Wilczek as saying "these are very peculiar jellies. They can interpenetrate each other. Also, they look the same whether you're moving through them or not — that's certainly not true of ordinary jelly." Have your students go through the entire essay, examining each analogy to discover its uses and limitations.

Cole also uses what scientists call *Gedanken* or thought-experiments, such as the imaginary telescope proposed in paragraph 11. Ask your students how this image helps them to envision the vacuum. Do they understand why one can imagine "turning off" the neutrinos, cosmic rays, and microwave background, but not the Higgs field? In general, ask them to assess how much they learned about vacuums by reading this essay, and to identify which methods were most effective in producing that understanding.

Additional Activities

Cole shares some of Gould's problems, or at least mentions them: she quotes Wilczek on the distinction between a fertile theory and one that is "just talk" (para. 14); and she finds vacuums "worth talking about because they seem like good ways of solving long-standing problems" (para. 27). She, like Gould and Eiseley, sees that everything in the universe is connected. But although she mentions the potential danger of "tweaking our present vacuum" in order to see what happens when the Higgs field is turned off, she doesn't dwell on the very real possibility that physicists might destroy our world in an attempt to understand how that world was created. You might use Cole's essay, and the contrast provided by the other two essays in this chapter, to set off a discussion of the moral implications of scientific research.

You might also want to examine Cole's language in this essay. What is the effect on the reader of her wordplay and her often colloquial tone? Does it help to draw in an audience who might otherwise be intimidated by science, especially such an abstract branch of science? Where does her tone work against her? Can your students point to places in the text where she sacrifices rigor to maintain her tone, and ends up being unnecessarily vague or difficult to understand?

Generating Writing

If any science majors are in your class, assign them the task of writing an accessible essay on a scientific discovery for a lay audience. Let them choose the topic for themselves, but if they ask for help, you might suggest that they take on the task of explaining how modern field theory differs from the old ether theory before Einstein. Or ask them to clarify any other question that arose in your mind, or your nonscience-major students' minds, as you read Cole's essay. For this purpose, you might field suggestions from the class on essay topics they'd really like to see someone address comprehensibly.

WRITING ABOUT THE CHAPTER

1. Modern science has just recently acknowledged that a truth about novels and movies also applies to scientific theory: the point of view of the observing subject affects the object that is being observed; that is to say, no "reality" is completely uncontaminated by point of view. Assign an essay in which students analyze the effect of the writer on the essays in this chapter. Which of the writers try to play down their own existence, and which take it into account more directly? How does their handling of this issue affect the way in which their essay is read?

2. Have your students reread the drafts they wrote before reading the selections in this chapter. Each of the authors in this chapter includes numerous references to belletristic texts in his or her essay: both Eiseley and Gould quote poetry, for example, and Cole includes Shakespearian allusions. Assign an essay in which your students analyze these essays as sites of encounter between the two large segments of human knowledge.

3. Alternatively, your students might want to try their hand at curricular reform: have them write an essay, in the form of a proposal to the vice chancellor, outlining a plan by which the connections between humanities and sciences would be taught to undergraduates. Their plan could take the form of a core curriculum, a sequence of courses, pairings of courses in different departments, a detailed plan for one seminar, or any other form they can imagine.

37

Understanding Horror

Edgar Allan Poe, The Tell-Tale Heart

Harper's Magazine, In Pursuit of Pure Horror

WORKING WITH THE CHAPTER

Teaching Strategies

In a world where real-life terror and tragedy seem to occupy an ever larger share of our awareness, the popularity of horror entertainment is at an all-time high. Why are we fascinated with horror? What function does it serve in our society? Students can hardly fail to have an interest in horror, for most horror film and literature is primarily directed at young adults. Ask for their own definitions of horror. What contact have they had with the genre over the past week? The past month? The past year? Encourage them to challenge one another's definitions. See if class input can be refined into a consensus on the nature of horror.

The chapter is focused on Edgar Allan Poe, the first great American creator of horror. Ask the class how familiar they are with Poe's work. Many students may have read his short stories in high school. Others might have seen movies based on his work. You may want to give a synopsis of his life and career (which seem like one of his own plots). Discuss the Richard Wright epigraph. (Remind students that Wright was the author of *Native Son,* with which they may be familiar.)

What does Wright mean when he says that horror would have invented Poe? Does "horror" exist outside of cultural contexts? What cultural differences might there be in understanding and creating horror?

William James's view might be helpful here. Inform students that he was the father of American psychology (and the brother of "The Turn of the Screw" author as well). This quotation is from his great work of 1902, *The Varieties of Religious Experience.* What does horror have to do with religion? Does horror express our society's moral and metaphysical views? Is James's comment as true today as it was almost a century ago?

One way to segue from a discussion of these epigraphs to Stephen King's might be to bring up the idea of an American tradition of horror. What does the class think that might be? Most will probably be experts on King and his work. What characteristics do they feel his writing exemplifies? How is his view of horror's function similar to James's? How does it differ? Discuss with the class the possible motivations behind King's statement. How is it in his interest to stress the psychological usefulness of horror as a genre? You might want to introduce catharsis here. Do students agree that horror entertainment provides a socially acceptable outlet for fear and anxiety? Why do they go to horror movies or read the literature of horror? Why do they think others might?

Because the center of the chapter is "The Tell-Tale Heart," it might be wise to make certain students have read and understood the story before discussing the chapter as a whole. How do students feel the story fits in with King's definition of horror? With James's? Of what common psychological quirks is Poe's narrator a terrifying exaggeration? How does the narrator's exaggerated manifestation of universal anxieties help us face our own fears?

Once students fully comprehend "The Tell-Tale Heart," have them go on to the panel discussion, "In Pursuit of Pure Horror." Ask them how the panel's members seem to define horror and its social purposes. How do these definitions differ from King's and James's? From the class's? How are they similar? Do the panel members share Wright's view of Poe? Encourage some discussion of these issues. What might others — authors of the epigraphs, other authors or directors in the horror industry, or class members themselves — have contributed to this discussion? What might Poe himself have offered?

A Writing-before-Reading Exercise

Invite students to think about their own sense of horror. One way into the topic might be to read them the description of Room 101 in Orwell's *1984* (book 3, chapter 5). Ask them to write, for their own eyes only, a brief description of their own greatest fear or fears. When they have completed this exercise, ask them to turn this fear into the plot of a projected big-budget horror movie. Have them describe the production in one or two paragraphs, making it sound attractive and potentially successful. Ask the class to reflect on how the creative process transforms a personal fear into a shared experience of entertainment, and perhaps even education.

WORKING WITH THE SELECTIONS

Edgar Allan Poe

The Tell-Tale Heart

Teaching Strategies

Encourage students to read "The Tell-Tale Heart" closely. You may want to read it aloud in class, or have people take turns with it; presenting the story in this way may focus the class's attention on the narrator and his voice. Ask them to characterize the narrator briefly. How does the class diagnose his problem? Does he remind them of types and characters from today's horror fiction (or even fact)?

Some students may have trouble with Poe's style or language. Ask them to list passages they find unclear, and discuss them in class. What do students think of Poe's style? How does his tone affect them?

Why, in their opinion, does the narrator kill the old man? What might their relationship have been? How does the narrator identify himself with his victim? For example, the narrator says he recognizes his victim's "groan of terror" because "it has welled up from my own bosom." Ask students to find the passages in which the narrator and the old man seem almost to be doubles. The double is one of the most frequent themes in the American tradition of horror, from Hawthorne to *Invasion of the Body Snatchers*. Why? How is the double frightening? What common anxieties might it symbolize?

Why is disposal of the old man's corpse so briefly and uninformatively described? How might a treatment of this theme written today differ? Ask students if they find the narrator's matter-of-fact tone here more disturbing than grisly details might be. How is the speaker's distance from his crime alarming?

Discuss the narrator's perception of his encounter with the police. How does Poe undermine the speaker's credibility? What story about the questioning and arrest can we reconstruct by reading between the lines? How is the first-person point of view necessary to the story's effect? Ask students to imagine what a third-person omniscient retelling of the story might be like. How would the story be changed if it were told by the old man (until his murder) and then by the detectives? Why might Poe have chosen to tell this story from the murderer's perspective?

You might want to connect this story with the class's work on Chapter 8, "Bridging Distances." How does Poe's story dramatize the danger of interpersonal alienation? Discuss the narrator's splitting the old man from his eye. Why does he justify his crime by stating that he really loved the old man — it was only the eye he hated? Can this be seen as a metaphor for social prejudice, fear, and hate?

Additional Activities

You might wish to view the film version of this story if it is available, and discuss with the class how the adaptation was done. How do Poe's effects depend on genre?

Assign students to read other stories by Poe and give the class brief oral reports. What themes does he share with today's writers of horror? How does his work, as a whole, differ?

Generating Writing

1. Who is the "you" the speaker is addressing? Ask students to identify this individual, giving reasons for their opinion. Then invite them to imagine they are the addressee. Have them write a short report on their "interview" with Poe's narrator. They may want to discuss their opinion of his sanity, the enormity of his crime, his appearance and self-presentation, or other aspects of his deeds and character.

2. How does Poe use images of light and vision in the story? What do these images suggest? How do they complement the images of sound? What other patterns of imagery appear, and how do these advance the narrative?

Harper's Magazine

In Pursuit of Pure Horror

Teaching Strategies

Students may not be familiar with *Harper's* magazine or its regular panel-discussion features. Each month, the magazine presents a forum for opinion on one issue; the participants are journalists and others with a professional or personal interest in the topic. Ask the class what they think the strengths of this format might be. What drawbacks could it have?

Discuss the panel members with the class. Which points of view are represented? Which might not be? Do students know the work of any participants? Many may have seen *Psycho*, and Gahan Wilson's cartoons appear in a number of magazines, including *The New Yorker* and *The National Lampoon*. You might want to assign interested students to briefly research participants' work and give short reports to the class.

Why did *Harper's* precede this piece with the headnote about the murderer Albert Fish? Ask students to come up with some reasons. What kind of media coverage do murders receive? What is the public attitude toward murderers? Does the intensity of coverage vary with the circumstances of the murder? With the social roles and positions of murderer and victim? Why are we so fascinated by real-life murders and murderers?

What do students think about the way in which the discussion is structured? Why, in their opinion, did *Harper's* choose "The Tell-Tale Heart" to be the center of this debate? Would they have made the same selection? Talk about the idea of rewriting a classic story for today's audience. What kinds of changes do the panel members make automatically? What things do they take for granted about the public's interest and taste?

During the debate, Robert Bloch says, "There is no question at this table that this story should be done for the big screen." Discuss the panel's tendency to approach the "Tell-Tale Heart" project as a movie script, rather than as a novel or short story. Why did they make this decision? What reasons might they give for it when questioned? Ask the class how genre can influence presentation. What kinds of things can literature do that film cannot? What can film do better than literature? You might want to talk about current movies or television miniseries made from adaptations of books. How do stories make the transition between media? Have the class list the qualities that make a good horror film, and qualities that make good horror writing. How do the lists differ? How are they the same?

Which themes does the panel select as important? Do students agree or disagree with these choices? Ask them to talk about how the panel's interpretations seem to differ from their own. What agendas do panel members seem to have? Are they always focused on Poe's work and the development of his character, or do they seem to have their own visions of the story and its protagonist? Whose contributions, in students' opinion, stay closest to the spirit of Poe's work?

Gahan Wilson refers to random violence as "a modern, Eighties monster." Do specific times have specific monsters? You might want to discuss some trends in horror movies, such as the conjunction of the McCarthy era and the tremendous growth of the "alien" theme, or the convention of postapocalypse scenarios. One interesting example is *Mad Max* (1979; directed by George Miller), whose vision of a lawless world in which ruthless criminals kill for scarce gasoline is a perfect mirror of late-1970s social and environmental anxieties. What might the monsters of the 1990s be?

The panel devotes much time to discussing the serial killer Ted Bundy and his crimes. Refresh students' memories of the case; an interesting account is in *The Stranger Beside Me* by Ann Rule (1987). Which of our society's fears and worries do serial killers represent? Why are we fascinated by them? Why does it seem such an American phenomenon?

Ask students to evaluate the panel's proposal for *The Tell-Tale Heart, II*. Does it seem like a movie they would want to see (or a story they would want to read?) What would they add to or subtract from the panel's ideas? Try to re-create the atmosphere of the discussion in class, inviting students to try out their own ideas while you act as moderator. Write class input on the board, and try to agree on a scenario. You might then want to take the role of a studio executive and ask the class to sell you the project. Encourage them to defend it as worthwhile and potentially successful entertainment. What do they see as its strongest selling points? Which, in their opinion, are its weakest features?

Additional Activities

Ask students to use the group-discussion approach to develop an original horror scenario. (The Writing-before-Reading exercise might be revisited here.) Have them assume unlimited budget and casting and staffing opportunities, and state-of-the-art special effects. What things must be taken for granted? What kinds of compromises must be made? You might want to spend an entire class period on this project, make notes on class input, and distribute a summary of the discussion. Have the class critique its own project. How do its approach and creations reflect the group's terrors and anxieties? How do they reflect society at large? How might the group's project differ from an individual's approach?

Generating Writing

1. Invite students to imagine that a copy of *Harper's* carrying this discussion has fallen through a time warp into Poe's day. Ask them to draft a letter from Poe responding to the panel's interpretations and ideas.

2. Ask the class to write a review of *The Tell-Tale Heart, II.* How interesting, ultimately, is the story invented by the *Harper's* panel? Instruct them to approach the assignment as though they were writing for a fairly challenging publication; they should include a discussion of the work's relationship to Poe, as well as an attempt to situate it in current social thought and conditions.

WRITING ABOUT THE CHAPTER

1. Have students write a short essay on what horror means to them. Have these readings and discussions changed their views of horror? In what way or ways? They should refer to their Writing-before-Reading exercise, and discuss how they might now revise their presentation. Ask them to explicitly engage the Stephen King epigraph. Has their work on the chapter made his assertions about horror seem more or less convincing?

2. Ask students to compare and contrast Poe's narrative with the panel's, focusing on the psychology of horror. Have them use the William James epigraph as the core of their inquiry. How do Poe's approach and the panel's differ? How are they the same? How do they transform the experience of fear and revulsion into imaginative creation? How might the differences between Poe's work and the panel's reflect social changes over the past century? How much might they reflect participants' individuality? In their opinion, how much of the literature of horror is a personal statement? A social statement?

3. Some students may be interested in a research project on Poe. Ask them to read several of his works and offer an interpretation of his style and approach. Are the panel's comments on "The Tell-Tale Heart" equally applicable to Poe's other writing? How does the panel oversimplify or misrepresent Poe? What might be their motivation? The class might also view various film adaptations of Poe's work (*The Pit and the Pendulum*, with Vincent Price [1961; directed by Roger Corman] is perhaps the best) and discuss how the demands of film force changes in the literature on which it is based.

38

Origins

WORKING WITH THE CHAPTER

Myth making is perhaps the most essential of all creative activities. Myths help shape the structure of our perceptions; the modern world's philosophies continue to map themselves according to the patterns these primal narratives describe. Our sciences, too, draw on the language of myth for illustration. Religious and cultural traditions take strength from myth, and writers, painters, composers, and sculptors translate myth into art.

Teaching Strategies

Ask students how feel myth has affected their lives. Do myths shape their own experience at times? You may want to talk about myths of development or of heroism; do they see these kinds of stories as helping to explain the conflicts and challenges they face?

Creation myths are especially revealing; they reveal the fundamental assumptions of the culture that produces them, and also provide an arena for a society's self-definition. The creation myth can often seem a microcosm of a people's thought. The chapter supplies creation myths from three widely differing cultures, and the epigraphs give perspectives on the idea and experience of creation myths.

Before starting work on the chapter, you may want to brainstorm a class definition of *mythology*. You might assign students to look the word up in different dictionaries and encyclopedias, or ask them to think about the word and its meaning in their own lives. Write their contributions on the board, and encourage them to challenge and defend their ideas.

The best way into the chapter might be with a class discussion of the Graves and Sproul epigraphs. Have students read the passage from Graves carefully. Discuss his opening sentence with the class. How accurate do they find this representation? Remind students that Graves was writing in, and for, an England of several decades ago, when relatively few religious viewpoints were represented. (They may not be aware, for instance, that England has an official state religion.) How might his statement not apply to today's United States? Many religious groups in this country hold beliefs contradictory to those of other groups; would we classify some of those beliefs and not others as mythologies? How would we go about classifying them? Graves goes on to discuss the omission of Western religious ideas from the category of "mythology"; does that distinction apply for us today? Why, or why not? (You may need to tell students that "hagiologies" means "saints' lives.")

Sproul's epigraph seems more rooted in contemporary life. How does her view differ from Graves's? Ask students how accurate they find her assessment that this is "a time when old myths are being rejected and faith is under attack." Are our old myths being rejected? What new myths are being made to replace them? Discuss Sproul's opening sentence with the class. What do they make of the phrase "the absolute dimension of the relative world"? Dissect this idea with the class. How hospitable do students find Sproul's rejection of "the worldly"? How is this attitude consonant or disjunctive with their own religious training and experience? Do they feel that the struggle for transcendence is the central idea that all religions share? How would students paraphrase Sproul's statement that myths "show how life is a symbol to be lived"?

The Isaac Bashevis Singer epigraph makes personal the issue of creation mythologies. You may want to give students some background on Singer and his work; you should certainly remind them that Singer is an author in whose work religious ideas, both of questing and of faith, are a leading impetus. Ask students if this incident reminds them of experiences in their own life. Do they receive religious instruction or advice from parents or grandparents? Can generations ever clash over the issue of faith? How might the class respond to Singer's father's argument? Which is more convincing, the argument itself, or Singer senior's faith in it?

The excerpt from Genesis might well be taught in conjunction with the Graves and Sproul epigraphs. Would Graves see this story as mythology? Would Sproul? How might these passages from Genesis support Sproul's contention that myths present life as "a symbol to be lived"? What moral and ethical principles have Judaism and Christianity drawn from Genesis? How does the narrative shape the lives of individual Christians and Jews?

Students should be encouraged to examine the Bering Strait Eskimo myth together with Genesis. (This discussion may require a bit of delicate handling, to avoid offending those who may hold fundamentalist Christian or Jewish beliefs.) How are these creation narratives similar? How do they differ? What goals do they seem to share? Ask the class if Sproul's characterization of myth applies to each selection equally. How do they fulfill Graves's criteria for myth?

Ask the class to compare and contrast the selection from Plato's *Symposium* with Genesis and the Eskimo myth. How does Plato's agenda differ from those of the others? What social conditions might this creation myth reflect? How does the existence of this kind of creation story lead us to reevaluate some features of others?

A Writing-before-Reading Exercise

Have students briefly outline their own conception of life's origins. How does this idea influence their view of the world and of others? If their creation stories were to change, how might that affect their feelings and actions?

WORKING WITH THE SELECTIONS

Plato

From Symposium

Teaching Strategies

You may need to give students some background for this selection. Several recent editions of the *Symposium* (our selection comes from *The Works of Plato,* selected and edited by Irwin Edman. Modern Library Edition, © 1928, Benjamin Jowett translation) include informative prefaces and notes. The shortest way into the selection might be simply to tell students that it is part of a long philosophical dialogue on the nature of love. The class may be unfamiliar with the tradition of philosophical dialogue; one helpful way of describing it is that the characters in a dialogue, like those in a work of fiction, can express varied viewpoints on the issue without forcing the author into taking one specific position or having to contradict himself. Ask the class how close they feel this tradition is to modern philosophy. Does it survive more fully in fiction and the arts? Do they see any connection between the tradition of dialogue and our love of political and philosophical debate?

Remind students that when Plato mentions "Love" he means both an abstract concept and its personification, the god Eros or Cupid. How might that reading shape Plato's (or Aristophanes' idea of love? The class may want to discuss Greek mythology and its roots in personification more generally; how do all mythic and religious traditions transform abstractions into characters in their narratives?

Ask the class to read closely Aristophanes' support for his claim that the sexes were originally three. What do they make of the justification for the number: "because the sun, moon, and earth are three"? Do we think of these three as in opposition? How might we divide them? Aristophanes goes on to say that "the man was originally the child of the sun, the woman of the earth, and the man-woman of the moon, which is made up of sun and earth." Do these divisions seem natural to us? What might be the motivation for them?

The real-life Aristophanes was a playwright known for his cynical satire; some of his plays parodied religious beliefs of his time (*The Frogs* includes a comic depiction of the afterlife and the journey through the underworld). How might Aristophanes' reputation influence his contemporaries' reactions to statements made by a character of the same name? How seriously might the reader of Plato's time be disposed to take the statements made here about religion?

Does the first half of Aristophanes' creation story seem sympathetic to the class? Ask what poetic truth they find in the description of love as the yearnings of halves for a whole. How is that mythology reflected in our popular culture? People often refer to their spouses as "my better half," for instance. Is the image of division and union powerful for us today?

What reaction do students have to the second idea Aristophanes raises, that men who love men are the most truly masculine? You may want to get to this discussion by asking students how Aristophanes dismisses heterosexuals and lesbians so quickly. What does the focus suddenly become? Why does Aristophanes switch the discussion from human love to masculine love? Does this move in the argument surprise them? How does this attitude demonstrate the cultural difference between our society and ancient Athens? What social needs might be served by this rationale for a homosexual life-style?

How are we to take Aristophanes' statement that the reason for our division into half-beings was "the wickedness of mankind?" How does this notion echo the structure of other creation myths? Discuss his warning that humanity must respect the gods or it is in danger of being split again. What is this caution meant to achieve? What kind of actions is Aristophanes encouraging? He states that "he is the enemy of the gods who opposes [Love]." Might Aristophanes' creation fable be seen as a justification for particular behaviors? What larger meanings might it have? What changes in attitude does Aristophanes seem to want his narrative to inspire?

Additional Activities

Oral reports might be assigned with this selection; students could research other Greek creation myths and present them briefly to the class. How does Plato's myth differ from others in the Greek tradition? How are they similar? What aspects of the Greek view of life's origin inform our outlook today?

You may want to look at this selection together with Chapter 9, "Affirmations of Love." How might Weinberg, Leavitt, and Allison react to Plato's fable? What identities could it help shape or support? What might feminists' reactions be? bell hooks's essay "Feminism: A Transformational Politic" (Chapter 18), might be an interesting counterpoise to Plato's male-centered mythology. What might hooks see as the motivation underlying the *Symposium's* myth making?

Generating Writing

1. Ask students to write their own fables about the origin of the genders. Have them read their own work critically; what attitudes do their myths reveal? What view of the relationship between the sexes does their story express? Now ask them to imagine their work as part of the *Symposium,* where characters are constantly critiquing one another's position. What kind of critique might Aristophanes offer in response to their myth?

2. Have the class list the assumptions in Aristophanes' argument. (Among the foremost are polytheism, the sun, earth, and moon as a triad of primary entities, and the notion that human suffering is the product of human wickedness.) How many of these assumptions does contemporary American society share? How many does it reject? How might these parallels affect our evaluation of this creation narrative?

How are we to approach the narrative symbolically? For what might this story be a metaphor? Again, how does the difference between our society's assumptions and those of ancient Athens affect our interpretation of this myth?

Genesis

Chapters One, Two, and Three

Teaching Strategies

Most students, regardless of their religious background, will be at least slightly familiar with the Genesis story. Discuss in class the meaning of the word *genesis.* How does the title's abstraction show our culture's assumptions about the universality of this myth? Remind students that the word *bible* is taken from the Greek and Latin for *book.* What does that tell us about our society's history of religious tolerance?

The class might benefit from being encouraged to focus on the cultural circumstances surrounding the writing of the Genesis narrative. Talk about the nomadic ways of ancient Hebrew society; other desert cultures such as the Berbers still survive in much the same way as we assume the author or authors of Genesis did — herding sheep and goats, migrating seasonally to provide the best food supply for people and animals. How might these circumstances shape a society's view and presentation of the origins of life?

Ask students to discuss the differences between the Genesis view of the earth and our own. For example, the narrative presents the earth and the sky as equally tangible and equal in importance if not in size. What disparities in society and situation might this conception reflect? How are heavenly bodies arranged? Genesis says that God "made two great lights" — the sun and the moon — and that "he made the stars also." What relative importance do today's creation narratives assign to sun, moon, and stars? Why might an earlier astronomical focus differ so greatly from ours?

Why are birds and fish created on the fourth day, but land animals on the fifth? Does our society preserve a distinction between animals that travel in water and on air, and those which live on land? What might be gained by making this distinction?

The passages in Chapter One that have most deeply influenced the world are those relating to the creation of human beings. Discuss 1:27, "So God created man in his own image." How can this verse be seen as a key to the Judeo-Christian tradition? What place in creation does it assign to humanity? God makes humankind's role plain in 1:28, where he tells man to "have dominion over the fish of the sea, and over the fowl of the air, and over every living thing that moveth upon the earth." Does our society still enshrine this principle? How might this aspect of the West's religious heritage engender cultural differences from societies like India's, where both persons and animals are seen as souls trapped on a wheel of reincarnation? How has this view of our origins and purpose influenced our relationship with the world around us?

Chapter Two gives more specific details about the creation. What benefits might be gained by placing the myth in a familiar geographical context? (The four rivers named are all near to or within ancient Israel.) Genesis describes Adam's function in naming the animals; how are human skills seen as complementing God's? What does the myth seem to say about the origin and uses of language? Finally, Chapter Two describes the creation of the genders; what assumptions does the description of women as formed from the bodies of men reveal? If Adam is to name her, too, then how is she equated with the animals? This seems like a point that will inspire passionate discussion; you might want to invite students to debate whether Genesis 2:21–25 holds the roots of Western sexism. How can religious ideas inspire actions and attitudes that seem to contradict their basic principles?

Chapter Three gives us the story of the Fall, an event of great mythic as well as theological importance. The story of man's first disobedience is a powerful one, and Westerners of all religious outlooks are quick to use it as a structure for narrating and ordering experience. Shakespeare's Henry V compares his friends' treason to the Fall; Milton's Paradise Lost is one of the primary documents in English literature, inspiring imitations, allusions, and parodies even today. What principles does this story illustrate? Discuss the outcome of human disobedience. What was Adam and Eve's life like before tasting the fruit? Which of the sorrows and inconveniences of our lives are depicted here as resulting from their action? What purposes might be achieved by describing human shame, fear, pain, and labor as the consequences of a challenge to divine authority? What might be gained by attributing our own mortality to this original defiance?

Another aspect of this story that has profoundly influenced both religious and secular thought in the West is naming the serpent an evil tempter. What other Judeo-Christian ideas does this story foreshadow? Our society's moral and metaphysical view is still shaped today by the Genesis view of evil as a force lurking even in ideal surroundings, waiting to lure us to bad or unwise actions. Ask the class how powerful this idea of evil is in their own life. How do they see it reflected in our culture?

The final image of Adam and Eve shut out from the garden by a flaming sword is a powerful one. Throughout history, Western artists and thinkers have depicted humanity as in perpetual exile from an idyllic original peace. Is this image alive today? How has it formed on our religions and cultures?

Additional Activities

Students might be encouraged to research various translations and interpretations of Genesis throughout Western history. How do individual Jewish and Christian sects interpret the story differently? Do their idiosyncratic beliefs and circumstances affect their approach to the narrative? One group project that might be fun would be a class viewing of the film *The Bible* (1966; directed by John Huston), if it is available. How is the story affected by being dramatized?

This selection could be approached together with Chapter 12, "Family Stories." Is Genesis the West's leading story of the human family? How has the narrative shaped our interactions and view of each other? To which family tensions might it contribute? Which might it lessen?

Generating Writing

1. Have students write a short essay on their own experience with the Genesis narrative. They might wish to express individual religious beliefs, or give examples of the story used as a metaphor in popular culture. What are their feelings about Genesis? How close is it to their own views about the origins of human life? Do they find it to be either literally or symbolically true?

2. Ask students to return to Graves's definition of myth's two main functions. How does Genesis serve the first function — to answer big, "awkward" questions about the nature and meaning of life? How does it fulfill its second goal — to justify social structures and rituals? Does Genesis provide support or challenge to Graves's explanation of myth?

Bering Strait Eskimo Creation Myth

The Time When There Were No People on the Earth Plain

Teaching Strategies

Students may want more information on the Bering Sea Eskimos; the *Handbook of North American Indians* (United States Government Publications Office, 1983) is a good place to start, as are Smithsonian Institution publications. You might ask colleagues in anthropology to recommend a short film introduction to Eskimo culture; Robert Flaherty's classic *Nanook of the North* (1926) is often available on film and video. How familiar are students with Native Americans of the North? Their contribution to our culture is often overlooked.

Discuss the opening sentence of the Bering Strait myth: "It was in the time when there were no people on the earth plain." What shared cultural assumptions does this opening take for granted? Would not a people living near the Arctic be expected to view the first landscape as a plain, rather than as a garden? Ask the class what philosophies of life might be reflected in the description of humanity as arising from the plant world? How is this idea alien to Western traditions?

Why might the myth depict the first man's first experience as one of thirst and drinking? For what aspects of our nature might this depiction be a shorthand? His second experience is an encounter with the supernatural order, in the person of Raven. Raven is a powerful spirit that chooses to take the form of a bird when on earth; what relationship between humanity and the animal world might this image indicate? How might the depiction of man's creator in the form of a bird reinforce the Bering Strait culture's ideas about man's duty to nature? Raven's encounter with man prompts him to change into his own, more closely human form; he is surprised that "this strange new being was so much like himself in shape." How might a world view wherein the Creator can, and does, shift his shape from a bird's to a man's differ from our own? How might we view our own physical incarnation differently?

Raven's first act is to settle man in a place he feels might be more advantageous. He proceeds to feed man, and to supply him with other animals that are to be useful to him.

How do the Bering Strait Eskimos draw on their everyday experience in creating this part of the myth? For what factors in their lives does the myth offer an explanation?

The creation of woman is another of Raven's services to man. How do students react to this depiction of women's role in the universe? Remind them that a number of other cultures' creation myths show women as the first human creatures, and men as created by or for them. How might a society with that primary narrative differ from that of the Bering Strait Eskimos, or from our own?

The life of the first human beings on the earth plain is seen as idyllic; Raven seems devoted to their every need and wish, and the natural world around them is drawn as perfect and welcoming. Discuss how this image of original life might be related to the Eskimo's everyday reality. Why do most creation myths seem to share the theme of a golden age in the world's first days? Is the natural tranquility that surrounds the first human beings a metaphor for an ideal of human interaction with the environment?

How might students characterize Raven's role in the creation myth? How does it differ from that of other mythic creators? A great deal of his function seems to be teaching; what kind of social models might the narrative inspire and reinforce? How does the class react to his almost playful rationale for the "shrew-mouse," which is not for food but for decoration? In other myths of northern Native Americans, Raven is presented as a spirit with a love of mischief. Does he evince that aspect of his personality here?

Additional Activities

A good research assignment might be to have students examine other Native-American creation stories. One excellent presentation of a culture's view of the world and its origins is Frank Waters's *The Book of the Hopi* (Penguin, 1977). How do a people's geographical circumstances shape its creation myths? How do their narratives justify their social and religious traditions?

This selection should be looked at together with N. Scott Momaday's "A First American Views His Land," in Chapter 28, "Visions of the Land," as well as that chapter's Chief Joseph epigraph. How do the Bering Strait Eskimos differ from the North American Indians described by Momaday in their view of humanity's place in the natural world?

Generating Writing

1. Ask students to extrapolate from the Bering Strait Eskimos' creation myth a list of some of their social goals and priorities. How do their ways of structuring experience seem to differ from our own? What features of the natural world do they display that we might overlook or ignore?

2. Have students write a brief creation myth explaining the existence and habits of animals in their own lives, just as the Bering Strait Eskimos explain reindeer, sticklebacks, and the "shrew-mouse." How might the animals important to them be described? How is the genesis of the natural world an essential element in a myth about the origins of human life?

WRITING ABOUT THE CHAPTER

A traditional comparison-and-contrast essay could profitably be assigned in this chapter; it would give students an opportunity to work in a standard essay form and could also encourage the class to examine the universal features of the creation myth, as well as its cultural specifics. Ask them to think about such issues as who the creators were and their relationship to humanity; the role of humanity in nature; the ordering and presentation of life forms; and the moral and ethical injunctions stated or implied in the creation narratives.

Ask students to return to the chapter epigraphs. Which of the myths presented here is the closest to embodying Graves's ideas about myth? Which is the closest to Sproul's? Which do they feel most closely corresponds to their own definitions?

How has their work on this chapter changed students' perception of myth and creation narrative? How have the selections challenged, if at all, their own views on the origins of life? How might they defend their own creation narratives against challenges from Plato, the author of Genesis, or the Bering Strait Eskimos?

The Search for Truth

Francis Bacon, Idols of the Mind

René Descartes, Stripping the Mind of Its Beliefs

Shunryu Suzuki, Emptiness

WORKING WITH THE CHAPTER

How can we attain truth and enlightenment? One way recommended by philosophers from Francis Bacon to Ludwig Wittgenstein is to clear the mind of common errors and received opinions. In a classic statement, Bacon called these errors and opinions "idols of the mind." For Bacon, unthinking worship of these "idols" led to superstitious beliefs and fictitious views of both human beings and the natural world. Only if we submit the mind, he wrote, to "its purgation and dismiss its idols" can we find "access to truth."

Around the same time that Bacon was describing the mind's idols, a twenty-three-year-old Frenchman had a dream (it was on November 10, 1619), which transformed the history of philosophy. Descartes thought his dream had come from God; in it, he saw that it was possible to combine mathematics and logic and thus reach a level of certainty previously unknown. In his famous *Discourse on Method* (1637) Descartes uses a narrative-memoir form to describe his mental development. For many people formal schooling is the beginning and end of their education; but for Descartes — who realized when he finished school that he knew nothing — it was only the beginning. Searching for a bedrock of indubitable truth, Descartes devised a daring philosophical plan, with which Francis Bacon would have agreed: "I could not do better than to undertake to rid myself, at least once in my life, of all the opinions I have hitherto accepted on faith."

With their scientific and experimental orientation, Bacon and Descartes form the origins of modern Western philosophy. But stripping the mind of its preconceived ideas has long been a tradition in Eastern philosophy and religion. In his talks on meditation, the Zen master Shunryu Suzuki also recommends a version of mental purgation. "When you study Buddhism," he says, "you should have a general house cleaning of your mind."

Teaching Strategies

Though intellectually challenging, the selections in this chapter should appeal to students and could offer them valuable philosophical insights. Your students may instinctively believe that philosophy is something arcane and remote (an example of a "preconceived idea"), and something that one learns by laborious acquisition of knowledge. The selections, therefore, may surprise them. The point they share is that philosophy is as much a method for getting rid of knowledge as for obtaining it. Much of our knowledge, these philosophers explain, is based on error or opinion or both. How much of what we think we know, have we actually tested for ourselves? How many of our indisputable truths are really dogmatic assertions? These are questions that students will need to ask throughout their education.

The three short epigraphs — two by famous philosophers and one by a famed philosophical comedian — introduce students to the intellectual contours of the chapter. The opening passage from Pascal's *Pensées* confronts the idea of skepticism: for diehard skeptics the search for truth is absurd because truth is not possible to attain. (The biggest difficulty with that position, of course, is that in claiming we can't know the truth, the skeptic presumes to know the truth; in other words, what gives the skeptic the basis for knowing that we can't know? The true skeptic would need to be skeptical of skepticism. As students will see, none of the thinkers in this chapter is a total skeptic.) Pascal's view is directly opposed to that of Descartes; Pascal believed that the bedrock of truth, the "first principles," eluded reason and could be known only by the "heart," or what we might call intuition. Reason by itself is powerless to prove or demonstrate these principles. Descartes, on the other hand, sets out to show that reason is the only sure way in which these first principles can be known. You might use this epigraph also to compare the skeptic's view of dreams to the way in which Descartes regards dreams at the conclusion of the selection from *The Discourse on Method*.

Have students consider the epigraph by the German philosopher, Friedrich Nietzsche: "Convictions are more dangerous enemies of truth than lies." The quotation is at the heart of this chapter. Students should be able to discuss Nietzsche's meaning in some depth, examining the danger of convictions and whether the observation is really accurate (what if our conviction is true?). Lies, of course, can be exposed and often seen for what they are; whereas those who hold convictions may not be willing to see them exposed. Nietzsche's comment is closely related to Bacon's *Idols*, especially those ideas "which have immigrated into men's minds from the various dogmas of philosophies. . . ."

Woody Allen is no professional philosopher, but he knows how strange philosophy sometimes sounds. In the passage from his collection *Getting Even*, he parodies philosophical reasoning and terminology with expressions and logical connectives ("Finally," "That is not to say," "Therefore," "So, then," "thus," and so on) to assemble meaningless sentences that simulate the philosophical style of argument. In the characteristic style of stand-up comedy, Allen also follows each seemingly serious statement with an undercutting remark. Because students may think this passage is funny but not be sure why, you might want to discuss a few of his comic techniques. But the main point of the epigraph is its burlesque of philosophical language. It should alert students to be dubious about important-sounding abstractions.

A Writing-before-Reading Exercise

To get students writing about this topic right away, invite them to draft an essay in which they discuss the Nietzsche quotation on convictions. They should examine the quotation from a variety of angles, asking themselves what it means, whether convictions are indeed a greater enemy to truth than lies, and whether convictions might instead be an important part of our intellectual life. Along the way, they might want to say what they believe is the most dangerous conviction that stands in the way of truth today.

WORKING WITH THE SELECTIONS

Francis Bacon

Idols of the Mind

Teaching Strategies

This well-known selection by the first English essayist, Francis Bacon, was originally written in Latin in the form of 130 "Aphorisms Concerning the Interpretation of Nature and the Kingdom of Man." The twenty-three aphorisms reprinted here as "Idols of the Mind" are aphorisms 39–61 in the standard text. Caution students that this is an excerpt from a longer work, which explains some references in the final aphorisms.

You might start by asking what *idols* are; some will know that the meaning is false gods. Bacon's purpose in these aphorisms, of course, is to alert his readers to tendencies of the mind that lead naturally to erroneous mental images or conceptions. Bacon believes that all of us are susceptible to distorted ideas, and he describes four categories of weakness, which he defines with special names: the idols of the tribe, the cave, the market-place, and the theatre. These labels, however, are metaphorical; invite class discussion by asking students to describe each "idol" in their own words. This examination will take time; Bacon's categories seem to overlap and some of his terminology is dated. Still, with some work, students should begin to get his point about the various ways in which we distort facts and deceive ourselves. For Bacon, distortion and deceit are built directly into our minds, perceptions, and temperaments (you might say we're wired for error) and therefore the way to truth is constant awareness of our intellectual vulnerability.

As you examine the idols one by one, see if the class can discover ways in which Bacon's warnings apply to contemporary forms of deceit or propaganda. They might see that aphorism 8 applies to superstitions marketed in astrology columns or in sensationalist stories headlined in weekly tabloids like the *National Enquirer*. They might see, too, that aphorism 9 applies directly to many advertising strategies meant to construct memorable associations in the consumer's mind. It could be both challenging and fun to match Bacon's aphorisms with as many types of contemporary propaganda as students can think of. This classroom exercise demonstrates the general applicability of Bacon's thinking (it could also be a writing assignment; see below).

Because they're about language, Bacon's aphorisms 21 and 22 may stimulate productive discussion that will tie in with other issues. Bacon warns us that this idol is the "most troublesome of all." Look closely here so that everyone understands his warnings about how the names of things can hinder our understanding. Unfortunately, Bacon's example in aphorism 23 no longer illustrates his point, for most of his meanings for *humid* are now obsolete. But have the class consider a current word that cannot be "reduced to any constant meaning."

Remind students about Nietzsche's comment on the danger of convictions. Bacon, too, concentrates on the mind's way of attaching itself to some ideas, especially those we seem to be in natural agreement with. In aphorism 20, he introduces a rule summarizing his attitude toward pet ideas: "And generally let every student of nature take this as a rule — that whatever his mind seizes and dwells upon with peculiar satisfaction is to be held in suspicion. . . ." Students should consider this comment carefully. Bacon does not simply mean that we ought to be skeptical of received opinions but that we should be skeptical even of ideas we have developed on our own and feel sure of. To follow Bacon's rule would mean to live with constant resistance to our own beliefs. Do students think such mental effort is achievable, and have they ever encountered anyone who thought as Bacon recommends? Certainly, they have been exposed to enough instructors to see that entrenched ideas, inflexible viewpoints, and unreflecting adherence to causes or ideologies are all around. But have they ever seen the contrary?

In conclusion, it might be a good idea to point out how large a part the idea of deceit plays in this selection. Ask students to run through the aphorisms and list every word that refers to error: *figments, distorts, fictions,* and others. List with these, too, all that refer to sly manipulation: *insinuation, mischief, feigns, steal,* and so on. In that way, they'll understand how much Bacon cares about our capacity to be easily misled and misinformed. Point out, however, that Bacon's mistrust of our perceptions and intelligence does not lead him to philosophical skepticism. He believes that we *can* discover the truth; but it requires trained observation, constant vigilance, and willingness to toss overboard all the baggage of worthless opinion.

Additional Activities

Bacon, of course, was one of the great English essayists. He opened his famous collection with the essay "Of Truth," reprinted here. You might want to pass around copies of the essay to stimulate additional discussion. Invite students to read the essay in class (it's short enough) and then discuss in what ways it resembles and differs from the ideas Bacon expresses in "Idols of the Mind."

Of Truth

What is truth? said jesting Pilate, and would not stay for an answer. Certainly there be, that delight in giddiness, and count it a bondage to fix a belief; affecting free-will in thinking, as well as in acting. And though the sects of philosophers of that kind be gone, yet there remain certain discoursing wits, which are of the same veins, though there be not so much blood in them, as was in those of the ancients. But it is not only the difficulty and labor, which men take in finding out of truth, nor again, that when it is found, it imposeth upon men's thoughts, that doth bring lies in favor; but a natural, though corrupt love, of the lie itself. One of the later school of the Grecians, examineth the matter, and is at a stand, to think what should be in it, that men should love lies; where neither they make for pleasure, as with poets, nor for advantage, as with the merchant; but for the lie's sake. But I cannot tell; this same truth, is a naked, and open day-light, that doth not show the masks, and mummeries, and triumphs, of the world, half so stately and daintily as candle-lights. Truth may perhaps come to the price of a pearl, that showeth best by day; but it will not rise to the price of a diamond, or carbuncle, that showeth best in varied lights. A mixture of a lie doth ever add pleasure. Doth any man doubt, that if there were taken out of men's minds, vain opinions, flattering hopes, false valuations, imaginations as one would, and the like, but it would leave the minds, of a number of men, poor shrunken things, full of melancholy and indisposition, and unpleasing to themselves?

One of the fathers, in great severity, called poesy *vinum dæmonum,* because it filleth the imagination; and yet, it is but with the shadow of a lie. But it is not the lie that passeth through the mind, but the lie that sinketh in, and settleth in it, that doth the hurt; such as we spake of before. But, howsoever these things are thus in men's depraved judgments, and affections, yet truth, which only doth judge itself, teacheth that the inquiry of truth, which is the love-making, or wooing of it, the knowledge of truth, which is the presence of it, and the belief of truth, which is the enjoying of it, is the sovereign good of human nature. The first creature of God, in the works of the days, was the light of the sense; the last, was the light of reason; and his sabbath work ever since, is the illumination of his Spirit. First he breathed light, upon the face of the matter or chaos; then he breathed light, into the face of man; and still he breatheth and inspireth light, into the face of his chosen. The poet, that beautified the sect, that was otherwise inferior to the rest, saith yet excellently well: *It is a pleasure, to stand upon the shore, and to see ships tossed upon the sea; a pleasure, to stand in the window of a castle, and to see a battle, and the adventures thereof below: but no pleasure is comparable to the standing upon the vantage ground of truth* (a hill not to be commanded, and where the air is always clear and serene), *and to see the errors, and wanderings, and mists, and tempests, in the vale below;* so always that this prospect be with pity, and not with swelling, or pride. Certainly, it is heaven upon earth, to have a man's mind move in charity, rest in providence, and turn upon the poles of truth.

To pass from theological, and philosophical truth, to the truth of civil business; it will be acknowledged, even by those that practise it not, that clear, and round dealing, is the honor of man's nature; and that mixture of falsehoods, is like alloy in coin of gold and silver, which may make the metal work the better, but it embaseth it. For these winding, and crooked courses, are the goings of the serpent; which goeth basely upon the belly, and not upon the feet. There is no vice, that doth so cover a man with shame, as to be found false and perfidious. And therefore Montaigne saith prettily, when he inquired the reason, why the word of the lie should be such a disgrace, and such an odious charge? Saith he, *If it be well weighed, to say that a man lieth, is as much to say, as that he is brave towards God, and a coward towards men.* For a lie faces God, and shrinks from man. Surely the wickedness of falsehood, and breach of faith, cannot possibly be so highly expressed, as in that it shall be the last peal, to call the judgments of God upon the generations of men; it being foretold, that when Christ cometh, *he shall not find faith upon the earth.*

Generating Writing

To demonstrate how applicable Bacon's idols are to today's world, the class could take one of the idols and write an essay showing how it relates to a current opinion or attitude. The essay should interpret the selected idol as clearly as possible, and explain how Bacon's definitions and illustrations are relevant to the contemporary example.

René Descartes

Stripping the Mind of Its Beliefs

Teaching Strategies

Hegel called Descartes "the grand initiator of modern thought," and many other thinkers refer to him as the founder of modern philosophy. Like Bacon, Descartes took all knowledge as his province, and like Bacon he hoped to put philosophy on a solid experimental and scientific foundation. He also resembled Bacon in his resistance to dogmatism and received opinions. But the differences between these two thinkers are significant. Whereas Bacon reasoned mainly by induction (he believed firmly in observation and inference), Descartes hoped to establish a system of philosophy based on deduction from first principles. This approach accounts for the importance of the external world (nature and humankind) in Bacon as opposed to the interiority of Descartes, whose philosophy begins with the word "I."

Introduce students to these two great thinkers by pointing out that both believed truth could be reached but each took a different path (in fact, each uses the "path" metaphor). Students should know that their names are closely linked in the history of philosophy — despite their different approaches — because each thinker in his own way and at around the same time tried to make philosophy more scientific and more certain.

Students shouldn't have a great deal of trouble reading the Descartes translation. His prose is straightforward and at times crystal clear. He also deliberately put his philosophical discoveries into the readable form of an autobiographical narrative (like the religious-conversion narratives popular in his time). Students should also find grounds for identifying with Descartes. Here is a young person who finds that his expensive education has taught him little, that it has left him more confused than enlightened. He decides to set out on a quest for certainty in a world of clamorous and divided opinion. He travels to see new cities and other cultures; he meets many kinds of people and listens to many strange ideas. But all along he has one ambition, a goal he never deviates from: he wants to clear all the mental clutter and replace it with ideas he can truly trust. It was a noble experiment.

And it was an *experiment*. His predecessor Montaigne (whom Descartes often echoes) called it an *essai*, a test, a trial. Descartes subjects *himself* to experiment; he gives up the study of books and instead studies himself. His search into himself is like that of another contemporary, though Rembrandt explored himself in painting, not in philosophy.

You might begin discussion of *The Discourse on Method* by asking students if they find anything strange about the ideas in Descartes' opening two paragraphs. They will be fully prepared to agree that we are all equal (politically, legally, and so on) but many will be unprepared to accept Descartes view that we're all equal in our power of reasoning (his opening sentence is slightly satirical — all people seem satisfied with their good sense). Students must see that Descartes doesn't mean that everyone thinks alike or thinks equally well. Through discussion bring out that Descartes means all human beings possess the power of reason — that "it is whole and entire in each of us" — and the main causes of inequalities in thinking are the *methods* of reasoning we use. Descartes' main claim in this selection is not that he has found a new philosophy but rather a new method of thinking upon which to base a philosophy. As you discuss these opening paragraphs, also ask why it's important for Descartes' method that we accept this premise of equality in reason. They should see that if we found major differences among people in reason — if we believe that different cultures have different kinds of reason, say (though the differences would still be subsumed under the same species) — then Descartes' method would have limited applicability.

Descartes' agenda should require little explanation, for his account of his progress is fairly clear. He wants to strip his mind of all opinions and ideas that he does not think are certain — practically everything he's learned — in order to find some bedrock of truth upon which to build. In solitary reflection, he finds that foundation in one of philosophy's most quoted sentences: "I think, therefore I am." Volumes have been written on this proposition and a composition class may not be the place to analyze it properly; still, you might explore the statement in class. Why shouldn't introductory students respond to Descartes' ideas just as he responded to the ideas of others?

Take a deep breath and ask the class to consider what "I think, therefore I am" means? Does it seem obvious to them? Redundant? Will any wonder why the proposition can't be reversed: "I am, therefore I think." And can they speculate about what Descartes might mean by the word *think* here? Does he mean "I reason," or "I reflect," or "I have consciousness," and so on? You might want to explore, too, why the proposition is so essential to Descartes' philosophy. What does it prove to him with certainty? What other proofs does he build upon it?

But try looking, too, at the selection from a literary and compositional point of view. First, ask the class to identify Descartes' metaphors. They might list several: the path or road, buildings and architecture, and books themselves. Notice how important these metaphors (often developed to the point of analogy) are to Descartes' reasoning. He sees his search for truth as traveling, and thus he pursues a road or path and aims toward a clear destination. He sees philosophy as architectural structure, in which he needs to lay a solid foundation to build from; he abandons his books only to turn to the world and himself and study them as though they were in fact books. You might also point out his problematic use of *fable:* in paragraph 5, he calls his memoir a *story* or a *fable*, thus giving it a literary more than a philosophical shape; and yet later in paragraph 8, he is critical of fables for their fictional extravagances. Do students detect any inconsistency or tension between Descartes' philosophical methods and his literary methods?

Descartes claims to have rejected education, history, and even culture to derive a universal human rule upon which to construct — through a chain of reasons — a philosophy that would be wholly certain. In conclusion, do students think Descartes did in fact rid himself of these inherited opinions, or do they think he never quite escaped them? This question could lead to another point suggested by the *Discourse:* do students think Descartes' goal is possible to achieve?

Additional Activities

To expand discussion you might want to compare and contrast Descartes' Four Rules (para. 22) with Bacon's Four Idols. They will provide a number of differences and similarities, but perhaps most important, the comparison will enable you to introduce the distinction between inductive (Bacon) and deductive (Descartes) thinking.

Generating Writing

Why not invite your class to do what Descartes attempted to do? In a reflective essay they should try to come up with a truth they think is indisputable, something they believe is certain. They should try to write the paper in a narrative form that will demonstrate the steps in their reasoning. It might be instructive afterward to discuss the essays to see how much people disagree about "indisputable" truths.

Shunryu Suzuki

Emptiness

Teaching Strategies

The connection between Suzuki's two short essays and the Bacon and Descartes selections is immediately apparent in Suzuki's first sentence: "If you want to understand Buddhism it is necessary for you to forget all about your preconceived ideas." Here, too, is a method for reaching truth that requires stripping the mind of its beliefs and inherited wisdom. Nearly every concept dealt with in Bacon and Descartes is also addressed in Suzuki, but from a vastly different perspective.

For Descartes, stripping the mind of its beliefs in the search for truth led directly to predication of his own existence as a fundamental idea; for Suzuki (who died in 1971), one must "give up" that very notion of existence if one is to arrive at the truth. "The usual view of life," Suzuki maintains, "is firmly rooted in the idea of existence." Yet, we must learn to see that "life includes both existence and non-existence." There is mystery here, and part of the difficulty that we may have with this paradoxical view of life comes from ingrained mental habits that derive from our own culture and philosophy. After all, whether we have systematically read Bacon and Descartes or not, our modern consciousness has been constructed from their influential ideas.

But Suzuki proposes a different intellectual journey. If Descartes reasons, "I think, therefore I am," Suzuki might say, "I don't think, therefore I truly am," for his philosophy rejects the deductive, directed thinking that Descartes associates with existence. Descartes couldn't imagine the mind coming to a stop — with no thinking — but Suzuki feels we can stop our thinking if we want to. In this way we can find freedom. Descartes' philosophy, furthermore, is entirely based on a separation of body and mind, but Suzuki also rejects that notion of duality. And unlike Bacon, who demands scientific observation, Suzuki believes we can observe something better if we do not try too hard to watch it.

Invite students to reflect on emptiness. Can they? Do they have a sense of what Suzuki means by it? When they try to reflect on it do they do so in the style of thinking promoted by Bacon or Descartes? Do they think it is possible to develop "mindfulness" — which is *not* the wisdom of Bacon or Descartes? Remind students that Suzuki, like Descartes, is discussing a *method* for reaching wisdom. Yet his is not a method of reasoning but a meditative practice called *zazen*. For Suzuki, it is only through this practice that mindfulness can be achieved.

You might close with discussion about Suzuki's relevance. How do students perceive the value of his philosophical views? Do they think his views are enlightening? escapist? resigned? If any students are Buddhist or have practiced zazen you might want to elicit their views. Though the brief selections from Suzuki demand much more context and background than can be provided here, they will prove a stimulating contrast to the traditional views of Western philosophy.

Additional Activities

A worthwhile and thought-expanding exercise is to set up a panel in which students report on aspects of Zen Buddhism — its origins, practices, history, and philosophy. Students could look in the many books on the subject, and also into Suzuki's other work. Suzuki's is only one line of thought, however, and so students should be sure to cover the differences among Zen practices and beliefs.

Generating Writing

Invite students to reflect on one of Suzuki's essential points: what does he mean when he says "The bird exists and does not exist at the same time"? They might try answering this question in a reflective essay in which they try to understand this view of life. Encourage them to do further reading from Suzuki's works in preparation.

WRITING ABOUT THE CHAPTER

1. If you first asked your students to draft the essay on the dangers of intellectual convictions before reading the selections, they could now go back over it and revise accordingly. They might want to support their essay with further examples in the manner of Bacon; or they might want to restructure their essay into a narrative similar to that of Descartes. Then, too, Suzuki's little essays may have awakened a few new ideas or altered their perspective.

2. Invite students to consider each of the selections from a personal point of view. They should select the piece they feel intellectually closest to and say why. This explanation needn't be an argument. They should read over the selections and identify the style of thinking that most conforms to their own belief and temperament. Do they prefer the inductive manner of Bacon; the deductive style of Descartes; or the mindfulness of Suzuki? Whichever they chose, they should explain why they find that manner of thinking most agreeable.

40

Why We Write

Joan Didion, Why I Write

Bernice Johnson Reagon, Nurturing Resistance

Francine du Plessix Gray, I Write for Revenge against Reality

Rudolfo A. Anaya, B. Traven Is Alive and Well in Cuernavaca

WORKING WITH THE CHAPTER

Students rarely have a sense of themselves as part of a larger community of readers and writers. They are, of course, part of such a community, and they need to be made aware that other writers share their preoccupations, challenges, and joys. This chapter presents some views from the inside: authors trying to explain their motivation, a history of their struggle toward self-expression.

Teaching Strategies

The chapter epigraphs are the best place to begin class discussion. The passage from Orwell succinctly recounts his approach to a literary project. How familiar are students with Orwell's work? Most will have read *Animal Farm,* as well as "Politics and the English Language" (Chapter 32) and "Shooting an Elephant" (Chapter 3). Does his description of his motives seem valid when we consider these works? What does the class feel is the balance between artistic and political interests in his writing? In their own? Ask them to assess the claims of style and content in their writing. What other forces shape their work?

In Toni Cade Bambara's view of the writing process, she seems to focus almost exclusively on its political aspect. What does the class feel she means by "the Family"? Have students return to her story, "The Lesson" (Chapter 16). Might Bambara's comments apply specifically to this work? Might it be described as a "transformation" of experience into "usable wisdom"? How effective is this as a model for describing all writing? Ask the class to discuss Bambara's characterization of "those disciplines whose split . . . predisposes us to accept fragmented truths and distortions as the whole." What does she mean? How does writing serve as a bridge between seemingly opposed ideas?

The passage from Annie Dillard sketches the basic motivation for writing, a love of words. What do students make of the writer's question, "Do you like sentences?" Ask them to explain how this is an answer to the aspiring student. Do they like sentences? Which, if either, do they find more important in their own writing, a love of language or a love of ideas? Have them look back at Dillard's "Seeing" (Chapter 35). How does the essay reflect the matters expressed in this paragraph? Would the class say that Dillard liked sentences?

Joan Didion's "Why I Write" should be looked at together with the Orwell epigraph. What does the class make of Didion's reference to Orwell and his essay? Didion says of her borrowed title, "One reason I stole it was that I like the sound of the words" (para. 1). What might some of her other reasons be? How is Didion's experience of writing unlike Orwell's? One place to focus might be on the writers' different estimates of the role of politics in their work. Where does Didion mention politics? How important a motivation does that seem to be for her work? What might Orwell think about her political involvement? Both Didion and Orwell are known as novelists and essayists; although Orwell's novels *1984* and *Animal Farm* are perhaps his best-known works, the focus of his career was mainly essays and nonfiction writing. Didion, on the other hand, is equally well-known for her fiction, to which she chiefly refers in this essay. Might the two authors' choice of genres reflect their different aims in writing? Which do students see as more effectively political, fiction or nonfiction? Which do they see as dealing more with aesthetics?

Ask the class to compare Didion's essay with the Dillard epigraph. Are Didion's views compatible with those of Dillard's well-known writer? Are Didion's "grammar" and Dillard's "sentences" one and the same? How do they differ? Is Didion's intoxication with images costly to her intoxication with words, or do the two complement each other? What might Didion make of Dillard's metaphor equating words and paint?

Bernice Johnson Reagon's essay seems a perfect expression of the ideas sketched in Toni Cade Bambara's epigraph. How might the two authors disagree? Do their views on African-American culture seem to differ? What interests do they not seem to share? Compare Reagon's description of making political art with Orwell 's . How do they differ? What part might such variables as nationality, race, gender, and class have in that difference? Reagon is a songwriter and performer writing about her art that, as a public experience, is somewhat different from the art of the novel or essay discussed by the chapter's other authors. What comment might the other writers have on this difference? How is the interaction between performer and audience unlike that between writer and reader? How are they similar?

Francine du Plessix Gray and Joan Didion offer interestingly complementary perspectives on the drive to write. How might Didion's description of writing as "the act of saying *I*" describe Gray's own experience of writing as a defense against an inimical environment? Would Gray agree with or reject Didion's view that writing is inherently an aggressive or hostile act? What view does the class hold? Both authors describe writing as an intensely personal act. Do they seem to see the personal in the same way? Didion describes her own work as motivated by the power of visions and images; Gray views her writing as the product of strong emotion. How do the essays themselves reflect these different approaches?

Rudolfo A. Anaya's short story is a fictional treatment of the themes dealt with by all the chapter's authors: the drive to write, the place of writing in society, and the transformation of real-life experience into literature. How might Joan Didion view this story? What elements does it share with her own fiction, as she describes it? What might Francine du Plessix Gray make of it? Does Anaya's narrator seem to be in the grip of powerful emotions? How does he seem to understand his relationship to B. Traven? What might Orwell, Bambara, and Reagon make of the politics in this story?

A Writing-before-Reading Exercise

Ask students to write a brief in-class essay answering the question, "Why do I write?" They may want to talk about experiments in fiction, poetry, or drama, or perhaps their work on a student newspaper or magazine. Is their work in this course, and their other courses, satisfying to their urge to write? How do they find it unsatisfactory? What constraints do the structure of assignments, essay questions, and grades put on their self-expression? What changes would they like to see in the way writing is assigned and evaluated? What changes might they make in their own approach to render their work more effectively personal?

WORKING WITH THE SELECTIONS

Joan Didion

Why I Write

Teaching Strategies

Didion, in her essay, treats the process of writing in an intensely personal way. Does the class find her tone intimidating? Ask someone to read the first two paragraphs of the selection aloud. How does Didion's tone reflect her description of writing as "an aggressive, even a hostile act" (para. 5)? Have students examine the structure of Didion's prose. What is the subject of most of the sentences? Does this focus on the first person reinforce her ideas about writing as an extension of the self?

Ask the class what they think of the distinction Didion makes between "ideas," with which she claims to be uncomfortable and inept, and "pictures in my mind" (para. 10), which we might classify as observation or experience. Are the two as sharply defined as she makes them out to be? Why might Didion be oversimplifying here? What might be at stake?

One of the most important tools a writer has is grammar. Didion writes, "All I know about grammar is its infinite power. To shift the structure of a sentence alters the meaning of that sentence . . ." (para. 12). Talk about this statement with the class. How can grammar change the meaning of a sentence? Have students come up with examples. Ask them to look through Didion's essay for instances in which grammar makes meaning. How might the class characterize Didion's use of grammar?

Didion's discussion of her novels' origins in isolated scenes illustrates how she seems to feel the writing process works. Have the class pull out her comments on how writing happens — "It tells you" (para. 13), for instance, or "the picture that shimmered and made these other images coalesce" (para. 19) — and talk about them. Do they agree with Didion that the writer is more or less a tool of the story? How do they think stories get made and told? What do they make of Didion's narratives about writing? Do they sympathize with her? Have they had similar experiences?

Some of Didion's references might need to be explained to the class. Ask students to write down names and phrases they don't understand and define them in class; they may not know what a bevatron is, or that Jax was a women's boutique in Beverly Hills, or that Jack Valenti is president of the Motion Picture Association of America. How do these "inside" references heighten Didion's personal style?

Additional Activities

Students interested in Didion's work may want to read the novels discussed and present brief reports to the class. How did the author's description of the books' origins affect their perceptions of them? What similarities do they find between Didion's voice as an essayist and as a novelist? How does her style change with the genre?

Ask the class to go back to Didion's essay in Chapter 1, "On Keeping a Notebook." From the two selections, how would students describe Didion's attitude toward experience? Toward writing? What differences do they see between the selections? How does the idea of an audience seem to affect Didion's approach?

Generating Writing

1. Have students write a brief essay discussing Didion's distinction between "the tangible" and "the abstract." Do they agree or disagree with this distinction? Ask them to

give examples of each category, if they agree with Didion, or, if they disagree, to cite instances in which the division between things and ideas is transcended or crossed. Which, in their opinion, is more valuable to the writer?

2. Bring in several photographs (from advertising, perhaps, or magazine articles, or from collections of photographs) and give students time to look at them. Have them select one of the photographs and write a brief (one or two paragraphs) story about it. What aspects of the image "shimmered" for them? How did the picture itself seem to determine the story they told about it?

Bernice Johnson Reagon

Nurturing Resistance

Teaching Strategies

Ask students how familiar they are with Reagon's work in Sweet Honey in the Rock. You may want to bring in one of the group's albums for class members to hear. What do students know about the traditions of music as protest? The class may be aware of such early artists as Woody Guthrie; they may also be familiar with the work of such 1960s figures as Pete Seeger and Bob Dylan. Ask what contemporary protest music they listen to; many rap artists, for example, comment on society in their work (KRS One, Public Enemy, Queen Latifah), as do such rock musicians as Sting, U2, and Sinead O'Connor. How can music be an effective form of protest? Have songs and performers inspired students to rethink prejudices and attitudes?

What does the class think of Reagon's straightforward statement about her song, "Ode to the International Debt" — "I wanted to see if I could sing progressive contemporary analysis" (para. 1)? Are they disappointed to find a songwriter approaching composition with such a clear-cut agenda?

How does Reagon think the circumstances of her own life have affected her artistic development? Ask the class to read closely and come up with a list of social conditions, events, and individuals Reagon sees as powerful influences on her voice. How many of these are specific to her personal history? How many of them are specific to her generation, race, class, status, and gender? How many of them might be shared by anyone in this country? by anyone in the industrialized nations? in the world?

Discuss Reagon's ideas about "re-imagining America" (para. 13) with the class. Is her statement, "I operate out of the assumption that I am the United States of America and that I am central to anything that is really happening in this country that is worthwhile" (para. 11) a bold one? What might she mean by saying that she is "a secret"? Do our media (news, television, advertising) usually portray middle-aged, left-wing, African-American women as "central"? Why not? How does the denial of Reagon's experience by our mass culture parallel the ways in which the United States denies the experience of other cultures? What "mythology" does Reagon want to "smash"? Why might she want to reject this mythology?

How does Reagon reconcile the cultural specificity of her own history and outlook with the internationalism that is her political goal? What difficulties might lie in this resolution? How might Reagon respond to them?

Ask the class to discuss Reagon's ideas about communities united for change. What does she see as the link between individual and social goals? How does she characterize personal and public contributions to political movements? What is the artist's role in this model of social change? How might students agree or disagree with Reagon's views of political struggle?

Additional Activities

Some students may want to research and report on protest music. Ask them to briefly summarize the issues the songs discuss or refer to. What position does the song's author take? Who is his or her intended audience? What action is the song meant to inspire? How dangerous might this protest be? How aware would the average listener be of the song's political content?

A number of other essays in the text would be interesting juxtaposed to Reagon's work. You might ask students to compare and contrast Reagon's ideas about reimagining this country and this continent with Ishmael Reed's in "America: The Multinational Society" (Chapter 7); or they might want to look at Reagon's view of African-American women's culture with Paule Marshall's ("From the Poets in the Kitchen," Chapter 30).

Generating Writing

1. Reagon cites numerous examples of people, circumstances, and events that shaped her artistic voice. Ask students to write a brief personal essay discussing the individuals and situations that have shaped their own voices as writers. What effects, positive and negative, have these had on their writing? On how they feel about themselves as writers?

2. Have the class discuss, and write on, Reagon's view of our nation's place in the world. Do they agree or disagree with her condemnation of the attitude she sees as our cultural imperialism? What do they make of her proposals to reimagine America? Do they feel America needs to be "re-imagined"?

Francine du Plessix Gray

I Write for Revenge against Reality

Teaching Strategies

Gray, like Didion, seems to consider writing a highly personal act. What do students make of her connections between her personal and her artistic development? Are they confused or alienated by her autobiography? It may be necessary to go over the incidents in Gray's life with the class, and discuss some of the events (her father's death in the Resistance, her migration to the United States) and persons (Charles Olson, Blake, Marvell) she mentions. What do students make of her life and career? Are they familiar with her novels or other writing?

Talk about Gray's portrayal of how she came to write her first novel (para. 14). What events motivated her to begin the work? She makes its ties to her own life quite clear: the first chapter is from a story "about my governess." What do students make of Gray's confession that completing the novel "entailed a solid and delicate psychoanalysis" (para. 14)? Is the connection between the two processes clear to them? Are they surprised that Gray so closely links her art and her self-discovery? Ask the class to discuss this paragraph's concluding sentence, "I may have had to bury my father to set my tongue free." What does Gray mean here, specifically? What general truth might she be expressing?

Ask students what they think of Gray's assessment of her own career. Why might she be so anxious about the size of her output? What do they make of her simultaneous idealization and fear of the novel and novel writing?

Have the class read Gray's course description closely. (You might want to briefly characterize the assigned books for them.) Would they want to take a course with Gray? Ask them to look at her advice to students, "shed all narcissism." Does this suggestion seem paradoxical coming from such a personal writer? What might the differences between self-examination and narcissism be? What do they make of her description of the writing process as one of perseverance, "dreadful draft after dreadful draft" (para. 19)?

Ask students to summarize the reasons Gray gives, in her six concluding paragraphs, for writing. How many of these are personal? How many of them are a response to social and historical conditions? How many of them seem determined by Gray's race, class, nationality, education, age, and gender? Do students share any of Gray's reasons for writing, or do they have parallel motivations? For example, one of the reasons Gray writes is that her husband reads and critiques her work; do students have family or friends who take an interest in their writing? Gray also states that she has "faith in the possibility that I can eventually surprise myself" (para. 28). What might this declaration mean? Do students hope that their writing will surprise them? Would they like it to surprise others?

Additional Activities

How does Gray's essay compare, as a "family story," to the selections in Chapter 12? Students might want to focus on a comparison between Gray's work and Maxine Hong Kingston's "No Name Woman," or perhaps to discuss Gray's essay along with Elizabeth Stone's "Stories Make a Family." What role did Gray's family have in her development as a writer? How is her "family story" essential to her work?

You might also want to ask students to compare Gray's depiction of her mother and father with the images of mothers and fathers in Chapters 19 and 20. With which of these writers does Gray seem to have most in common? What kind of influence do parents seem to have on literary development?

Generating Writing

1. Ask students to read the essay closely and write a brief description of the author. How do they perceive her? How does she seem to perceive herself? Have students identify one feature of Gray's style. How would they explain her use of language? How would they describe her tone?

2. Have the class write a short personal essay on writing as "revenge against reality." How does Gray use the concept? Against what aspects of reality is her writing a revenge? Upon what, and whom, would students like to avenge themselves? How might writing help them to achieve that?

Rudolfo A. Anaya

B. Traven Is Alive and Well in Cuernavaca

Teaching Strategies

Unlike the other selections in the chapter, this is a work of fiction. Discuss with the class the differences between the genres. Why might a short story be included in a chapter called "Why We Write"?

Who is the narrator of the story? What is his profession? How is he like Anaya himself? Discuss the narrator's and the story's audiences. Are they the same? Talk about the difficulty of differentiating between author and narrator in this story. How does this difficulty fit in with Anaya's theme? How does the multiplicity of B. Travens — the historical B. Traven, the figure of B. Traven in this story, and the B. Traven character who appears at the story's end (not to mention the B. Traven impostor described by the narrator's friend) — demonstrate the need and impossibility of distinguishing between an author and his work?

This story seems to be about writing stories. What else is it about? What possible literary subjects does the narrator encounter and discard? Why, for example, does he focus on Justino instead of the friend for whom Justino works? The narrator also alludes briefly to the political situation in Mexico, but does not discuss it in detail. Why might that be? Why is the narrator so sparing with information about himself? Might his own mysteriousness be an attempt to be like B. Traven?

Discuss with the class Anaya's style and language. How do the voices of the narrator and the other characters differ? Is the narrator formal or informal? Is his tone appropriate in a story about how stories come to us?

What does Mexico seem to mean to the narrator? What does it seem to mean to Anaya? Both Anaya and the narrator are Mexican-Americans; how might a figure like B. Traven have a specific significance for them? Discuss the storyteller's use of Mexican mythology. How does the narrator react to Justino's story of La Llorona? What does his own addition to the myth, the figure of El Mero Chingon (Mr. Complete Failure) say about his view of mythology? Of himself? Does this incident explain the narrator's attitude toward women, and perhaps give a motivation for his trip to Mexico and his writer's block? What might Anaya imply here?

Is the story Justino tells about the Pozo de Mendoza a false lead for the reader? Ask students if they were surprised that the narrator failed to go with Justino on his search for treasure. Of what might the treasure be a symbol? Of what might the story about the treasure be a symbol? What things keep the narrator from accompanying Justino? Is Anaya making a statement about the difficulties writers face when trying to become fully involved in experience? The old man at the reception says of his trip to the pozo, "Not a very good story. Never came to anything" (para. 86). Does the narrator, in choosing not to go to the pozo, make a better story? After his encounter with the possible B. Traven, he says, "I understood now what the pozo meant, why Justino had come into my life to tell me the story" (para. 91). What might the narrator mean?

How does the last paragraph represent writers and writing? The narrator says, "Somewhere in the background I heard the tinkling of glasses and the laughter which came from the party, but that was not for me" (para. 92). Are writers isolated from the world around them? Might B. Traven, the mysterious exile, be seen as a symbol for all writers? Is his spirit, as the narrator's friend believes, with us?

Additional Activities

Interested students might want to read and report on some of B. Traven's works. Which of Traven's recurrent themes are represented in Anaya's story? What attitudes do the two authors seem to have in common? You may also want to watch the film of Traven's novel, *The Treasure of the Sierra Madre* (1948: directed by John Huston) with the class or assign it for individual viewing. What themes do the film and the story share? Does the end of this story contradict the nihilism of the film's final scene?

Students might also want to compare this short story with some of the other short stories in the text. How is Anaya's narrator different from the narrator of Updike's "A & P" (Chapter 3)? from the narrator of "The Lesson" by Toni Cade Bambara (chapter 16)? How do these first-person short stories illustrate the themes of the chapters in which they appear?

Generating Writing

1. How would students describe Anaya's narrator? What is he like? What is his voice like? On which aspects of his experience does he focus? Which does he overlook? Which of his own qualities does he ascribe to the mysterious B. Traven?

2. Using the narrator's addition to the myth of La Llorona as a model, ask students to write a brief essay updating a myth by adding a new character. What does that character represent? How does the change in the myth relate to their own experience? (Students might want to use Greek and Roman myths as their source, or perhaps such traditional European fairy tales as "Sleeping Beauty," "Cinderella," or "The Three Bears.")

WRITING ABOUT THE CHAPTER

1. Each author in this chapter discusses or alludes to the personal side of writing. How do writers' lives shape their literary voices? How do their experiences affect their work? their goals? Ask students to choose two writers from the chapter and compare and contrast how personal experience influences their work. Do the authors freely acknowledge the connection between their lives and their writing?

2. All writing is the public expression of private thoughts. Have the class write a brief essay on the tension between the public and the private in writing, and how this conflict is presented by the chapter's authors. Which of the writers represented here seem to care most about writing's private side? Which seem to consider its public side more important? How is this bias reflected in the authors' work? With whose view of this issue would students ally themselves?

3. Ask students to write a personal essay on the purpose of writing, using the chapter selections as a jumping-off place. What are the goals of a writer? What does a writer owe to the community in which he or she lives? How can authors contribute to society? Invite students to imagine that they had unlimited time, ability, and motivation to write one literary work that would be a guaranteed best seller. What issues would it address? How would they hope to change public opinion?

41

The Act of Reading

Richard Wright, *From* Black Boy

Eudora Welty, A Sweet Devouring

Donald Hall, Four Kinds of Reading

Lin Yutang, The Art of Reading

WORKING WITH THE CHAPTER

Teaching Strategies

As English instructors, we have grown accustomed to speaking of writing as consisting of process and product. The epigraphs and selections in this chapter, taken as a whole, suggest that we speak of reading in the same format. The children whose acts of reading are represented here (two little girls) both focus on reading as pure process. Eudora Welty consumes series after series of books in "a sweet devouring"; even when the content of the book, right down to the illustrations, is disappointing, she writes, "But I liked *reading* the book all right — except that I finished it." Edna Buchanan finds so much "shared warmth and adventure" in the books that are read to her that she searches the neighborhood for someone — anyone — who will share the process with her.

When Richard Wright, at age nineteen, obtains a bootleg library card, his reading is as indiscriminating as that of the little girls. Like them, he is experiencing a world of books for the first time, and he can't seem to get enough. He writes, "I gave myself over to each novel without reserve, without trying to criticize it." Of course, the reading process can produce a product with or without the reader's conscious cooperation, and Wright finds himself, as a result of his reading, "able to calculate my chances for life in the South as a Negro fairly clearly now." We can assume that the clarity he gained from reading — both the clear vision of his social environment and the clarity of expression — contributed to his eventual career as a writer.

In an epigraph to this chapter, Vladimir Nabokov describes both the physical process of reading, "laboriously moving our eyes from left to right," and that of rereading, when we "behave towards a book as we do towards a painting." Donald Hall, too, distinguishes between the mechanical kinds of reading we do when we just want to gather information or lose ourselves in the plot of a book, and the reading of literature, which he describes as "slow and sensual, a deep pleasure that begins with touch and ends with the sort of comprehension that we associate with dream." Both Nabokov and Hall focus on reading as a process, as does Henry David Thoreau, who refers to reading the classics as a "noble exercise." Thoreau explicitly links the reading to the writing process when he says that "Books must be read as deliberately and reservedly as they were written."

Both Lin Yutang and Malcolm X emphasize the liberating power of reading. Lin speaks figuratively of the "man who has not the habit of reading," as "imprisoned in his immediate world, in respect to time and space," whereas Malcolm X speaks from his experience in prison, where reading opened up "new vistas" for him. Coming as they do from very different worlds, Lin and Malcolm X see the product of writing differently. Malcolm X sees it as political: he never wastes time that might be spent in "studying something I feel might be able to help the black man." Lin Yutang speaks more about the reader's "cultivation of personal charm of appearance and flavor in speech." But no matter what the differences in background, Lin Yutang, Malcolm X, and the other writers in this chapter can all be seen as the products of their own lifetimes of reading.

A Writing-before-Reading Exercise

Ask students to think back to their childhood, and try to recall their earliest memory of reading or being read to. Ask them to narrate the incident, telling what happened, who was there, how they felt. What images and feelings do they now associate with reading that they can trace back to that early memory? Such rough drafts are especially good to read to one another in groups, because almost everyone takes an interest in the humor and poignancy of childhood memories.

WORKING WITH THE SELECTIONS

Richard Wright

From Black Boy

Teaching Strategies

This excerpt from Richard Wright's autobiography will give your students a glimpse at a world that they're not likely ever to know at first hand. Memphis in the late 1920s was strictly segregated, as students will see when they read about the parks, playgrounds, and libraries that were closed to blacks. (Similar testimony comes from Itabari Njeri, in "Granddaddy," who writes about the first black swimming pool in the southern town where her grandfather was killed.) Under these circumstances, it is no wonder that Wright prized every book that he could get his hands on. The amazing reality is the courage and determination that marked his efforts to gain access to these books.

To understand Wright's reaction to the books he read, your students will have to recognize his position as a black man in the South fifty years ago. How does the South's assigning him "the role of a non-man" affect his way of reacting to what he reads? Might his status have contributed to his reading "without trying to criticize"? Ask your students what standpoint a non-man could have from which to criticize. Of course, even though he says that "the impulse to dream had been slowly beaten out of me by experience," he does have some outlook from which to relate to the voices and ideas he encounters in books. Ask students to identify the personal connections Wright finds in the books he gets from the library. And how does reading broaden his experience, so that he can understand more and more kinds of people?

Ask your students if they can tell why southern whites would try to keep the blacks out of libraries. Why is the librarian on her guard against blacks who might want to "use" books themselves? (John Edgar Wideman, in "The Language of Home," also alludes to the white man's stake in keeping the blacks ignorant.) Wright describes the cumulative effect of his reading: "My tension returned, new, terrible, bitter, surging, almost too great to be contained" (para. 75). No doubt this is precisely the reaction that, among other things, the "Kluxers" feared. In fact, Wright's own initial reaction to reading was contaminated by fear: when he considers using words as a weapon, as Mencken has done, he thinks, "Then, maybe, perhaps, I could use them as a weapon? No. It frightened me." Ask students why he was frightened. They may point to the frequent lynchings mentioned (para. 91). And why does he have such a hard time conquering his "sense of guilt" (para. 66) for his clandestine reading? You will probably want to discuss the extreme difficulty involved in living as one of a minority in an oppressive culture without being affected by that culture's beliefs about your ethnic group. Other essays in the reader that touch on this issue include Shelby Steele's "On Being Black and Middle Class," and Kesaya Noda's "Growing Up Asian in America" (both in Chapter 6).

It's important not to play down the physical hardships suffered by minority groups such as blacks. Some students might have the romantic notion that if one has access to books and pen and paper, one has everything necessary to be a writer. Wright includes the important detail of his can of pork and beans, heated by running hot water on it, and another, that he could read faster once he began eating regular meals. Virginia Woolf spends a good deal of time in *A Room of One's Own* contrasting the food the men ate at their college with the food the women ate at theirs. She makes the point that the mind cannot soar on coarse and ill-prepared food. Of course, many more obstacles confronted Wright's career as an author as well. See how many of them your students can identify.

Additional Activities

If the students would like a chance to see why Wright reacted as he did to Mencken's prose, they might go to the library and check out one or both of the books that the librarian gave to Wright on his first foray into the library with Mr. Falk's card. How does Mencken's prose seem to them? Does it strike any chords for them as it did for young Richard Wright? How might the books have struck Wright if he had been reading for content rather than tone?

Generating Writing

Assign an essay in which your students analyze the effect of reading upon Richard Wright. On the one hand he says that his reading "had created a vast sense of distance between me and the world in which I lived"; on the other hand he also says "I now felt I knew what the white men were feeling." In what sense could it be true that his reading simultaneously created and collapsed the distance between Wright and the other inhabitants of Memphis?

Eudora Welty

A Sweet Devouring

Teaching Strategies

This autobiographical piece is a delight to read. Eudora Welty manages to capture a child's-eye view of books in language that echoes the child's vocabulary, while conveying keen psychological insights. Ask students to describe the point of view in this essay. Of course, it is the grown-up Welty who addresses us in these pages, but she tells us very little that she didn't know as a child. Have students point to details that they had to infer for themselves because it would have been out of character for nine-year-old Eudora to know them. What, for example, is probably the answer to her initial question? And why is she so disappointed with the illustration of "the crusty old gentleman" who was supposed to give Simple Susan a guinea?

Have students examine the character sketches provided in the essay — of the librarian, or the little girl who wrote the book of poems, or of Welty's mother. What can they tell about these people from the observations by one sharp little girl and one sharp writer, her adult counterpart?

For the child in the essay, it is the sheer act of reading, and not the quality or even the content of the book, which counts — a preference that, were it to appear in an adult reader, would throw Donald Hall into a fit. When the child's taste improves, the essay comes to an end. You might ask students why this seems a natural stopping place. Also ask what the child loses when she gains literary taste. Do your students ever feel the enthusiasm for books that she describes? Do books live for them, as if they were "generations of everybody," instead of mere series? Do they ever find access, no matter how brief, to the faith that Welty felt as a child, that books hold all that one seeks? Do they still have a good appetite for reading, with correspondingly high gratification? Why is it that Welty claims that appetite and gratification sail "closer together" in childhood "than ever again in . . . growing up"? Have your students ever felt the appetite, only to discover a disappointing measure of gratification? What is it about growing up that makes this disillusionment happen? One great thing about reading this essay is that it can reawaken long-dead feelings about reading and about life. It's inspirational: ideally it will make your students think, "If Eudora Welty can remember those feelings so clearly, then maybe I can, too."

Additional Activities

"A Sweet Devouring" derives some of its humor from the little girl's coming up with pretty sophisticated literary theories, which are recognizable despite the childish diction and syntax as the same insights offered by such renowned theorists as Vladimir Propp and Roland Barthes. When she reduces fairy tales and Maria Edgeworth's novels to the bare bones of formula, she echoes the work of the structuralists. And look at her insight about series: "As long as they are keeping a series going, I was afraid, nothing can really happen. The whole thing is one grand prevention." If your students read S/Z, by Barthes, they will see the same insight in different language. To any students interested in literary theory, you might suggest an extra-credit project in which they report on one book of theory that they have found particularly helpful or fascinating. Along with this chapter they might try The Act of Reading, by Wolfgang Iser; Reading for the Plot, by Peter Brooks; or the aforementioned S/Z.

Generating Writing

Have your students go to the library and find one or more of the children's books that Welty mentions in her essay. Have them read these books and analyze them. What kinds of messages about moral behavior do such books transmit to children? How would they describe the structure of the books? The plot? The characterization? They may want to compare and contrast one book from Welty's childhood with a contemporary children's book. Alternatively, they may wish to look back at some of the books they read and loved as children, and analyze those instead.

Donald Hall

Four Kinds of Reading

Teaching Strategies

Donald Hall expresses strong opinions about reading in this selection — and not everyone will agree. The mere act of cataloguing the "four kinds of reading" is not likely to raise an argument: taxonomies created by different people seldom mesh exactly, but then again, few people are willing to ride into battle over the slight differences among them. But some of the pronouncements Hall makes along the way are certainly controversial. Ask your students, for example, if any other authors in this chapter might disagree with Hall's statement that the "piety" about reading is "silly." On what grounds would they disagree?

Hall makes a political argument about the source of that piety: it used to be a "mark of social distinction, separating a small portion of humanity from the rest." In fact, as it turns out, the distinction reflects not only classism but also sexism, as Hall implies, "When he says that his wife is interested in books and music and pictures, he is not only enclosing the arts in a female world, he is saying that he is rich enough to provide her with the leisure to do nothing." Ask students if Hall himself is free of the twin taints of classism and sexism. How would they account for his remark about the "opium of the suburbs" (para. 6), or for his hypothetical college student (para. 7) being a "boy"?

Similarly, why does he place the study of "literature" above the "minor discipline called the history of ideas"? Because he criticizes the intellectuals and the professors of English, it's not easy to label him an intellectual snob. How might your students characterize his attitude? What blind spots does his attitude produce? You might look at his discussion of the Chaucer exam he took at the University. It was an exercise in identification, and Hall apparently did quite well, whereas students who were "well-informed about the great chain of being" had a difficult time. Why doesn't Hall question the validity of the exam? He just takes it for granted that the kinds of questions he excels in are the only true test of a person's knowledge of literature.

Ask your students if they can infer a definition of *literature* from Hall's essay. Although he never explicitly defines it, it's clear that he considers some books literature and some decidedly not. What books does he mention when he's talking about literature, and what books does he mention in a derogatory tone? You might use this essay as a jumping-off place for discussing the literary canon, and the recent challenges to the closely guarded ivory tower where the canonical texts were protected.

Generating Writing

Ask students to write an argumentative essay taking on one or more of Hall's assumptions or statements. They might decide to analyze and refute his stand on television and books. Or they might like to reassess the significance of Woolf's comments on *Twelfth Night:* how else might one see the reading of a play, besides labeling it "narcissism"?

Assign an essay in which your students identify and describe several varieties of something other than reading. They should use Hall's form, not his content, for their model. Make sure they understand that they should be making a larger point as well, not simply categorizing for the sake of creating more categories in a world already replete with them.

Lin Yutang

The Art of Reading

Teaching Strategies

Lin Yutang considers the enjoyment of books one of the greatest "charms of a cultured life," but he gives no indication of believing that only the members of a chosen class can or should lead the cultured life; rather, he talks of "giving [oneself] that privilege." Anyone can enjoy the charms of reading, anyone can widen his or her horizons by reading. Lin Yutang, like Henry David Thoreau, finds that reading puts "one in touch with one of the best talkers in the world," the author of the book. Like Malcolm X, he sees books as a passkey that opens the door to a "prison" that's otherwise impossible to escape. (You might want to discuss the difference in effect between Lin Yutang's metaphorical prison and Malcolm X's literal one.)

Despite these similarities between the ideas expressed in "The Art of Reading" and in the epigraphs by American writers, the cultural difference does create some differences in Lin's ideas as expressed in this essay. Whereas Western writers may cite authorities to support their points, originality is still more highly praised in the West than is tradition. Lin, however, follows the Eastern practice of valuing shared ideas, especially those shared with sages and poets, most highly. He states that both "Mencius and Ssema Ch'ien, China's greatest historian, have expressed the same idea." He also talks of such things as "dead spirits" and reincarnation. Ask students if they can discover ways of relating to these concepts, whether or not they believe in reincarnation. The art of "the cultivation of personal charm and appearance and flavor in speech" is certainly not a concept that is alien to our Western perspective, but we would probably interpret it in a more superficial sense than Lin means; he refers to "something other than physical beauty." Also, "flavor in speech" here in twentieth-century America would probably refer to idiosyncratic or original ways of speaking, whereas Lin talks of absorbing the author's style, until the reader's "own voice and manner and way of smiling and way of talking become like the author's own." If you do discuss the cultural differences between Lin's assumptions and those of the other authors in this chapter, you will of course be sure that students use this as an opportunity to learn about the ways of cultures other than their own, an opportunity to widen their own horizons.

Additional Activities

You might ask students to identify and discuss the various metaphors Lin Yutang uses in his essay. These include metaphors from nature, such as the tree and the river, and metaphors about love and other spells. What do his metaphors say about his attitude toward reading?

Some seeming contradictions arise in this essay: Lin says that "There can be . . . no books that one absolutely must read"; later in the same paragraph he modifies that thought when he writes, "Even if there is a certain book that everyone must read, like the Bible, there is a time for it." Similarly, he first refers to the discovery of one's favorite author as a "crucial event," comparable to love at first sight, whereas he later admits that many people have many favorite authors — and lovers — in a lifetime. Ask your students what they make of these discrepancies. Lin seems to be making up his mind, revising his thinking, as he goes along. What is the effect on the reader of his shifts?

Generating Writing

Ask students who have a favorite author to write an essay describing the moment when they discovered that special affinity. Did it happen the first time they read one of his or her books, in accordance with the love-at-first-sight pattern? Did they instantly recognize their own thoughts in the author's writing? Or did their realization of the affinity form gradually, as they became more and more familiar with the author's work? Have they remained faithful to one favorite author, or do they remember past favorites fondly even though they have been replaced by authors who are more compatible with their present stage of maturation? Invite them, if they'd like, to try to capture the echo of their favorite writer's style in their own essay about him or her.

WRITING ABOUT THE CHAPTER

1. Give your students the option of revising the rough drafts they wrote before reading the epigraphs and selections that make up this chapter. They will probably find Eudora Welty's essay most helpful as a model for their revision, because Welty deals with early memories of reading, and she captures the young reader's enthusiasm so well. If they decide to revise this draft, suggest that they examine Welty's style closely before doing so.

2. Richard Wright, Lin Yutang, and Eudora Welty all use the metaphor of eating — devouring, digesting, and so on — for reading. In fact, the metaphor seems so natural as to almost warrant cliche status: people regularly "gobble up" books. Suggest an essay in which students explore the implications of this metaphor. What is it about eating that suggests such a powerful connection with the act of reading? They may want to look at the passage from *Metaphors We Live By*, by George Lakoff and Mark Johnson, in Chapter 33, for ideas on how to analyze and talk about metaphor.

Writing Informally about Reading

A journal is a great place for students to experience the process of writing. Because journals are not graded, they don't create the sense of pressure associated with most college writing assignments. Students also know they don't have to worry about mechanics such as grammar and spelling, and can often direct their unfettered energy to the pursuit of ideas. Journals and other informal writing assignments can be the best cure for writer's block.

If you decide to assign journals, you have several ways of going about it. After reading these comments and suggestions, you'll be in a good position to settle on a method that will work best for you and your students.

Many instructors collect and read their students' journals once a week, although you can also set two or three deadlines during the semester, when all journals are due. Because journals can give you access to the pulse of the class, teachers who prefer to check that pulse often will prefer the first method. The weekly collection has an advantage for students in that it prevents extreme forms of procrastination. If they are in the habit of waiting until the night before an assignment is due before getting started, the pressure of writing five weeks' worth of journal entries in one night will destroy one reason for writing in a journal in the first place. If your schedule arranges that your slack times come twice or thrice in a semester, however, you might try the second method. Also, to keep students feeling as if they are writing the journal primarily for themselves, and secondarily for you, the infrequent due dates might help.

Because these journals are not diaries — because, that is, they are assigned rather than taken up voluntarily — the audience will almost inevitably extend beyond the writer of the journal. To create an opportunity for students to write their journals purely for themselves, and simultaneously inspiring trust, you might try *not* collecting or reading the journals, instead informing your students at the beginning of the semester that they will be responsible for handing you a written report at the close of the term on their success at keeping a journal. They should not only assess the frequency of their entries but also discuss the experience of journal writing, and give an opinion on the advantages and disadvantages of being its sole reader. Here is a less radical plan that still takes into account the possibility that students may not want or need a wider audience. When they hand in their journals, have them fold in half lengthwise any page they would prefer you not look at. In this way you can make sure they've done the assignment and still ensure their right to privacy.

How might you respond to the journals you do read? Some instructors write nonjudgmental comments in the margins of journal entries, setting up a dialogue by responding to the subject — that is — to the ideas in the entry rather than to their mechanical trappings. This is one good way to simultaneously get to know your students and help them think of new directions in which to push their ideas. Other instructors don't make a mark on the journals, because they take seriously the idea that the journal is the student's own place to write. The students are less likely to see their journal writing as a performance; they may even be able to forget about the audience and write for themselves. Your decision on whether or not to write in the margins will obviously involve a trade-off: do you want to give each the personal touch of a dialogue and some guidance in their thinking, or do you want to give them a chance to see what they can accomplish on their own, and perhaps gain a sense of their own authority? (If you're not satisfied with the thought of giving up either option, you might try assigning team journals, which are described below.)

How do the journals figure into grades? Even though the journal entries themselves must be ungraded for the students to receive the benefit of writing a journal, it's a good idea to give credit for simply having done it. If you make it clear at the beginning of the semester that regularly writing in the journal — *not* the quality or even the quantity, but merely the act of participating — will affect their grade, they will be more likely to at least go through the motions. And students who start out just going through the motions often get something out of the exercise in spite of themselves. After all, exercising their minds and hands is part of the idea in writing journals in the first place. A good way to compute grades for journal writing is to give each student one point for each week in which he or she writes in the journal. Then assign a letter grade to correspond to each number — twelve entries could equal an A, eleven an A–, down to an F for zero entries. When you make up the final course grade, give the journal-writing grade the same weight you would give to a polished paper. If you make it clear that you will compute the final grade in this way, you give tangible proof that you value the writing as well as its product.

What should your students write in their journals? This question, too, has many possible answers. You might give them complete freedom to choose their subject. This option works well if you see the journal primarily as a place for finger exercises, a place for them to practice writing without external restrictions or pressures. Or, if you'd prefer to make sure that students move past purely narrative accounts of daily life in the dorm, you might define the journal more narrowly. You could call it a *reading journal,* suggesting that they use it as a place in which to record their responses to the readings for your course. You could define it as a *writer's notebook,* in which they can write down bits and pieces of ideas for papers, a safe place to explore those ideas for themselves, free of a critical reader's gaze. You could suggest that the journal is a good place to write down personal responses to ideas brought up in class, responses that may not be appropriate for class discussion, but are nonetheless relevant to the subject. Or you might describe the journal's possibilities as combining any or all these options.

TEAM JOURNALS

We learned about this exciting variation on the basic journal from Elizabeth Renfro, of California State University at Chico, and we have used her idea many times with great success in our own classrooms. The primary audience for a team journal is not you, and not the individual writer, but the group of four to six students composing the team. Because you do not write in the team journals — not even in the margins — your students very quickly forget that you are reading them, and begin to address their entries to their teammates. The responsibility for their ideas, and their interaction, shifts to them, and they gradually gain the sense of their own authority that is so essential to their development as writers.

Here are instructions for setting up team journals. Divide the students on your class list into groups of equal size. (Five students per group works well, but four or six will also work.) Make the groups heterogeneous in gender, ability, and so on. If any students regularly attend workshops or tutorials together, or if you have put students in permanent peer-editing groups, break these groups up to form the teams for journals. The idea is to bring each student into contact with as many others as possible in your many classroom and out-of-class activities, so that they will see the class as a group of friends, people with whom it is possible to carry on discussions without fear of ridicule.

Bring several new spiral-bound notebooks to class, one for each team. Divide students up into the teams you have arranged, and give each team a notebook with a blank label stuck to the cover. Have them come up with a name for their journal, and write it on the label. They should also write all their names inside the cover. Then they hand the journals back to you. You explain to them that they will be expected to write in the journal once a week, and that they are to address their comments to their teammates. Give any instructions or suggestions you want about their journal during the semester so that it best fits their needs. Say that you will read their journals once a week, just to make sure they're doing them, and specify exactly the hour you set aside for your weekly journal reading. You must be consistent about when you read the journals, not only because that time will precisely define the limit of each week (the deadline) but also because no students may have the journal checked out at that time.

Now tell students where they will find the journals — say, in the reserve book room of your campus library. Draw a map on the board if necessary, and explain the procedure for checking out books on reserve. After class, take the journals to the library and put them on two-hour reserve. Use the titles created by the student groups when you list the journals in the card catalogue. Explain to the librarian that your students have been *instructed* to write in these books. (One teacher had a difficult time persuading librarians to ignore the usual rule against writing in library books.) If possible, arrange to have librarians give you all journals at the specified time each week; otherwise you will have to fill out several charge cards each time you come in to read the journals.

And be prepared to be delighted. Instead of lugging home a stack of conventional journals each week, and reading through entry after entry written by students who often don't have a clear sense of audience ("Am I writing this for me or for the instructor?") or a clear sense of what to write ("I wonder if *this* is what my instructor wants."), you will find yourself watching a fascinating journey of discovery and communication. Your students will set the tone for their journals, and they will set the intellectual pace, stimulating one another to push harder and harder on their ideas, and to explore new avenues — probably more avenues than you, with your one mind, would have thought of. And if a student writes a sexist or racist remark, you will no longer be responsible for trying to figure out a way to set it straight. Team journals are self-sufficient universes: teammates will respond as only peers can, each adding his or her voice to the discussion of the issue.

As with any other method, you may have to do some troubleshooting in the first few weeks. If some students persist, despite your instructions, in addressing journal comments directly to you ("I was absent today because my roommate twisted her ankle, but don't worry — it won't happen again"), you may have to make a second announcement in class, reinforcing the principle behind the journal's audience. If one or two groups have set low standards for themselves, writing only short, uninspired entries, you could break their cycle early by showing them an example from a productive journal. Ask the members of an active, lively team for permission to photocopy and distribute a few pages from their journal, or for permission to allow members of another group to check out their journal once to get an idea of how other group journals are working. If you continue to use team journals in your classes, consider photocopying model entries, again with permission, to use as examples in following semesters. You'll want to photocopy a series of entries, at least one from each team member, to capture the spirit of communication and exchange of ideas that goes on in team journals at their best. Use these models sparingly, though, to leave enough room for each group to conceive of the journal in its own format.

At the end of the semester, let each group decide what to do with its own journal. Some will say that you can have it. Others will want to make a copy for each team member. (Copies may be too light if they've written in pencil; warn them in advance.) You may receive more creative suggestions, such as an auction or a raffle. The most satisfying conclusion — admittedly rare — comes when a group decides to continue to write in its team journal after the semester has ended, either by leaving it on reserve or by mail. This continuation is an extreme manifestation of the general effect of team journals, and the best reason to assign them. Team journals help your students take charge of their own education, to discover their own sense of authority.

QUESTION PAPERS

The idea for this genre of exploratory writing came to us from teachers in the Bay Area Writing Project, particularly John McBratney and Jane Juska. Question papers, like journals, provide a safe environment in which your students can take intellectual risks. Also like journals, question papers do not receive a grade, but that the student has written one should be registered in the final grade.

Here are instructions for a question paper. Have each student think of a question about the text you are reading, something he or she has been wondering about, and really wants to know. Have them write that question at the top of a sheet of paper, and then write a possible answer to it. That answer should lead to more questions that test the limits of the first answer. Then the student should consider another possible answer to the initial question, or to a question that evolves from the first one. The questions and answers should dovetail, forming a flexible dialogue in which the student talks with himself or herself in writing. Impress on them the need to try several answers to the questions. A common problem student writers have is settling too quickly for the first answer that comes to mind, grateful to have found any answer at all. This desperate attitude is not conducive to developing ideas or complex, sophisticated essays. The spirit of inquiry they exercise while writing question papers helps enhance their ability to develop ideas in polished essays as well.

After your students have written as many answers — and follow-up questions, and answers to those — as they can, instruct them to read over what they have written, and underline the hot spot, a surprising or intriguing idea that may have appeared. This hot spot might become the starting point for a subsequent question paper; it might become the thesis statement for a formal paper; or it might come to no utilitarian end at all. Students need to understand that they are writing these question papers primarily to explore and develop their response to the text as fully as possible. If they get the impression that all question papers are ultimately mere fodder for polished essays, the old hierarchy of product over process will be reinstated.

The first time you assign a question paper, you may want to make it an in-class writing assignment, because it is a new form and students may not understand the assignment. After the class has had a few minutes to think of questions, ask for volunteers to read theirs aloud. Consider reading your question aloud, too, as one model among the others. Give them, and yourself, thirty minutes or so in which to write the dovetailing questions and answers, then call again for volunteers to read theirs aloud.

Collect their papers at the end of the hour. Your written response to their question papers will ideally take the form of an extension of their own activity of writing them: ask any questions that occur to you when reading their papers, and mark any hot spots that they might not have noticed — or merely applaud a hot spot they *have* chosen. Once they have the hang of this new form, you can assign question papers as homework often. We find it beneficial to alternate question papers with polished papers on our schedule of assigned writing. If you are in the habit — as we are — of assigning a rough draft before every polished essay, continue to do so. The question paper is not a substitute for the rough draft; each form has its own uses and advantages. And your students will surely discover the advantages of question papers: many who learned about them in our classes have gone on to use them to question texts assigned by teachers who had never heard of question papers. When students voluntarily adopt a strategy such as the question paper, you can be sure that they have judged it worthwhile.

The Selections as Rhetorical Examples

ANALOGY

Max Apple, *Bridging*
James Baldwin, *Stranger in the Village*
K. C. Cole, *Much Ado about Nothing*
Loren Eiseley, *The Star Thrower*
James Fallows, *Viva Bilingualism*
Vivian Gornick, *Who Says We Haven't Made a Revolution?: A Feminist Takes Stock*
Pete Hamill, *Crack and the Box*
June Jordan, *Waiting for a Taxi*
Lin Yutang, *The Art of Reading*
N. Scott Momaday, *A First American Views His Land*
Susan Sontag, From *AIDS and Its Metaphors*
Shunryu Suzuki, *Emptiness*
Marie Winn, *TV Addiction*

ARGUMENT AND PERSUASION

Barbara Lazear Ascher, *Mothers and Sons*
Russell Baker, *Happy New Year?*
Wendell Berry, *The Journey's End*
Judy Brady, *I Want a Wife*
Susan Brownmiller, *Let's Put Pornography Back in the Closet*
René Descartes, *Stripping the Mind of Its Beliefs*
Fyodor Dostoyevsky, *Confession of Faith*
Gerald Early, *Baseball: The Ineffable National Pastime*
James Fallows, *Viva Bilingualism*
Henry Louis Gates, Jr., *2 Live Crew, Decoded*
Nikki Giovanni, *On Holidays and How to Make Them Work*
Vivian Gornick, *Who Says We Haven't Made a Revolution?: A Feminist Takes Stock*
Stephen Jay Gould, *Sex, Drugs, Disasters, and the Extinction of Dinosaurs*
Bob Greene, *Mr. President*

Pete Hamill, *Crack and the Box*
Harper's Magazine, *In Pursuit of Pure Horror*
Václav Havel, *Words on Words*
Ho Chi Minh, *Declaration of Independence of the Democratic Republic of Viet-Nam*
bell hooks, *Feminism: A Transformational Politic*
Thomas Jefferson, *The Declaration of Independence*
June Jordan, *Nobody Mean More to Me than You and the Future Life of Willie Jordan; Waiting for a Taxi*
Martin Luther King, Jr., *I Have a Dream*
William Severini Kowinski, *Kids in the Mall: Growing Up Controlled*
Lin Yutang, *The Art of Reading*
Walter Lippmann, *The Indispensable Opposition*
Nancy Mairs, *A Letter to Matthew*
George Orwell, *Politics and the English Language*
Edgar Allen Poe, *The Tell-Tale Heart*
Ishmael Reed, *America: The Multinational Society*
Richard Rodriguez, *Toward an American Language*
Anne Roiphe, *The WASP Sting*
Phyllis Rose, *Shopping and Other Spiritual Adventures in America*
Richard Selzer, *What I Saw at the Abortion*
Charlene Spretnak, *Ecofeminism: Our Roots and Flowering*
Elizabeth Cady Stanton, *Declaration of Sentiments and Resolutions*
Brent Staples, *Just Walk on By: A Black Man Ponders His Power to Alter Public Space*
Shelby Steele, *On Being Black and Middle Class*
Shunryu Suzuki, *Emptiness*
Jonathan Swift, *A Modest Proposal*
Lewis Thomas, *Natural Man*
Judith Jarvis Thomson, *A Defense of Abortion*
Henry David Thoreau, From *The Maine Woods*
Alice Walker, *In Search of Our Mothers' Gardens*
George Weinberg, *The Madness and Myths of Homophobia*
Ellen Willis, *Putting Women Back into the Abortion Debate*
Virginia Woolf, *Thoughts on Peace in an Air Raid*

CAUSE AND EFFECT

Sherwood Anderson, *Discovery of a Father*
Barbara Lazear Ascher, *Mothers and Sons*
Russell Baker, *Happy New Year?*
Bering Strait Eskimo Creation Myth, *The Time When There Were No People on the Earth Plain*
J. Hector St. Jean de Crèvecoeur, *What Is an American?*
Bruce Curtis, *The Wimp Factor*
René Descartes, *Stripping the Mind of Its Beliefs*

COMPARISON AND CONTRAST

Pete Hamill, *Crack and the Box*
Harper's Magazine, *In Pursuit of Pure Horror*
Langston Hughes, *Salvation*
Nancy Mairs, *A Letter to Matthew*
N. Scott Momaday, *A First American Views His Land*
Joyce Carol Oates, *Shopping*
Phyllis Rose, *Shopping and Other Spiritual Adventures*
Philip Roth, *My Baseball Years*
Scott Russell Sanders, *The Men We Carry in Our Minds*
Susan Sontag, From *AIDS and Its Metaphors*
Shelby Steele, *On Being Black and Middle Class*
Amy Tan, *Two Kinds*
Lewis Thomas, *Natural Man*
Alexis de Tocqueville, *How the Americans Understand the Equality of the Sexes*
Mark Twain, *The Damned Human Race*

DEFINITION

Francis Bacon, *Idols of the Mind*
Judy Brady, *I Want a Wife*
K. C. Cole, *Much Ado about Nothing*
J. Hector St. Jean de Crèvecoeur, *What Is an American?*
Paul Gruchow, *Seeing the Elephant*
June Jordan, *Nobody Mean More to Me than You and the Future Life of Willie Jordan*
Walter Lippmann, *The Indispensable Opposition*
Gloria Naylor, *A Question of Language*
Kesaya E. Noda, *Growing Up Asian in America*
Anne Roiphe, *The WASP Sting*
Susan Sontag, From *AIDS and Its Metaphors*
Sallie Tisdale, *Neither Morons nor Imbeciles nor Idiots: In the Company of the Mentally Retarded*
Marie Winn, *TV Addiction*

DESCRIPTION

Paula Gunn Allen, *Where I Come from Is Like This*
Michael Arlen, *Ode to Thanksgiving*
Russell Baker, *Gumption*
Toni Cade Bambara, *The Lesson*
Wendell Berry, *The Journey's End*
David Bradley, *Ringgold Street*
Judy Brady, *I Want a Wife*
Judith Ortiz Cofer, *Casa: A Partial Remembrance of a Puerto Rican Childhood*

Toi Derricotte, *Diary: At an Artist's Colony*
Annie Dillard, *Seeing*
Gretel Ehrlich, *The Solace of Open Spaces*
Loren Eiseley, *The Star Thrower*
Mary Gordon, *More than Just a Shrine: Paying Homage to the Ghosts of Ellis Island*
Paul Gruchow, *Seeing the Elephant*
Langston Hughes, *Salvation*
Barry Lopez, *The Stone Horse*
N. Scott Momaday, *A First American Views His Land*
Bharati Mukherjee, *Fathering*
Joyce Carol Oates, *Shopping*
George Orwell, *Shooting an Elephant*
Richard Selzer, *What I Saw at the Abortion*
Henry David Thoreau, From *The Maine Woods*
Sallie Tisdale, *Neither Morons nor Imbeciles nor Idiots: In the Company of the Mentally Retarded*
John Updike, *A & P*
E. B. White, *Once More to the Lake*

DIVISION AND CLASSIFICATION

Francis Bacon, *Idols of the Mind*
David Bradley, *Ringgold Street*
Judy Brady, *I Want a Wife*
Susan Brownmiller, *Let's Put Pornography Back in the Closet*
David Elkind, From *Teenagers in Crisis*
Donald Hall, *Four Kinds of Reading*
Jamaica Kincaid, *Girl*
George Lakoff and Mark Johnson, From *Metaphors We Live By*
Desmond Morris, *Territorial Behavior*
Kesaya E. Noda, *Growing Up Asian in America*
George Orwell, *Politics and the English Language*
Adrienne Rich, *Split at the Root: An Essay on Jewish Identity*
Scott Russell Sanders, *The Men We Carry in Our Minds*
Charlene Spretnak, *Ecofeminism: Our Roots and Flowering*
Amy Tan, *Two Kinds*
Sallie Tisdale, *Neither Morons nor Imbeciles nor Idiots: In the Company of the Mentally Retarded*
George Weinberg, *The Madness and Myths of Homophobia*
Eudora Welty, *A Sweet Devouring*

The Selections as Rhetorical Examples

EXAMPLE

Maya Angelou, *"What's Your Name, Girl?"*
Michael Arlen, *Ode to Thanksgiving*
Francis Bacon, *Idols of the Mind*
Russell Baker, *Gumption*
Bruce Curtis, *The Wimp Factor*
Toi Derricotte, *Diary: At an Artist's Colony*
Joan Didion, *On Keeping a Notebook; Why I Write*
Annie Dillard, *Seeing*
Fyodor Dostoyevsky, *Confession of Faith*
Gerald Early, *Baseball: The Ineffable National Pastime*
Thomas Edison, *The Woman of the Future*
Nora Ephron, *A Few Words about Breasts*
Vivian Gornick, *Who Says We Haven't Made a Revolution?: A Feminist Takes Stock*
Cynthia Hamilton, *Women, Home, and Community: The Struggle in an Urban Environment*
Harper's Magazine, *In Pursuit of Pure Horror*
Václav Havel, *Words on Words*
S. I. Hayakawa, *Words with Built-in Judgments*
Ho Chi Minh, *Declaration of Independence of the Democratic Republic of Viet-Nam*
Langston Hughes, *Salvation*
Susan Jacoby, *Unfair Game*
Thomas Jefferson, *The Declaration of Independence*
Jamaica Kincaid, *Girl*
William Severini Kowinski, *Kids in the Mall: Growing Up Controlled*
Jonathan Kozol, *Distancing the Homeless*
George Lakoff and Mark Johnson, From *Metaphors We Live By*
Nancy Mairs, *A Letter to Matthew*
Mary McCarthy, *Names*
George Orwell, *Politics and the English Language*
Walker Percy, *The Loss of the Creature*
Ishmael Reed, *America: The Multinational Society*
Richard Rodriguez, *Toward an American Language*
William Safire, *On Keeping a Diary*
Susan Sontag, From *AIDS and Its Metaphors*
Elizabeth Cady Stanton, *Declaration of Sentiments and Resolutions*
Judith Jarvis Thomson, *A Defense of Abortion*

NARRATION

Dorothy Allison, *Don't Tell Me You Don't Know*
Rudolfo A. Anaya, *B. Traven Is Alive and Well in Cuernavaca*
Sherwood Anderson, *Discovery of a Father*

Maya Angelou, *"What's Your Name, Girl?"*
Max Apple, *Bridging*
Russell Baker, *Gumption*
James Baldwin, *Stranger in the Village*
Toni Cade Bambara, *The Lesson*
Bering Strait Eskimo Creation Myth, *The Time When There Were No People on the Earth Plain*
Judith Ortiz Cofer, Casa: *A Partial Remembrance of a Puerto Rican Childhood*
Toi Derricotte, *Diary: At an Artist's Colony*
René Descartes, *Stripping the Mind of Its Beliefs*
Joan Didion, *On Keeping a Notebook; Why I Write*
Frederick Douglass, *Learning to Read and Write*
Genesis, *Chapters One, Two, and Three*
Gerald Early, *Baseball: The Ineffable National Pastime*
Gretel Ehrlich, *The Solace of Open Spaces*
Loren Eiseley, *The Star Thrower*
Nora Ephron, *A Few Words about Breasts*
Doris Kearns Goodwin, *From Father, with Love*
Mary Gordon, *More than Just a Shrine: Paying Homage to the Ghosts of Ellis Island*
Francine du Plessix Gray, *I Write for Revenge against Reality*
Paul Gruchow, *Seeing the Elephant*
Harper's Magazine, *In Pursuit of Pure Horror*
Ho Chi Minh, *Declaration of Independence of the Democratic Republic of Viet-Nam*
Langston Hughes, *Salvation*
June Jordan, *Nobody Mean More to Me than You and the Future Life of Willie Jordan*
Maxine Hong Kingston, From *A Song for a Barbarian Reed Pipe; No Name Woman*
David Leavitt, *Territory*
Barry Lopez, *The Stone Horse*
Paule Marshall, *From the Poets in the Kitchen*
Mary McCarthy, *Names*
Bharati Mukherjee, *Fathering*
Itabari Njeri, *Granddaddy*
Joyce Carol Oates, *Shopping*
George Orwell, *Shooting an Elephant*
Grace Paley, *The Loudest Voice*
Plato, From *Symposium*
Edgar Allan Poe, *The Tell-Tale Heart*
Adrienne Rich, *Split at the Root: An Essay on Jewish Identity*
Philip Roth, *My Baseball Years*
Gloria Steinem, *Ruth's Song (Because She Could Not Sing It)*
Elizabeth Stone, *Stories Make a Family*
Amy Tan, *Two Kinds*
Henry David Thoreau, From *The Maine Woods*
Sallie Tisdale, *Neither Morons nor Imbeciles nor Idiots: In the Company of the Mentally Retarded*

PROCESS ANALYSIS

The Selections Arranged by Compositional Element

PURPOSE

To Explain

Bruce Curtis, *The Wimp Factor*
J. Hector St. Jean de Crèvecoeur, *What Is an American?*
Joan Didion, *On Keeping a Notebook; Why I Write*
David Elkind, From *Teenagers in Crisis*
Francine du Plessix Gray, *I Write for Revenge against Reality*
Genesis, *Chapters One, Two, and Three*
Stephen Jay Gould, *Sex, Drugs, Disasters, and the Extinction of Dinosaurs*
Pete Hamill, *Crack and the Box*
George Lakoff and Mark Johnson, *Metaphors We Live By*
George Orwell, *Shooting an Elephant*
Walker Percy, *The Loss of the Creature*
Plato, From *Symposium*
Bernice Johnson Reagon, *Nurturing Resistance*
William Safire, *On Keeping a Diary*
Susan Sontag, From *AIDS and Its Metaphors*
Charlene Spretnak, *Ecofeminism: Our Roots and Flowering*
Shelby Steele, *On Being Black and Middle Class*

To Inform

Paula Gunn Allen, *Where I Come from Is Like This*
Francis Bacon, *Idols of the Mind*
J. Hector St. Jean de Crèvecoeur, *What Is an American?*
René Descartes, *Stripping the Mind of Its Beliefs*
Alexis de Tocqueville, *How the Americans Understand the Equality of the Sexes*
Joan Didion, *Why I Write*
Frederick Douglass, *Learning to Read and Write*
Bob Greene, *Mr. President*
Cynthia Hamilton, *Women, Home, and Community: The Struggle in an Urban
  Environment*

To Reflect

Philip Roth, *My Baseball Years*
Brent Staples, *Just Walk on By: A Black Man Ponders His Power to Alter Public Space*
Gloria Steinem, *Ruth's Song (Because She Could Not Sing It)*
Elizabeth Stone, *Stories Make a Family*
Amy Tan, *Two Kinds*
John Updike, *At War with My Skin*
Alice Walker, *Beauty: When the Other Dancer Is the Self*
Eudora Welty, *A Sweet Devouring*
E. B. White, *Once More to the Lake*
John Edgar Wideman, *The Language of Home*
Virginia Woolf, *Thoughts on Peace in an Air Raid*
Richard Wright, From *Black Boy*

To Entertain

Rudolfo A. Anaya, *B. Traven Is Alive and Well in Cuernavaca*
Michael Arlen, *Ode to Thanksgiving*
Russell Baker, *Happy New Year?*
David Bradley, *Ringgold Street*
Judy Brady, *I Want a Wife*
Gretel Ehrlich, *The Solace of Open Spaces*
Nora Ephron, *A Few Words about Breasts*
Nikki Giovanni, *On Holidays and How to Make Them Work*
Doris Kearns Goodwin, *From Father, with Love*
Bob Greene, *Mr. President*
Harper's Magazine, *In Pursuit of Pure Horror*
Mary McCarthy, *Names*
Grace Paley, *The Loudest Voice*
Walker Percy, *The Loss of the Creature*
Edgar Allan Poe, *The Tell-Tale Heart*
Phyllis Rose, *Shopping and Other Spiritual Adventures in America Today*
Philip Roth, *My Baseball Years*
William Safire, *On Keeping a Diary*
Mark Twain, *The Damned Human Race*
John Updike, *A & P*
E. B. White, *Once More to the Lake*

To Analyze

Dorothy Allison, *Don't Tell Me You Don't Know*
Francis Bacon, *Idols of the Mind*
James Baldwin, *Stranger in the Village*
Wendell Berry, *The Journey's End*
David Bradley, *Ringgold Street*
René Descartes, *Stripping the Mind of Its Beliefs*
Joan Didion, *On Keeping a Notebook*

Annie Dillard, *Seeing*

Fyodor Dostoyevsky, *Confession of Faith*

Gerald Early, *Baseball: The Ineffable National Pastime*

Henry Louis Gates, Jr., *2 Live Crew, Decoded*

Vivian Gornick, *Who Says We Haven't Made a Revolution?: A Feminist Takes Stock*

Paul Gruchow, *Seeing the Elephant*

Harper's Magazine, *In Pursuit of Pure Horror*

June Jordan, *Waiting for a Taxi*

William Severini Kowinski, *Kids in the Mall: Growing Up Controlled*

David Leavitt, *Territory*

Desmond Morris, *Territorial Behavior*

Joyce Carol Oates, *Shopping*

Walker Percy, *The Loss of the Creature*

Anne Roiphe, *The WASP Sting*

Phyllis Rose, *Shopping and Other Spiritual Adventures in America Today*

Susan Sontag, From *AIDS and Its Metaphors*

Charlene Spretnak, *Ecofeminism: Our Roots and Flowering*

Shunryu Suzuki, *Emptiness*

Gloria Steinem, *Ruth's Song (Because She Could Not Sing It)*

Lewis Thomas, *Natural Man*

John Updike, *At War with My Skin*

Alice Walker, *In Search of Our Mothers' Gardens*

John Edgar Wideman, *The Language of Home*

To Criticize

Maya Angelou, *"What's Your Name, Girl?"*

Michael Arlen, *Ode to Thanksgiving*

Francis Bacon, *Idols of the Mind*

Toni Cade Bambara, *The Lesson*

Judy Brady, *I Want a Wife*

Susan Brownmiller, *Let's Put Pornography Back in the Closet*

Bruce Curtis, *The Wimp Factor*

Toi Derricotte, *Diary: At an Artist's Colony*

René Descartes, *Stripping the Mind of Its Beliefs*

Alexis de Tocqueville, *How the Americans Understand the Equality of the Sexes*

Fyodor Dostoyevsky, *Confession of Faith*

Gretel Ehrlich, *The Solace of Open Spaces*

Nikki Giovanni, *On Holidays and How to Make Them Work*

Stephen Jay Gould, *Sex, Drugs, Disasters, and the Extinction of Dinosaurs*

Cynthia Hamilton, *Women, Home, and Community: The Struggle in an Urban Environment*

Susan Jacoby, *Unfair Game*

June Jordan, *Nobody Mean More to Me than You and the Future Life of Willie Jordan*

Maxine Hong Kingston, *No Name Woman*

Walter Lippmann, *The Indispensable Opposition*
Itabari Njeri, *Granddaddy*
George Orwell, *Politics and the English Language*
Walker Percy, *The Loss of the Creature*
Richard Rodriguez, *Toward an American Language*
Charlene Spretnak, *Ecofeminism: Our Roots and Flowering*
Jonathan Swift, *A Modest Proposal*
Lewis Thomas, *Natural Man*
Henry David Thoreau, From *The Maine Woods*
Mark Twain, *The Damned Human Race*
John Updike, *A & P*
George Weinberg, *The Madness and Myths of Homophobia*
Virginia Woolf, *Thoughts on Peace in an Air Raid*

To Satirize

Michael Arlen, *Ode to Thanksgiving*
Russell Baker, *Happy New Year?*
Judy Brady, *I Want a Wife*
Nora Ephron, *A Few Words about Breasts*
Nikki Giovanni, *On Holidays and How to Make Them Work*
Mary Gordon, *More than Just a Shrine: Paying Homage to the Ghosts of Ellis Island*
Langston Hughes, *Salvation*
George Orwell, *Shooting an Elephant*
Jonathan Swift, *A Modest Proposal*
Mark Twain, *The Damned Human Race*

To Convince or to Persuade

Michael Arlen, *Ode to Thanksgiving*
Barbara Lazear Ascher, *Mothers and Sons*
Francis Bacon, *Idols of the Mind*
James Baldwin, *Stranger in the Village*
Wendell Berry, *The Journey's End*
Judy Brady, *I Want a Wife*
Susan Brownmiller, *Let's Put Pornography Back in the Closet*
Bruce Curtis, *The Wimp Factor*
J. Hector St. Jean de Crèvecoeur, *What Is an American?*
René Descartes, *Stripping the Mind of Its Beliefs*
Annie Dillard, *Seeing*
Fyodor Dostoyevsky, *Confession of Faith*
Gerald Early, *Baseball: The Ineffable National Pastime*
Thomas Edison, *The Woman of the Future*
James Fallows, *Viva Bilingualism*
Henry Louis Gates, Jr., *2 Live Crew, Decoded*
Pete Hamill, *Crack and the Box*

Václav Havel, *Words on Words*
bell hooks, *Feminism: A Transformational Politic*
Susan Jacoby, *Unfair Game*
Thomas Jefferson, *The Declaration of Independence*
Jamaica Kincaid, *Girl*
Martin Luther King, Jr., *I Have a Dream*
William Severini Kowinski, *Kids in the Mall: Growing Up Controlled*
Jonathan Kozol, *Distancing the Homeless*
Walter Lippmann, *The Indispensable Opposition*
Nancy Mairs, *A Letter to Matthew*
Ho Chi Minh, *Declaration of Independence of the Democratic Republic of Viet-Nam*
George Orwell, *Politics and the English Language*
Walker Percy, *The Loss of the Creature*
Edgar Allan Poe, *The Tell-Tale Heart*
Richard Rodriguez, *Toward an American Language*
Phyllis Rose, *Shopping and Other Spiritual Adventures in America Today*
Scott Russell Sanders, *The Men We Carry in Our Minds*
William Safire, *On Keeping a Diary*
Richard Selzer, *What I Saw at the Abortion*
Charlene Spretnak, *Ecofeminism: Our Roots and Flowering*
Elizabeth Cady Stanton, *Declaration of Sentiments and Resolutions*
Shelby Steele, *On Being Black and Middle Class*
Shunryu Suzuki, *Emptiness*
Jonathan Swift, *A Modest Proposal*
Judith Jarvis Thomson, *A Defense of Abortion*
Sallie Tisdale, *Neither Morons nor Imbeciles nor Idiots: In the Company of the Mentally Retarded*
Lewis Thomas, *Natural Man*
Judith Jarvis Thomson, *A Defense of Abortion*
Mark Twain, *The Damned Human Race*
George Weinberg, *The Madness and Myths of Homophobia*
John Edgar Wideman, *The Language of Home*
Ellen Willis, *Putting Women Back into the Abortion Debate*
Marie Winn, *TV Addiction*
Virginia Woolf, *Thoughts on Peace in an Air Raid*

POINT OF VIEW

Tone (Personal)

Dorothy Allison, *Don't Tell Me You Don't Know*
Sherwood Anderson, *Discovery of a Father*
Wendell Berry, *The Journey's End*
David Bradley, *Ringgold Street*
Judy Brady, *I Want a Wife*

Tone (Humorous)

Tone (Ironical)

Shunryu Suzuki, *Emptiness*
Jonathan Swift, *A Modest Proposal*
Amy Tan, *Two Kinds*
Sallie Tisdale, *Neither Morons, nor Imbeciles, nor Idiots: In the Company of the Mentally Retarded*

Tone (Impassioned)

Judy Brady, *I Want a Wife*
Susan Brownmiller, *Let's Put Pornography Back in the Closet*
Fyodor Dostoyevsky, *Confession of Faith*
Gretel Ehrlich, *The Solace of Open Spaces*
Nora Ephron, *A Few Words about Breasts*
Pete Hamill, *Crack and the Box*
Susan Jacoby, *Unfair Game*
June Jordan, *Nobody Mean More to Me than You and the Future Life of Willie Jordan*
Martin Luther King, Jr., *I Have a Dream*
Jonathan Kozol, *Distancing the Homeless*
George Orwell, *Politics and the English Language*
Edgar Allan Poe, *The Tell-Tale Heart*
Marie Winn, *TV Addiction*
Virginia Woolf, *Thoughts on Peace in an Air Raid*

Tone (Hard-edged)

Judy Brady, *I Want a Wife*
Susan Brownmiller, *Let's Put Pornography Back in the Closet*
Mary Gordon, *More than Just a Shrine: Paying Homage to the Ghosts of Ellis Island*
Susan Jacoby, *Unfair Game*
Thomas Jefferson, *The Declaration of Independence*
Jonathan Kozol, *Distancing the Homeless*
Walter Lippmann, *The Indispensable Opposition*
Ho Chi Minh, *Declaration of Independence of the Democratic Republic of Viet-Nam*
Elizabeth Cady Stanton, *Declaration of Sentiments and Resolutions*
George Weinberg, *The Madness and Myths of Homophobia*

DICTION

Formal

Francis Bacon, *Idols of the Mind*
Susan Brownmiller, *Let's Put Pornography Back in the Closet*
J. Hector St. Jean de Crèvecoeur, *What Is an American?*
René Descartes, *Stripping the Mind of Its Beliefs*
Frederick Douglass, *Learning to Read and Write*

Mark Twain, *The Damned Human Race*
E. B. White, *Once More to the Lake*

Technical

Jonathan Kozol, *Distancing the Homeless*
Desmond Morris, *Territorial Behavior*

Dialect

Maya Angelou, *"What's Your Name, Girl?"*
Toni Cade Bambara, *The Lesson*
June Jordan, *Nobody Mean More to Me than You and the Future Life of Willie Jordan*
Jamaica Kincaid, *Girl*
Paule Marshall, *From the Poets in the Kitchen*
Bharati Mukherjee, *Fathering*
Amy Tan, *Two Kinds*

Dialogue

Dorothy Allison, *Don't Tell Me You Don't Know*
Rudolfo A. Anaya, *B. Traven Is Alive and Well in Cuernavaca*
Maya Angelou, *"What's Your Name, Girl?"*
Max Apple, *Bridging*
Michael Arlen, *Ode to Thanksgiving*
Russell Baker, *Gumption*
Toni Cade Bambara, *The Lesson*
Fyodor Dostoyevsky, *Confession of Faith*
Harper's Magazine, *In Pursuit of Pure Horror*
Maxine Hong Kingston, From *A Song for a Barbarian Reed Pipe*
David Leavitt, *Territory*
Mary McCarthy, *Names*
Bharati Mukherjee, *Fathering*
Itabari Njeri, *Granddaddy*
Joyce Carol Oates, *Shopping*
Grace Paley, *The Loudest Voice*
Amy Tan, *Two Kinds*
Sallie Tisdale, *Neither Morons nor Imbeciles nor Idiots: In the Company of the Mentally Retarded*

Figurative Language

Francis Bacon, *Idols of the Mind*
René Descartes, *Stripping the Mind of Its Beliefs*
Annie Dillard, *Seeing*
Gretel Ehrlich, *The Solace of Open Spaces*
Loren Eiseley, *The Star Thrower*

Henry Louis Gates, Jr., *2 Live Crew, Decoded*
Paul Gruchow, *Seeing the Elephant*
Maxine Hong Kingston, From *A Song for a Barbarian Reed Pipe*
David Leavitt, *Territory*
Paule Marshall, *From the Poets in the Kitchen*
Walker Percy, *The Loss of the Creature*
Plato, From *Symposium*
Charlene Spretnak, *Ecofeminism: Our Roots and Flowering*
John Updike, *A & P; At War with My Skin*
Virginia Woolf, *Thoughts on Peace in an Air Raid*

STRUCTURE

Order (General to Specific)

Sherwood Anderson, *Discovery of a Father*
Michael Arlen, *Ode to Thanksgiving*
Joan Didion, *Why I Write*
Frederick Douglass, *Learning to Read and Write*
Thomas Edison, *The Woman of the Future*
Pete Hamill, *Crack and the Box*
Cynthia Hamilton, *Women, Home, and Community: The Struggle in an Urban Environment*
bell hooks, *Feminism: A Transformational Politic*
Thomas Jefferson, *The Declaration of Independence*
Jonathan Kozol, *Distancing the Homeless*
George Lakoff and Mark Johnson, *Metaphors We Live By*
Lin Yutang, *The Art of Reading*
Ho Chi Minh, *Declaration of Independence of the Democratic Republic of Viet-Nam*
Desmond Morris, *Territorial Behavior*
William Safire, *On Keeping a Diary*
Susan Sontag, From *AIDS and Its Metaphors*
Elizabeth Cady Stanton, *Declaration of Sentiments and Resolutions*
Lewis Thomas, *Natural Man*
Alice Walker, *In Search of Our Mothers' Gardens*
Marie Winn, *TV Addiction*

Order (Specific to General)

Susan Brownmiller, *Let's Put Pornography Back in the Closet*
Nora Ephron, *A Few Words about Breasts*
Paul Gruchow, *Seeing the Elephant*
Susan Jacoby, *Unfair Game*
William Severini Kowinski, *Kids in the Mall: Growing Up Controlled*
George Orwell, *Shooting an Elephant*

Walker Percy, *The Loss of the Creature*
Ishmael Reed, *America: The Multinational Society*
Phyllis Rose, *Shopping and Other Spiritual Adventures in America Today*
Brent Staples, *Just Walk on By: A Black Man Ponders His Power to Alter Public Space*
Henry David Thoreau, From *The Maine Woods*
John Updike, *A & P; At War with My Skin*
Alice Walker, *Beauty: When the Other Dancer Is the Self*
Virginia Woolf, *Thoughts on Peace in an Air Raid*

Order (Chronological)

Rudolfo A. Anaya, *B. Traven Is Alive and Well in Cuernavaca*
Bering Strait Eskimo Creation Myth, *The Time When There Were No People on the Earth Plain*
René Descartes, *Stripping the Mind of Its Beliefs*
Nora Ephron, *A Few Words about Breasts*
Genesis, *Chapters One, Two, and Three*
Francine du Plessix Gray, *I Write for Revenge against Reality*
Plato, From *Symposium*
Richard Selzer, *What I Saw at the Abortion*
Henry David Thoreau, From *The Maine Woods*
John Updike, *At War with My Skin*
Alice Walker, *Beauty: When the Other Dancer Is the Self*

Order (Question and Answer)

Russell Baker, *Happy New Year?*
David Bradley, *Ringgold Street*
K. C. Cole, *Much Ado about Nothing*
René Descartes, *Stripping the Mind of Its Beliefs*
Joan Didion, *Why I Write*
Fyodor Dostoyevsky, *Confession of Faith*
Harper's Magazine, *In Pursuit of Pure Horror*
William Safire, *On Keeping a Diary*

Order (Transitions)

Max Apple, *Bridging*
Francis Bacon, *Idols of the Mind*
René Descartes, *Stripping the Mind of Its Beliefs*
Annie Dillard, *Seeing*
Gerald Early, *Baseball: The Ineffable National Pastime*
Gretel Ehrlich, *The Solace of Open Spaces*
Genesis, *Chapters One, Two, and Three*
Paul Gruchow, *Seeing the Elephant*
Václav Havel, *Words on Words*

EFFECTIVE PARAGRAPHS

Topic Sentence (Expressing a Controlling Idea)

Coherence

Russell Baker, *Gumption*

Judy Brady, *I Want a Wife*

René Descartes, *Stripping the Mind of Its Beliefs*

Joan Didion, *On Keeping a Notebook*

Gretel Ehrlich, *The Solace of Open Spaces*

David Elkind, From *Teenagers in Crisis*

Pete Hamill, *Crack and the Box*

Cynthia Hamilton, *Women, Home, and Community: The Struggle in an Urban Environment*

Thomas Jefferson, *The Declaration of Independence*

Martin Luther King, Jr., *I Have a Dream*

William Severini Kowinski, *Kids in the Mall: Growing Up Controlled*

Jonathan Kozol, *Distancing the Homeless*

Walter Lippmann, *The Indispensable Opposition*

Nancy Mairs, *A Letter to Matthew*

Ho Chi Minh, *Declaration of Independence of the Democratic Republic of Viet-Nam*

Walker Percy, *The Loss of the Creature*

William Safire, *On Keeping a Diary*

Susan Sontag, From *AIDS and Its Metaphors*

Elizabeth Cady Stanton, *Declaration of Sentiments and Resolutions*

Shunryu Suzuki, *Emptiness*

Jonathan Swift, *A Modest Proposal*

Judith Jarvis Thomson, *A Defense of Abortion*

Mark Twain, *The Damned Human Race*

George Weinberg, *The Madness and Myths of Homophobia*

John Edgar Wideman, *The Language of Home*

Support

Michael Arlen, *Ode to Thanksgiving*

Francis Bacon, *Idols of the Mind*

Russell Baker, *Happy New Year?*

James Baldwin, *Stranger in the Village*

David Bradley, *Ringgold Street*

René Descartes, *Stripping the Mind of Its Beliefs*

Joan Didion, *On Keeping a Notebook*

Fyodor Dostoyevsky, *Confession of Faith*

Frederick Douglass, *Learning to Read and Write*

David Elkind, From *Teenagers in Crisis*

Donald Hall, *Four Kinds of Reading*

Václav Havel, *Words on Words*

Susan Jacoby, *Unfair Game*

Thomas Jefferson, *The Declaration of Independence*

Martin Luther King, Jr., *I Have a Dream*

EFFECTIVE BEGINNINGS

Establishing the Importance of the Subject

Establishing a Setting

Pete Hamill, *Crack and the Box*
Jonathan Kozol, *Distancing the Homeless*
Mark Twain, *The Damned Human Race*

Posing a Central Question or Problem

Russell Baker, *Gumption*
Toi Derricotte, *Diary: At an Artist's Colony*
Fyodor Dostoyevsky, *Confession of Faith*
Frederick Douglass, *Learning to Read and Write*
Nikki Giovanni, *On Holidays and How to Make Them Work*
Harper's Magazine, *In Pursuit of Pure Horror*
bell hooks, *Feminism: A Transformational Politic*
Jonathan Kozol, *Distancing the Homeless*
George Lakoff and Mark Johnson, *Metaphors We Live By*
Walter Lippmann, *The Indispensable Opposition*
George Orwell, *Politics and the English Language*
Gloria Steinem, *Ruth's Song (Because She Could Not Sing It)*
John Updike, *At War with My Skin*
George Weinberg, *The Madness and Myths of Homophobia*
Virginia Woolf, *Thoughts on Peace in an Air Raid*

EFFECTIVE CONCLUSIONS

Summarizing Essential Points

René Descartes, *Stripping the Mind of Its Beliefs*
Desmond Morris, *Territorial Behavior*
Walker Percy, *The Loss of the Creature*
Shunryu Suzuki, *Emptiness*
Ellen Willis, *Putting Women Back into the Abortion Debate*

Framing (Returning to the Beginning)

Paula Gunn Allen, *Where I Come from Is Like This*
Barbara Lazear Ascher, *Mothers and Sons*
Russell Baker, *Gumption*
Joan Didion, *On Keeping a Notebook*
Francine du Plessix Gray, *I Write for Revenge against Reality*
James Fallows, *Viva Bilingualism*
Paul Gruchow, *Seeing the Elephant*
Václav Havel, *Words on Words*
June Jordan, *Waiting for a Taxi*
Nancy Mairs, *A Letter to Matthew*
Desmond Morris, *Territorial Behavior*

Gloria Naylor, *A Question of Language*
Itabari Njeri, *Granddaddy*
Grace Paley, *The Loudest Voice*
Walker Percy, *The Loss of the Creature*
Amy Tan, *Two Kinds*
Henry David Thoreau, From *The Maine Woods*

Stimulating Further Discussion

James Baldwin, *Stranger in the Village*
Judy Brady, *I Want a Wife*
Vivian Gornick, *Who Says We Haven't Made a Revolution?: A Feminist Takes Stock*
Jonathan Kozol, *Distancing the Homeless*
George Orwell, *Shooting an Elephant*
Ishmael Reed, *America: The Multinational Society*
Susan Sontag, From *AIDS and Its Metaphors*
Judith Jarvis Thomson, *A Defense of Abortion*
Richard Wright, From *Black Boy*

Offering Recommendations, Solutions, or Answers

David Bradley, *Ringgold Street*
René Descartes, *Stripping the Mind of Its Beliefs*
Henry Louis Gates, Jr., *2 Live Crew, Decoded*
Nikki Giovanni, *On Holidays and How to Make Them Work*
Pete Hamill, *Crack and the Box*
bell hooks, *Feminism: A Transformational Politic*
Susan Jacoby, *Unfair Game*
Thomas Jefferson, *The Declaration of Independence*
William Severini Kowinski, *Kids in the Mall: Growing Up Controlled*
Walter Lippmann, *The Indispensable Opposition*
Nancy Mairs, *A Letter to Matthew*
Ho Chi Minh, *Declaration of Independence of the Democratic Republic of Viet-Nam*
George Orwell, *Politics and the English Language*
Charlene Spretnak, *Ecofeminism: Our Roots and Flowering*
Elizabeth Cady Stanton, *Declaration of Sentiments and Resolutions*
Brent Staples, *Just Walk on By: A Black Man Ponders His Power to Alter Public Space*
Shunryu Suzuki, *Emptiness*
Amy Tan, *Two Kinds*
Lewis Thomas, *Natural Man*
Sallie Tisdale, *Neither Morons, nor Imbeciles, nor Idiots: In the Company of the Mentally Retarded*
George Weinberg, *The Madness and Myths of Homophobia*
John Edgar Wideman, *The Language of Home*
Virginia Woolf, *Thoughts on Peace in an Air Raid*

Creating a Dramatic Example, Anecdote, or Phrase

Michael Arlen, *Ode to Thanksgiving*
Toi Derricotte, *Diary: At an Artist's Colony*
Joan Didion, *Why I Write*
Annie Dillard, *Seeing*
Paul Gruchow, *Seeing the Elephant*
Martin Luther King, Jr., *I Have a Dream*
Maxine Hong Kingston, *No Name Woman*
Barry Lopez, *The Stone Horse*
Nancy Mairs, *A Letter to Matthew*
Brent Staples, *Just Walk on By: A Black Man Ponders His Power to Alter Public Space*
Elizabeth Stone, *Stories Make a Family*
Amy Tan, *Two Kinds*
Lewis Thomas, *Natural Man*
Sallie Tisdale, *Neither Morons, nor Imbeciles, nor Idiots: In the Company of the Mentally Retarded*
Alice Walker, *Beauty: When the Other Dancer Is the Self*
Eudora Welty, *A Sweet Devouring*
E. B. White, *Once More to the Lake*

Building a Dramatic Conclusion

Rudolfo A. Anaya, *B. Traven Is Alive and Well in Cuernavaca*
Maya Angelou, *"What's Your Name, Girl?"*
Toi Derricotte, *Diary: At an Artist's Colony*
Gretel Ehrlich, *The Solace of Open Spaces*
Mary Gordon, *More than Just a Shrine: Paying Homage to the Ghosts of Ellis Island*
Donald Hall, *Four Kinds of Reading*
June Jordan, *Nobody Mean More to Me than You and the Future Life of Willie Jordan*
Mary McCarthy, *Names*
Edgar Allan Poe, *The Tell-Tale Heart*
Amy Tan, *Two Kinds*
Henry David Thoreau, From *The Maine Woods*
John Updike, *A & P*
E. B. White, *Once More to the Lake*
Marie Winn, *TV Addiction*

INCORPORATING INFORMATION

Quotation

K. C. Cole, *Much Ado about Nothing*
Bruce Curtis, *The Wimp Factor*
Gretel Ehrlich, *The Solace of Open Spaces*

David Elkind, From *Teenagers in Crisis*
Bob Greene, *Mr. President*
Cynthia Hamilton, *Women, Home, and Community: The Struggle in an Urban Environment*
Susan Jacoby, *Unfair Game*
June Jordan, *Nobody Mean More to Me than You and the Future Life of Willie Jordan*
William Severini Kowinski, *Kids in the Mall: Growing Up Controlled*
Jonathan Kozol, *Distancing the Homeless*
William Safire, *On Keeping a Diary*

Paraphrase

Sherwood Anderson, *Discovery of a Father*
Francis Bacon, *Idols of the Mind*
Susan Brownmiller, *Let's Put Pornography Back in the Closet*
René Descartes, *Stripping the Mind of Its Beliefs*
David Elkind, From *Teenagers in Crisis*
Maxine Hong Kingston, *No Name Woman*
William Severini Kowinski, *Kids in the Mall: Growing Up Controlled*
Jonathan Kozol, *Distancing the Homeless*
N. Scott Momaday, *A First American Views His Land*
Charlene Spretnak, *Ecofeminism: Our Roots and Flowering*
Sallie Tisdale, *Neither Morons, nor Imbeciles, nor Idiots: In the Company of the Mentally Retarded*
George Weinberg, *The Madness and Myths of Homophobia*

Data (Evidence)

Bruce Curtis, *The Wimp Factor*
Frederick Douglass, *Learning to Read and Write*
Mary Gordon, *More than Just a Shrine: Paying Homage to the Ghosts of Ellis Island*
Cynthia Hamilton, *Women, Home, and Community: The Struggle in an Urban Environment*
William Severini Kowinski, *Kids in the Mall: Growing Up Controlled*
George Lakoff and Mark Johnson, *Metaphors We Live By*
Desmond Morris, *Territorial Behavior*
George Orwell, *Politics and the English Language*
Ishmael Reed, *America: The Multinational Society*
Susan Sontag, From *AIDS and Its Metaphors*
Sallie Tisdale, *Neither Morons, nor Imbeciles, nor Idiots: In the Company of the Mentally Retarded*
George Weinberg, *The Madness and Myths of Homophobia*

McQuade/Atwan

AUTHOR

The Winchester Reader
TITLE Resources for Teaching

DATE DUE	BORROWER'S NAME

DEMCO